Y0-BVR-602

POCKET *A*DVENTURES
PANAMA

Patricia Katzman

HUNTER

HUNTER PUBLISHING, INC,
130 Campus Drive, Edison, NJ 08818
732-225-1900; 800-255-0343; fax 732-417-1744
www.hunterpublishing.com

Ulysses Travel Publications
4176 Saint-Denis, Montréal, Québec
Canada H2W 2M5
514-843-9882, ext. 2232; fax 514-843-9448

Windsor Books
The Boundary, Wheatley Road, Garsington
Oxford, OX44 9EJ England
01865-361122; fax 01865-361133

Printed in the United States

ISBN 1-58843-529-6

© 2006 Hunter Publishing, Inc.

Cover photo: Sailboats in the San Blas Islands © 2006 Maxine Cass
Index by Nancy Wolff & Mary Ellen McGrath

Maps by Kim André & Lissa K Dailey, © 2006 Hunter Publishing, Inc.

1 2 3 4

www.hunterpublishing.com

Hunter's full range of guides to all corners of the globe is featured on our exciting website. You'll find guidebooks to suit every type of traveler, no matter what their budget, lifestyle, or idea of fun.

Adventure Guides – There are now over 40 titles in this series, covering destinations from Costa Rica and the Yucatán to Tampa Bay & Florida's West Coast, Switzerland, Paris and the Alaska Highway. Complete with information on what to do, as well as where to stay and eat, *Adventure Guides* are made for the active traveler, with comprehensive coverage of the area's history, culture and wildlife, plus all the practical travel information you need. Details on the best places for hiking, biking, canoeing, horseback riding, trekking, skiing, watersports, and all other kinds of fun, are included.

Alive Guides – This ever-popular line of books takes a unique look at the best each destination offers: fine dining, jazz clubs, first-class hotels and resorts. In-margin icons direct the reader at a glance. Top-sellers include *St. Martin & St. Barts*, *The US Virgin Islands* and *Aruba, Bonaire & Curaçao*.

And Hunter has long been known for its **one-of-a-kind** travel books that focus on destinations and vacations rarely found in travel books. These include *The Best Dives of the Caribbean; The Virginia Handbook; Cruising Alaska; A Traveler's Guide to the Galapagos* and many more.

Full descriptions are given for each book at www.hunterpublishing.com, along with reviewers' comments and a cover image. You can also view pages and the table of contents. Books may be purchased on-line via our secure transaction facility.

Acknowledgments

It would require a full chapter to acknowledge all those who provided the assistance, encouragement and, best of all, friendships that made this book and the *Panama Adventure Guide* a reality. I thank everyone. A special mention to Virginia and Frances, whose delightful hostal, La Casa de Carmen, became my Panama City "home away from home;" insightful Jorge Loiza of Decameron Resorts provided gracious respite that kept me plugging along. Quique Pesantez of Pesantez Tours introduced me to some delightful folks and whisked me to places I might otherwise have missed, as did Panama City Tours' Amalia and Jesús (Jesús, you're the best driver I have ever entrusted with my life). Dinners shared with Ana Royo of Experience Panama Tours provided companionship, information and sheer relaxation. I am truly grateful to valued friends Ana Maria Sanchiz and Jorge Sanchiz of Casa de Campo. Kathy Herold of Panama Explorer Club and Carlos Alfaro of Los Quetzales - thank you for your gracious hospitality. Last, but certainly not least, a big thank you to Kim André for giving me the opportunity to author the original *Panama Adventure Guide*.

Contents

◆ Maps

DEDICATION

This guide is dedicated to Ariadna Sanchez, my beloved friend. Thanks Ariadna, for your faith, time, patience and all else you contributed, including the loan of your car, and all those introductions!

Introduction

Author Graham Greene, who returned again and again to Panamá, described perfectly my sentiment when he wrote, "I already felt oddly at home in this small remote country of my dreams, as I had never felt in any country of Latin America before."

Panamá is an oxymoronic blend of modern big city sophistication, rural tradition and ancient pre-Columbian life ways. Although rated one of the hemisphere's safest countries for visitors, it hasn't seen many – and that is truly surprising. Fortunate travelers will find its paths less beaten, a wealth of adventures in tune with nature, and a developed infrastructure that includes good public transportation – a boon for those on budgeted time. The predominant Spanish Caribbean culture melds indigenous, European, African, Chinese, Indian, North American and more into a vivacious mélange of inhabitants, and while Panamá City is as vibrant and cosmopolitan as any world capital, you'd be hard-pressed to find people further removed from "civilization" than the Darien's indigenous Emberá and Wounaan, or more independent than the colorful Kuna.

Panamá lies on an isthmus, the diverse and heart-stoppingly beautiful land bridge that connects South and Central America. Since its formation, plant and animal species have migrated over the land bridge, converging here to bequeath Panamá with a biodiversity greater than that of any other Central American country – including Costa Rica, its famed eco-destination neighbor. Exotic wildlife, some found nowhere else on earth, is abundant and visible. There are more bird species here than in the US and Canada combined, and more plant and tree species than in all the US, Canada and Europe. There are lush lowland rainforests and high mountain cloud forests, wide rivers and sparkling streams, and endless miles of tropical beaches. Adrift in its crystal seas are more than 1,500 Caribbean and Pacific islands and cays – some covered in rainforest, others mere specks of dazzling white sand and a few rustling coconut palms.

Best known for its canal, Panama fairly bursts with extraordinary adventures: Swoop through the jungle canopy; transit the famous canal; dive two oceans in one day; run whitewater rapids through jungle-enclosed canyons; rappel a sheer rock cliff or seek out the rare cloud forest-dwelling resplendent quetzal, the hemisphere's most beautiful bird. Take in a folkloric ballet at the magnificently restored National Theatre, a trendy nightclub's evening of jazz, or throb to the gut-thumping rhythms of pounding Congo drums. Stalk the ramparts of ancient Spanish forts, kayak a primordial island maze; enjoy world-class dining; hike over the continental divide, surf some serious waves and shop for gold jewelry – exact replicas of the idols revered by long-ago pre-Columbian kings. Like Greene, I return again and again. Perhaps you will too.

❖   WHAT'S IN A NAME?

The word Panamá is said to mean "abundance of butterflies" or "abundance of fish" in the language of its pre-Columbian inhabitants – at least that is what promotional materials claim. According to an early Spanish account, when asked where he lived, a native pointed into the distance and replied, Pa-na-maa, which was taken to mean "over there" or "far away." In 1516, Pedro Arias de Avila, then-governor of the region, wrote to the Spanish court, "Your highnesses should know that Panamá is a fishery on the coast of the South Sea and the fishermen there are called Panamá." A century and a half later, a Catholic bishop wrote to his superiors, "The city is called Panamá, after a beautiful tree that grows here."

Using this Guide

Adapted from the larger *Panamá Adventure Guide*, this portable version has less history, a little less detail, and a few less places to stay and eat listed than in the original. However, it does include a smattering of new information. Since most visitors arrive by air and spend at least a day or two in the capital and its environs, this guide begins there. Whether getting around by driving yourself, by bus, commuter flights (frequent and inexpensive) and/or water craft, you'll find all the information necessary to plan your time and activities. The Pan-American Highway – called **InterAmericana** here – is the only highway or road of any sort that runs (almost) the country's entire length, from the Costa Rica border east to the town of Yaviza in Darién. The only break in the 16,000-mile/25,800-km roadway from Alaska to the southern tip of South America is in Panamá – between Yaviza and the Columbian border, a 54-mile stretch of wilderness called the Darién "Gap."

> **AUTHOR NOTE:** *The tour operators, hotels and lodges that have chosen to operate with ethical conservation and preservation standards get special mention in this guide. But here, like anywhere else, merely hanging a sign emblazoned with "eco-whatever" does not necessarily mean a place adheres to sustainable standards.*

This is a country on the move, and things are changing rapidly. Prior to the official Panamá Canal reversion during the last days of 1999, 50,000 US military and civilian personnel vacated the country – a mass exodus that left thousands of acres of land abandoned and thousands of buildings deserted. Some have been converted to office or entertainment complexes, shopping or educational centers: Sprawling Fort Clayton now houses The City of Knowledge, an installation dedicated to learning and research; the capital's domestic airport moved to the former US Air Force Albrook airbase that now also includes a gigantic new bus terminal and a megamall with more than 100 shops, restaurants and entertainment venues.

History

Panamá's history boils with plundering and pandering, treachery and intrigue. Reminders of the turbulent past are still visible – in massive stone forts, sunken galleons, ancient cathedrals, and in the famous Panamá Canal. But history didn't begin with the conquistadors; it began thousands of years before when indigenous people first settled here. In keeping with this guide's "pocket portability," history has been reduced here to a timeline. If you would like to know more about the country's past – or present — refer to *Recommended Reading*, page 289.

◆ Timeline

Prehistoric to Pre-Columbian Times

By 11,000 BC: Nomadic Paleo-Indian peoples had migrated to the isthmus.

By 9500 BC: Plant cultivation had begun.

By 6000 BC: Expanding agriculture led to permanent settlements and the start of slash and burn farming.

By 3000 BC: Central America's first known pottery is made on the Azuero Peninsula.

By 1000 BC: Class ranked societies had evolved. Pottery and burial practices grew increasingly more sophisticated. Slash and burn farming had deforested areas of the Pacific Coastal Plains.

By 900 BC: First painted pottery had appeared. Witchcraft and shamanistic cults flourished.

1-500 AD: Powerful chiefs ruled class-ranked warrior kingdoms. The art of metallurgy arrived from South America and the first gold objects were made. Agriculture and trade continued to expand. Migrants from central Costa

Rica established the Barilles culture near Barú Volcano in (what is now) western Panamá.

500–1501: Panamá's classic period. Mythical, ritualistic and shamanistic designs dominated intricate gold effigies (*huacas*) and painted pottery. Gold was an established trade commodity. Barú Volcano erupted around 600 AD, burying the Barilles culture beneath lava and ash.

1501 AD: The Spanish arrive with the dawn of the 16th century to find the isthmus populated with dozens of separate indigenous groups, each with its own language and culture.

The Conquest to Colonial Times

Strategically located in the New World's very center, the isthmus provided the shortest land route from the Pacific to the Caribbean (Atlantic). Soon after the Spanish arrived, it became the stage for one of the New World's most rapacious and bloody dramas – one that ran for centuries.

❖ THE PLAYERS

First to appear were the indigenous people, followed by the Spanish invaders. The cast grew to include African slaves, English slave traders, pirates and buccaneers from every nation. No records were kept of the numbers of the indigenous and no one knows now how many there might have been. Pedrarias' orders to enslave or exterminate them, European diseases and the priesthood's "convert or die" policies wiped most from the stage.

The Cimmarones: Thousands of African slaves were brought to the isthmus – most by English slave traders – to replace indigenous Indians who died under their staggering burdens or chose suicide over slavery. It was estimated that 300 of every 1,000 Africans brought here escaped into the jungles. They developed communities deep in the Darién, and were called Cimmarones, an early Spanish term for wild men. Intent on murdering the hated Spanish, the Cimmarones organized gangs and raided treasure caravans along the Camino Real. And, like many indigenous people, they later joined forces with plundering English pirates. A few Cimmaron communities still exist in Darién. Today, they're known as Dariénites.

The Pirates, Privateers and Corsairs: Pirates were outlaws that operated independently and illegally. Privateers were financed by commercial ventures, often with the approval of their country's government. However, some of the privateers also operated illegally as pirates. The French trader-pirates were called corsairs.

The Buccaneers: The Spanish abandoned Hispaniola near the end of the 16th century, leaving escaped criminals and deserters stranded on the island. These rag-tag men of all nationalities banded together to become the "buccaneers." Owing allegiance to no one but themselves – and then only when it suited them – the buccaneers plundered Spanish towns and captured ships, killing the crews or incorporating them into their ranks. Their trademark triangular black banner, inscribed with a white skull and crossbones – the fearsome "Jolly Roger" – struck terror in the hearts of all who saw its approach. The buccaneers disbanded soon after the 1697 Treaty of Ryswick ordered them captured and executed. Some retired, and many were hunted down and killed. One who escaped was a Dutchman named **John Esquemeling**, whose memoirs attempted to glorify the brutal escapades of the buccaneers. Although the group terrorized the New World for only three-quarters of a century, Esquemeling's exaggerated accounts are still being published.

AUTHOR NOTE: *Hispañola's cannibalistic **Carib Indians** preserved meat by drying it over open fires. They called the dried meat* bucan. *European criminals and deserters, abandoned on Hispaña, adopted the practice and came to be called "bucan eaters." The word eventually evolved into "buccaneer."*

1501:	Spaniard Rodrigo de Bastidas is the first European to visit the Caribbean shores of what is now Panamá. A young seaman named Vasco Nuñez de Balboa is among his crew.
1502-1503:	Columbus arrives on the Caribbean coast during his fourth and last voyage.
1510:	Santa Maria del Darién, the first New World colony, is founded. Balboa assumes its unofficial leadership. Nombre de Dios is founded.
1513:	Balboa "discovers" the Pacific Ocean.
1514:	Pedro Arias de Avila, (Pedrarias) arrives to govern Veragua, as the region was then known.
1519:	Pedrarias accuses Balboa of treason. After a sham trial, Balboa is judged guilty and executed. Pedrarias founds Nuestra Señora de la Asunción de Panamá, the first European city on the Pacific coast.

> ❖ **PEDRARIAS THE CRULE**
>
> Pedrarias ruled Castilla de Oro from 1514 until his death in 1530. During that time, he caused the death or enslavement of more than two million native people, earning him the nickname, "Pedrarias the Cruel."

1595: English corsair Francis Drake destroys Nombre de Dios.

1597: Portobelo replaces Nombre de Dios as Spain's principal Caribbean port.

> ❖ **EL CAMINO REAL**
>
> Following the route of a former Indian trail, the Camino Real (Royal Road) was paved by the Spanish with stone and used to transport looted treasure from the Pacific across the isthmus to the Caribbean. By 1600, more than 200,000 tons of silver had crossed the Royal Road. No records survive to tell of the tons of gold and jewels.

1670-71: Buccaneer Henry Morgan destroys Panamá.

1673: A new city of Panamá (Nueva Panamá) is founded.

1739: Spain decrees the isthmus part of its Viceroyalty of New Granada. English pirate Edward Vernon destroys Portobelo. Soon after, Spain begins to withdraw from the isthmus, rerouting its trade and treasure ships around Cape Horn.

1748: The last Spanish galleon arrived on the isthmus.

Post-Colonial Times

1819: Panamá declares its independence from Spain, joining with Peru, Columbia, Ecuador and Venezuela, as part of Simon Bolívar's Republic of Gran Columbia.

1830: Gran Columbia collapses. The isthmus lapses into a back water of Columbia.

1848: The California gold rush begins. Tens of thousands of gold seekers (forty-niners) swarm the isthmus on their way to the gold fields.

1850: Construction of the Panamá Railroad begins.

AUTHOR NOTE: *More than 12,000 workers died during the railroad's construction, most from malaria and yellow fever. They were dying in such numbers that railroad officials began to pickle the bodies in barrels and sell them to medical schools. Proceeds from the sales were used to build a hospital.*

1855: The railroad is completed.

1881:   Ferdinand de Lesseps' French Canal Company arrives to build a sea-level canal across the isthmus.

1888:   de Lesseps abandons the attempt. Never realizing that a sea-level canal across the isthmus was technically impossible; his stubborn folly cost 22,000 lives and 1,200 million Francs, almost bankrupting France.

Modern Times

"Panamá was born with the US Navy for a midwife"
Kenneth C. Davis, *Don't Know Much about History*

1903:   With US warships guarding its shores, Panamá declares its independence from Columbia.

1904:   The Hay Bunau-Varilla Treaty grants the US rights to build a canal across the isthmus and to maintain it "into perpetuity." Construction of the Panamá Canal begins.

1914:   The Panamá Canal is completed, ahead of schedule and under budget.

AUTHOR NOTE: *The Panama Canal couldn't have been built without the railroad. The French Canal Company hadn't realized its importance, but US canal engineer John Stevens did. After new rails were laid and much-needed repairs were made, the railroad was used to transport workers, food, heavy equipment, and fresh water. Thousands of flatcars moved heaps of rock and debris dug from the canal channel during construction.*

1968:   President Arnulfo Arias Madrid is ousted in coup led by General Omar Torrijos Herrera.

1977:   US President Jimmy Carter and Torrijos sign the Panama Canal Treaties.

1981:   Torrijos dies in a suspicious plane crash.

1983:   Manuel Antonio Noriega, a Bush supported CIA informant and later accused drug trafficker, gains control of the country.

AUTHOR NOTE: *Noriega's handpicked military force was called the Dignity Battalion. Panamanians insultingly called them the "Dingbats.*

1989:   US troops invade to remove Noriega. The invasion, code named "Operation Just Cause," causes the deaths of more than 3,000 Panamanians. Noriega is taken to the US, convicted of drug trafficking and sentenced to 40 years in a federal penitentiary.

1994:   Panamá's military is abolished by constitutional amendment.

1999:	Mireya Moscoso, widow of Arnulfo Arias Madrid, becomes Panamá's first woman President.
1999:	The Panamá Canal and its territories revert to Panama.
2004:	Martin Torrijos, son of Omar Torrijos Herrera, is elected to succeed Moscoso.

Geography

Panamá lies on the isthmus connecting South and Central America. It is Central America's southernmost country, at the center of the Western Hemisphere, bordered by Costa Rica on the west and Colombia on the east. It curves like an "S" toppled sideways between 1,000 miles/1,610 kilometers of Pacific shoreline to the south and 800 miles/1,288 kilometers of Caribbean (Atlantic) shores to the north. With a length of 480 miles/773 kilometers, Panamá is far longer than it is wide, measuring a mere 37 miles/60 kilometers at its narrowest point and 110 miles/177 kilometers at its widest. With a land area of 29,762 square miles/77,381 square kilometers, it's slightly smaller than South Carolina, but its varied landscape makes it seem much larger. In geological terms, Panamá is one of the Western Hemisphere's youngest lands.

> **AUTHOR NOTE:** *Panamá lies east to west rather than north to south. As if to confound the directionally challenged – and those who are not — this "sideways" position makes the sun appear to rise in the west and set in the east.*

◆ The Land Before Time

The Earth's surface is made up of rigid plates that have been shifting since its beginning, a process called plate tectonics. About 250 million years ago, these plates fused the earth's subcontinents into a giant land mass, a super continent called Pangea. Over passing eons, as the earth continued to invent and reinvent itself, the plates began to pull apart, like the pieces of a giant puzzle. By 20 million years ago, North and South America were separated by an oceanic gap called the Panaminic Seaway, a vast waterway that halted all plant and animal land migrations between the divided continents. Even as Atlantic and Pacific waters mingled through this vast open waterway, unstable crustal plates continued to slide, collide and rupture, causing a massive volcanic arc to develop and spread east from what is now Mexico. This undersea violence pushed up the granite cliffs and a chain of volcanoes that formed Central America's rugged backbone.

> **AUTHOR NOTE:** *As recently as 1947, forests covered 70% of Panamá's land area. Today, that figure has dwindled to less than 30%.*

◆ Land Bridge of the Americas

Between 11 and six million years ago a chain of islands along what is now Panamá's Caribbean coast pushed up from the sea. Over the next eight million years or so, an archipelago developed between North and South America to form Panamá's eastern **San Blas** and **Tierra Llorna** (Crying Land) mountain ranges. Between six and three million years ago, the continuing eruptions and upheavals had closed the seaway. A narrow land bridge – the **Isthmus of Panamá** – reconnected the North and South American continents. This rerouting of the seas brought about dramatic worldwide climatic changes and great floods that repeatedly submerged the isthmus until about 2.5 million years ago. The seas finally receded, leaving Panamá's wide coastal plains in their wake.

Topography

Panamá is one of the world's most geographically complex lands, dominated by a spine of rugged mountains and hills of the continental divide. The Cordillera de Talamanca, commonly called **Cordillera Central** (Central Mountains) runs eastward from Costa Rica to the lowland canal basin, and the **Cordillera de San Blas** rises from east of the basin to Darién. The Panamá Canal runs through an 18.5-mile/30-km wide strip of this relatively low land, dividing the country in two as it slices almost 50 miles/80 km across the isthmus in a roughly northeast-to-southwest direction.

Wide coastal plains border both coasts, sloping upwards to an average of 4,900 feet/1,470 meters in the mountainous interior. The summit of 11,401-foot/3,475-meter **Volcán Barú** in northwestern Chiriquí Province is Panamá's highest peak.

Large areas of virgin rainforest blanket Caribbean slopes and banana plantations spread across north Bocas del Toro's coastal plains. Tracts of evergreen and deciduous forests still cover the drier Pacific side's mountain interior, although coastal plains and rolling hills have suffered severe deforestation from being cleared for farms and cattle pastures. Long before the conquest, indigenous peoples practiced intensive farming in the region, beginning the semi-arid conditions of the **Arco Seco** (dry arch) that stretches along the Pacific coast from Coclé Province through the Azuero Peninsula. The **Sarigua Desert's** red, crumbling earth testifies to the destruction caused by deforestation and land overuse.

More than 1,500 islands lie off Panamá's coasts – including the Pacific's **Isla Coiba**, **Isla Taboga** and **Islas de las Perlas** (Pearl Islands), and the Caribbean archipelagos of **San Blas** (Mulatupo) and **Bocas del Toro**. Southwestern **Darién Province's** rugged mountains, rainforests, network of rivers and low-lying swamps protect Central America's largest remaining tracts of primary forest.

Five hundred rivers network down from Panamá's mountainous interior. Of the 350 emptying into the Pacific, most important are the **Bayano**, **Chucunaque** and **Tuira**. The remainder flow to the Caribbean, most notably the **Changuinola**, **Indio** and the mighty **Chagres**, a primary water source for the Panama Canal.

Climate

◆ Almost Paradise

Panamá lies below the hurricane belt, spared from the devastating storms that wreak havoc on its northern neighbors. The worst weather one can expect here are heavy rainstorms that blow in during rainy season. The country is at the tail end of the Pacific **Ring of Fire** – the chain of active volcanoes arching through North and Central America – and hasn't experienced appreciable volcanic activity since giant Volcán Barú in northwestern Chiriquí last exploded rock and ash more than 600 years ago.

The climate is tropical, with only two distinct seasons; **summer** (*verano*), mid-December to mid-April, and **winter** (*invierno*), the rainy or "green" season, from mid-April to December. Temperatures throughout the country remain fairly constant year-round, averaging 80°F/27°C in the hot and humid lowlands. Lowland humidity takes getting used to, especially during rainy season, when you might be dripping even when the skies aren't! Highland temps are perpetually spring-like with balmy days and cool nights. Elevations above 3,000 feet/900 meters can get chilly after sunset, with temps sometimes dropping to the low 50s (around 12°C).

TEMPERATURE & RAINFALL		
MONTH	**DAILY TEMP (MAX / MIN)**	**RAINFALL (INCHES)**
JANUARY	88° / 71° F	1.0
FEBRUARY	89° / 71° F	0.4
MARCH	90° / 72° F	0.7
APRIL	90° / 74° F	2.0
MAY	87° / 74° F	8.0
JUNE	86° / 74° F	8.4
JULY	87° / 74° F	7.1
AUGUST	87° / 74° F	7.9
SEPTEMBER	86° / 74° F	8.2
OCTOBER	85° / 73° F	10.0
NOVEMBER	85° / 73° F	10.2
DECEMBER	87° / 73° F	4.8

Source: *The Traveling Woman*, New York Times Company

Expect a shower or two every day during winter – except perhaps along the drier Pacific coast, called the Arco Seco (Dry Arch). Lowlands receive more precipitation than highlands, and more rain falls on the country's Caribbean side than its Pacific due to a low-pressure air mass that drifts up from the southeast every year from about May to December. This low pressure stalls above the Central Mountains and, by interrupting northeasterly trade winds, causes torrents of rain to fall on Caribbean slopes. If you've never experienced a tropical downpour, you'll wonder where all that water comes from. Take heart; storms arrive in the afternoon and don't usually last long.

> **AUTHOR NOTE:** *Bajareques are light rains that can occur at any time of year in highland regions. More often than not, they are as fine as gentle veiling mists.*

Flora & Fauna

Panamá is blessed with an extraordinary variety of plant and animal species, some of them found nowhere else, others yet to be discovered. To protect fragile ecosystems and rare creatures, almost 29% of the country's terrain has been set aside in national parks and reserves. The rich biodiversity contains 12 of the world's 38 established life zone categories and as many more sub-categories. Of the 5,000 animal species known to exist in the world, fully 1,500 of them live in Panamá. Among the thousands of identified plant species are more than 1,200 native orchids, one with blooms so tiny you need a magnifying glass to see them.

> **AUTHOR NOTE:** *Two-and-a-half acres (one hectare) of temperate forest usually support no more than 10 tree species. The same amount of rainforest land supports about 100, and frequently as many as 200 different species.*

◆ Plants

Panamá has 14,000 identified plant species – ferns, vines, lianas, orchids, bromeliads, mosses and more. Native peoples have relied on medicinal plants to cure or relieve the symptoms of illness for thousands of years. Used in various formulations, they combat headaches and stomach aches, provide antiseptics for wounds, and even prevent bad dreams. In fact, almost half of the modern medicines available from your local pharmacy are derived from jungle plants and trees. Research facilities throughout the world are continually studying and testing tropical plants that may hold the secret to curing cancer and other devastating diseases.

> **AUTHOR NOTE:** *Panamá's national flower is the beautiful, waxy white orchid called **Flor del Espíritú Santo** (Flower of the Holy Ghost).*

Trees

An amazing number of Panamá's 1,500 identified tree species produce gorgeous flowers and edible fruit. The towering **Panama tree** grows to 120 feet/36 meters tall and produces a nut-like fruit that possesses medicinal properties. In contrast to its "elephant foot" trunk base, the **jacaranda** flowers a glorious violet blue. Trek a jungle pathway and you're sure to encounter a giant **ceiba** (kapok or silk-cotton) that was here before the conquistadors arrived. The ancient Maya revered these magnificent trees, which have crowns that spread as wide as 131 feet/40 meters. Another giant you may come across, the spreading **corotu**, dresses up in fluffy white pom-pom flowers. The shimmering gold of a blooming **guayacan** makes this beautiful tree a real standout. An **espave** can grow as tall as 131 feet/40 meters, and rare harpy eagles nest in **cuipo** branches above the jungle canopy. Native people use juice from the **jagua** tree's fruit to make body paint that also repels insects. There are trees that "walk," trees with spines, and the roots of more than a dozen **mangrove** species provide safe haven for tiny sea creatures. The roots and leaves of the **jobo** tree are used to cure colds, heal wounds and reduce fevers. Dozens of **palm** species provide edible fruit, fibers for weaving hats and baskets, and material for thatching roofs. The **Angel's Trumpet** is named for its beautiful, foot-long white flowers shaped like upside-down trumpets, which are reputed to contain a narcotic.

"Rainforests cover less than 2% of the Earth's surface,
yet they are home to some 50-70% of all life forms on our planet.
The rainforests are quite simply, the richest, oldest,
most productive and most complex ecosystems on Earth."
Rainforest Action Network

◆ Birds

Panamá's wild lands protect almost 1,000 identified bird species, and only 124 of them are migratory. The long list of avian inhabitants includes five **macaw** and 52 **hummingbird** species, two species of **toucan** (the jolly Froot Loops birds), hawks, herons, vultures, mot-mots, woodpeckers, aricaris, parrots and parrotlets. Tiny **dacnis** array themselves in neon blue, **tanagers** in every imaginable shade. **Oropendola** nests sway from the trees like hundreds of dirty brown socks hung out to dry. Panamá's national bird, the endangered **harpy eagle**, is the world's most powerful bird of prey. A harpy's wingspans can expand to seven feet, and its talons grow as large as bear paws. The rare **resplendent quetzal** has been called the most beautiful bird in our hemisphere. Spot a showy male with 30-inch-long glittering iridescent green tail feathers and you'll see why. This exquisite avian is Guatemala's national bird – but you'll see many more of them in Panamá's cloud forests!

BIRD SEEKERS: *A Panamanian saying boasts that 20 tourists in Costa Rica try to see one quetzal, while in Panamá, one tourist tries to see 20 of these gorgeous birds.*

◆ Mammals

Magnificent, elusive **jaguars** (*Panthera onca*) are the largest of five cat species that include puma, jaguarundi, margay, and ocelot. Stealthy and shy of humans, they are, like all cats, nocturnal, and more active at night. Fully grown jaguars average 200 pounds/90 kilos, and a large adult male can weigh as much as 300 pounds/135 kilos. Their pelts range from buff to golden orange, with irregular black "donut hole" spots. A few jaguars are solid black with slightly darker spots. Because of this rare "tone-on-tone" coloration, they are sometimes mistakenly called panthers. Jaguars are strong swimmers that don't hesitate to dive into the water after their prey. Killed for their beautiful pelts and pushed from their hunting territories by farmers and developers, these regal animals are highly endangered.

Pumas once ranged from Argentina to British Columbia. These solitary yellowish to gray-brown cats with buff-colored bellies weigh from 148 pounds/67 kilograms to 227 pounds/103 kilograms. Their habitats vary more than the jaguars and they're also endangered.

Because of their color – dark gray/brown to almost chestnut – and facial appearance, **jaguarundis** are often called "otter cats." They're usually found near rivers and streams, as fish is a preferred meal. These little cats range throughout South and Central American and weigh from nine to 17½ pounds/two to four kilograms when fully grown.

Shy, blundering **Baird's tapirs** have stout, compact bodies and long mobile upper lips. They resemble small elephants with short trunks but are more closely related to the horse and rhino. Tapirs are solitary vegetarian animals, usually found alone unless a mother with her baby. They are agile swimmers and when frightened usually head for water. Hunted by native peoples – and jaguars – for their meat, these gentle, defenseless herbivores, which can weigh up to 500 pounds, are tottering toward extinction.

Most of Panamá's 350 **bat** species dine on fruit, small fish or insects. Only the tiny **vampire bat** – whose body size averages only 3.2 inches/80 mm – feeds on fresh, warm blood. Vampires rarely bother humans but, if you're camping in the jungle and wake up with an exposed toe trickling blood, you can assume a vampire has enjoyed a midnight snack. No, you won't turn into a Count (or Countess) Dracula, but may risk an infection. Tent-making bats actually chew through the tough veins of large plant leaves, causing the leaves to collapse down into tent-like shapes. The little bats then roost inside.

Five **monkey** species live in Panamá; **howler**, **capuchin**, **Geoffrey's tamarin**, **spider** and **lemurine night**. Howlers are the most often observed – and heard. When these guys roar, the sound carries up to three miles/4.8 kilometers. It's enough to shake the leaves from trees and guaranteed to send shivers down your spine. Adult howlers have blackish-brown fur and can weigh up to 22 pounds/9.9 kilograms. They are interesting to watch, but don't get too close. When howlers feel threatened, they've been known to pelt invaders with feces. An adult lemurine night monkey weighs only 2.21 pounds/1 kilogram. They're cute little critters, with big round shining eyes. Because of their hooting call, they're also called owl monkeys.

Although you may never see a jaguar, a tapir or a tiny vampire bat in the wild, your chances of spotting **agoutis** (*ñeque*), two- and three-toed **sloths** (*peresoso*), vested **anteaters** (*tamadua*), **coatimundis** (*gato solo*) and monkeys are excellent. **Armadillos**, those little armored pigs, are also around, but don't expect to see them during the day as they're also nocturnal. **Pacas** are attractive little vegetarian rodents with reddish spotted fur and squirrel-like faces. They're shy night foragers that average about 22 pounds/10 kilograms when fully grown.

Other common mammals are collared and white-lipped **peccaries, capybaras, giant anteaters, deer, kinkajous, tayras, rabbits** and **raccoons**, to name only a few. None of them will throw anything at you. Peccaries may look like harmless little pigs, but an enraged herd of these smelly animals should be avoided at all costs.

◆ Reptiles & Amphibians

Snakes

The **fer-de-lance**, a pit viper that grows up to eight feet/2.4 meters in length, is Panamá's most infamous reptile. Females give live birth to as many as 100 babies at a time. Although seldom encountered by tourists, this deadly snake is numerous throughout Central America. Young fer-de-lances are more aggressive than adults.

> **AUTHOR NOTE:** *In Mexico, the fer-de-lance is called "tres minutos" (three minutes) – an exaggeration of how long one might survive after having been bitten. In Belize, it's called "tommygoff"; in Honduras, "barba amarilla." Panamá's indigenous people call it "X snake," because of the diamond-shaped markings on its back.*

The larger **bushmaster** is also poisonous, but quite rare. Tiny venomous **coral snakes** are pretty little creatures with bright red, yellow and black bands around their bodies. Their fangs are much too tiny to pierce shoe leather, so they don't pose any danger unless you attempt to pick up one or walk through the forests barefoot or in open sandals. Yellowish-green **eyelash vipers** are equally pretty, but they, too, are venomous. Panama's largest snake, the non-poisonous **boa constrictor**, may bite if molested, although it isn't usually dangerous unless you're a small, warm mammal. Well, maybe not so small. Just exercise a bit of caution and don't poke your hands or feet into places you can't see. Then rest easy, as snakes prefer to avoid humans, and most are harmless.

Turtles

Five **sea turtle** species nest on Panamá's shores and all are endangered – **hawksbill**, **olive ridley**, **loggerhead**, **Atlantic green** and **leatherback**. These harmless creatures are hunted for their meat and for their shells, which are made into jewelry.

Most endangered of all is the massive leatherback, named for the tough rubbery-textured carapace covering its back in place of a shell. Adults average eight to 10 feet in length and can weigh more than a ton (1,016 kilos). Leatherbacks are the world's largest reptiles and they've been around since the time of the dinosaurs – about 100 million years. It might shock you to know that in only the last 20 years, their numbers have declined by fully two-thirds and today, they are on the edge of extinction. Many are drowned in fish and shrimp nets; nesting grounds are lost to development. Wild pigs, dogs, humans and other predators rob eggs from their nests; and seabirds prey upon hatchlings so tiny, one fits easily in the palm of your hand. Because the leatherback's diet consists almost exclusively of jellyfish, it often mistakes floating plastic bags and other debris for a meal. The result is devastating.

Sea turtles come ashore along Panamá's Pacific and Caribbean coasts from July through December to lay their eggs in the sand. To watch thousands of tiny turtles pop out of their nests in the sand and struggle toward the sea is a never-to-be-forgotten adventure. Their numbers are decreasing so rapidly that, in 1998, the presidents of Panamá, Costa Rica and Nicaragua signed a tri-partite agreement outlining conservation measures to protect them. Sadly, illegal poaching of both turtles and their eggs continues almost unabated.

By attaching depth recorders to leatherback turtles, scientists have learned these huge creatures can dive more than 3,300 ft/1000 meters below the sea's surface.

River turtles are far more numerous. You'll see them sunning along the banks of rivers and streams and clustered on exposed rocks.

◆ Crocodiles & Caimans

There are no alligators in Panamá, only caimans or crocodiles (*lagartos*) that are seldom seen during the day unless in captivity. Gamboa Rainforest Resort and Panagator Crocodile Park are two places to see them close up. Two crocodilian species inhabit the isthmus, the large **American Crocodile** and the smaller **Common Caiman**. A large full-grown male American crocodile (sometimes called *lagarto blanco*) can measure 16 feet/five meters in length; an adult male common caiman, only about eight feet/2½ meters. These most vocal of all reptiles use a wide range of sounds to communicate, including hisses, bellows, several differently pitched coughs, and a squawk of distress that sounds much like a crow's caw. They may appear lethargic, but when they choose, these big reptiles encased in lumpy hides can move lightening fast.

◆ Frogs & Toads

Panamá has more than 140 frog species. Peek into a few bromeliads during your jungle trek and you might see a tiny one paddling around in the water that collects inside these plants – perfect swimming pools for the little guys. The **red-eyed tree frog** is a charming fellow with a deep green body, a yellow belly, big feet and bulging bright red eyes. He's a popular model for advertising materials.

Two species of **poison dart frog**, found nowhere else in the world, inhabit Bocas del Toro's islands. Red Frog Beach got its name from the fingernail-size crimson frogs that are known to exist in only one small patch of nearby jungle. While poisonous frogs are beautiful and brightly colored, **Bufo toads**, also poisonous, are big, brown and lumpy. Bufos exude poison from their backs, so don't go around biting or squeezing them. Dogs and cats, unfortunately, do bite them occasionally.

◆ Lizards

Darting lizards are everywhere. All are harmless and most are only a few inches long. Largest are the three-foot black or **green iguanas** that are hunted for food. Called "tree chickens" because their meat tastes like chicken, those penned in a back yard might be destined for the dinner table. Other more fortunate captives are "farmed" to ensure their continuation. No matter how adventurous your taste buds, please don't eat one!

◆ Insects & Arachnids

Like all tropical regions, Panamá is plentifully supplied with bugs. They are beautiful, ugly, annoying, useful, curious, fascinating or downright nasty. Among the 1,500 species butterfly (*mariposa*) species are the exquisite **blue morphos** with iridescent six-eight-inch/15-20-cm wings that flutter in rippling slow motion. Spend a few hours in the jungle and you're sure to encounter **leaf-cutter ants** (*hormigas*) scurrying along tiny worn pathways with chunks of leaves waving like green umbrellas above their tiny bodies. Roving brigades of "soldiers" guard the little ants as they travel miles in single file. The gathered bits of leaves are toted back to the nest where the ants chew them into mulch to be planted in underground "gardens." The mulch sprouts a mold that supplies their food.

Whistling inch-long **paraponara ants** are interesting to observe, but these big brutes pack a painful bite. And don't panic if you encounter a huge, hairy **tarantula** spider. They are actually quite gentle and seldom bite. Pesky **mosquitoes** carry serious diseases and harmless dung beetles are useful and, well…yucky. Blood-sucking **ticks** come in a variety of species, some smaller than pinheads. These little invaders are extremely unpleasant as they tend to seek out the body's warm, moist places.

AUTHOR NOTE: *As many as eight million leaf-cutter ants live in a single underground colony that can be as long as 18 ft/three meters and contain up to 3,000 chambers.*

◆ In the Waters

The Caribbean reefs lying off Bocas del Toro harbor more than 79 coral species, and the western central Pacific's largest coral reef system stretches along Panamá's northwestern coast. The reefs teem with small fish, **octopi**, **crabs** and **lobsters**. **Starfish** congregate by the thousands in the warm waters of Bocas del Toro and Kuna Yala. Other aquatic creatures include **sharks**, **rays**, **sea turtles**, dozens of **fish** species, **eels**, **dolphins**, **manatees** and migrating **orca** and **humpback** whales.

More world sportfishing records have been set in Panamá than anywhere else has on earth. **Blue marlin, black marlin**, **sailfish**, **dorado**, **roosterfish**, **wahoo** and **yellowfin tuna** are regularly caught and released in Caribbean and Pacific waters. **Rainbow trout** fairly burst from Chiriquí's cold mountain streams, and **peacock bass** have literally overrun Gatún Lake. Neither the bass nor the trout are indigenous – man transported both here. The trout haven't caused any difficulty, but the bass have reproduced so rapidly, they've crowded out native species.

Preservation

Unfortunately, many of the world's most exotic and useful animals and plants are highly endangered. The World Conservation Monitoring Association has "red-listed" – meaning their continued survival is precarious – more than 100 of Panamá's creatures. Small colonies of frogs, particularly vulnerable to air and water pollution, might disappear in an instant. Panamá's fabled **golden frog** has become a rarity.

Parrots captured for sale on the international black market often don't survive the trauma. **Macaws** and **quetzals** are killed for their beautiful feathers; **iguanas** for their meat; **sea turtles** are killed for meat and shells and their nests plundered for eggs. **Lobsters**, once plentiful throughout San Blas, have almost disappeared from that area, and are traded for a few paltry dollars to end up as expensive dinners on the mainland.

Jaguars and other big cats are doubly threatened; slaughtered for their pelts and by loss of habitat. Ancient, irreplaceable trees and rare plants are cut, burned, razed and bulldozed out of existence to make way for cattle ranches, logging concerns, roads, subsistence farms, and developments. Greedy poachers, native peoples and hungry peasants hunt indiscriminately and thoughtlessly – to feed their families or merely for profit.

◆ Sustainable Travel

Panamá's population density is low and concentrated largely in cities and towns. For these reasons, its wilderness heritage and ancient indigenous cultures have been well preserved. Follow a few simple rules that will make your adventures more rewarding while helping to preserve wild lands, animals and local cultures.

- ❖ When in a fragile environment, don't wander from marked trails. Your foot, dainty as it may be, can crush a tiny frog, frighten a bird from its nest or destroy delicate mosses.

- ❖ Remove nothing. Picking a flower or fruit might deprive a plant of the seeds necessary to continue its species, or a hummingbird its lunch.

- ❖ Don't litter. A single plastic bag tossed on the beach might strangle a critically endangered sea turtle.

- ❖ Local and indigenous people may have views and beliefs quite different from your own. Instead of making judgments, ask questions and listen to the replies. You'll gain perspective and understanding.

- ❖ Purchase gifts and souvenirs from local people – but only those crafted from renewable resources.

- ❖ Hire local guides who will share knowledge and insight while leading you to experiences you might have missed otherwise. Bear in mind that people who can earn more money from tourism than from killing a jaguar for its pelt, a sea turtle for its shell or a macaw for its feathers are more likely to spare these magnificent creatures.

- ❖ We like to be generous, but skewing the local economy doesn't help local people. Try not to under tip or over tip for services. Take note of when it's okay to bargain and when it is not. Don't belittle an artisan by demanding a discount for an item that may have taken days or weeks to craft.

- ❖ Don't give money unless in exchange for goods or services. (It's okay to donate to a worthwhile non-profit organization.) If you want to give gifts when visiting remote areas, take pencils, crayons, paper and coloring or picture books – but not candy — for the kids. Adults appreciate small useful items; fishhooks, needles and thread, pocket knives or lighters. Many delight in a simple Polaroid photograph. If you've visited places where children chase and plead with tourists for money, you can guess how this humiliating custom came about.

A few years ago, Panamá commissioned an "Eco-development" plan called T-C-R (Tourism-Conservation-Research) to promote sustainable tourism. It will take years to gauge its success. A handful of conservationist landowners and hoteliers have already taken measures to sustain their lands. These include growing only organic foods, providing training and work for local people, replanting native forests, buying biodegradable cleaning products in refillable containers, and using of energy-saving devices. In the Central Mountains of Coclé province, a rare albino hummingbird species, unseen for half a century and thought to be extinct, suddenly reappeared after previously barren cattle pastures had been reforested. Endangered golden frogs are also making a comeback in these high mountain forests where lizards sing.

On the other hand, a "reforestation" concession promising huge benefits to landowners is resulting in a proliferation of teak forests. Highly valued for its lumber, teak is fast-growing so investors – many of them foreign — don't wait long to reap financial benefits. If unchecked, this might prove disastrous since teak doesn't provide the nuts, fruits, seeds, nesting places or ground cover for the protection and survival of wildlife. .

National Parks

Panamá's national parks are administered by the government agency **ANAM** – Autoridad Nacional del Ambiente. Most are open to visitors, but a few can be visited only with advance permission from ANAM; ☎ 507-229-7885 in Panamá City. A small fee (currently $3 per person and $10 per person for marine parks) is charged to visit the parks. Camping is usually permitted, and some parks have rustic accommodations for overnight stays. No fees are charged to visit other protected areas.

◆ Panamá Province

Parque Nacional Camino de Cruces/Trail of the Crosses National Park: Enclosing a portion of the old Spanish route and part of the biological corridor connecting Soberania and Chagres national parks, this 11,337-acre/4,590-hectare park protects the Panamá Canal's eastern banks. Popular for its hiking and bird watching opportunities, it is home to red and green macaws, rare slaty-tailed trogons, crested eagles, iguanas, red brocket and white-tail deer, coatimundis, howler monkeys and pacas.

Parque Nacional Chagres/Chagres National Park: Parts of the Spanish Las Cruces Trail and the Camino Real run through this 337,500-acre/129,000-hectare park, established to protect the Chagres River's watershed that supplies 80% of the Panama Canal's fresh water as well as Panamá City's drinking water. Lake Alajuela, the Chagres River, and several Emberá communities are within its boundaries. Visits to the communities, hiking, bird watching, camping and fishing are a few of its attractions for visitors. Access is from Panamá City or Cerro Azul. See page 115.

Parque Nacional Altos de Campana/Campana Heights National Park: Panamá's first national park was created in 1966. Its 12,000-acres/4,925 hectares include spectacular cliffs and mangrove estuaries, and its 32 mammal species include two- and three-toed sloths, pacas, vampire bats and coatimundis. Orchids, bromeliads and epiphytic plants are abundant, and golden frogs can still be found here. The park protects the watersheds of three important rivers. There are good hiking trails and spectacular views. See page 121.

◆ Colón Province

Parque Nacional Soberanía/Soberanía National Park: One of the world's most accessible rainforests is a half-hour from the capital. Soberanía's 47,772 undulating acres (19,341 hectares) protect the Panama Canal watershed, 105 mammal species including jaguars, capybaras, black-handed spider and howler monkeys and 525 bird identified bird species. The park, particularly along Pipeline Road, is one of the world's prime bird watching areas. Naturalists and hikers will find several excellent trails. See page 114.

Parque Nacional Portobelo/Portobelo National Park: This 88,744-acre/35,929-hectare park and UNESCO World Heritage site includes the ruins of the ancient Spanish City, Portobelo, rugged interior rainforests and a 43.4-mile/70-kilometer coastline that includes coral reefs, beaches, estuaries and mangrove forests. Attractions include touring the ruins, scuba diving, hiking and trekking. See page 140.

Parque Nacional Omar Torrijos Herrera/Omar Torrijos Herrera National Park (Coclé Province, page 166): Most often called "El Copé" for a nearby town and a tree species common to the area, this magnificent cloud-forest park spreads over the continental divide. All five of Panamá's cat species live within its 54,845 acres/25,275 hectares, as do white-lipped and collared peccaries, Baird's tapirs, white-tailed deer and several endemic bird species. Activities include hiking, bird watching and naturalist adventures.

◆ Azuero Peninsula

Parque Nacional Sarigua/Sarigua National Park (Herrera Province, page 180): Sarigua's 20,000 acres/8,000 hectares includes three distinctly different areas – semi-desert, sea and fragmented soil. The semi-arid sections of the park stand in mute testimony to the destruction caused by over-use of the land. The park contains important archeological sites, a small amount of remaining forest and mangrove stands along the coast.

Parque Nacional Cerro Hoya (Los Santos and Veraguas provinces): This 80,415-acre/32,557-hectare park at the extreme end of the Azuero Peninsula protects the hydrographic basins of several important rivers, mangroves, tropical humid and rainforests, as well as an area of continental shelf, coral reefs and small islets. There are spectacular waterfalls and the peninsula's last remaining tropical forest. Endemic bird species include the painted parakeet and fishing eagle.

◆ Veraguas Province

Parque Nacional Coiba/Coiba National Park: Coiba's 650,000 acres/ 270,000 hectares protect three different habitats, island, reef and marine. Largest of an island group within the park, Coiba Island, part sanctuary and part penal colony, is the Panamanian Pacific's largest island and one of the country's last refuges for endangered scarlet macaws (see page 198.

◆ Chiriquí Province

Parque Internacional La Amistad/La Amistad International Park (Chiriquí and Bocas del Toro Provinces; pages 233 and 249): Shared with Costa Rica, La Amistad is a UNESCO World Heritage Site and the world's first bi-national Biosphere Reserve. Slightly more than half of the park lies within Panamá in the rugged Talamanca Mountains. 95% of its 517,000 acres/207,000 hectares are in Bocas del Toro Province and 5% are in Chiriquí. Jaguars, Baird's and Andean tapirs, giant anteaters, harlequin frogs, harpy eagles and resplendent quetzals are some of the endangered animals living in the park, and three indigenous tribes make their homes here.

Parque Nacional Volcán Barú/Volcán Barú National Park: This dramatic park's 36,000 acres/14,322 hectares roughly follow the contours of its most striking feature, massive Volcán Barú. Rising from the mountains that surround it, Barú's 11,401-foot/3,405-meter summit is Panamá's highest peak. Among the rare endemic birds found here are the volcano junco and the bare-necked umbrella bird. See page 232.

Parque Nacional Golfo de Chiriquí: More than two dozen islands and islets lie in the Pacific waters of this park's 36,407 acres/14,740 hectares, the largest of which is Isla Parida. The island's wildlife includes red-lored Amazon parrots, scarlet macaws, tiger herons, black and green frogs, and many, many iguanas; five sea turtle species nest on its beaches. White-tip sharks, angel rays and dozens of spectacular fish species are found in the park's waters.

◆ Bocas del Toro Province

Isla Bastimentos National Marine Park: Bastimentos conserves island, coral reef, sea and mangrove habitats in Almirante Bay off the northern Caribbean coast. The white-sand-bordered Zapatilla Cayes and part of Bastimentos Island lie within its 32,668 acres/13,325 hectares, slightly more than half of which are marine zones. Scuba diving, snorkeling, surfing and wildlife watching are the main attractions. See page 254.

◆ Darién Province

Parque Nacional Darién/Darién National Park: Bordered by Columbia's Katio National Park, Panamá's largest national park (1.5 million acres/576,000 hectares) protects several endemic wildlife species and Central America's largest remaining tracts of primary forests. Declared a UNESCO World Heritage Site and Biosphere Reserve in 1981, its varied landscapes include Atlantic and Pacific coastlines, mangrove stands, rivers, rainforests, marshes, and mountain ranges with peaks up to 8,200 ft/2,490 meters above sea level. Kuna, Wounaan and Emberá (also called Chocó) comarcas (autonomously ruled lands) lie within the borders of this vast wilderness that offers extraordinary cultural, bird and wildlife watching, and trekking adventures. See page 282.

Government

Panamá is a **republic** with a constitution that guarantees its citizens freedom of speech and religion. Citizens 18 years and older have the right to vote in elections. The government is headed by a president and two vice-presidents elected by the people to a five-year term. Twelve appointed ministers of state make up the cabinet Council. The legislative assembly's 72 members, elected by popular vote, also serve a five-year term. The Supreme Court's nine-member judiciary, appointed by the president, serves for 10 years.

Panamá's nine provinces are **Darién**, **Panamá**, **Colón**, **Coclé**, **Los Santos**, **Herrera**, **Veraguas**, **Bocas del Toro** and **Chiriquí**; each has a governor appointed by the executive branch. There are also five indigenous *comarcas* – lands administered autonomously by Panamá's native peoples. They are: the Kuna *comarcas* of **Wargandi**, **Madungandi**, and **Kuna Yala**; **Comarca Ngöbe-Buglé**; and **Comarca Cemaco** (Emberá/Wounaan). Although they are independently governed, citizens of the *comarcas* vote in the country's elections and can have representatives in the congress.

Economy

Panamanians enjoy the highest per capita income in all Central America, and almost two-thirds are urban dwellers. Commerce and trade have fueled the economy since 16th-century Conquistadors first hauled looted treasure across the isthmus. The country's present service-based economy developed along this same corridor in the late 19th and early 20th centuries during construction of the Panamá Railroad and the US Canal.

The canal continues to be the most important single factor in the economy, with revenues generated by tolls and the jobs it provides, both directly and indirectly. More than one-half of the population now lives and works at either end of the "corridor" in or near Panamá City and Colón. Due to a convergence of fiber optic networks here, the cities are fast emerging as Internet and telecommunications hubs. Although 25% of workers are employed in agriculture, most are subsistence farmers. Bananas are the largest export crop, followed by sugar, coffee and tobacco. Panamá is an international banking center, hosting 100 international banks that provide 11,000 jobs, while the Colón Free Zone continues to expand with an annual turnover of about $12 billion.

Because of an historical dependence on commercial activity, tourism was not a priority until the late 1990s, when it began to slowly increase. After the 1999 elections and new tourism officials were installed, the number of visitors dwindled, despite a staggering increase in promotional budgets. Almost simultaneously, the economy suffered a devastating blow with the Panamá Canal reversion as 50,000 US military and civilian personnel departed the country, evaporating an estimated $300,000,000 generated annually by their presence.

But things are looking up. Those huge promotional expenditures and a lot of recent play in the press have put Panamá back in the spotlight: The canal reversion made headlines around the world; the 2002 Miss Universe is Panamanian; Donald Trump's 2003 Miss Universe Pageant was held in the capital; a 2004 US edition of the popular *Survivor* television series was filmed in the Pearl Islands and new ports are luring more and more cruise ships to include the country as a port of call. In 2004, Martín Torrijos, son of legendary Omar Torrijos Herrera, was elected president and internationally famed musician and actor Rúben Blades garnered the tourism institute's (IPAT) top slot. Panamá is once again on the brink of discovery — this time not by plunderers and treasure seekers, but travelers in search of natural adventure

Panamá's People

Panamá's turbulent history bequeathed it a legacy of vibrant cultures and people so diverse it's impossible to make more than a few generalizations about them. On the whole, they are easygoing and genuinely friendly, exuberantly patriotic and exceedingly loyal and tolerant. The old "machismo" still prevalent in many Latin American countries is fading into the past as more and more women professionals enjoy work place equality.

Differences are respected; family and friends treasured; babies, children and great-aunts adored. Although extremely hardworking, Panamanians know how to relax and enjoy life. No excuse is needed for a celebration and there seems always to be a birthday, anniversary, quince, graduation or housewarming that requires one. Don't be surprised if a new acquaintance invites you to share the fun. By all means go – and find yourself cocooned with new friends as diverse and exotic as Panamá's landscapes and as warm and welcoming as its tropical sunshine.

◆ Their Origins

Panamá is a delicious stew of races, ethnic backgrounds and religions. **Mestizos** (called "Cholo" in Central Mountain regions), mixed Spanish and Amerindian, make up about 70% of the citizenry, although **Blacks** and mixed **Black-Amerindian** (14%) and **European** and **North American whites** (10%) are well represented. Triply blessed **Criollos** are a mixture of Black, European white and indigenous backgrounds. About six percent of the population are unmixed indigenous Amerindian, and smaller communities of Chinese, Indians, Jews and Arabs have made important contributions to the country's economy and cultural diversity.

> **AUTHOR NOTE:** *According to the latest published census in 2003, Panamá's population is estimated at 2,960,784; 52% live in or near Panamá City and Colón.*

◆ Indigenous Peoples

When the Spanish arrived at the beginning of the 16th century, the isthmus was heavily populated with indigenous peoples. No records remain to tell us how many there might have been or how many died. Today, only seven groups survive – the **Kuna Ngöbe-Buglé, Emberá, Wounaan, Bri-Bri, Teribé** and **Bokata**.

Ngöbe-Buglé

Panamá's largest indigenous group consists of two closely related peoples, the Ngöbe and Buglé. So closely related, in fact, that they share a *comarca* (independently governed lands) and are called collectively Ngöbe-Buglé or sometimes Guaymí. About 125,000 of these stately, handsome people live autonomously in small family groups in the Central Mountains of Chiriquí, Veraguas and Bocas del Toro provinces. Many of these traditional subsistence farmers must now migrate for economic reasons to labor on coffee plantations and vegetable farms.

Kuna (Tulé)

Second-largest but more widely recognized are the Kuna, or Tulé, numbering about 50,000. Anthropologists trace their origins to the Darién jungles – the warriors that accompanied Balboa on his trek to the Pacific may have been Kuna. Resistant to outside interference, these fiercely independent people gained autonomous rule over their lands after a bloody civil uprising in 1925. Their territories, called Kuna Yala or Dulenega (Land of the Kuna), include a mountainous strip of jungle stretched along the Caribbean coast from Colón Province to Columbia and the 200-mile/322-km San Blas Archipelago, a paradisiacal island chain.

Emberá & Wounaan

Only a slight language variation separates the Emberá and Wounaan who migrated up from South America to the Darién jungles. Both groups live in traditional villages of open-sided homes on stilts above the riverbanks. Over the last 30 years or so, a few Emberá have migrated north to the jungles bordering the Chagres River, a scant two hours north from the capital. Tourism now plays an important part in their economy and visitors are warmly welcomed to their villages. Go, if you possibly can. The first thing you'll notice is the stunning beauty of the women and children; or perhaps the blue-black paint adorning their bodies like tattoos.

Bri-Bri, Naso (also called Teribé) & Bokata

Small populations of Bri-Bri (related to Costa Rica's Talamancas) and Naso (Teribé) inhabit Bocas del Toro's wet tropical forests near the headwaters of the Teribé and Yorkin rivers. The Naso work hard to keep their ancient traditions alive as they assimilate into the modern world. Sadly, the Bokatas have lost most of their culture and assimilated into the local Mestizo population – a process greatly accelerated by Christian missionaries during the 1950s.

◆ Other Ethnic Groups

Afro-Antilleans & Congos

The Congos trace their lineage to African slaves brought to the isthmus during colonial times. The name is derived from "Congo," a traditional dance of African origin. Although small in numbers, most of these fun-loving folks live along Caribbean shores in and around historic Portobelo. Masked Congo dancers in costumes decorated with tree bark and trailing feathers take part in Panamá's important celebrations and, even now, five centuries after the Conquest, their dances still poke fun at the conquistadors.

French-speaking Blacks from Martinique and Guadeloupe immigrated to Panamá during the 1880s to work on the construction of the failed French canal. Waves of English-speaking immigrants, mostly from Barbados and Jamaica, arrived between 1848 and 1914 to labor on the Panama Railroad and the Panama Canal, and to work in banana plantations along the northern Caribbean coast.

Chinese

The Chinese arrived to provide the bulk of labor for the Panama Railroad's construction. Brought to the country as indentured servants, most arrived during 1854 and 1855. Of all the nationalities brought to work on the railroad, they proved the hardest working and most efficient. A second, smaller wave of Chinese immigrants came to work on the French canal project and, during the 1980s, more arrived seeking political freedom. There are today about 80,000 Chinese in Panamá.

Europeans

Since the time of the conquistadors, Panamá has attracted Europeans and North Americans. Some came to settle the rich farmlands of Chiriquí Province, while others arrived to work on the railroad, the French canal and the US canal. They found the country to their liking and remained here. Panamá's pleasing climate, high standard and reasonable cost of living continues to attract North American and European retirees.

◆ Education

Panamá's literacy rate is 93% and rising. Education is highly valued, and most young people look forward to attending college or university. Public elementary and secondary schools are free and, although university tuition is surprisingly inexpensive, many that can afford it complete their education in the US, with a few going to Europe. You'll meet Panamanians who speak English without a trace of an accent. Visit a doctor or dentist while you're here, and chances are he or she trained in the US.

◆ Language

Although **Spanish** is the official language, **English** is widely spoken in the capital and in large resorts – and it's the unofficial language of the Caribbean coast. Many well-educated citizens speak two, three, or more languages. English is taught in the schools, but a recent movement to make it an second official language failed: Many voters thought it unpatriotic. **Spanglish**, a mixture of Spanish and English, is also spoken, so don't be surprised to hear it in a sentence like, "Quiere va el mall?" – meaning, of course, "Do you want to go to the mall?" In the interior, few people speak anything other than Spanish.

◆ Religion

About 80% of Panamanians are wholeheartedly **Catholic**, although many young people find weekend visits to "el interior" or the beaches more attractive than attending formal services. Another 14% are **Protestant**, due largely to an onslaught of foreign missionaries. The rest are of all religions and beliefs. You won't have any difficulty in finding a mosque, temple or shrine in which to worship during your visit. A dwindling few indigenous people still hold animistic beliefs, but most are Catholic and some have converted to Protestant faiths because of an unrelenting barrage of evangelical missionaries.

◆ Traditional Culture

The customs of old Spain blended with those of Native America and Africa to produce Panamá's traditional folk culture. Modernization came slowly to the central provinces of Coclé, Veraguas, Los Santos and Herrera, where traditions originated during the 16th and 17th centuries are still very much alive. Frequent festivals are held with age-old abandon and you'll hear more traditional music than pop, salsa or rock blaring from the radios. As they have been for centuries, rural homes are built by hand of whitewashed mud bricks and hand-made clay tiles. Mounted cowboys still work cattle ranches and rural farmlands, but oxcarts are fading into memory, replaced now by imported Japanese pick-up trucks. Until a few decades ago, the traditional peasant dress, called *pollera* for women and *camisilla* or *montuño* for men, was worn daily. Now it's donned only for festivals or whenever there is an opportunity to display the national costume.

Customs and traditions are rooted in religious beliefs, and every town and village has its **patron saint**, honored each year with a festival (*patronal*). Patronales begin with nine days of prayer in the local church and end with a solemn procession of the faithful following the saint's statue through the streets. After the statue is returned to the church, the party begins. The delicious scents of roasting corn and meats mingle with the sounds of laughter as cadenced drumbeats and the cry of the mejorana (a small four-string guitar native to the region) accent three days and nights of traditional music and dance, fireworks, contests and *corridas* (bullfights).

> ### ❖ LOCAL LORE
>
> **Muñecos** are life-size effigies made in December and burned on New Year's day. Usually stuffed with straw, these huge dolls might express one's displeasure toward someone – usually a political figure – or something, or they are made simply for fun. The tradition had begun to die out, but is now enjoying a revival.

Food & Drink

Don't expect your eyes to tear from hot, spicy food. Traditional Panamanian dishes rely heavily on garlic, culantro and onions for delicious subtle flavors. If you prefer more zing, ask for a bottle of *salsa piquante* (hot sauce) and sprinkle it on.

◆ Traditional Dishes

Panamá's national dish, **sancocho**, is the traditional Sunday meal in the central provinces. It's a steaming bowl of heavenly chicken soup delicately flavored with garlic, oregano, and culantro (a member of the parsley family, similar to cilantro), served with rice on the side. Sometimes corn on the cob is added. It varies only slightly by region and is on menus throughout the country. Be sure to try it.

Meals usually include a side of **patacones** made from green plantains (*platanos*), a banana-like fruit inedible when raw. This dish is prepared by slicing the plantains into "coins," frying them, smashing them down, then frying again until crisp. Add a dash of picante and crunch away. Sweet **platanos en tentación** are ripened plantains sliced lengthwise and baked slowly with butter, brown sugar and cinnamon. Other favorite dishes are:

- ❖ **Yuca frita** – French fries made from yuca instead of potatoes; to me, they're tastier.
- ❖ **Arroz con pollo** – Panamá's version, a popular lunch dish, is boneless chicken cooked with rice, garlic and bits of vegetables.
- ❖ **Tasajo** – delicious sun-dried smoked beef, usually accompanied by vegetables.
- ❖ **Tamal de ola** – This dish combines large, tasty corn tamales stuffed with meat and vegetables and sprinkled with hot pepper sauce. Raisins or tomatoes are sometimes added before the mixture is baked in a huge clay jar (*ola*).
- ❖ **Ropa vieja** (old clothes) – It isn't what the name implies but a dish common throughout Latin America. Panamá's version is a piquantly spiced casserole of shredded beef, rice, tomatoes, bell peppers, onions, garlic and green olives simmered or baked in a large pot.
- ❖ Bocas del Toro's inspired West Indian cooks use coconut, coconut milk and hot peppers to flavor foods. Sample **coconut rice**, **flan coco** and **fufu**, fried fish cooked in coconut milk with yams and plantains.
- ❖ For dessert, opt for flan, **pudin de arroz** (rice pudding), a piece of sweet **très leches** (three-milk cake) or any number of delicious local specialties. Popular **pastel de manzana** (apple pie) and **pastel de queso** (cheesecake) are not the same as mom used to make and may disappoint.

◆ Seafood

Seafood lovers will glory in Panamá's bountiful fruits from the sea. Delicious **corvina** is a firm white fish usually grilled or broiled with a choice of sauces. Personal favorites are *corvina al ajillo* (with garlic) and *corvina* drenched in a delicate herbed cream sauce with chunks of lobster. **Red snapper** (*pargo*), **guabina** (similar to corvina but slightly more delicate) and **grouper** are also prepared in dozens of innovative ways. Liberal doses of garlic, spices, limes and butter flavor many seafood dishes. *Pulpo* (octopus) baked in a buttery garlic sauce is one of the most popular. **Camarones** are the average-size shrimp you'll find in dishes like paella, seafood pastas and served over rice. *Langostinos* are succulent prawns, so large that four or five make a filling entrée.

Tantalizing **ceviche** – raw fish or shellfish "cooked" (marinated) in lime juice with garlic and onions – are made with *corvina*, octopus or shrimp, or all three in combination. **Crab** (*congrejo*) and **lobster** (*langosta*) are grilled, boiled or broiled and succulent **clams** (*almejas*) no bigger than your thumbnail are eaten cold with cocktail sauce, added to paella or simmered in garlic and spices. **Oysters** (*ostiones*) aren't as common as other shellfish, but delicious when they're available. A couple of oddities found near the Azuero Peninsula's Pacific coast are *longarones*, four-inch-long tube-shaped shellfish, and *concha negra*, baseball-sized black clams. At least I think they're clams.

◆ Street Food

You won't find as much street food here as in other Central American countries. *Palitos de carne* (meat on a stick) is, well, chunks of barbecued meat on a stick. *Carimañolas* are meat-stuffed pastries made from yuca flour and fried to make a tasty finger-food snack. Similar *empanadas* are usually made from cornmeal flour stuffed with meat or cheese and baked. Sausages are called *salchichas*. *Bollos* are sold only in poorer districts. They are boiled cornmeal with a little oil added and wrapped in corn husks or banana leaves. Those little paper cones filled with crushed ice and fruit syrup hawked by street vendors are delicious *raspados*. Refreshingly cool and light, they taste best on hot, sunny afternoons. Choose a familiar raspberry, strawberry or cherry flavor, or one flavored with exotic papaya, soursop or tamarindo.

◆ Fruits & Veggies

Just about everything grows in Panamá – and it grows big. You'll find all the familiar fruits and vegetables and perhaps a few unfamiliar ones. *Name*, *otóe*, and *yuca* are starchy root vegetables. Little round *pixbae* are palm nuts that are eaten raw or pickled and often added to salads. They're very popular here, so try them. Personally, I think they taste like compressed sawdust. Fruits you'll encounter include huge **papayas**; juicy **strawberries**; sweet **oranges** and **pineapples**; **lemons**; **limes**; huge **raspberries**; luscious **mangoes**; **chirimoyas**; **avocados**; **melons**; **carambola** (starfruit, also called *fruita china*); **guavas** (*guayaba*); small and sour **nancé** (usually made into jam, or sweetened and used in milkshakes and other drinks); **soursop**; **noni** (a green fruit said to have medicinal properties); **plaintains**; **breadfruit;** and several varieties of **bananas**.

◆ Liquid Repasts

Panamanians are confirmed **coffee** drinkers. And no wonder, some of the world's finest coffee is produced here. The best is usually exported, but you can still find a good cup of java, especially if you prefer it strong, strong, strong. If you don't, ask for *café Americano* or *café con leche*, half coffee and half hot milk. You'll find the best in Chiriquí, where it's grown and freshly roasted. Herbal teas are popular as well.

Chicheme is a thick, nourishing drink made from ground corn, milk, sugar, cinnamon and vanilla, while *horchata* is made from rice, milk, sugar, cinnamon and vanilla. Both are combined and blended with ice.

Chicha is fresh fruit juice with water and sugar – "fruit-ade." It's still called *chicha* when fermented into a slightly sour alcoholic state.

Good water, or so it's said, makes good beer, and perhaps that's why Panamá's *cervezas* (beers) are of such high quality. If you like yours light, order a bottle of excellent Panamá, Soberana or Balboa. Atlas is heavier and stronger with a lingering taste. Carta Vieja and Ron Cortez are very good local **rums**.

> **AUTHOR NOTE:** *Be sure to sample thick, creamy* **batidos** *(milkshakes), made with plenty of fresh fruit blended with milk and rice. Yum.*

Seco, another popular alcoholic sugarcane derivative, is mixed with fruit juice and rum to make a drink called *chichita*. *Guarapo*, also called *guaro*, is Panamá's moonshine – a nasty, throat-scalding swill that packs a mule's kick.

> **AUTHOR NOTE:** *Milk, juices and other drinks are sold by the pint, quart, half-gallon and gallon – rather than by the liter.*

Holidays & Celebrations

◆ Holidays

◆ Festivals & Events

Carnival is the granddaddy of all festivals, a riotous country-wide cele-bration. Beginning the Saturday before Ash Wednesday, this four-day whirlwind of float parades, masked dancers and stomping *diablicos sucios* (dirty devils – also called *diablicos rojos* for their red costumes) fly-ing confetti, swirling *polleras* and throbbing congo drums competing with salsa, murga and traditional rhythms. Costumed celebrants party all day and all night. Panamá City hosts the biggest party; Las Tablas, the most traditional.

> **AUTHOR NOTE:** *The tourism institute, Instituto Panameño de Tourismo (IPAT), can provide more information and exact dates for events listed below – and many others. They can also pro-vide brochures, maps and other information. See page 40 for a list of regional offices or call their Tourism Hot Line toll-free from the US and Canada, ☎ 800-231-0568.*

◆ JANUARY

Fair of Flowers and Coffee (Boquete, Chiriquí Province, page 218) – Flower farms and coffee plantations surround the little highland town of Boquete in Chiriquí Province. This lovely 10-day fair started out on the Fair of Flowers grounds and has spread through the town. Perfumed flowers of ev-ery shade and hue blend with the scent of roasting coffee. A highpoint of the fair is a prestigious "cupping" (coffee tast-ing). Food, music and dancing add to the festivities.

◆ MARCH

David Fair (David, Chiriquí Province) – This gigantic inter-national fair, officially called Feria de San José de David, draws exhibitors and attendees from throughout Central America. In addition to livestock and technology exhibits, there are folkloric dance contests, traditional music, crafts displays and vendors, rodeos and horse shows. There's food in wonderful variety, rides and more. A don't miss if you're in the area the second and third week of March. For exact dates, check www.pananet.com/feria.

◆ APRIL-MAY

Azuero Fair (Villa de Los Santos, Los Santos Province, Azuero Peninsula) – National dance performances, craft exhibits, bullfights and horse shows highlight this huge agri-cultural and industrial fair. There are also cockfights and re-ligious ceremonies.

♦   JUNE

Corpus Christi Festival (Villa de los Santos, Azuero Peninsula) – This festival featuring religious parades and elaborately masked dancers re-enacting the life of Christ hasn't changed much since medieval times.

El Toro Guapo Festival (Antón, Coclé Province) – The "handsome bull" gets to dance once a year during this colorful celebration of regional music and dance. Of course, El Toro Guapo makes a fool of himself, but it's all in good fun.

San Juan Bautista (Isla Grande, Colón Province) – Isla Grande's patron saint festival is a waterfest of canoe races and swimming competitions.

♦   JULY

Festival de la Pollera/Pollera Festival (Las Tablas, Los Santos Province, Azuero Peninsula) – This veritable feast of the country's lovely national woman's dress is held during the Festival of Santa Librada. Nowhere else in the country will you be able to see so many of these beautiful dresses, typical music, and dances all in one place at one time.

♦   SEPTEMBER

Festival of the Black Christ (Portobelo, Colón Province) – Every September 21st, thousands of supplicants converge on the historic Caribbean town of Portobelo to pay tribute to the "miraculous" statue believed to answer prayers.

Festival of the Mejorana (Guararé, Los Santos Province, Azuero Peninsula) – Folkloric groups from all of Panamá gather in this historic heartland town to present traditional dances and music during the country's largest folkloric festival.

Bocas del Toro's big party is the annual **Fiesta del Mar** (Sea Fair), held in mid-September. A local beauty is queen of this party, featuring seafood, music, dance and exhibits.

♦   OCTOBER

Feria de Río Tigre/Río Tigre Fair (San Blas Islands, Kuna Yala) – This colorful four-day fair features typical Kuna food, dance and music.

♦   NOVEMBER

Panamá celebrates two **Independence Days** this month. **Independence from Spain** on November 3rd and **Independence from Colombia** on November 28th. Bands throughout the country practice for months to be ready for parades held in every town. All offices and most businesses close on these national holidays.

Shopping

You can find almost anything – designer clothing, fine leather goods, crystal and china, perfumes, jewelry, house wares, artworks and electronics from around the world – in the fashion-conscious capital, usually for less than you might pay at home.

> **AUTHOR NOTE:** *If leaving the country by air, you'll find some of the country's best buys on jewelry, watches, leather goods, luggage, perfumes and cosmetics, liquors and cigarettes and cigars at* **Tucumen International Airport's Duty Free Mall**.

◆ What to Buy

Artesanos/Handicrafts

Prized by collectors, Kuna *molas* are squares of bright cotton fabrics, layered, cut and finely stitched in reverse appliqué to resemble paintings made of cloth. Most often framed as wall décor, they are Panamá's best known handicraft.

Emberá and Wounaan women weave beautiful **baskets** from naturally dyed plant fibers; some are so tightly woven that they can hold water. The men are famed for intricate **carvings** made from rock-hard cocobolo wood and for tiny, intricate tagua carvings. Tagua is a small palm nut, slightly larger than a golf ball. It's soft and easy to carve when fresh, but becomes rock-hard when dry. Taguas are valued collectibles.

Ngöbe-Buglé women weave beautiful *chacara* **bags** using natural fibers colored with natural dyes. These remarkably strong bags – used to tote everything from babies to coconuts – are woven in a variety of sizes and colors with beautiful designs. Adopted by farmer-settlers during Colonial times, *chacaras* were used by men to carry seeds when planting their fields. Over the centuries they evolved to become part of Panamá's traditional men's dress. Pick up a few to cart back home the treasures you've bought during your visit. *Chaquiras* are large, beaded collars adapted from those once worn by native warriors. Today, they're a woman's fashion accessory.

Pottery displayed along the Azuero Peninsula's La Arena village roadside replicates vividly painted pre-Columbian designs or is suited to more modern tastes. The region's fantastic folk-art festival masks have evolved from those made in Spain centuries ago.

Coffee

Some of the world's finest coffees are produced in Panamá and the place to buy it is directly from the farms in Veraguas and Chiriqui provinces. If not visiting these provinces, buy yours from a specialty shop in the capital.

Most of the best is exported and supermarkets don't stock the highest quality.

Cigars

Famed Cuban cigars are available and perfectly legal, but smoke them before traveling to the US where they are contraband. In the little town of La Pintada, famed for its pintado hats, there is a factory that produces excellent local cigars.

Panamá Hats

Panamá's famous **sombreros pintados** (also called *pintaos*) are made near the town of La Pintada. Equally famous **sombreros Ocueños** are handcrafted in Ocú. If visiting either of these central province towns, buy a hat directly from its maker; otherwise, they're sold in some of Panamá City's finest gift shops.

> **AUTHOR NOTE:** *Be sure to ask for* sombreros pintados *or* sombreros Ocueños *by name. If you ask for a "Panamá hat," you might end up with one made in Ecuador!*

Official Matters

◆ Documentation

US and Canadian citizens need only a valid **passport** and a **tourist card** that can be obtained from your inbound air carrier when you check in for your flight. Tourist cards are also available upon arrival in Panamá, but lines are often long and the wait can be frustrating. All visitors require an ongoing or return ticket. If coming by road from Costa Rica, you can buy the card at the border. The cost is $5, and cards are valid for up to 90 days. Note that there is a $20 airport departure tax when you leave the country.

Foreign driver's licenses are valid for 90 days.

◆ Emergency Telephone Numbers

Police (*Policia*) . . . . ☎104
Fire Department (*Bomberos*) . . . . ☎103
Ambulance Alerta, S.A. . . . . ☎ 507-264-4522
SEMM (ambulance) . . . . ☎ 507-264-4122

◆ Hospitals

The following hospitals are in Panamá City:
Centro Medico Bella Vista . . . . ☎ 507-277-4022

Centro Medico Nacional . . . . ☎ 507-264-5444
Centro Medico Plaza Paitilla . . . . ☎ 507-265-8800
Clinica Hospital San Franciso . . . . ☎ 507-229-1800

AUTHOR NOTE: *Hospital Nacional,* ☎ *507-204-8100, features a department specifically for tourists. The staff is multi-lingual and most insurance is accepted.*

Health & Safety

I've traveled throughout the country at all times of year and have had only one small concern: a spider bite that swelled and oozed for a couple of days. Don't let this discourage you – these nasty arachnids search me out. I've been bitten in Florida and in New York too. Those common intestinal upsets, dreaded by travelers to Latin America, are very rare here due to exceptionally high standards of sanitation. And I have never once feared for my safety, been the target of, or witnessed a crime of any kind.

◆ Diseases & Discomforts

Transmitted by mosquitoes, **malaria** is a serious illness indicated by fever, chills, aching joints and fatigue. Although completely wiped out in the Canal Zone during the Panama Canal's construction, a few cases have been reported in San Blas, Darien and Bocas del Toro provinces. Consider taking an anti-malarial medication if you'll be spending much time in these regions. Consult your physician in advance as the pills must be started two weeks prior to arrival. Under most circumstances, all you need is a good insect repellent.

Dengue fever, also carried by mosquitoes, is far less serious. A few cases have been reported in Central America recently, but since there is no preventative, your best defense is mosquito repellent. Mosquitoes that carry dengue are most active during the day, those that carry malaria, at dawn and dusk.

Ticks cause irritating bites but, other than a possible infection caused by scratching the affected area, they pose no danger; Lyme disease hasn't arrived here. Discourage them by wearing long pants tucked into socks and apply insect repellent to clothing and exposed skin. Tiny, flying **no-see-ums** zero in on unprotected tender areas. Once again, the best preventative is insect repellent. Ditto, to repel **sand fleas**. **Spider bites** are extremely rare. If you are bitten, see a doctor if there is pain, itching, swelling or oozing.

Traveler's **diarrhea** is rare here and unless you're really, really foolhardy, your chance of contracting it is almost nil. It's irritating but not infectious and usually clears up in day or two. You can speed the process by taking an over-the-counter medication. **Dysentary**, also rare, is serious. If you have diarrhea that doesn't clear up in a day or two, have a fever or pass bloody stools, get to a doctor pronto. Preventatives for both include washing your hands often, avoiding street food or food that isn't piping hot, and by drinking purified water when in rural areas.

Tetanus inoculations should be kept up to date. If you haven't had one in the last 10 years, I recommend you do so. Hepatitis A, most often contracted by ingesting contaminated food, can be picked up anywhere. It is extremely unpleasant and debilitating and may last as long as six months, but unlike hepatitis B and C, is seldom fatal. Disastrous hepatitis C is spread by blood to blood contact and Hepatitis B is spread through sexual or blood contact with an infected person. You should get vaccinated immediately if looking for love in all the wrong places or might somehow be stabbed by a used needle or sharp instrument.

> **AUTHOR NOTE:** *To put your mind at ease before you travel, check out the US **Centers for Disease Control** Travelers' Health information at www.cdc.gov/travel, and the **World Health Organization** site, www.who.int.en, for up-to-date advisories.*

❖   TIPS FOR AVOIDING ILLNESS OR ACCIDENT

- ❖ Wear a hat to prevent sunstroke and drink plenty of water to avoid dehydration.
- ❖ Slather on sunscreen to prevent sunburn.
- ❖ Wear sturdy leather hiking boots when in the jungles or hiking in rural areas and don't hike remote regions alone. If you should have an accident, it may be days before other hikers happen by or rescue arrives.
- ❖ Avoid swimming where there are riptides. They are the biggest danger you're likely to face.
- ❖ Don't stick your hands or shuffle your feet under leaves or logs in the jungles. In fact, don't stick them anywhere without looking first.

◆ Crime

Panamá is one of the Western Hemisphere's safest countries for visitors. This is assuming, of course, that you won't go wandering around in the capital's Chorillo and Caledonia slum neighborhoods after dark or Colón City at any time of the day or night. Casco Antiguo is still emerging from a slum and side streets and alleys can be unsafe after dark. This doesn't mean you should miss out on the fine dining and exciting nightlife here, just stay in well-lit areas where there are plenty of people. The friendly, helpful Tourist Police have a strong presence, but most speak only Spanish.

Although the country is a known drug transshipment area, most of this illicit action takes place offshore, particularly around the more remote San Blas Islands. In regions other than Darién (which you should visit only with a knowledgeable guide), use the same common sense precautions here as you would anywhere and you shouldn't experience difficulties. Crimes against tourists are virtually unheard of here.

❖ SAFETY TIPS

- ❖ Don't carry all your cash at one time; try to keep some separate.
- ❖ Whenever possible, leave your passport locked in your hotel's safe and carry a copy of the identification pages.
- ❖ Don't flaunt expensive cameras or jewelry.
- ❖ Never leave your purse, wallet, backpack or camera bag unattended.
- ❖ Park your rental car in an attended lot or hire someone to watch it. Always keep it locked.
- ❖ Keep all valuables, luggage, cameras, shopping bags and the like out of sight or locked in the trunk.

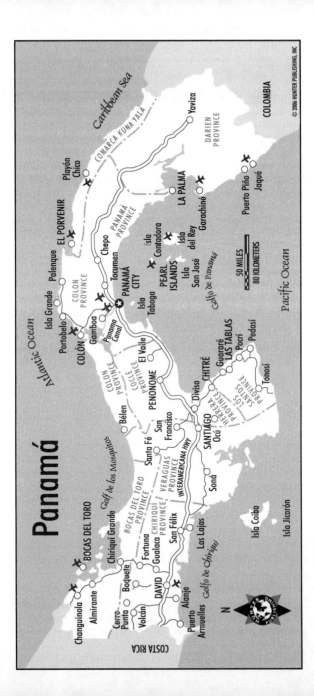

Travel Information

Quick Facts

- ❖ Panamá's population is estimated at 3.2 million.

- ❖ Spanish is the official language, although about 14% of the population speak English.

- ❖ Currency is the US dollar, often called "Balboa," and written as either $ or B/.

- ❖ The country's area code is 507; no need to dial it when making in-country calls.

- ❖ Panamá's time is the same as US Eastern Standard; five hours behind Greenwich Mean Time. There is no daylight saving time.

- ❖ Electric voltage is 110w-60Hz, same as in the US. Electrical surges are frequent, so if taking a laptop or other sensitive electrical equipment, you may want to include a surge suppressor.

- ❖ A flight from Miami or Ft. Lauderdale to Panamá City takes less than three hours; one from Houston, less than four; from London, about 14.

- ❖ The longest time it will take to fly from Panamá City to the most distant in-country destination is about one hour.

- ❖ There are more than 100 airplane runways throughout the country, about 46% are paved.

- ❖ *Modern Maturity Magazine* rated Panamá one of the World's Top 10 retirement havens.

- ❖ Most pay phones here accept only phone cards.

When to Go

Panamá is a year-round destination. Rainfall is heavier and more frequent from about mid-May to mid-December (Green Season), but showers usually pass quickly and puddles soon evaporate in heavily forested regions that never completely dry out. Downpours can turn dirt roads into rivers of mud and dissolve trails to ankle-deep muck. However, diving and snorkeling in Bocas del Toro, whitewater rafting in Chiriquí and Coclé, and adventuring in Darién are best during this time.

Information Sources

◆ Tourism Offices

Panamá's tourism bureau, **Instituto Panameño de Tourismo** (IPAT) can supply you with brochures, maps and other important information. You can call IPAT's toll-free Tourism Hot Line from the US and Canada, ☎ 800-231-0568. Regional offices are listed below.

❖ IPAT REGIONAL OFFICES	
Main office, Panamá City	☎ 507-226-7000
Panamá City Tourism Information	☎ 507-225-3544
Vila de Los Santos	☎ 507-966-8040
Bocas del Toro	☎ 507-757-9642
Boquete	☎ 507-720-4060
Coclé (Farallón)	☎ 507-993-4141
Colón	☎ 507-441-9644
Chiriquí (David)	☎ 507-775-4120
El Valle de Antón	☎ 507-983-6474
Portobelo	☎ 507-448-2073
Veraguas	☎ 507-998-3929

◆ Newspapers & Magazines

There are no printed edition English-language newspapers in Panamá at present, so log on to *The Panamá News*, www.thepanamanews.com, to get local news and entertainment information. *The Wall Street Journal*, *Washington Post*, *The New York Times*, *The Miami Herald* international edition, *USA Today*, *Time* and *Newsweek* can be found in many large hotel newsstands. Walk into most large hotels and restaurants and pick up a free copy of the twice-weekly English-language tabloid called *The Visitor*, ☎ 507-225-6638 (Focus Publications), which has information for tourists. Published by the same company and full of tourism facts and figures, *Focus Panamá* is a slick little 5x7 magazine, and is also found in major hotels.

Communications

◆ Telephones

Phone service in Panamá is excellent; the country code is **507**. If you're in Panamá and want to call someone in another country, first dial the international access code of 00, then the country code for the place you wish to reach (the US is 1, UK 44, Germany 49, etc.), followed by the phone number. For example, to call someone in the US from Panamá, first dial 00, then the US country code 1, followed by the area code and seven-digit number you're calling. Conversely, to call a Panamá number from the US or Canada, dial the international access code (011) then the country code (507), followed by the phone number (which, in Panamá, also has seven digits).

If you are in Panamá and you don't know the access code for the country you want to call, dial 106 to reach an international operator.

Pay phones are common throughout the country, but most can be operated only with a phone card. Cards in denominations from $1 to $20 can be purchased from shops and markets throughout the country. Calls cost 15¢ for the first three minutes.

◆ Internet

You can't walk more than a couple of blocks in Panamá City's business districts without passing a few Internet cafés. They're now everywhere in the country, except for the smallest towns and remotest villages. Expect to pay between $1.50 to $3 for an hour's use.

◆ Mail & Shipping Services

Post offices are open from 7 am until 6 pm on weekdays and from 7 am to 3 pm on Saturdays. Postcards sent to the US cost 25¢. Airmail letters weighing up to 0.7 ounce cost 35¢. If sending to Canada, the cost is 40¢; to Europe, 45¢. Regular mail sent to the United States can take a week or more to arrive. Many hotels sell stamps and will post your letters or cards.

Although it happens infrequently, packages can be lost. If you have packages to send home, considering using a courier service. To find the nearest locations, **FedEx**, ☎ 507-800-1122; **DHL**, ☎ 507-271-3451; or **UPS**, ☎ 507-269-9222. **Mailboxes, Etc.**, ☎ 507-261-1748, has locations in Patilla, Albrook, the banking area of Panamá City, and in some Super 99 supermarkets.

There are 60 **Western Union** offices, ☎ 507-800-2274, in Panamá.

Money, Currency & Banking

Panamá's paper currency is the **US dollar**, interchangeably called dollar or Balboa (written B/). Coins are minted in the same size and denomination as US coins and they're interchangeable. As in the US, many establishments won't accept $50 or $100 bills, so try not to carry bills larger than $20. It's best to use only US currency, as changing foreign currency can be a hassle and banks will charge you for the privilege.

Panamá City banks are open from 8 am until 1 pm, some until 3 pm. You will find ATMs everywhere in the cities and in most towns. Look for signs reading **Systema Clave** – and ATMs with a "Cirrus" or "Plus" sign.

Although **Traveler's Checks**, preferably American Express, should be in US dollars, they're not well accepted in Panamá. Banks are the only places you'll be able to change them. Most large shops, hotels, restaurants and resorts will accept **credit cards** but, outside of the capital, don't depend on being able to use them. "Cash only" is often the rule in many small towns and villages.

◆ Tipping

It's customary to tip restaurant servers 10% of your total bill. A few restaurants include the tip on your check, but others don't, so look it over before paying. Bellhops and porters should receive $1 for each bag carried; hotel maids, $1 for each night stayed. Taxi drivers don't expect tips. When taking a guided tour, it's also customary to tip your guide.

What to Take

You can find almost anything here, usually cheaper than in North America or Europe, except perhaps for some specialized sports equipment or clothing. The sultry lowlands dictate cool cotton or fast-dry fabrics designed to wick away perspiration. In cooler highland regions where nights get downright chilly, you'll appreciate a sweater, sweatshirt or windbreaker. Jeans are okay in the temperate highlands but too hot and heavy elsewhere – and they take up valuable luggage space. Some sports are rough on your duds, so if you don't use specialized clothing, take a few old T-shirts, pants and shorts and dump them when they become disreputable. Leave good jewelry at home. If surfing, take your board; snorkel and fins are available to rent. Collapsible kayaks and scuba gear should be brought with you, except for the tanks that can't be transported aboard aircraft.

> **AUTHOR NOTE:** *Panamá's commuter flights limit passengers to 25 pounds of baggage. Anything above that is charged as overweight.*

◆ The Basics

These clothing items should be ample for a one- or two-week visit:

- ❖ Hiking boots, waterproof sport sandals or walking shoes (sneakers are okay for casual sightseeing but not on slippery or steep terrain)
- ❖ 3 pairs absorbent cotton socks
- ❖ 2 pairs lightweight pants or slacks
- ❖ 2 pairs lightweight shorts
- ❖ 3 T-shirts
- ❖ 1 skirt and 1 blouse ensemble for women for city wear (you can always substitute a nice T-shirt for a second blouse)
- ❖ 1 or 2 short-sleeve sport/dress shirts (for men)
- ❖ 1 bathing suit
- ❖ 1 hooded rain slicker/poncho (heavy-gauge material if you'll be in the jungles)
- ❖ 1 jacket or windbreaker (if visiting the highlands)
- ❖ 1 wide-brimmed hat (preferably one that rolls up to pack)
- ❖ 1 pair protective sunglasses
- ❖ 1 light cotton sleepwear
- ❖ 1 pair flip-flops (useful on the beach, as slippers, in the shower)

Don't overload on fragile toiletries. Cosmetics and personal items are readily available in Panamá. Try taking shampoos and cosmetics in sample sizes, then toss the packaging (into a recycling bin) after the contents are used. Suggested items:

- ❖ Prescription medications
- ❖ Personal hygiene products
- ❖ Insect repellent (Bug-Stop or 3M work best)
- ❖ Pain reliever (aspirin, Tylenol, Bufferin, etc)
- ❖ Antibiotic ointment
- ❖ Band-aids
- ❖ Sunblock
- ❖ Cosmetics
- ❖ Toilet paper (rural bathrooms don't always provide it)
- ❖ Hand sanitizer or small bar of soap
- ❖ Rubber sink stopper
- ❖ Hand and body lotion
- ❖ Moleskin (for blisters)
- ❖ Toothbrush, hairbrush/comb, razor, other daily grooming aids

AUTHOR NOTE: *Panamá's supermarkets sell laundry deter-gent in little plastic packages intended for one washing machine load. They're easy to carry – you can squeeze a couple into the corners of your luggage or backpack – and come in handy for washing items in the bathroom sink.*

◆ Other Stuff

- ❖ Documents: Passport, driver's license, tourist card
- ❖ Credit card and ATM card (or traveler's checks)
- ❖ A few $1 bills for tipping upon arrival
- ❖ Concealed money belt
- ❖ Pocket size high-intensity flashlight
- ❖ Camera (film for traditional cameras; extra battery and memory card for digital ones)
- ❖ Pocket-size Spanish dictionary, preferably with phrases if you don't speak the language.
- ❖ Small notebook and ball-point pens
- ❖ Resealable plastic bags (to keep your camera dry and your cosmetics from leaking)
- ❖ Reading material
- ❖ Itty-bitty book light
- ❖ Binoculars

❖ TIP: TAKE BANDANNAS!

Pack three or four 100% cotton bandannas. They're easy to hand-wash and they dry quickly. Here are a few of the uses I've found for them:

- ❖ Roll or fold one and tie it low around your forehead to keep sweat out of your eyes when hiking.
- ❖ Tie one over your hat to keep it from blowing off.
- ❖ Use to dry your hands where there are no towels.
- ❖ Wet one and tie it around your neck to cool off during a hot trek.
- ❖ Wrap one around your camera or binoculars when you want to keep them handy and safe from flying sand or dust.
- ❖ Dry the outside of your pack, camera, binoculars, etc. if dampened accidentally.
- ❖ Wipe the fog from glasses.
- ❖ Use as a handkerchief.

AUTHOR NOTE: *Make a photocopy of your passport. Leave the original locked in your hotel's safe and carry the photocopy when sightseeing.*

Customs & Courtesies

◆ Dress & Manner

Panamanians are warmly formal and exceptionally courteous, and they are more likely to be prompt (usually, anyway) than many other Latin Americans. People dress to suit the occasion and appearance is considered important. Evening attire ranges from casual office wear to dressy. If you're invited out or to someone's home, ask your host or hostess what to wear. Shorts and T-shirts are not acceptable attire when dining out, and shorts should not be worn when visiting cathedrals and churches.

◆ Photography

It is considered rude to photograph people without first asking permission.

Special Considerations

◆ Travelers with Disabilities

Although it is slowly improving, Panamá is not the easiest country for adventurers with disabilities to negotiate. Some city sidewalks are steep or broken, and many lodgings do not have ramps or elevators. I've made it a point to list handicap-accessible facilities and attractions in this guide.

◆ Traveling with Children

Panamá is a very kid-friendly country. Playgrounds are numerous, many hotels and resorts have specially equipped play areas, children's pools, and some offer supervised activities.

◆ Gay & Lesbian Travelers

There is still some stigma attached to alternative lifestyles, although less so in the capital than in rural areas. You won't find Panamá City's gay bars listed in the telephone book and most clubs, even the big, flashy ones, don't post signs outside. The old "machismo" hasn't quite died out, and you will almost never see affection between same-sex partners shown openly in public. Your best resource for all-around current information is online at www.gaypanama.com. A listing of gay- and lesbian-oriented clubs is in the Panamá City *Entertainment* section, page 105.

◆ Resources

Fantasy Tours, an IGLTA member, ☎ 507-260-2832 or 260-5818 (201-840-1827 in the US), www.fantasytoursonline.com, arranges travel throughout the country and the world. They're also a good resource for current local information.

Turkos Masculinos Gay Baths, Calle 54, ☎ 507-264-5986.

Momentum Cabañas and B&B, ☎ 507-720-4385, www.momentum-panama.com, a lovely resort in the mountains near Boquete, caters to both the straight and GLB communities.

A new gay-friendly bed and breakfast, **La Boca Inn**, is scheduled to open in Panamá City's Balboa neighborhood. For information, ☎ 507-264-5939.

Getting Here

◆ By Air

Scheduled passenger flights from the United States, the Caribbean and South America, and charters from Canada and Europe arrive at **Tocumen International Airport**, 13 miles/21 kilometers east of Panamá City.

> **AUTHOR NOTE:** *Taxi fees are set at US $25 from the international airport to Panamá City. If you've reserved a hotel, ask if they provide shuttle service, if not, ask if they have an arrangement with a taxi driver for a lower fare. Many do.*

COPA Airlines (www.copaair.com, see Web site for phone reservation numbers for each city) flies non-stop from Miami, Orlando and Los Angeles; **Continental** (☎ 800-523-3273 in the US, www.continental.com) flies non-stop from Houston and Newark; **American Airlines** (☎ 800-433-7300, www.aa.com) from New York and Miami; **Delta Air Lines** (☎ 800-221-1212 in the US, www.delta.com) from Atlanta. **TACA** (☎ 800-535-8780, www.taca.com) flies direct from Miami; **US Airways**, ☎ 800-428-4322 in the US, www.usairways.com, non-stop from Ft. Lauderdale. Check a phone directory or an airline's website for local telephone numbers, and if calling from outside the US or Canada.

> **AUTHOR NOTE:** *In flight jargon, a **non-stop flight** is just that – no stops between your departure and destination cities. A **direct flight** makes one or more stops without a change of planes. A **connecting flight** means there will be at least one change of planes before you arrive at your destination.*

◆ By Land

If you are arriving overland from Costa Rica, there are border crossings at Paso Canoa on the Pacific side and Guabito/Sixaola on the Atlantic. You cannot arrive by land from South America.

◆ By Sea

If you're traveling aboard a cruise ship that will dock in Panamá for a few hours and want to see a little of the country, check the list of local tour operators on page 52. Before the advent of the Colón 2000 cruise port and Panamá City's new Fuerte Amador Resort and Marina port, Panamá began actively wooing the cruise lines to add the country to their itineraries. By the time you read this, more cruise lines may have added Panamá as a port of call.

TRAVEL INTRODUCTION

❖ CRUISE LINES CALLING IN PANAMÁ

- ❖ **Princess Cruises**, ☎ 800-PRINCESS, www.princess. com.
- ❖ **Carnival Cruise Lines**, ☎ 888-CARNIVAL, www.carnival.com.
- ❖ **Celebrity Cruises**, ☎ 800-722-5941, www.celebrity cruises.com.
- ❖ **Royal Caribbean**, ☎ 800-398-9819, www.royalcaribbean.com.
- ❖ **Crystal Cruises**, ☎ 877-226-2731, www.crystal-cruises.com.
- ❖ **Windjammer Barefoot Cruises**, ☎ 800-327-2601, www.windjammer.com, has six-day cruises through the San Blas islands.
- ❖ **Lindblad Expeditions**, ☎ 800-EXPEDITION, www. lindblad. com, specializes in small ship naturalist adventure cruises and touring.

Getting Around

◆ On Foot

Except for specific treks and unless you have all the time in the world, you probably won't want to get around on foot. On the other hand, walking is customary in many small towns and villages in the interior, so once you're there, it's often the only way to explore them – and the surrounding countryside.

Hitchhiking is not customary here and unless you're puffing along a dirt road in the interior, no one will stop for you.

◆ On Wheels

By Bus

Getting around the country by bus is easy and inexpensive. Buses go almost everywhere and they go frequently. Destinations are printed across the top of the windshield and sometimes on the back and/or sides of the bus. Most have conductors who will make sure you're getting on the right one and off at the correct stop. If you don't plan to make stops, opt for an express bus. The fare is a little more, but well worth it for the time you'll save. They're plusher, air-conditioned and some have toilets and TVs. Minibuses, called *colectivos* (collectives), serve rural towns and villages – and if your destination is a remote village, you might find your seat is a bench in the bed of a 4x4 pick-up!

> **AUTHOR NOTE:** *That motorcycle policeman you see lurking beside the highway ahead might – or might not – be a painted plywood cut-out! Whichever he is, please obey posted speed limits; for your own safety and that of others.*

By Car

The recently widened InterAmericana (Pan-American Highway) is a fairly smooth ride west from Panamá City all the way to the Costa Rica border. Highways and most secondary roads are paved and in good condition. Exceptions are the interior's unpaved dirt side roads and steep, deeply rutted mountain roads that can become rivers of mud during the rainy season. You'll need a high-clearance 4x4 vehicle to navigate many of them even when dry.

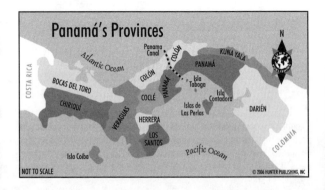

MILEAGE CHART	COLON	DAVID	PANAMA CITY	PENONOME	SANTIAGO
AGUADULCE	266	251	190	41	59
BOQUETE	549	35	473	327	277
CHIRIQUI GRANDE	592	106	516	370	270
CHITRE	326	271	250	101	79
COLON	-	514	76	225	325
DAVID	514	-	438	289	192
EL VALLE	200	373	124	81	181
PANAMA CITY	76	438	-	149	249
PENONOME	225	289	149	-	100
PORTOBELO	43	537	99	248	348
SANTIAGO	325	192	249	100	-
VOLCAN	571	57	495	349	249

Note: To convert kilometers to miles, multiply by 0.62.

Driving yourself will give you more freedom and choices than public transportation, but there are drawbacks. First of all, car rental is expensive. A no-frills compact rents for about $30 a day plus insurance, and a fully equipped SUV will run you around $70 a day. To be on the safe side, you'll want to take out all the insurance offered. Gasoline prices hover around $3 a gallon, sometimes higher. What you want to do and the time you have to do it are also considerations. For instance, if you plan to go directly from Panamá City to one of the highland towns like Boquete or Volcán, the drive, with one rest stop, will take six to eight hours. You can shave 4½ to five hours off that by flying to David and taking a bus from there, or you can pick up your rental at the David airport.

AUTHOR NOTE: *Be sure to fasten your seat belt. It's the law here. If not wearing one, you can be stopped and ticketed.*

❖ AUTO RENTAL AGENCIES

Those listed below are all in Panamá City. Regional offices are listed in each chapter. You must be 21 to rent a car and will need your driver's license, passport, and a deposit of approximately $300, usually applied to a credit card. Drivers under 25 are often charged an additional cash deposit. Check with individual rental companies for requirements, and always ask if there are any special rates available.

❖ **Alamo Rent A Car**, Marbella, Panamá City, ☎ 507-265-3786, fax 507-223-5802.

❖ **Avis:** Central Reservations, ☎ 507-264-0722; Tocumen International Airport, ☎ 507-238-4056; Hotel Intercontinental, ☎ 507-214-1532; Panamá City, ☎ 507-213-0555, fax 507-254-0222.

- ❖ **Barriga Rent A Car**, Tocumen International Airport, ☎ 507-238-4495, fax 507-264-2903.
- ❖ **Budget:** Via España, ☎ 507-263-8777, fax 507-263-7721; Tocumen International Airport, ☎ 507-263-9190, fax 507-238-4092; Marcos A.Gelabart (Albrook) Airport, ☎ 507-238-4069.
- ❖ **Central Rent A Car:** Calle 50 ☎ 507-223-5165; Tumba Muerto, ☎ 507-230-0447; Albrook Airport, ☎ 507-238-4936, fax 507-223-6941 (same for all locations).
- ❖ **Discovery Rent A Car**, Tocumen International Airport, ☎ 507-239-4820, fax 507-236-8191.
- ❖ **Dollar Rent A Car:** Calle 50, ☎ 507-220-0535; Tocumen International Airport, ☎ 507-238-4032, fax 507-238-4032 (same for both locations).
- ❖ **Hertz**, Tocumen International Airport, ☎ 507-238-4031; Albrook Airport, ☎ 507-315-0418.
- ❖ **National:** Calle 50, ☎ 507-265-0222; Tumba Muerto, ☎ 507-237-5777; Tocumen International Airport, ☎ 507-238-4144, fax 507-263-6881 (same for all locations).
- ❖ **Shellane's Rent A Car**, El Cangrejo, ☎ 507-269-3532, fax 507-265-3870.
- ❖ **Thrifty**, Tocumen International Airport, ☎ 507-214-7677, fax 507-264-7419.
- ❖ **Tico Rent A Car**, El Carmen (city), ☎ 507-229-5259, fax 507-265-3870.

AUTHOR NOTE: *Although gas, milk, and other liquids sold in Panamá are usually measured in gallons, quarts, etc., distances are given as metric measurements, usually in kilometers. To convert them to miles, multiply the number of kilometers by .62.*

◆ By Air

With more than 100 landing strips – some paved, some not – Panamá's inexpensive commuter flights are real timesavers. They'll get you to outer islands and regions where there are no roads. All of the country's domestic airlines also offer charters. Check with the ones below for rates and schedules.

- ❖ **Aeroperlas**, ☎ 507-315-7500. Flies to David, Colón Free Zone, Bocas del Toro, Changuinola, Chire, Bahia Pina, Contadora, La Palma, El Real, Jacque, Garachiné, Sambú, Contadora.
- ❖ **Aero Taxi**, ☎ 507-315-7250. Services San Blas.
- ❖ **Ansa**, ☎ 507-315-7251. Services San Blas.

- ❖ **Aviatur**, ☎ 507-315-0307. Flies to San Blas, Sambú, Garachiné, La Palma, Pina, Contadora, San Miguel, Changuinola.
- ❖ **Aero Mapiex**, ☎ 507-315-0888. Offers flights to David, Bocas del Toro, Changuinola.
- ❖ **Helipan**, ☎ 507-315-0452, offers helicopter charters and tours; and **Helix**, ☎ 507-264-5155, has only helicopter charters.

◆ By Water

Offshore islands are accessed by water taxis, ferries, scheduled marine express services and private boat. There are also some crewed or bareboat "live aboard" accommodations available. Look under *Getting Here* and *Adventures On Water* for each chapter.

Tour Operators

❖ IN ONE WEEK, YOU CAN...

Spend two to three days sightseeing/adventuring in the capital and Canal Zone corridor (see Panama and Colón Province chapters) and still have time for one or two of the following:

- ❖ Visit the islands of Bocas del Toro or San Blas (Kuna Yala);
- ❖ Fly to Chiriquí and tour coffee plantations, climb massive Barú Volcano, go whitewater rafting/birding/hiking in the Eastern or Western Highlands;
- ❖ Fly to Cana, deep in the Darién wilderness, a once-in-a-lifetime naturalist adventure;
- ❖ Drive or bus to El Valle to hike the Cordillera, go river rafting, mountain biking, wet rappelling, explore the jungle canopy and the country's best Sunday market;
- ❖ Explore the Azuero Peninsula, Panama's heartland;
- ❖ Combine a spa retreat with bird watching, hiking, kayaking and cultural adventures;
- ❖ Go by Land Rover and cayuco (or by air) and spend a night or two in a Darién indigenous village;
- ❖ Spend a few days at an all-inclusive mountain or beach resort;
- ❖ Cruise an archipelago of paradisiacal islands on a live-aboard vessel;
- ❖ Experience some of the world's best sportsfishing.

◆ In Panamá

By using the services of a local tour operator or guide, you'll get to see and do more while saving time, aggravation and, quite possibly, money! Listed below (in alphabetical order) are some of the best tour companies that adhere to sustainable tourism standards and employ bilingual or multilingual guides. All are headquartered in Panamá City. Check their websites; most provide specialty services or will prepare an itinerary to specifications. A few more with local or regional offices are listed in corresponding chapters.

Ancon Expeditions, ☎ 507-269-9415, www.anconexpedtions.com. Panamá's foremost naturalist operator, a spin-off from a leading conservationist organization, offers a veritable feast of educational, natural and cultural experiences. Their exceptional specialist guides – who rank with the world's best – will take you places few others will ever see.

Ecocircuitos, ☎ 507-314-1586, www.ecocircuitos.com. Preservationist Ecocircuitos offers an excellent variety of eco-sensitive adventures and cultural experiences. Conservation and understanding are first priorities.

Exotics Adventures, ☎ 507-223-9283, www.exoticadventures.com. This fine small company specializes in cultural and high adventure travel. They're so good that National Geographic chose them to assist when filming in Darién, one of their featured destinations.

Cristian Moreno, ☎ 507-671-1343, cmorenog@hotmail.com. You won't find a better or more knowledgeable naturalist guide than independent Cristian. He will help you plan and guide you to unforgettable ecological adventures.

Panamá City Tours, ☎ 507-263-8918, www.panamacitytours.com. This top-notch company features a vast range of itineraries throughout Panamá – and a full-service travel agency to boot.

Panamá Explorer Club (PEX), ☎ 507-215-2330, www.pexclub.com. Panamá's first and finest active and extreme sports specialists also offer soft adventure and cultural tours.

Panamá Surf Tours, ☎ 507-236-8303, www.panamasurftours.com. These dedicated surfers know where and when to find the best rides.

Panoramic Panamá, ☎ 507-314-1417, www.panoramicpanama.com, is a unique company offering personalized services and tailored itineraries to visitors or those considering a move to Panamá.

Pesantez Tours, ☎ 507-263-8771/223-5374, www.pezanteztours.com. This long-established operator is one of the country's most respected and, as its first full-service agency, has set the standard for superior service.

◆ In the US and UK

If you prefer to work with a company in your home country, here are a few reliable specialists that offer package tours to Panamanian destinations.

Holbrook Travel, ☎ 800-451-7111, www.holbrooktravel.com, offers naturalist, cultural, and birding tours.

Wildland Adventures, ☎ 800-345-4453, www.wildland.com, has natural history, wildlife, cultural, birding, and adventure tours.

Tara Tours, ☎ 1-800-327-0080, www.taratours.com, has a variety of nature, adventure, and cultural tours.

Victor Emanuel Nature Tours, ☎ 800-328-VENT (8368), www.vent-bird. com, specializes in trips for bird-watchers.

Lindblad Expeditions, ☎ 800-EXPEDITIONS, 397-3348, www.expeditions.com, has small ship cruises that focus on nature and natural history.

Tropical Travel, ☎ 800-451-8017, www.tropicaltravel.com, specializes in birding and adventure tours.

Field Guides, ☎ 800-728-4953, www.fieldguides.com, has a variety of birding tours.

Panama Travel Experts, ☎ 877-836-5300, www.panamatravelexperts. com, has sightseeing, historical, cultural, and naturalist trips.

The Travelling Naturalist, ☎ 44-1305-267994, www.naturalist.co.uk, offers bird watching, wildlife and cultural excursions.

Where to Stay

Resorts outside the capital tend to fill up on weekends, but might be virtually deserted — and less expensive – during the week. The opposite is true in the capital, where hotels that cater to business travelers frequently offer lower weekend rates.

Many hotels quote only their highest "rack" rates, but usually have cheaper promotional rates that are offered only if you inquire. Make it a point to ask for the lowest rate. Although a few hotels and resorts charge the same rates year-round, expect to pay more during "high season" from mid-December to mid-May and consider an aparthotel if traveling with family, friends, or plan to stay more than a few days. Backpackers, sociable types and those traveling "on the cheap" might prefer a comfortable hostel or bed and breakfast. Panamá's are usually a step up from most in other Central American countries.

Some hotels do not offer single rates. If traveling solo, ask for a discount. You might get one.

> **AUTHOR NOTE:** *Guest facilities are licensed by Panamá's government tourism bureau,* **Instituto Panameño de Tourismo** *(**IPAT**), which levies a 10% tax on room rates. Sometimes the tax is included in quoted rates, and sometimes it's not, so you should ask.*

◆ Hotels & Resorts

Hotels offer rooms and/or suites. Panamá's can be five-star luxurious or low-end economy. Some offer nothing more than basic rooms. Others provide an endless list of amenities that can include restaurants and lounges, swimming pools, casinos, tennis courts, several dining options, room service, airport transportation, spas or health clubs, shopping arcades, business centers and butler service. Intercontinental, Holiday Inn, Country Inn and Suites, Marriott, Sheraton, Melia and Rosewood are some of the internationally recognized hotel names with properties in Panamá.

Usually located away from the cities, resorts and resort hotels offer vacationers an opportunity to relax and enjoy activities such as golf, diving or relaxing on the beach. All-inclusive resorts include your room, meals and a host of other amenities such as snacks, drinks (yes, even alcoholic), entertainment, activities, use of sporting equipment and perhaps even a local tour or two.

◆ Bed & Breakfasts, Hostals & Pensiones

Most confusingly labeled are the hostals and pensiones. As expected, some are the typical dormitory style, shared bath accommodations with kitchen privileges, while others offer private air-conditioned rooms, laundry services, in-room TV, on-site restaurant, spa facilities, local tours and more. In short, don't overlook a property simply because it's called a pensione or hostal; it might be a lovely country inn and spa. Even true "hostels" are no longer for only young backpackers on tight budgets, but well-suited to many of us older folks.

❖ THE PASSIONATE PUSHBUTTON MOTELS

Some hotels here resemble North American motels, but true motels, other than those called "pushbuttons" haven't caught on. Pushbuttons, if you haven't already guessed, are one-story, motel-like affairs designed for well, affairs or illicit trysts. They're almost always hidden from the highway behind high hedges or fences with locked gates. Those roadside signs displaying a cute little cupid shooting his arrow into a big red heart announce a concealed pushbutton. To enter, push the button next to the gate and, when it swings open, drive to the cashier's window, pay, collect your key and continue on to the enclosed garage connected to your room. It's all very anonymous. If you've a hankering, you can stay an entire night, but expect to pay an hourly, rather than a nightly rate.

◆ Campgrounds & RV Resorts

Owing to Panamá's geographic location and its proliferation of beach and mountain resorts, recreational vehicles are an uncommon sight. As of this writing there is only one true RV resort in the entire country! The tourism bureau had no classification for such an oddity, couldn't figure out how to classify it, and therefore held up its licensing for an interminable period of time. Private campgrounds too, are few and far between, but they're gaining in popularity and you'll find a few very nice ones. The national parks are administered by the **Autoridad Nacional del Ambiente** (**ANAM**), and most permit camping. The cost is $5, plus a $3 entrance fee.

Top 20 Attractions

THE PANAMA CANAL: This Eighth Wonder of the World stretches almost 50 miles across the isthmus from the Atlantic to the Pacific. There are observation towers for you to watch the lock systems operate as giant ships are raised and lowered as they pass through the Miraflores or Gatún Locks. Better yet, get an insider's view by taking a full or partial canal transit. See page 74.

PANAMÁ LA VIEJA: Fires consumed this fabled first city of Panamá (also called *Panamá Viejo*) during pirate Henry Morgan's raid in 1671. There's enough left to give you an idea of its former splendor. See page 69.

CASCO ANTIGUO ("OLD COMPOUND"): This historical "city within a city" is a treasure trove of historical architecture dating from the 17th century. By the dawn of the 20th century, the New World's wealthiest city had lapsed into a tenement neighborhood that is only now returning to its former glory. Enjoy a walking tour through its ancient cobbled streets and take time to dine in a trendy new eatery. See page 64.

BARRO COLORADO ISLAND: Nature trails on this 3,865-acre/1,564-hectare island, isolated in Gatún Lake for almost a century, offer an insider's view of a New World tropical forest. It's a great introduction to tropical ecology, and you can expect to see – and hear – forest creatures. The island has hosted a Smithsonian Tropical Research Institute facility since 1923. See page 78.

ISLA GRANDE: Water sports are the main attraction for visitors to this jewel of an island plopped in the Caribbean. It's a laidback little place, only a few minutes boat ride from the mainland. Folks here are mostly of African origin so you'll hear as much Congo and reggae as salsa. See page 142 .

PORTOBELO: Pirates and buccaneers have faded into history, but Portobelo's rusty cannons remain vigilant. Once the New World's richest treasure port, Portobelo slumbers under the Caribbean sun, waking once a year to celebrate the annual Festival of the Black Christ. If you want to pay your respects, you'll find the treasure-bedecked statue residing in the town's Church of San Felipe. Make a stop here on the way to Isla Grande. See pages 136.

SCUBA DIVING: Panamá's got it all – fantastic coral reefs, plunging walls, neon fish and warm tropical waters. Dive the Caribbean in the morning, the Pacific in the afternoon or spend a few days in each. You probably won't find Francis Drake's lead casket, but you might recover a long-lost piece-of-eight. If diving is your thing, see the *On Water* sections in each chapter.

SAN BLAS ISLANDS: The San Blas Archipelago's 377 white-sand-fringed islands stretch 200 miles along Panamá's southern Caribbean coast. Kuna Indian inhabitants say there is "an island for every day of the year." Spend a couple of days on one to enjoy a decidedly different cultural experience and a glorious dose of sun, sand and sea. See the *San Blas* chapter beginning on page 267.

EL VALLE DE ANTÓN: Magical "El Valle" nestles in the crater of an extinct volcano high in the refreshingly cool mountains of the Cordillera Central. Take a second look at this charming resort community and you'll discover that it's a terrific place to test your adventure and survival skills. Zip above the rainforest canopy suspended on wires, brave the rapids with white-water rafting, rappel a waterfall or climb a rock wall. Tamer pursuits include visits to ancient petroglyphs and hot springs, bird watching, hiking, and collecting local folklore. As an added bonus, El Valle hosts Panamá's largest and most colorful Sunday market. See page 148.

SOBERANÍA NATIONAL PARK: Enter a rainforest world only 30 minutes from downtown Panamá City. Walk the Spanish treasure trail, watch birds in one of the world's best places to see record numbers of avian critters, listen to howler monkeys and introduce yourself to a sloth or two. Ride a silent tram through the jungle canopy, get up close and personal with lolling crocodiles, or stay in a quietly elegant hotel recycled from a former US military radar tower, now considered one of the world's top eco-resorts and one of the best bird watching sites.

SPORTFISHING: More world records for catching the big ones have been set and broken here than anywhere else on Earth. Fish practically virgin waters for marlin, wahoo, sailfish, tuna and more – many more.

VOLCÁN BARÚ NATIONAL PARK: Climb to the top of Panamá's highest peak, majestic Volcán Barú. And, if the weather cooperates, look out over both the Caribbean and Pacific.

LA AMISTAD INTERNATIONAL PARK BIOSPHERE RESERVE: This is nature at its most impressive. One million acres of spectacular mountain landscape enclosed in cloud forest wilderness. See pages 233 and 249.

COFFEE PLANTATIONS: Almost everyone in highland Chiriquí seems to have a few coffee plants. Take a plantation tour to learn how coffee cherries are processed to end up as the precious liquid in your cup. At harvest time, colorful Ngöbe-Buglé Indians flood the plantations to pick the bright red coffee "cherries." See page 219.

WHITE-WATER RAFTING: Panamá's white-water rafting originated on Chiriquí's challenging rivers. It's catching on fast in Coclé. Spectacular scenery comes with the ride. See page 221.

BIRD WATCHING: If you've never considered this activity, you might find it's much more interesting and exciting than you had imagined. You'll encounter an incredible variety of birds in Panamá. Birders have been flocking here for years, hoping for – and getting – a glimpse at some of Panamá's rare species. See sections for *On Foot*.

DARIÉN NATIONAL PARK: The largest national park in all Central America is as wild as when Balboa stumbled through on his way to discover the "Southern Sea." This virtual laboratory of biodiversity is a majestic cathedral of unspoiled natural wonders. See page 282.

FINCA DRACULA: Many orchids prefer a cool, moist climate. Finca Dracula's 1,200 species appear content in their cloud forest home. You might even spot a quetzal or two on the grounds. See page 231.

BASTIMENTOS NATIONAL MARINE PARK & THE ZAPATILLA CAYES: You can't get much closer to paradise than this protected area of palm-fringed white-sand islands floating in the crystal waters of the Caribbean. Hire a boatman in Bocas town and go for the day. Stop for lunch or dinner in a *bohio* built over the sea, where the fish is so fresh it's not only prepared to order, it's also caught to order! See page 254.

BOCAS TOWN: It could be said that Bocas is much like other Central American towns along the Caribbean coast. It's easy-going and relaxed and folks here are friendly, but it seems to have more of everything – more lodging and dining choices, more to do, and an eclectic mix of locals and expats. The new arrivals, most from North America and Europe, include so many Italians you may find yourself exclaiming, "Mama mia, that's good pizza!" Ride the waves at a nearby surfing beach, go scuba diving, get close up and personal with a bat colony, count starfish, watch frolicking dolphins or just hang out. See pages 249.

TRAVEL INTRODUCTION

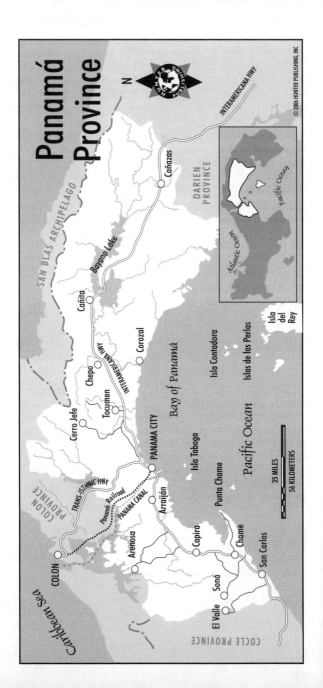

Panamá Province

Panamá City

Modern Panamá City is as cosmopolitan as any world capital, a bustling metropolis of almost one million people, about one-third of the country's population. Proud residents call it three cities in one – the ruins of Panama la Vieja, Colonial Casco Antiguo; the modern downtown area; and suburban neighborhoods. The capital's 262-square-mile metro area sprawls approximately 16 miles/10 km along the Pacific coast from the Panama Canal east to the ruins of Panama la Vieja. Panamá Bay curves to the south, between colonial Casco Antiguo and Punta Paitilla's glittering skyscrapers with 19,341-acre/47,772-hectare Soberanía National Park bordering it to the north. The downtown area includes Via España's fine shopping, the nearby banking and restaurant district and lovely Avenue Balboa, lined with graceful palms, skirts the bay. Proximity to the Panama Canal and Colón Free Zone make this sophisticated city that is chock-full of superb dining and entertainment venues, one of the world's best for shopping.

History

◆ Timeline

1519:   Founded by Pedrarias as Nuestra Senora de la Asuncion de Panamá (Our Lady of the Assumption of Panamá)

1521:   Spain officially decrees Panamá the capital of Castilla de Oro.

1533:   Pizarro begins the conquest of Peru. Treasure looted from the great Inca Empire arrives here en route to Spain.

1671:	Fires destroy the city during an attack by Buccaneer Henry Morgan. To this day it is unknown whether the fires were set by Morgan's men or the residents.
1673:	A new city of Panamá (Nueva Panamá) is founded.
1740:	The city sinks into decline as Spain withdraws from the isthmus.
1848:	The California gold rush revives the city.
1881-present:	The Panamá railroad, the French and then the American canal builders, and finally, World War II, bring construction and revitalization. By 1970, Panamá had become an international trade and banking center. The city continues to grow and prosper.

Getting Here

International flights arrive at **Tocumen International Airport**, 13 miles/ 20 kilometers east of the city. Two new expressways have helped to alleviate traffic in and out of the city. **Corridor Sur** (South) runs to/from Tocumen International Airport, and **Corridor** Norte (North) runs north to/ from Colón. As of this writing, the northern corridor has been completed only about halfway across the isthmus, but even that much saves a lot of time and irritation. The other road to Colón, called the **Transithmica** (also called the Trans-Isthmic Highway), is clogged with traffic during rush hours and heavily traveled all of the time. Tolls for both corridors are $2.50 for passenger vehicles.

> **AUTHOR NOTE:** *Street numbers are not used or published in the phone book. A typical address will read "Via España at the corner of Via Brasil," and sometimes the name of a familiar landmark or building nearby will be listed. If in doubt, call ahead for directions.*

Getting Around

If you are driving, you'll discover that getting into and out of the city is a lot easier than getting around in it. Most, but not all, of the capital's **streets** (*calles*) run north to south and most, but not all, **avenues** (*avenidas*) run east to west. To further confuse matters, many streets change names as they run through the city; for example, Avenida Balboa becomes Via Israel east of the Punta Paitilla traffic circle, and beyond that, it changes to Cincuentenario. Via España turns into Avenida Central and so on. Fortunately, all main arteries are indicated on maps, so be sure to pick one up from any tourist information office, major hotel, or other large store if you aren't familiar with the city.

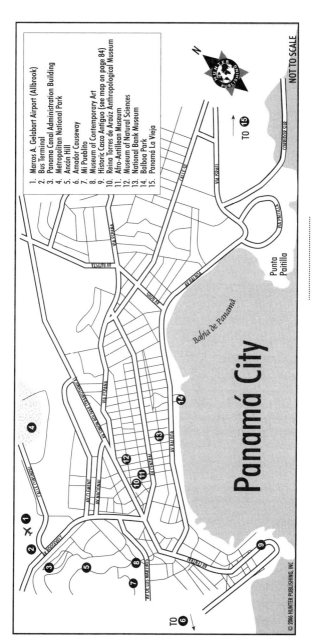

1. Marcos A. Gelabart Airport (Allbrook)
2. Bus Terminal
3. Panama Canal Administration Building
4. Metropolitan National Park
5. Ancón Hill
6. Amador Causeway
7. Mi Pueblito
8. Museum of Contemporary Art
9. Historic Casco Antiguo (see map on page 84)
10. Reina Torres de Araúz Anthropological Museum
11. Afro-Antillean Museum
12. Museum of Natural Sciences
13. National Bank Museum
14. Balboa Park
15. Panamá La Vieja

NOT TO SCALE

PANAMA PROVINCE

TO 15

Punta
Paitilla

Bahía de Panamá

Panamá City

TO 6

© 2006 HUNTER PUBLISHING, INC

AUTHOR NOTE: *The best map you'll find is a fold-out in the freebie tourist magazine called* **Focus**, ☎ *507-225-6638. Pick one up at the airport on arrival or from the front desk in any large hotel.*

◆ Public Transportation

Buses

Hundreds of retired exhaust-belching US school buses barrel through Panamá City's streets. On the plus side, you can get almost anywhere in the city for only 25¢ a ride. Destinations are emblazoned across the top of the front windshield and easy to see. You won't find any bells or buzzers to signal the driver to stop, so when you want to get off, just yell "parada." On the negative side, buses are owner-operated so the more passengers that can be squeezed in, the greater the profit. The older buses don't have air conditioning and make many, many stops. If you're traveling a short distance, taking the bus is a good way to save a buck, but if you're in a rush to get somewhere or even the slightest bit claustrophobic, take a taxi instead.

> ❖ **THE RED DEVILS (DIABLOS ROJOS)**
>
> Those roaring buses that dominate Panamá City's main streets are called "red devils," although most are not red but multi-colored. These highly amusing – and highly precarious – means of transport are brightly and creatively painted in an assortment of designs that usually include a portrait representing the driver's girlfriend, favorite movie star, saint, cartoon character, or a combination of any of these. A few have neon lights flashing above their windshields or all around them, huge steer horns attached to the hoods or flying tassels affixed almost anywhere. The most expensively decorated buses are airbrushed works of art. They operate on the "no mercy" rule and some blast deafening salsa or rock music from loudspeakers. Unfortunately, the best paint and customizing jobs are very expensive, and the high cost may soon put an end to this amusing tradition that is already fading.

Taxis

Taxis are plentiful and inexpensive. Cabs are not metered, but average in-town fares run only a dollar or two. Although most drivers are honest, I've run into a couple that take advantage of obvious tourists. I was once charged $5 for a ride that I knew should have cost only $1.50. It was my own fault. I hadn't asked the fare when telling the driver where I wanted to go. Now, I make it a point to ask first. If told an amount I know is incorrect, I say "no thanks," and hop out. Taxis are ubiquitous on city streets and another will be along in about two seconds – unless it's raining. Drivers are usually courteous and will take pains to get you to your destination. All licensed taxis have yellow license plates, and those waiting outside hotel lobbies, the "tourist" taxis, are permitted to charge double or triple the fare charged by those hailed from the street. These tourist taxis can be recognized by the "SET" on their license plates.

◆ Driving

Panamá City streets are woefully congested, more so during rush hours when the mildest milquetoast transforms into "the fast and the furious" behind the wheel. Afternoon rush hour, by the way, runs from about 4 to 7 pm. Mildly put, it's a free-for-all of unmarked one-way streets, ignored stop signs, blocked intersections and blaring horns. Worse yet, a few streets reverse traffic flow during peak hours. If you don't know where they are, you might zip around a corner and find yourself facing oncoming traffic. And keep in mind that landmarks are used in place of street numbers. Still want to drive in the city? If you do, and don't know your way around, try to stick to main thoroughfares and mark out your route on a map before starting out. My advice? Taxis are cheaper and faster, and the drivers (usually) know where they're going.

◆ Bicycles & Motorbikes

You'll see few bicycles or motorbikes in the city. The reason becomes obvious after you've read the sections above for getting around by bus, car and taxi. The little scooters you'll see occasionally belong mostly to fast-food delivery folks. If you plan to get around on a bike or motorbike, be prepared for some hair-raising experiences.

Sightseeing & Touring

> ### ❖ TIME MANAGEMENT
>
> If you have only one full day in the capital, it's time enough for one or two of the following:
>
> ❖   An in-depth tour of modern Panamá City, Panamá la Vieja and Casco Antiguo;
>
> ❖   A full- or half-day Panamá Canal transit;
>
> ❖   Bird (or wildlife) watch along famed Pipeline Road in Soberanía National Park;
>
> ❖   Hike along jungle-enclosed Camino Real, the Spanish Gold Route;
>
> ❖   Spend a half-day on Barro Colorado Island, a naturalist's Garden of Eden;

PANAMA PROVINCE

❖   Ride the Panamá Railroad to Colón, visit Gatun Locks and Fuerte San Lorenzo;

❖   Go by boat to Isla Taboga, the Isle of Flowers;

❖   Kayak the Panamá Canal and/or the Chagres River;

❖   Go by dugout canoe to an indigenous Emberá village;

❖   Dive Pacific reefs, the Panamá Canal or both;

❖   Savor the flavor of one or two of the city's fine restaurants;

❖   Mountain bike Metropolitan National Park's steep trails;

❖   Take a city at night tour aboard an open-sided *chiva parrendara* (party bus)

◆ Casco Antiguo Walking Tour

Casco Antiguo ("old compound") is the second Panamá City (Nueva Panamá), and was founded in 1673 to replace the city destroyed during Henry Morgan's 1671 raid. Once the New World's wealthiest city, it declined after the Spanish began sending their ships around Cape Horn instead of across the isthmus. Casco Antiguo enjoyed a revival during the California gold rush and again during its occupation by the French Canal Company. However, it didn't begin to spread beyond its ancient walls until the early 20th century and, as Panamá City began to spread eastward, Casco Antiguo lapsed into a forgotten slum neighborhood. Recently recognized as an historical and architectural gem, UNESCO declared it a World Heritage Site in 1997, and this once-opulent neighborhood is undergoing a renaissance. Many of its magnificent Spanish Colonial, French, neoclassic and Caribbean-style buildings have been restored or are under restoration. Elegant restaurants, sidewalk cafés and trendy clubs have taken up residence along its cobbled streets and plazas.

AUTHOR NOTE: *Consider hiring a good guide. They know the way around and provide interesting historical facts and fables. You'll find a list of them on page 52.*

If coming from the city center, take Avenue Balboa west and turn left onto Central Avenue. This will bring you into Casco Antiguo. There's very little parking, so your best bet is to go all the way to the peninsula's tip and park in front of the French Plaza. Better yet, avoid the difficulty of maneuvering Casco Antiguo's narrow congested streets and take a taxi.

AUTHOR NOTE: *Although it's a not-to-be-missed attraction, keep in mind that Casco Antiguo is only now emerging slowly from a slum, and many of its once-magnificent old mansions are still dilapidated, crowded tenements. If touring without a guide, exercise a bit of caution and avoid unsavory-looking side streets. I make it a point to "dress down," don't carry anything I can't afford to lose, and don't flash an expensive camera. Take a few simple precautions and you shouldn't have any problems.*

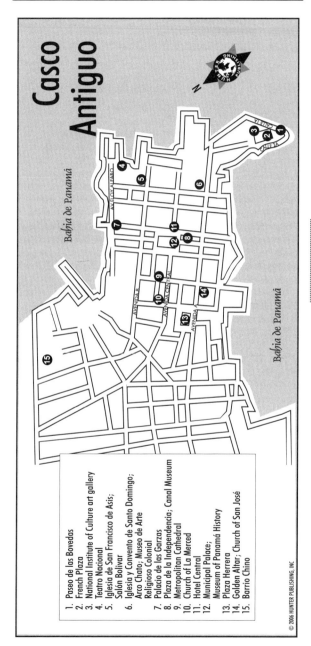

Casco Antiguo

Bahía de Panamá

Bahía de Panamá

N

1. Paseo de las Bovedas
2. French Plaza
3. National Institute of Culture art gallery
4. Teatro Nacional
5. Iglesia de San Francisco de Asis;
   Salón Bolivar
6. Iglesia y Convento de Santo Domingo;
   Arco Chato; Museo de Arte
   Religioso Colonial
7. Palacio de las Garzas
8. Plaza de la Independencia; Canal Museum
9. Metropolitan Cathedral
10. Church of La Merced
11. Hotel Central
12. Municipal Palace;
    Museum of Panamá History
13. Plaza Herrera
14. Golden Altar; Church of San José
15. Barrio Chino

A good way to begin your tour is with a stroll along **Paseo de las Bovedas** ("Promenade of the Vaults"), also called Esteban Huertas Promenade, at the southern tip of the peninsula. This vast walkway curves above a massive stone defensive sea wall built by the Spanish. The cannons are long gone, replaced by arching bowers of flowering red bougainvillea and gentle sea breezes. There are wonderful views of the modern capital from one side and, from the other, the arching Bridge of the Americas and the islands connected by the causeway.

> **AUTHOR NOTE:** *Local artists set up shop along the walkway, and you can find some surprisingly good watercolors of Casco Antiguo and other traditional Panamanian scenes. Most are priced between $5 and $10.*

Just below the wall is the lovely **French Plaza**, dedicated in 1923 to commemorate the 22,000 workers who died during de Lesseps' attempt to build a canal. A magnificent towering obelisk crowned with a Gallic cockerel serves as its centerpiece. Twelve marble plaques embedded in the wall relate the French canal history, and the principal characters involved are portrayed in a semicircle of bronze busts. On one side of the plaza, **Las Bovedas**, the vaults or jails, date from early colonial times. Nine of the vaults were restored in 1982 and now house an elegant French restaurant, also called Las Bovedas, and the **National Institute of Culture's (INAC) art gallery**. The imposing building next to the vaults was originally the **Palace of Justice**. Partially destroyed during the 1989 US invasion, "Operation Just Cause," it's since been restored and now houses INAC's offices. The lovely early 20th-century French-designed building opposite the plaza with flowering bougainvilleas dripping from its balconies is occupied by the **French Embassy**.

Walk up Avenue A when leaving the Plaza to the corner of Avenue 3, to find the remains of 18th-century **Iglesia y Convento de Santo Domingo** (Church and Convent of Saint Domingo). Only the walls and chapel (now the Museum of Colonial Religious Art) of this ruined church still stand. Its main attraction, the amazing Arco Chato, a 50-foot-long flat arch above the entrance, collapsed in late 2003. The former chapel has been restored to house the **Museo de Arte Religioso Colonial** (Museum of Religious Colonial Art), ☎ 507-228-2897. Don't miss this small museum with its exquisite, artfully displayed relics. The charming lady docents will pridefully describe each piece or let you wander about quietly on your own. Admission is only $1. It's open Monday through Friday, 9 am to 4 pm. Closed Saturday and Sunday.

> **AUTHOR NOTE:** *The Arco Chato (Flat Arch) was a determining factor in the US choosing Panamá for its canal: The arch had remained in place for centuries – proof that earthquakes are of no consequence here. On the eve of November 7, 2003, the Arco Chato collapsed. All Panamá mourned its loss.*

Turn north on Avenue 3, and just past the imposing Ministry of Government and Justice Building is the magnificent neoclassical **Teatro Nacio-**

nal (National Theater), first opened in 1908. Tiers of red velvet and gilt seating, a glittering crystal chandelier, and busy rococo décor make it almost decadently opulent. Its most important feature is a breathtaking, magnificent domed ceiling depicting the birth of the Republic and recently restored murals painted by artist Roberto Lewis. There is no admission fee, but you will need to ask the security guard to let you in. If you'd like to attend a performance – the national ballet and national orchestra frequently perform here, check the billboard, or call the ticket office, ☎ 507-262-3525.

> **AUTHOR NOTE:** *If you can speak or write a little Spanish and want to know about upcoming events in Casco Antiguo, call ☎ 507-228-3329, or e-mail informacion@cascoantiguo.gob. pa. Depending on who is working when you call or send a message, you might or might not get a reply in English.*

Opposite the theater, across from Bolívar Park, **Iglesia y Convento de San Francisco de Asis** (Church and Convent of Saint Francis of Asisi) complex seethes with history. First built as a monastery in 1678, it was twice destroyed and rebuilt. In 1826, Simón Bolívar, in his attempt to unite all of Latin America, called together representatives of Central America, Colombia, Peru, Venezuela, Argentina, Mexico and Panamá to a meeting in the church's schoolroom annex to write the Isthmus Protocol. While the initial attempt failed, Bolívar eventually liberated Colombia, Bolivia, Ecuador, Venezuela, and Peru into the unified state of Gran Colombia. In 1890, the church was transformed into a religious school. Panamá's first congress met here to write the country's constitution in 1904. Between 1923 and 1924 it was used to train a military regiment, and later became the Foreigner's Hospital. After a long and careful restoration, the magnificent convent section has reopened, and now houses Panamá's Ministry of Foreign Relations. It has been renamed **Salón Bolívar** in honor of the "Great Liberator." Visits to the annex can be arranged by calling the Bolivarian Society, ☎ 507-262-2947.

Cross from the park to Eloy Alfaro Street on the bay and you'll come to the heavily guarded Presidential Palace, called **Palacio de las Garzas** (Palace of the Herons) for the great birds that strut its grounds. Built in 1673, its opulent interior reflects an exotic blend of colonial and Spanish-Moorish style. Although Panamá's President lives on the top floors, visits can be arranged Tuesday through Friday by appointment, ☎ 507-227-9840 or 227-9874, fax 507-227-4278. There is no fee.

Walk south from the Palace to **Plaza de la Independencia**. During colonial times, this was the city's central plaza, and today it's a hub of activity. Trendy new restaurants and sidewalk cafés border its perimeters and, on weekends, vendors hawk *raspados* (crushed ice with fruit syrup), soft drinks, cotton candy, hot dogs and *salchichas* (sausages). This is a good place to take a break for lunch or dinner while watching passersby that might include groups of nuns, backpackers, tourists, neighborhood children and well-heeled ladies at lunch. Construction of the massive **Metro-**

PANAMA PROVINCE

politan Cathedral, which dominates one side of the plaza, began in 1688, but wasn't completed until 1796 – 108 years later!

Directly opposite the cathedral across the park is the 19th-century neoclassical **Hotel Central**. Once the city's most opulent hotel, it had deteriorated into a flophouse. It's since been resurrected, along with the surrounding neighborhood. Facing the cathedral to your left, you'll see the **Municipal Palace**, designed by Italian architect Genaro Ruggieri and built in 1910. Its lovely neoclassic design carries a strong Italianate influence. The **Museum of Panamá History**, ☎ 507-228-6231, on the top floor, displays mostly historical documents.

Next door to the Museum of Panamá History is the **Panama Canal Museum's** newly restored building; ☎ 507-211-1650, www.canalmuseum.com. It is one of the city's finest examples of Classic French architecture, built in 1875 as the Grand Hotel by George Lowe, who sold it to the French Canal Company in 1881. It served as company's headquarters until 1904, when it was transferred to the US, and served the same purpose until 1912, when it was purchased and restored by Panamá's President Belasario Porras, for government use. Both the building's interior and exhibits are exceptional and range from the isthmus' creation to the present day canal, along with ancient documents and artworks. Don't miss the fine gift shop. There is no fee to visit, but guides will appreciate a tip.

Head back on Avenue Central to Avenue 9 and walk one block west to **Plaza Herrera**, named for Military leader General Tomas Herrera. There's an equestrian statue of Herrera in this plaza where bullfights were once held, but nothing more of interest. To see the famous **Golden Altar**, which was moved to the **Church of San José** after fire destroyed Panamá la Vieja in 1671, walk up Av Central to Calle 9. The church isn't all that impressive, but the altar is a masterpiece. If you're carrying a carrying a camera, don't be surprised if you're accosted by giggling schoolchildren on the street outside, begging to have their photos taken.

The Church of La Merced, estimated to have been built in 1592, is three blocks east of the Church of San José, on Av Central and Calle 10.

There are some interesting things to see near Casco Antiguo's entrance. The narrow street that runs from Central Avenue to Avenue B is called **Salsipuedes**, which translates as "get out if you can." Back in the 18th century, or so the story goes, it was notoriously dangerous, but today, it's only an alley narrowed by flea market stalls selling fruits and vegetables, medicinal plants, plastic housewares and an assortment of usual and unusual junk. The only danger is from pickpockets, so stash that cash and anything else of value before visiting.

A brightly painted oriental arched portal marks the entrance to **"Barrio Chino"** (Chinese Neighborhood) between Juan Mendoza Street and Avenue B. Beginning in 1850, the first waves of Chinese immigrants arrived to work on the Panama Railroad. Some brought their families and many settled in this area. You might want to sample some authentic Chinese food in one of the small eating establishments or peruse the local supermarket's shelves. Stalls of military supplies, cooking utensils, camping gear and the odd saddle, some new and some used, are sold in the row of stalls near the market on Calle E, close to the waterfront.

You'll find plenty of dining and nightlife in the renovated areas bordering **Plaza de la Independencia**, the **French Plaza**, and scattered along nearby streets. When visiting after dark, take a taxi or park close by in a well-lighted area. And if a scruffy character approaches with an offer to watch your vehicle, by all means take him up on it and pay him a dollar or two when you leave. It's the custom here and he will guard it well. Keep in mind that most of the narrow, cobbled streets support only one-way traffic.

◆ Panamá La Vieja Walking Tour

Massive stone walls and heaps of age- and fire-blackened rubble are about all that's left of Panamá's once opulent first city, called Panamá La Vieja (Old Panamá), which was destroyed by fire in 1671. The conflagration consumed all of its wooden buildings, sparing only the stone walls of the most impressive structures. Just one escaped the flames, the Convent and Church of San José, with its legendary golden altar. Centuries of neglect took a further toll on the abandoned city and, when restoration began a few years ago, only its cathedral bell tower remained largely intact. With a good guide, you can visualize the long-lost grandeur of this huge city that spread west and north from the cathedral plaza on a promontory above the sea. The site is hauntingly beautiful, partly shaded by giant trees – including some ancient and beautiful Panamá trees.

The city's cathedral, **Catedral de Nuestra Señora de la Asunción**, built between 1610 and 1626, and the neighboring **Bishop's House** (Casa Alarcon) are the two best-preserved structures, both near the ruins' main entrance. Restoration of the cathedral's three-story bell tower is well underway, but there is little chance that Panamá la Vieja can ever be fully restored – too much has been lost and part of its outlying district now lies beneath a modern slum neighborhood.

The fine **Panamá Viejo Museum** is at the main entrance, in the same building with a cooperative craft market. Visit the museum before entering the ruins to get an idea of what the city was like in its heyday. During the recent restorations, archaeologists have uncovered a collection of 16th- and 17th-century Spanish artifacts and a much older indigenous burial ground dated to the first century BC. One of these burials has been removed and now lies inside a glass case exactly as it was discovered, complete with the deceased's skeleton surrounded by earthenware pottery. Signs posted in English and Spanish explain the history of each artifact. Be sure to see the well-executed scale model of the city as it was in 1671. It has tiny lights, illuminated by an operator in coordination with a taped description of its principal buildings and features. The tapes are played in both English and Spanish. The museum is open Monday-Friday, 9 am-noon and 1:30-4:30 pm. Admission is $1.

Take time to browse the **crafts market**, in the same building as the museum. This cooperative venture helps provide income to Panamá's indigenous groups. You'll find a vast selection of outstanding baskets and tagua carvings made by Emberá and Wounaan people, Kuna molas, Ngöbe-Buglé chaquiras (beaded collars once worn by warriors) and woven bags, along with assorted pottery, wood carvings, paintings, and even T-shirts.

Panamá la Vieja (also known as Panamá Viejo) is on the outskirts of Panamá City, about four miles east of the city's downtown area. Head east from the city on Av Cincuentenario (also named Av Balboa or Via Israel, depending on where you get on) and stay on this main road until you come to the ruins. Panamá la Vieja is open Monday through Saturday, 9 am to 4 pm, and Sunday from 9 am to 1 pm. Your $1.50 admission fee includes a visit to the ruins. There is free parking in front of the building that houses the Panamá Viejo Museum and crafts market. A new, much larger museum on the highway west of the site may have opened by the time you read this. Watch for it on the right.

◆ Mi Pueblito (My Little Village)

Since this charming life-size recreation of a colonial village typical to Panamá's heartland opened in 1994, two more complexes have been added. Now a trilogy of Panamá's cultures, it's more appropriately called Mis Pueblitos. The recreated Afro-Antillean town pays tribute to the West Indian immigrants who came to work on the Panamá Railroad and later the canal, while the indigenous sector honors the country's three most prominent native peoples – the Emberá, Kuna and Ngöbe-Buglé (Guaymí).

Built around a central plaza, the charming "heartland" village replicates a rural village of a century or so ago. Its authentic little mission-style church is furnished with extraordinary care; the schoolroom appears ready for class to begin, and the tiny "typical" home features a parlor and outbuilding kitchen complete with 18th-century cooking implements and a wood-burning clay stove. There's a telegraph office, a pollera museum and a row of little shops that sell handicrafts, souvenirs and jewelry. Traditional fare is served inside the restaurant here or on its balcony overlooking the plaza where full dress traditional dance performances, including the lovely tamborito, the national dance, are held every Thursday evening.

Brightly painted Victorian-Caribbean architecture with lots of gingerbread highlights the colorful Afro-Caribbean complex and its lovely white chapel perched on a knoll. Two houses typical of the early 20th century illustrate the vast differences between the home of a prosperous West Indian merchant and one of the laboring class. Chat with the smiling musicians strumming away in front of the shops and sway down curving brick pathways in tempo to reggae music drifting on flower-scented air. The Afro-Caribbean restaurant painted an azure blue features excellent seafood; there's a bakery, a cafeteria and if it's coffee you crave, follow your nose to Luis Beitia's kiosk for a cup of Panamá's superb best.

Least fanciful is the indigenous enclave, a faithful illustration of the way Panamá's native peoples have lived for centuries. Meander wooded pathways and into typical Kuna, Emberá and Ngöbe-Buglé homes, a communal house and a council house. Watch ages-old rituals performed and artisans crafting molas, baskets, tagua and wood carving, flutes, drums and clothing. Craft items are available for purchase. And don't miss the lookout here that offers spectacular views of the capital.

Mis Pueblitos entrance is off Av de Los Martires near the base of Ancon Hill, on the city's west side. It's open from 10 am until 10 pm, Tuesday through Sunday. Admission is 50 cents and parking is free. ☎ 507-228-7178.

◆ Museums

Museo Antopologico Reina Torres de Araúz (Reina Torres de Araúz Anthropological Museum), Central Av at Plaza 5 de Mayo, ☎ 507-262-8338, is the country's premier museum, named in honor of its first and foremost woman archaeologist. Highlights include an exceptional display of Barilles culture stone statues, metates and grinding tools. Among an exquisite assortment of intricate pre-Columbian gold huacas is Central America's oldest-known piece of metallurgy, a copper and gold nosepiece dating from AD 180. The ethnology section's 10,000 artifacts (most recovered from looters), include several hundred pieces rescued from Noriega's home after his arrest. Built in 1913, the lovely neoclassic building housing the museum was once the city's main railway station. Open Monday through Friday, 9 am until 4 pm. Admission is $1 for Panamá residents, $2 for tourists.

Museó Afro-Antilleano (Afro-Antillean Museum), corner of Calle 24 West and Av Justo Arosemena, three blocks from the Anthropology Museum, ☎ 507-262-5368. Housed in an old Christian mission church, the collected photographs, artistic and domestic objects lovingly displayed in this special little museum offer a rare insight into the lives of the West Indian people who came to work on the railroad and the canal. Between 1904 and 1914, 20,000 arrived from Barbados alone, most as deck passengers aboard the USS *Ancón*, to build the Panama Canal. Admission is $1 for adults and 25¢ for children under 12 and students with ID.

Museó de Arte Religioso Colonial (Museum of Colonial Religious Art), in Casco Antiguo between Calle 3 and Av A (see *Sightseeing and Touring*, Casco Antiguo, page 64), ☎ 507-228-2897. A small but impressive collection of paintings, wood and polychrome carvings, and sacred artifacts are displayed in the restored chapel of the Church and Convent of Santo Domingo.

Museó del Canal Interoceánico (Panama Canal Museum), ☎ 507-211-1650 OR 211-1649, www.canalmuseum.com. This one is exceptional. Exhibits detail the history of the isthmus, the railroad, the failed

French canal, and the heroic efforts that resulted in the Panama Canal, known as "the path between the seas." Located on Plaza de la Independecia, Casco Antiguo. For more about this museum, see *Sightseeing & Touring*, page 68.

Museó de Ciencias Naturales (Museum of Natural Sciences), Av Cuba between Calles 29 and 30, ☎ 507-225-0625. There are exhibits of Panamá paleontology, entomology and marine biology, along with examples of flora and some stuffed mammals and reptiles found in Panamá. African and Asian exhibits feature antelopes, lions and tigers – also stuffed. Hours are 9 am until 4 pm, Tuesday through Saturday, and 9 am until 1 pm, Sunday. Admission is $1 adults, 25¢ for children.

Museó del Banco Nacional (National Bank Museum), Calle 34 at Av Cuba, ☎ 507-225-2640. The collection of coins, bills and stamps dating from the 16th century to the present will be of special interest to numismatists and philatelists. Hours are 8 am to 12:30 pm, and 1:30 pm until 4 pm, Tuesday through Friday, and 8 am until noon on Saturday. Admission is free.

Museó de Historia de Panamá (Museum of Panamá History), on the 3rd floor of the Municipal Palace building in Casco Antiguo, next door to the Panama Canal Museum, ☎ 507-228-6231. Five salons display historical documents, photographs, emblems and the like, dating from colonial times to the present. Open Monday through Friday, 9 am to 3:30 pm.

Museó del Arte Contemporáneo (Museum of Contemporary Art), Calle San Blas and Av de los Martires in the Ancón neighborhood, ☎ 507-262-3376. Permanent and revolving exhibitions of paintings, sculptures, photographs and graphic arts by Panamanian and foreign artists are displayed in this attractive museum where musical recitals are sometimes held. Ask if you can tour the restoration workshop. Hours are 9 am-5 pm, Tuesday through Sunday. Admission is $1 for adults, 50¢ for children.

❖   **GOLD HUACAS**

The word "huaca" is derived from the Spanish, huacal, referring to a burial. The word evolved to mean the items interred in pre-Columbian gravesites, so huacas might be jewelry, pottery, weapons or tools. Panamá's gold huacas were fashioned into pendants, earrings, nose rings, breastplates, cuffs and bracelets. The beautifully detailed pendants represented gods, animals, fantastic zoomorphic creatures and humans.

◆ Calzada de Amador (Amador Causeway)

The causeway stretches alongside the canal's entrance 1.5 miles/2.5 km into the Pacific, connecting the mainland's peninsular Amador neighborhood to the islands of Culebra, Naos, Perico and Flamenco. Strategic to protecting the canal, this beautiful area was occupied since 1919 by military installations, beginning with the US military's Fort Grant and, later, Fort Amador until 1979. During the 1980s, the now-disbanded Panamanian Military was based here, and in 1996, as outlined by the Carter-Torrijos Treaty, it reverted to Panamá. Its military background is fading into history as the causeway and islands emerge as one of the capital's most attractive and popular recreational areas.

Heading toward the causeway on Calle Amador, you'll pass on the right a pod of buildings transformed from military use to ultra-exclusive shops and, on the left, a lovely new **Country Inn and Suites**. **Pencas Restaurant**, on the right, serves good food and lovely views from its half-moon shaped 2nd-floor balcony. Downstairs, **Moses Bicycle** rents bikes ($2.10 per hour) and inline skates to cruise the causeway under your own steam. Also on the right is **Panama Canal Village**, a mega-luxury complex of condos, a five-star resort hotel, shopping and entertainment venues, and a massive new convention center, completed only days prior to hosting the 2003 Miss Universe Pageant.

Be sure to visit the Smithsonian Tropical Research Institute's **Centro de Exhibiciones Marinas** (Marine Exhibition Center) on Culebra Island if you've ever wanted to stroke a neon-orange starfish or wiggly little octopus. There are aquariums of Atlantic and Pacific marine critters, a few reptiles and among the excellent displays that focus on preservation is one that traces the isthmus' natural and human history from the time of its formation. Study the huge illustrations of sea-going vessels before gazing through the powerful telescope and you'll be able to identify many of the ships lined up to enter the canal. The center's three large buildings were once military bunkers and a machine shop while the small, glass-enclosed structure that now houses displays was built by Noriega for private entertaining. Those towering trees lining the shore and pathway to the exhibits are part of one of Central America's largest surviving tracts of Pacific Dry Forest. Signs at the base of each tree identify its species, and if you look high into the branches you might spot iguanas and a sloth or two up there with the birds. The center is open Tuesday through Friday from 1 to 5 pm, and Saturday and Sunday from 10 am until 6 pm. Suggested donation is $1 for adults, 50 cents for children 12 and under.

Next on the right, you'll find **ScubaPanama's** newest dive shop and **Mi Ranchito**, a long-established and very popular open-air restaurant that moved here recently from across the way. It's a great place to enjoy a cold beer and a heaping plate of camarones al ajillo (garlic shrimp).

The last and largest island, **Flamenco**, has been transformed from a former US military command post into the new **Fuerte** (Fort) **Amador Resort and Marina**. It is now one of the city's most exciting shopping and entertainment complexes, hosting Panamá's first full-service marina, a cruise port, upscale and duty-free shopping, outdoor bistros, restaurants and lounges, and entertainment centers. With all this and spectacular views of the sea and Panamá Bay, the causeway and the capital, Fuerte Amador is a great place to spend a day and/or a night. A casino and two five-star hotels are expected to open soon; the one to be built on the plateau atop the island's steep hill will offer breathtaking views.

PANAMA PROVINCE

❖ **IN THE WORKS...**

The Museum of Tropical Diversity, designed by world-renowned architect Frank Gehry, is scheduled to open near Amador Causeway's northern entrance in February 2006. Gehry has designed some of the world's most striking buildings, including the sinuous titanium Guggenheim Museum in Bilbao, Spain, and the Chiat-Day Building in Venice, California that has a pair of giant binoculars for its entrance. Gehry, who's been called the king of "pop" architecture, began using crumpled papers from his drawings to create models for some of his buildings. The model for the country's most talked-about museum looks like he used bent, rather than crumpled, paper. Its multi-layered, multi-shaped roofs in varying heights resemble handfuls of bent construction paper in shades of bright red, pink and blue. Like children's blocks, the complementing pastel outer walls are a jumble of triangles, cones, cylinders and cubes. It will certainly be eye-catching when complete! The Smithsonian Tropical Research Institution is expected to provide consultation for the exhibits.

◆ The Panama Canal

Mention Panamá and most people automatically think "canal." And no wonder. Since its completion in 1914, the "big ditch" has been considered the world's greatest feat of engineering. In 1904, the US acquired the failed French Canal Company's assets and began to build the canal that runs almost 50 miles/80 km across the narrowest part of the isthmus – from Colón City on the Atlantic to Panamá City on the Pacific. Although it took 10 years to dig through the continental divide, blast through mountains of rock, and divert and dam rivers to create a system of artificial lakes, the three lock canal was completed ahead of schedule and, at a cost of $387 million, under budget. To visualize the amount of rock and dirt that was removed from the channel, imagine it heaped on a train of flatcars long enough to circle the globe four times! Only freshwater can be used to operate the locks; salt water would corrode the machinery. For this reason, the canal's watershed, five mile-wide swaths of forest on both sides of the channel, had been left undisturbed for almost a century. However, during Moscoso's administration permits were issued to log almost 25,000 acres/10,000 hectares within the protected areas. I hope they've been revoked.

> **AUTHOR NOTE:** *Canal grass (pana canalera or elephant grass) was imported from Vietnam by the Americans in 1913 and planted alongside the canal to prevent soil erosion. It helped to avoid collapse of the canal's banks, but soon began to spread and choke out native plants. Today, you'll see this 10-foot/three-meters-tall grass throughout Panamá and Colón provinces. Steps are underway to control it.*

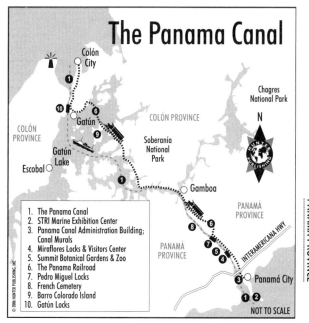

Ships transiting from the Atlantic to the Pacific pass through almost seven miles/11 kilometers of the channel to the first lock system, Gatún, where they are raised 85.9 feet/25.9 meters to the level of Gatún lake. After passing over a 15.8-mile/25.5-kilometer stretch of the lake and through the Gaillard (Culebra) Cut, they enter Pedro Miguel Locks, where they are lowered 30.8 feet/9.4 meters. The canal continues another 1.30 miles/2.1 kilometers to Miraflores Locks, where the ships are again lowered to the Pacific tidewater level before proceeding the remaining 2.48 miles/4 kilometers to the sea. It takes approximately eight to 10 hours for each ship to transit the canal from ocean to ocean, and more than half of that is across Gatún Lake, the world's second-largest man-made lake. Fifty thousand people were displaced as villages, forests and mountains were flooded during the lake's creation, and all those many islands rising above its surface are the tops of drowned mountains.

The canal contains three **lock systems** – Miraflores and Pedro Miguel on the isthmus' Pacific side, and Gatún on the Atlantic – each of which has two lanes.

Miraflores Locks are 20 minutes west of the city, just off the Gaillard Highway. As you head west, you'll see the clearly marked entrance on the left. The newly remodeled Miraflores Visitor Center reopened in late 2003, with three viewing platforms for watching the giant ships as they are raised and lowered to squeeze through the locks. Four indoor exhibition halls contain scale models of the canal, a navigation simulator, artifacts and historical information. Films depicting the canal's history are shown in the 182-seat theater and there are gift shops, snack bars and a restaurant. Bilingual guides are on hand. The center is open from 9 am to 5 pm daily. Admission for foreign nationals is $8 for adults, $5 for students and minors ages 8-12 with identification, and free for children age five and under. Parking is free. If coming by bus, take any one bound for Gamboa and ask to be dropped at the Miraflores entrance. Call **SACA Bus**, ☎ 507-262-7333 for schedules. Fare from the city is 35 cents.

The **Gatún Locks** near Colón do not have a visitor center, but there is a viewing platform and guides are available. There are no visitor facilities at **Pedro Miguel Locks**, which can be seen only from a distance. For more information, visit the Web site www.pancanal.com, or request specific information by phone, ☎ 507-272-1502, or by writing to ACP, PO Box 5411, Miami, FL, USA 33102-5413.

❖   PANAMA CANAL FACTS

- ❖   The first vessel to make a complete canal transit was a floating crane, the *Alexander La Valley*, on January 17, 1914. The canal was officially inaugurated on August 15, 1914, with the transit of the ship USS *Ancón*. Since then, more than 880,000 vessels have passed through.

- ❖   In July 1934, Franklin Delano Roosevelt became the first US President to transit the canal.

- ❖   Fifty-two million gallons of fresh water are used for every vessel that passes through the canal locks.

- ❖   Each transiting vessel pays tolls of approximately $48,000.

- ❖   In 1928, adventurer Richard Halliburton paid the lowest toll – 36¢ to swim the canal. It took him 10 days.

- ❖   The highest toll was $217,513.75, paid by the cruise ship *Coral Princess* during its inaugural cruise on January 17, 2003.

- ❖   The canal locks have a total of 40 pairs of miter gates, all dating back to its construction. The tallest of these gates are at Miraflores Locks; each one weighs 730 tons!

- ❖   French impressionist painter Paul Gauguin worked as a common laborer on the canal in 1887.

- ❖   The Panama Canal is the only place in the world where military commanders must relinquish control of their ships. Panama Canal pilots guide all ships through the canal.

BEST BET: *Get out there yourself with a full or partial **canal transit**. You can arrange it with one of the city's tour operators listed on page 52. Partial transits with buffet breakfast are offered every Saturday, 7 am to noon. The cost is $99 per person. Full transits with brunch are run every third Saturday, 7 am to 5 pm, and the cost is $149 per person.*

◆ The Panama Canal Murals

These beautiful murals portray in graphic detail the heroic efforts that resulted in Panama Canal, known as "the path between the seas." Mounted in the **Panama Canal Administration Building's** towering rotunda, the powerfully poignant 1,000-square-foot murals were painted by New York artist William Van Ingen, who created murals for the Library of Congress in Washington DC and the US Mint in Philadelphia. The four main murals illustrate the construction of Gaillard Cut at Gold Hill, where the canal passes through the continental divide; the Gatún Dam spillway that dammed the Chagres River to create massive Gatún Lake; construction of a lock miter gate; and the construction of the Miraflores Locks, near the canal's Pacific entrance.

> **AUTHOR NOTE:** *While in the rotunda, look closely at its eight towering marble columns. All but one were installed upside down! By the time anyone noticed, it was too late to correct the error.*

During two visits to the construction sites in 1914, Van Ingen and his assistants made charcoal sketches of the works in progress, then returned to New York to paint the boldly brush-stroked murals. Brought to Panamá in January 1915 and installed under Van Ingen's personal supervision, they are the largest grouping of murals by an American artist displayed outside of the United States. The aging murals were restored in 1993 by Anton Rajur, an art conservator from Madison, Wisconsin and rededicated in a ceremony held September 29, 1993.

The Administration Building dominates the side of Ancón Hill in the Balboa Heights district. A taxi from town will cost $3-$4. There are an astounding 113 steps up to the building from the plaza and the Goethels monument, built to honor George W. Goethels, the canal's chief construction engineer.

> **AUTHOR NOTE:** *Ships traveling from New York to San Francisco save 7,872 miles by transiting the Panama Canal instead of going around South America's Cape Horn.*

◆ Summit Botanical Gardens & Zoo

Established by the Panama Canal Company for the study of tropical plants, this 300-acre/120-hectare botanical garden was transferred to Panamá in 1985. Shady picnic areas, a playground, cafeteria and a small zoo are set in the midst of its lush greenery and flowering tropical and subtropical plantings. Follow the long pathway bordered by thick stands of tall bamboo to the harpy eagle preservation display – it may be your only chance of ever seeing a pair of these powerful raptors with talons as big as grizzly bear claws. It's estimated that only 20 pairs of the extremely endangered harpys still survive in Panamá's wildest and most remote regions. You'll learn all about their habits, habitats and preservation during a guided tour through the adjacent Harpy Eagle Rotunda, where films, lectures and displays are featured. Although the eagles are kept in an expansive enclosure, many of the zoo's less fortunate animals are incarcerated in distressingly small cages. This may bother you. It did me. Summit is 20 minutes from the city, off the Gaillard Highway on the way to Gamboa. Plenty of free parking is available. If coming by bus, you can take any that is bound for Gamboa (SACA Bus, ☎ 507-262-7333). The fare is 55¢. A taxi will cost about $4 each way. The entrance fee is 25¢ for adults, 10¢ for children. The complex is open Monday through Friday, 8 am until 4 pm, and Saturday and Sunday, 8 am until 6 pm; ☎ 507-232-4850.

◆ The French Cemetery

When headed west on the Gaillard Highway, you can't miss the hundreds of white crosses staggered down a grassy slope just past the little village of Paraiso. This is the final resting place of the French engineers and administrators who succumbed to malaria and yellow fever during de Lesseps' failed attempt to build a canal. There's no reason to stop unless you want to pay your respects.

◆ Barro Colorado Island

A day visit to this 3,865-acre/1,564-hectare island in Gatún Lake will give you an informative peek into the awesome diversity of tropical rainforest ecosystems. Fossils date back 30 million years and a magnificent ceiba tree that was old when the conquistadors arrived towers above the lianas, bromeliads, orchids, strangler figs, cashews, oaks, palms and trees that "walk." The ceiba, or "the big tree," as it is called, is so large that smaller trees are growing from its massive branches. Twenty men holding hands with arms outstretched would barely encircle its trunk.

Barro Colorado's steep, hilly forests host five monkey species, tapirs, coatimundis, anteaters, peccaries, sloths, ocelots, agoutis, rare red deer and 385 bird species. Howler and squirrel monkey troops are often encountered, and I once spent 10 minutes playing peek-a-boo with a young vested anteater that was too curious to run away. He kept me in wary sight as he sidled around and around his tree to prevent me from taking his photograph. Other identified creatures include 70 bat species, 40 frog species, 47 snake species, 22 lizard species, at least 300 butterfly species, and 200 identified ant species, including 14 of army ants.

Barro Colorado was created during the Panama Canal's construction when the Chagres River was dammed and an area almost the size of Barbados was flooded to create 166-square-mile/430-square-kilometer Gatún Lake. The process took four years, from 1910 to 1914. When it was completed, only the tops of the tallest hills remained above the water. Barro Colorado Island is the largest of these. In 1923, the island was declared a biological reserve and one of the New World's first protected tropical rainforests. Since 1946, it has been administered by the Panamá-based **Smithsonian Tropical Research Institute** (**STRI**), a world-renowned biological research facility with labs, libraries, and living quarters for the scientists who study here. In 1977, five small islands and adjacent peninsulas were added to create Barro Colorado Nature Monument.

Visits can be arranged only through STRI or one of its approved tour operators. The number of visitors is strictly limited and it's not uncommon for space to be reserved a year in advance. If you can't plan that far ahead, ask to be put on the waiting list for your requested dates – there are usually a few cancellations. The cost is $70 per person for international visitors, $40 for international students with ID. This includes round-trip boat transportation from Gamboa, a morning hike with a naturalist guide and a cafeteria lunch. The launch leaves Gamboa at 7:15 am on Tuesday, Wednesday and Friday and at 8 am on Saturday and Sunday. There are no visits on Mondays, Thursdays or some holidays. For reservations, contact Patricia Pinzon at the STRI-Tupper Building, Monday through Friday, 8:30 am-4:30 pm, ☎ 507-212-8026, fax 507-212-8148; e-mail visitSTRI@tivoli.si.edu. Inquire here about any special concerns and bus or driving information to the Gamboa pier. The Tupper Building, ☎ 507-212-8000, is in Panamá City's Ancón district, on Avenida de los Martires, across from the Legislative Palace. You'll need ID to enter. There's a good research library with very helpful attendants and an excellent bookstore here as well.

> **AUTHOR NOTE:** *The Smithsonian Tropical Research Institute offers free science lectures in English on Tuesdays at noon in the Tupper Building Auditorium.* ☎ *507-212-8000 for information.*

Adventures

◆ On Foot

Walking & Jogging

Four very popular places for walking and jogging are the Amador Causeway, on the city's west side, Parque Balboa on Balboa Avenue next to Panamá Bay, Parque Recreativo (Recreation Park) in the San Francisco district and Ancón Hill. All offer spectacular views.

The 1.5-mile/2.5-kilometer **Amador Causeway**, built of rock and sand dredged up during the Panama Canal construction, stretches into the Pa-

PANAMA PROVINCE

cific to connect **Naos**, **Culebra**, **Perico** and **Flamenco** islands. It's a long haul from one end to the other, so you may want to take time out to relax on a bench along the route and just soak up the views. On one side you'll see the arching Bridge of the Americas and ships entering the canal. The other side offers sweeping vistas of the city and Panamá Bay.

The **Smithsonian Institution Marine Exhibition Center** is on Naos, while the last and largest island, Flamenco, has been transformed from the former Fort Amador US military installation to one of the city's newest "in" spots, with a cruise port, marina, restaurants, lounges and an upscale shopping arcade. Those cooling sea breezes also stream across **Balboa Park**, between the elegant Miramar Intercontinental Hotel and Panamá Bay. The views here are just as fantastic, with the city on one side and the sea on the other.

Parque Recreativo has a natural dirt jogging track and a paved one. You can also rent a bicycle here. The park is just west of the Caesar Park hotel, facing Av Belisario Porras. Depending on how long you stop to gawk at wildlife along the way, it will take at least 20 minutes to hike the winding asphalt road to the top of **Ancón Hill** on the city's west side. Toucans, deer, monkeys, coatimundis and sloths are plentiful in this reverted suburban neighborhood. From the top of the hill, Panamá City's highest point, you can look down on the canal, the city and an expanse of the Pacific. Look for the huge Panamanian flag flapping at the hill's summit.

Hiking

Metropolitan National Park is one of the world's few wilderness parks within the boundaries of a capital city, and the only one in Latin America. Much of its 655 acres/265 hectares are composed of the country's largest remaining tracts of lowland Pacific forest, inhabited by 255 identified bird species, deer, raccoons, sloths, tamarin monkeys, coatis, turtles and iguanas. Stop first at the visitor center to pick up information and brochures and, if you wish, to enlist a guide ($6) before beginning your hike. Four main trails of varying terrain wind through the park: Steep **Mono Titi Trail** winds up through the forest to a lookout at the summit of Cerro Mono Titi (Mono Titi Hill), 492 feet/150 meters above sea level for fantastic views of the park, Panamá City, the bay and the canal. **Cieneguita** is a little shorter, winding around to connect with Mono Titi near the top of the hill. **Los Coobos** trail starts behind the visitor center and Momotides begins at the highway across from it. Inside the center, there's a permanent display of the park's history and flora and fauna, a library and a delightful gift shop devoted to preservationist goodies. There is an orchid garden outside. Metropolitan National Park is open every day from 6 am to 5 pm. The visitor center, ☎ 507-232-5552, opens at 8 am. Entrance fees are $2 for adult tourists, $1 for Panamanian nationals and foreign students under 17 with ID. The visitor center is 10-15 minutes from downtown, facing Av Juan Pablo II. As of this writing, new construction and several detours complicate driving directions. The work should be completed when you read this, but I still recommend calling the visitor center in advance for the best route. Taxis should have no problem.

◆ On Wheels

The Panama Railroad

This attraction doesn't stay in the city, but it does start here. Sip a morning coffee while gliding alongside the canal in a restored turn-of-the-century railroad car. Gleaming brass lighting fixtures, air conditioning, carpeting and boot seating complements these great old cars with wide, wide windows. The early morning ride past lakes and through the jungles is especially beautiful. You don't need to be a train buff to enjoy this nostalgic coast-to-coast journey aboard the train that played such an important role in Panamá's history. The Panama Canal Railway Company, a joint venture of the Kansas City Southern Railway Company, resumed passenger service in late 1991 after two years of construction and improvements. The train operates Monday through Friday, departing Panamá City at 7:15 am and departing Colón at 5:15 pm for the return trip. Travel time each way is one hour. Adult tickets are $20 one way or $35 round-trip. Children under 12 pay half-fare. Reservations are not necessary. From Panamá City, the train departs from the Corozal Passenger station – the old Canal Zone commissary, building T-376. The Colón Passenger Station is at the Port of Cristobal near the freight house. ☎ 507-317-6070; info@panarail.com.

> **AUTHOR NOTE:** *Since there is only one round-trip journey each day, book your ride with a tour operator and include visits to Fuerte San Lorenzo, Gatun Locks and an extravagant buffet lunch at Melia Panama Canal Resort; or you can spend all day at the resort.*

Metropolitan Park

Hard-core **mountain bikers** may want to have a go at Metropolitan Park's hard-packed earth and rock trails. Mono Titi Trail's five miles/eight kilometers (up and back) wind steeply up to the summit of Cerro Mono Titi. Catch your breath and take in the fantastic city views. You can rent a bike from Julio Arjona at **Panamá Adventure Bike**, ☎ 507-676-4023, panamaadventurebike@hotmail.com, or he'll take you on an informative cycling tour. Be advised; this one takes a lot of stamina. See Metropolitan Park under *Hiking* on the previous page.

Amador Causeway

The causeway is as popular with cyclists and in-line skaters as with walkers and joggers. Make a day of it by stopping at the **Smithsonian Marine Exhibition Center** before continuing to Flamenco, the last and largest island with shopping, restaurants, a cruise port, marina and some breath-taking city, sea and canal views. Rent a bike from **Panamá Adventure Bike**, ☎ 507-676-4023, in the city, or rent one on the spot from **Moses Bike Rental**, downstairs from Pencas Restaurant, near the causeway entrance.

Chiva Parrandera (Party Bus)

The word *chiva* means bus and *parrandera* means to party. Put them together and you've got a party bus. Tour the city at night while partying aboard a brightly painted, open-sided bus, complete with live typical music, snacks and open bar. This one is a lot of fun and a reasonable $30 for three hours. Reserve your ride with one of local tour operators listed on page 52.

◆ On Water

Kayaking

When friends ask if you saw the **Panama Canal** you can reply, "I sure did, and I kayaked it, too!" You won't get dangerously close to the massive ships transiting the canal, but you will be able to observe them during this two- to three-hour paddle from Diablo to the Miraflores Locks. Expect to see plenty of shorebirds – herons, cormorants, tiny diving ducks – and perhaps an iguana or two sunning on overhanging branches. The **Panamá Explorer Club (PEX)**, ☎ 507-215-2330, www. pexclub.com, arranges this one for $25 per person, including the guide and all equipment.

A seven-mile/11-kilometer paddle on the translucently green **Chagres River** winds through rainforest virtually untouched since the days of the Spanish conquistadors. The excursion starts just below Gatún Locks and ends at Historic San Lorenzo, near the river's Caribbean entrance. Watch for scolding toucans and howler monkeys whooping it up in the forest on this incredible journey offered by **Exotics Adventures**, ☎ 507-223-9283, www.panamaexoticsadventures.com.

Rent a kayak or arrange a variety of tours with Gamboa Rainforest Resort's **Gamboa Tours**, ☎ 507-314-9000, www.gamboaresort.com.

Rafting

The day-long **"Chagres Challenge" rafting** adventure begins on the Piedras River, a Chagres tributary, and continues down the Chagres through beautiful forests to Madden Lake. It has classes II and III rapids that require some stamina and a short trek along a jungle pathway. **Pesantez Tours**, ☎ 507-263-8771 and 507-223-5347; e-mail pesantez@sinfo.net.

❖ AN INDIGENOUS ADVENTURE

During the last 25 years or so, a few of Panamá's indigenous Emberá people migrated north from Darién to the jungles of Chagres National Park, where they live in small communities along the Chagres River's steep banks. A visit to these kind, gentle people requires travel on wheels, on water and on foot! It's an hour's drive from Panamá City to a Chagres riverbank, where you'll meet an Emberá boatman who will whisk you upriver through the jungle in a motorized dugout *cayuco* (canoe). River turtles, herons, hawks, toucans, oropendolas, howler monkeys, agoutis, iguanas and hundreds of butterflies are commonly glimpsed along the route. Upon arrival, you'll be welcomed and treated to a music and dance presentation and a delicious lunch of fresh fish served in smooth brown bowls – the hollow shells of a coconut-like fruit called *samtotomo*.

The Emberá create beautiful baskets and carvings of tagua and wood. They'll be displayed for sale, but no one will push you to buy. You can walk medicinal trails with a native healer or swim in the river.

This "soft" adventure provides an opportunity to meet a gracious people whose lifestyle has remained virtually the same for centuries. Arrange your visit with a local tour operator. The day trip costs about $125 for two persons — but a party of six costs only $75 per person, so ask if others will be going and form a group. Overnight and longer stays can be arranged.

PANAMA PROVINCE

Tubing

White-water tubing on the **Chagres River** with indigenous Emberá guides combines great fun with a unique cultural experience. Half that fun is getting there in a motorized *cayuco*, the hollowed out trunk of a giant tree. Wildlife abounds in this true wilderness. You're sure to spot a few stoic wading herons, sunning river turtles, startled agoutis, toucans, cormorants, macaws and butterflies skimming above the water. After a brief stop in Emberá Drua community to pick up the guides, it's another 45 minutes farther upriver to the tube launching point. By the time you've navigated the rocks and currents back down to the village, a delicious fresh fish and fried plantain lunch will be waiting. Arrange this adventure with a local tour operator.

Drift through a jungle-cloaked island maze and watch monkeys watch you. With a little luck, you'll see sloths, iguanas, agoutis and for sure, hundreds of amazing birds. Or shine a flashlight along the Chagres's banks at night and try to count all those glowing red crocodile eyes. These short adventures depart from Gamboa Resort's marina. **Gamboa Tours**, ☎ 507-314-9000, www.gamboaresort.com (click "Tour Desk").

Scuba Diving

PACIFIC COAST – Coral-encrusted cannons strewn along Pacific **Porto-belo Bay's Salmadina Reef** are grim reminders of the ships these rocks have claimed over the centuries. The colorful coral gardens near **Drake's Island** teem with reef fish, but the infamous pirate's lead casket, rumored to lie on the sea's sandy bottom, has yet to be discovered. Some of this area's best diving, with visibility usually about 80 feet, is found along the **Fallarones Reef**, seven miles out from the bay. Gargantuan denizens of the deep lurk near the distant Pacific Northwest's virtually untouched and unexplored reefs and around the many small islands lying off the **Azuero Peninsula**.

CARIBBEAN COAST – The best months for Caribbean diving are June through December, when tropical sunlight penetrates warm waters to a depth of 20 feet/six meters. The undersea environment surrounding Bocas del Toro's beautiful islands boasts 74 of the Caribbean's 79 coral species, a variety of sponges and a host of little invertebrate creatures. Shallows near **Crawl Caye** and the **Coral Islands** reach a maximum depth of 20 feet/six meters, while reefs near **Solarte Caye**, **Cristobal** and **Colón** islands begin about 10 feet/three meters and drop slowly to the 60-foot/20-meter sea floor. **Hospital Point** is favored for the sponge and coral platform at a depth of 15 feet/4½ meters.

PANAMA CANAL – Enter a historic, although somewhat spooky underwater world of abandoned French machinery and a train submerged during early attempts to build the canal. Distant thrumming vibrations made by monster ships moving through the canal intensifies the eerie experience. Don't even think about attempting this dive on your own; contact the experts at **ScubaPanama**, ☎ 507-261-3841 or 261-4064 in Panamá City, www.scubapanama.com, to arrange a dive. The company enjoys an excellent reputation as one of the best – and first – established dive operators. Owner Rene Gomez trained in the US and Panamá and holds every dive certificate it's possible to obtain. Scuba Panamá has several locations, offers complete dive shops, and holds classes in both English and Spanish. Among the assortment of underwater adventures offered is a "Dive two oceans and the Canal" one-day adventure that starts in the Caribbean, moves on to the Panama Canal and rounds out the day in the Pacific. This package, with divemaster, includes pick-up and drop-off at your city hotel, lunch, two tanks, and weights for $150 per person, based on a minimum of two. Dives in Drake's Bay (off Portobelo) include all the above, but cost only $96 per person, based on two divers. With four divers, it's $80 per person. For those interested in longer adventures, ScubaPanama provides additional packages that include accommodations, airfare and all land and water transportation.

Chartered Sailing

Ply the Caribbean San Blas Archipelago's waters and swim, snorkel, dive, fish and explore while you unwind during an incredible voyage aboard the custom-built 40-foot trimaran, *Naylamp*. When you're ready to test your shore legs, *Naylamp* drops anchor off the mainland for a hike into the jungle or visits to indigenous Kuna villages. A change of pace takes you kayaking up a jungle river or sunning on idyllic deserted white-sand beaches. This is a great family adventure, as there are plenty of activities for the kids. Everything is included – gear, meals, snacks, and drinks. You'll dine on gourmet Mediterranean-style seafood complemented by fine French or Spanish wines. And what can possibly taste better than an ice-cold beer after an active day at sea? All-inclusive rates for four or more are $125 per person, per day – much less than the cost of a hotel room, meals and entertainment. One-day cruises are $40 to $50 per person, depending on number of passengers. Naylamp's tri-lingual partners, Daniel Ayora and Elena Larranaga, have designed itineraries lasting from two to 14 days. Dan is a professional PADI diving instructor who has logged more than 30,000 nautical miles, and Elena is an educator and children's swimming instructor, as well as a gourmet cook. Enjoy a lunch or dinner cruise or opt for longer three- to four-day live-aboard luxury cruises in San Blas or among the Pacific's beautiful Pearl Islands. Contact **Naylamp Adventures**, ☎ 507-683-8841 or 682-6825, e-mail trinaylamp@hotmail.com.

The Panamá Yacht Club, ☎ 507-314-1109, fax 507-314-0904, www.panamayachtclub.com, offers an exciting inventory of ecological adventures geared for the whole family. Prices start at $99 per person for the dinner cruises, full-day cruises with snorkeling and shore excursions are $1,100 to $1,300 all-inclusive for up to six people, and $25 for each additional passenger. Four-day cruises, with gourmet meals, snorkeling and exploring, are $4,500 with a minimum of six passengers. You'll find the Panamá Yacht Club's office at Fort Amador Marina's main terminal, Office 20.

San Blas Sailing, ☎ 507-226-2005, fax 507-226-8565, offers a variety of itineraries aboard monohulls, catamarans or engine-powered yachts.

Fishing

FRESHWATER FISHING – Fish in Gatún Lake and your guide will guarantee a catch of peacock bass, which are locally called *sargentos* (sergeants) because of their striped markings. These fish are not indigenous to Panamá and have crowded out native species since their introduction into the lake in the late 1950s. They're great "eating" fish, and prized for the strong fight they put up when hooked. Captain Tony Herndon of **Panamá Fishing and Catching** (the name says it all), ☎ 507-622-0212, www.panamafishingandcatching.com, offers a Gatún Lake day charter that takes you through fantastic rainforests aboard a custom 24-foot

Super Panga. Two anglers can fish for $350 a day and everything is included from pick up at your hotel to the top quality gear. Or fish the Bayano River for snook and tarpon. Everything you'll need is included in this one too, and the rate's the same.

> **AUTHOR TIP:** *Man-made Gatún Lake is 85 feet/26 meters above sea level. Part of the Panama Canal system, it stretches 23.5miles/38 km between Gatún Locks and Gaillard Cut.*

DEEP-SEA FISHING – Responsible sportfishing operators and guides encourage catch-and-release fishing to ensure continuation of the ocean's bounty. All of these listed abide by the practice. Until a few years ago just getting to prime sportfishing waters off the Azuero Peninsula was like a trip to the ends of the earth. Today it's an easy day-trip to Playa Reina and **Río Negro Sport Fishing Lodge**, ☎ 912-352-7365 or 912-786-5926 (US), 507-646-0529 or 507-636-6777 (Panamá), www.panamasportsman.com. Stand-up fishing from 26- and 33-foot fiberglass pangas powered by 86HP Yamahas and 105HP Evinrudes is featured for catching plentiful roosterfish, cubara snapper, Pacific sailfish, big eye and albacore tuna, wahoo, snook and *corvina*. Conservationist Río Negro is a catch-and-release lodge, but they will accommodate guests by processing and freezing a reasonable amount of table-quality fish. Prices start at $300 per person for each day of fishing that includes two nights' double-occupancy accommodations, all meals, local beverages, boat, guide, fishing equipment and tackle.

Panamá Fishing and Catching, ☎ 507-622-0212, www.panamafishingandcatching.com, offers one-day Gulf of Panamá charters with everything – even pick-up and drop-off at your hotel – included for a reasonable $350 a day. Bring your bathing suit for this one. Or charter an excursion to the Pearl Islands. This two-day package starts from $500, depending on the boat used, whether you choose all-inclusive or bare boat, length of trip, and area fished.

Pesca Panamá, ☎ 800-946-3474 (US), fax 623-362-2732, www.pescapanama.com, will take you to the rich Hannibal Banks off Panamá's northwestern coast near Coiba Island. Week-long packages, priced from $2,298, include six days of fishing from 27-foot center-console Ocean Masters with fighting chair; seven nights' accommodations, five at their floating lodge and the first and last at the Marriott in Panamá City; and meals and transportation to/from the David airport. Pesca Panamá also offers one-day fishing trips from the David Marina; call to ask about longer or shorter package prices.

Tropic Star Lodge, ☎ 800-682-3424 (US), www.tropicstar.com, overlooking Piñas Bay on the Darién's southern Pacific Coast, is the crème de la crème of sportfishing resorts, ranked as the world's best. More than 200 world records have been broken here, many of them the lodge's own. Circular hooks are used to prevent fish from being gut-hooked and, with rare exceptions, game fish are released. Rooms, cabins and public areas are air-conditioned, meals are world-class, and, with 80 employees and a maximum 36 guests, you can imagine the level of service. It's not cheap but, for what you get, it's a darn good deal. Those who don't fish can kayak in the bay or the Piñas River, swim and sun on a lovely white-sand beach, trek jungle pathways and visit indigenous communities. All-inclusive one-week fishing packages start at $2,750 per person. Non-fishing three-day/four-night packages are available from $875 per person, double occupancy. The lodge will arrange transportation to/from Panamá City at additional cost.

> **AUTHOR NOTE:** *More deep-sea sportfishing records have been set and broken in Panamá than anywhere else in the world.*

Shopping

You can find almost anything in fashion-conscious Panamá City – designer clothing, fine leather goods, crystal and china, jewelry, and perfumes arrive from around the world, and frequently cost less than you would pay at home. Some of the city's popular shopping centers include **El Dorado Mall**, the **World Trade Center Centro Commercio**, **Punta Paitilla**, **Plaza New York**, and the **Fort Amador Mall**. Two **Los Pueblos Malls** each have more than 100 stores and shops. You'll The first (and older) Los Pueblos Mall 1 is east of Panamá City. Recently opened Los Pueblos 2, opposite the bus terminal at Albrook, is a $3 taxi ride from downtown. Glitzy clothing stores, electronics, jewelry, and the city's largest department stores are located on **Via España**, the city's main shopping street. As this book went to press, a row of former US military buildings at the entrance to Amador Causeway was being transformed into upscale shops to showcase merchandise from some of the world's finest designers.

◆ Avenida Central (Central Avenue)

Famous for bargains, Central Avenue's crowded pedestrian-only, brick-paved blocks are a raucous mélange of Panamá's many cultures. It's in the picturesque old Caledonia neighborhood near the entrance to Casco Antiguo, and worth a visit if only to people-watch and admire the architecture. Patchworked into the crowded street are bargain-hunters; sailors on shore leave; black-robed nuns and veiled Arab ladies; delicate Kuna women in exquisitely colorful costumes hiding their faces from tourists' cameras; and scantily dressed teens tottering on three-inch heels with groups of teenage boys ogling them. Salsa, rock and pop blasts from music and electronics stores, and shopkeepers shout into megaphones, regaling passersby to step into their shops. Tables heaped with plasticware, shoes, cheap clothing, $3 watches and doo-dads line this street filled with giggling preteens, vendors selling cotton candy, cell-phone accessories, and balloons. Go see it for yourself. To get here from downtown, take Via España heading west. Via España becomes Central Avenue just beyond Plaza 5 de Mayo.

◆ Artesanos/Handicrafts

Centro Artesenal, ☎ 507-211-0100, in the old YMCA building near the entrance to Amador Causeway, stocks a vast selection of replica preColumbian pottery, carnival masks, musical instruments, Ngöbe-Buglé chacara bags and beaded collars, Kuna molas, Emberá baskets, wood and tagua carvings.

There are two more artisan markets on **Avenida de los Martires**, near the entrance to Mi Pueblito, and another at the entrance to Panamá la Vieja. **Gran Morrison department stores** (Via España, Los Pueblos I, Casa Zaldo, Punta Paitilla, Transithmica, El Dorado) dedicate an entire department to local handicrafts and artworks.

◆ Jewelry

Reprosa, Avenue Samuel Lewis, next to Plaza Obarrio and Fuerte Amador Shopping Plaza, ☎ 507-269-0457, has been creating gorgeous replicas of Panamá's pre-Columbian gold and silver jewelry for more than 25 years. The beautiful huacas produced by their artisans are true to the ancient originals, and are displayed in some of the country's museums. A more recent line of fine jewelry re-creates Panamá's native orchids in gold or silver. Prices for the beautiful objects range from $10 to $10,000.

◆ Crocodile Leather Goods

Drilo, Fort Amador Shopping Plaza, ☎ 507-314-0961, sells exquisite handbags, briefcases, wallets, shoes and more, handcrafted from crocodile skin. They're the same folks who operate Panagator Crocodile Park (page 114) on the Trans-Isthmic Highway, and they are quite conservation-minded.

◆ Books & Magazines

If you're running out of reading material, stop by my favorite Panamá City bookstore, **Exedra Books**, ☎ 507-264-2442, Via España at the corner of Via Brasil. You will find an excellent selection of English-language fiction and non-fiction, paperback and hardcover books, and magazines. Relax and peruse your purchases in one of the quiet reading corners or enjoy a delicious cappuccino and pastry in the café.

The city's leading department store chain, **Gran Morrison**, has an excellent book and magazine department, with literally hundreds of magazines, many of them published in the US and Europe.

Arrocha, an upscale drugstore/department store chain with locations around the city, has an extensive selection of books and magazines. **Argosy Bookstore**, ☎ 507-223-5344, Via Argentina, carries books in English, French, and Spanish.

◆ Military Gear

If you're planning a last-minute trek into the wilderness and didn't bring the proper gear, pay a visit to **Salsipuedes** (which translates as "get out if you can") at the entrance to Casco Antiguo, just beyond the modern fish market. Rows of stalls are stocked with reasonably priced surplus military tents, mosquito netting, boots, camouflage clothing and more – both new and used.

> **AUTHOR NOTE:** *Secure your wallet and put your camera away before diving into the crowds at Salsipuedes. Pickpockets sometimes work this area.*

Where to Stay

The accommodations listed here are a sampling of the capital's many places to stay. City hotels that cater to business travelers frequently offer lower weekend, off-season or promotional rates. Be sure to ask.

❖ HOTEL PRICING	
Based on double occupancy	
No $	under $20
$	$20 to $39
$$	$40 to $79
$$$	$80 to $124
$$$$	$125 to $199
$$$$$	over $200

◆ Luxury Hotels

All of these high-end hotels have dual line phones, voicemail, dataports, international cable TV, safe, minibar, coffee maker, iron and ironing board, robe, toiletries, hairdryer, smoking and non-smoking rooms, executive floors, business center, 24-hour room service, concierge, laundry and dry cleaning services, and valet parking, unless otherwise noted. Some also include babysitting, translation, secretarial, courier or other services. Many offer special weekend or promotional packages – it doesn't hurt to ask.

Miramar Intercontinental, Miramar Plaza, Av Balboa at the edge of the banking and business district, ☎ 507-206-8888, www.miramarpanama.com, 204 rooms include 14 suites, business rooms, Intercontinental Club rooms with private pool and lounge. 3 telephones, high-speed Internet connection, Restaurants, lounge, pool, tennis courts, 24-hour valet, marina and heliport, beauty and barbershops, gift shop, car rental, transportation service, $$$$$. The Miramar rises like a glittering phoenix above Panamá Bay and its exceptional service is as outstanding as the magnificent bay and city views. Tastefully decorated rooms and suites with ultra-comfortable king beds vary in size. Bowls of fresh fruit, fluffy robes and distinctive toiletries are welcoming extras. If you want to go all out, there's an intriguing – and expensive – suite furnished in lavish Louis XV style, right down to the plump satin bed covers. In another, luxurious animal skin upholstery (it's fake), bright ethnic prints, art objects and accent pieces made of horn mimic the realm of an African emperor – with ultra-modern comforts, of course. Greenery surrounds the vast pool and terrace overlooking the bay and marina. There's outdoor poolside dining, or you can enjoy the views in air-conditioned comfort from the **Bayview Restaurant**. If you don't stay here, at least come for the Bayview's exceptional Sunday brunch or weekday luncheon buffet. **Miramar Seafood Restaurant**, ☎ 507-206-6545 (reservations suggested), specializes in gourmet seafood dishes and popular **Sparkles** bar has live music every night.

The Bristol, Av Aquilino de la Guardia, Bella Vista, ☎ 507-265-7844, fax 507-256-7829, www.thebristol.com, $$$$. The hotel has 56 guest rooms and suites, movies, CD player and CDs, personal bar, refrigerator, ceiling fans, individually controlled A/C, 24-hour room service, fitness center and butler service, free newspaper, and restaurant (but no pool). The Bristol is proof positive that great things come in small packages. This gorgeous five-star boutique hotel, one of the Rosewood chain, offers every conceivable luxury and convenience. Its interior walls are painted in soft, restful pastels, beautifully coordinated with comfortable traditional upholstered and mahogany furnishings. Original artworks decorate the walls and blooming orchids add a welcoming touch. Glass-enclosed showers in the stunning marble bathrooms are separate from bathtubs so deep and roomy, you can wallow up to your neck with ease. Each floor, with only seven rooms or suites, has its own butler. Shoes left outside your room at night are polished and returned before the morning wake-up call arrives with coffee or tea and the newspaper. The equally elegant first-floor dining room specializes in artfully arranged, delicious continental food.

Hotel El Panamá, Via España 111, ☎ 507-269-5000, fax 507-223-6080, www.elpanama.com, $$$, has 345 rooms and suites with individually controlled A/C, butler service and private lounge on executive floors, 24-hour room service, pool, gym, beauty salon, car rental, shopping arcade, casino, restaurants and bars, handicap-accessible rooms and facilities. The venerable El Panamá is more than a hotel, it's an institution, having been the first of Panamá City's fine hotels. Summit Hotels now operates it, and the once deplorable service is now excellent. During a recent stay, I felt completely pampered. El Panamá's vast lobby is wide open to the outside. Wicker seating upholstered in bright tropical prints, slowly revolving ceiling fans, and greenery conjure up an atmosphere of days gone by. One almost expects to find "our man in Panamá" conspiring behind the potted palms. El Panamá's gigantic rooms and suites have been redecorated recently; some are done completely in soothing monochromatic creams, others have soft pastel walls and quietly printed bedspreads and upholstered furnishings. In addition to a gorgeous pool area, there are five restaurants, two lounges, live music nightly and Panamá's largest casino here.

Hotel De Ville, Av Beatriz M Cabal, just off Calle 50 in the banking district. ☎ 507-206-3100 or 263-0303, fax 507-206-3111, www.devillehotel. com, $$$-$$$$. Thirty-three luxury suites ranging from Junior to Grand, with marble bathrooms and deluxe accessories. All the services one would expect of a top-notch hotel including local newspapers delivered to your room Unexpected services include social salons, medical and spiritual counseling. The DeVille's exterior looks more like a French manor house than a hotel. The gorgeous rooms, with antique oriental rugs and furnishings, some inlaid with mother-of-pearl, are much like what you would expect in the home of a long-ago wealthy merchant trader. Bed linens are custom-made of fine Egyptian cotton and the plump pillows of soft goose down. A few suites are connecting and one of the most attractive is a two-story with unusual interior balconies. Gorgeous etched-glass dividers set off the small bar and intimate Navigator Restaurant's simple bistro décor doesn't detract from the exquisite Mediterranean and French specialties. Be sure to leave room for pastries and desserts.

Radisson Royal Panamá, World Trade Center, Calle 53 East, Marbella, ☎ 507-265-3636, fax 507-265-3567, $$$-$$$$, has 128 rooms, with king, queen or two double beds, phones, bathrooms with tub/shower combination, limited room service, translation services. As of this writing, Radisson Worldwide no longer represents this hotel, although that may change – along with its name. It's a quiet hotel that attracts many business travelers due to its World Trade Center location. The very large suites vary in décor, while standard average-size rooms are done in restful muted earth tones. Bathrooms are large and well-lighted. There's a well-equipped gym opening to the rooftop pool and pool terrace, and an outdoor juice bar that opens sporadically. An attractive restaurant and bar/lounge are on the first floor.

Holiday Inn Hotel and Suites, Av Manuel E. Bautista, ☎ 507-206-5555, fax 507-223-9043, www.holidayinnpanama.com, $$$$, offers 150 rooms, 38 suites, pool, gym, car rental, tour desk, complimentary airport transportation, gift shop. This Holiday Inn is nothing like those you'll find scattered across the US. It's far more upscale, and the friendly, helpful staff and extensive services have made it one of the city's busiest properties. It has suites bigger than many apartments, with some that boast large, lovely terrace balconies. Memories is a true sports bar, right down to its wood floors and shining brass rails. The popular La Galeria Restaurant, open for breakfast, lunch, and dinner, serves an awesome buffet of typical Panamanian foods, and also offers à la carte dining.

Panamá Marriott, Calle 52 and Ricardo Arias, ☎ 507-210-9100, fax 507-210-9110, www.marriott.com, $$$$, has 296 rooms, eight suites, business and executive floors, weekday newspaper, 24-hour room service, gym, health club, handicap-accessible rooms, Hertz rental car office, Continental Airlines agency. This lovely hotel is right in the heart of the banking district, a two-block walk from Via España shopping. Rooms here are quite large and well appointed with pastel walls and coordinating soft floral and striped print fabrics. The bi-level Champion's Sports Bar specializes in casual, American-style food and the Marriott Café features fine international and local dining. A small pastry shop at the back of the soaring lobby sells scrumptious goodies.

Hotel Caesar Park, Via Israel and Calle 77, ☎ 507-270-0477 fax 507-226-2693, www.caesarpark.com, $$$$, features 353 rooms, eight suites, 24-hour concierge, four restaurants, extensive shopping arcade, gym and health club, pool, lighted tennis courts, casino, car rental and airline desk, handicap-accessibility. The executive floor private lounge includes complimentary breakfasts and cocktails. This fine hotel is across the street from the Atlapa Convention Center, away from the downtown area, it's close to the Corridor Sur and an easy drive to the international airport. The service here is the best you'll find anywhere and most of the unfailingly helpful and attentive staff is bilingual. Typical of the city's fine hotels, the rooms are unobtrusively decorated in shades of beige and pale rose, with traditional mahogany furnishings. Bathrooms are large and convenient. Guests and locals have made the Lobby Bar, with live music nightly, a popular meeting place. Downstairs, Bahia Restaurant's excellent extensive buffet breakfasts, lunches, and dinners always draw a crowd. The food here is as fine as the service. Casual dining options include indoor/outdoor Crostini's for pizza and light Italian fare; Las Hadas with true deli-style sandwiches, gourmet coffees and pastries; and Las Palmas Pool Bar for delicious grilled seafood and steaks. For fine dining, Monsoon's serves southeast Asian specialties, and offers a sushi bar and panoramic views.

Hotel Continental Riande, Via España at Ricardo Arias, ☎ 507-265-5114, fax 507-265-2380, www.hotelesriande.com, $$, has 363 rooms, executive floors, restaurants, bars, lounges, pool, gym, Jacuzzi, 24-hour room service, casino, handicap-accessibility, complimentary breakfast. This is the city's largest hotel and the star of Panamá's Riande chain. A new wing with an exterior glass elevator was added a few years ago and the existing rooms have been redecorated. They are huge and elegant with cream or pastel walls and traditional mahogany furniture, some with four-poster beds. There are also a few rooms adjacent to the lovely ground-level pool and terrace. Until recently, the Continental's 24-hour casino was the city's largest. There's a disco, and dining choices include Captain Jack's, which has excellent seafood, and 24-hour Café Rendez-vous, offering international specialties. One of the two bars, aptly named the Wurlitzer Bar, boasts a rare original Wurlitzer organ. Built in 1930, it's one of the world's two largest and still plays beautifully. The only drawback here is that service tends to be sporadic. Most of the staff is unfailingly helpful, but one or two are so nonchalant as to seem almost rude. In the hotel's favor, rates are much lower than those of other high-end hotels, the Via España location is as central as you can get and it's convenient to shops, restaurants and the banking center. It's a good value and special weekend rates are usually available.

◆ Mid-Range Hotels

Country Inn and Suites Amador, Av Amador and Av Pelicano, 98 rooms and suites, ☎ 800-456-4000 US reservations, 507-211-4500, fax 507-211-4501, www.countryinns.com, $$$, offers phones, dataport, fax and Internet service, cable TV, iron, ironing board, coffee maker, room service, complimentary newspaper (English or Spanish), lighted tennis courts, complete spa and gym, swimming pool, handicap-accessibility. This brand new property, on the edge of the sea at the entrance to Amador Causeway, offers tasteful rooms, junior suites, and fully equipped two-room apartment suites. All have private balconies for breathtaking sea views of the causeway islands, canal entrance and the arching Bridge of the Americas. Other extras include adults' and children's swimming pools, children's playground, and a small shopping arcade with lovely gift shops. Complimentary coffee is always available in the lobby and there's an on-site, very popular, TGI Fridays. Surrounded by green lawns, swaying palms and soft sea breezes, this friendly place seems far from the city's congestion, but in reality, it's only five minutes from downtown.

Hotel Las Huacas, Calle 53, El Cangrejo, 33 suites, ☎ 507-213-2222, fax 507-213-3077, www.lashuacas.com, $$, has telephones, minibars, suites with fully equipped kitchenettes, cable TV, hair dryer, business center, 24-hour room service, laundry, concierge, babysitting, travel agency and car rental services, handicap-accessibility. This is a drop-dead stunning little hotel. Every unusual suite is unlike any other and each is an imaginative reflection of the country's heritage. The Darién Suite transports you to the green jungle, the French Canal Suite to an elegant, classic French turn-of-the-century mansion, and the Azuero Suite to Panamá's folkloric heartland… and that's only the beginning. The staff and management are welcoming and considerate. Las Huacas' restaurant, in a building next door, hadn't yet opened when I visited. If it's like the hotel, it's bound to be superb.

La Estancia, Quarry Heights, Cerro Ancon, eight rooms, two one-bedroom apartments, ☎ 507-314-1417, www.panoramicpanama.com, $-$$, arranges airport transportation and includes breakfast. La Estancia's warm exterior is the color of a delectable tropical papaya, and inside it's as cool and comforting as a refreshing breeze. This lovely place "with rooms and apartments for nature lovers," opened in mid-2003, despite the distractions of scolding toucans, curious monkeys, a couple of nosy iguanas and visiting sloths. Only minutes from downtown's bustle, La Estancia's forested Ancón Hill location blesses it with cool breezes, fantastic views and an abundant wildlife population. There's a happily gurgling little fountain in the lobby, gorgeous hand detailed wood furniture in the rooms and apartments, two comfortable sitting rooms, viewing balconies and a dining room for guests. All of the rooms have private baths. The spacious two-room apartments have brand new, fully equipped kitchens, walk-in closets, laundry room and private gardens. La Estancia's detail-oriented proprietors own **Panoramic Panamá**, a very unusual tour company that specializes in providing unique personalized services.

Country Inn and Suites, Av Miguel Brostella, 23½B Norte, ☎ 507-211-4500, fax 507-211-4501, www.countryinns.com, $$-$$$, features 84 rooms and suites, phones, dataports, fax, copy, Internet service, cable TV, iron and ironing board, coffee maker, pool, room service, complimentary newspaper, handicap-accessibility. This pleasant, attractive place is typical of Country Inns everywhere. There's a lovely pool and pool terrace with lots of greenery and an on-site TGI Fridays restaurant and lounge. The complimentary continental-plus breakfast adds a nice touch.

◆ Suite Hotels & Aparthotels

Crystal Suites Hotel, Via Brazil at Av Samuel Lewis, ☎ 507-263-5111, fax 507-264-8125, www.crystalsuites.com, $$, has 54 suites with phones, dataport, hair dryer, TV, safe, business center, room service, dry cleaning and laundry service, restaurant, continental-plus buffet breakfast. Full-length mirrors and reading lamps positioned to avoid glare are two of the many well thought-out appointments you'll find in these lovely suites. Although size and décor vary, all are luxuriously furnished with sumptuous beds, well-equipped bathrooms, a kitchen and dining area. Some have private balconies. Los Cristales restaurant on the first floor is open until 11 pm. There's plenty of parking and an attractive pool and terrace. Crystal Suites is a rare find and an exceptional value with rates from $65.

Hotel Las Vegas, Calle 55 and Eusebio Morales, 80 studios and suites, ☎ 507-269-0722, fax 507-223-0047, www.lasvegaspanama.com, $-$$, offers direct-dial phones, dataports, cable TV, safe, and kitchenettes. Close to everything in the downtown area, with studio and one-bedroom suites opening to shaded exterior corridors and a lush interior courtyard. Some rooms and suites are nicer or more spacious than others. All are comfortable and offer great city views. The larger suites accommodate up to five adults, and some even have laundry rooms. Two of the city's most popular restaurants are located here: Café Pomodoro, famed for excellent pastas and pastries, and the intimate Wine Bar, a popular gathering place. Both open to the courtyard. A nifty glass elevator glides up and down through the courtyard's tropical greenery. This hospitable place has a delightfully helpful staff. Discounts are offered for longer stays.

Tower House Suites, Calle 51, #36, Bella Vista, ☎ 507-269-2244, fax 507-269-2869, www.towerhsuites.com, $-$$$, 30 rooms, 12 suites, phones, cable TV, refrigerators, room service, barbeque, restaurant, handicap-accessibility. Past the stunning open patio lobby, you'll find a selection of rooms and suites that are equally as tasteful and appealing. All rooms and suites have refrigerators and separate sitting areas. The two largest suites have completely equipped kitchens and living areas separated from the bedrooms. There is a lovely pool, wet bar and barbecue area on the mezzanine level. Seafood is the specialty in the very good restaurant, which is open from 6 am until 11 pm daily.

Hotel Costa del Sol, Via España and Federico Boyd, 242 Jr. suites, ☎ 507-206-3333, fax 507-206-3336, www.costadelsol-pma.com, $$, has all suites with fully equipped kitchenettes, two-line phones, voice mail, dataport, cable TV, non-smoking floors, room service, Internet café, washers and dryers on every floor, recreation room, gym, saunas, tennis court, rooftop restaurant, bar and pool. Costa del Sol is a bright and cheery place with a whole lot of amenities. The suites aren't new, but they are clean and homey and the beds are comfortable. Completely equipped kitchenettes that can be closed off from the rest of the suite are a nice feature. Dine above the city indoors or out in the lovely rooftop restaurant with views. Gray Line Tours has a convenient office next door to the first-floor lobby. This conveniently located place can be a bit pricey in high season, so ask about any promotional rates.

Suites Ambassador, Calle D, El Cangrejo, ☎ 507-263-7274, fax 507-263-7872, www.suitesambassador.com, $$$, has 40 studio and one-bedroom suites, phones, dataports, cable TV, clock radio, fully equipped kitchen or kitchenette, spacious bathrooms, pool, dry cleaning service, 24-hour reception area, iron and ironing board, washer & dryer. This favorite, on a quiet side street a block from central Via España, offers spacious studio and one-bedroom suites with kitchen or kitchenette. Furnishings are top quality and the beds – queen in the studios, king in the one-bedroom suites – are deliciously comfortable. The complimentary continental-plus breakfast includes coffee, tea, a variety of fresh juices, tropical fruits, yogurt, pastries and more. There's an attractive rooftop pool and coin-operated washers and dryers. The service here is excellent and corporate rates are available. This is a favorite and a best bet.

◆ Budget Hotels

Hotel Covadonga, Calle 29 and Av Peru, ☎ 507-225-5275, fax 335-4071, phones, cable TV, gym, restaurant, room service, laundry, $. This scrupulously clean, well-maintained 63-room hotel has comfortable, if a tad nondescript, rooms of average size. There's a lovely rooftop pool and terrace offering panoramic views of the city and a covered parking area. The small restaurant is pleasant and management is very friendly. It's a good value with rates as low as $27 double.

Hotel El Parador, Calle Eusebio A. Morales and via Benetto, 80 rooms, ☎ 507-214-4586, fax 507-214-4589, e-mail helparador@ cableonda.net, $, has air conditioning, telephone, cable TV, fax and Internet service, safe, restaurant and bar, room service, spa, pool. This hotel opened in early 2003, offering single to family-size rooms. While it's very clean and the beds are comfortable, the furnishings are rather dull and out of style. I've never understood the penchant for hanging framed prints only inches below the ceiling! Some of the rooms tend to be dark, so ask to see more than one. There's a restaurant with panoramic city views – I haven't sampled the food – and an attractive rooftop pool. You can probably make a deal here.

Hotel California, Via España and Calle 43, 60 rooms, ☎ 507-263-7736, fax 507-264-6144, www.hotel-california.ws, $, has air conditioning, phones, cable TV, Internet, restaurant and bar, room service, complimentary coffee. I doubt if the Eagles titled their song after this place, but it has been around for quite some time. It's clean and comfortable and very friendly. Surprisingly, the rates have recently dropped by a couple of dollars. Room décor is warm, although a bit dated, and service is good. The small ground-floor restaurant is open until midnight. It's popular with business people and backpackers. Discounted rates are often available.

Hotel Aramo, Via Brasil and Abel Bravo, 55 rooms, ☎ 507-269-0174/260-2355, fax 507-269-2406, $, offers minibar, phone, cable TV, room service, bar/restaurant, security boxes, laundry service, Internet and fax service, pool. The Aramo's staff is very friendly and helpful, and it's meticulously clean, but public areas are far more attractive than its austere, cramped rooms with small bathrooms and individual air conditioning units. There's a worn look to these rooms; furniture and beds have seen better days, bedside lamps are too small for reading, and wall décor consists solely of large wooden crosses. If you're feeling a bit monkish or of the evangelical persuasion, you'll fit right in but, if not, you can find a better deal elsewhere. The $38 and up rates are no bargain.

◆ Hostels

A best bet for budget travelers is **Hostal La Casa de Carmen**, Calle 1, El Carmen #32, ☎ 507-263-4366, www.lacasadecarmen.com, $ and under, has eight rooms and one apartment. It offers air conditioning, free Internet access, library and book exchange, safe, parking, self-service kitchen, self-service laundry and laundry service, iron, ironing board, lounge with international cable TV, complimentary coffee and tea all the time, and luggage storage. Full breakfasts are available, and it is handicap-accessible. This rare find is a block from Via España and within walking distance of shopping, restaurants, a supermarket and the city's best bookstore. Delightfully eclectic collections of Kuna molas, woven Ngöbe-Buglé chacara bags, cheerful painted plaques and unique maps of Panamá brighten cream-colored walls in the public areas. The neat and tidy rooms have remote-control air conditioners, and all but two have private baths. The one large dorm room will accommodate up to six and a fully equipped second-floor apartment comfortably accommodates four. There's a lending and reference library. A walled garden adjoins the covered outdoor dining terrace, which has tables and chairs painted in a gay batea-style that represent Panamá's cultures, flora and fauna. Hostesses Virginia and Frances will help with your travel arrangements, offer suggestions, and provide you with valuable information on what to see, and where and how to see it. Menus from nearby restaurants, tour and travel brochures, current event listings and more are posted for guests' convenience.

The New Voyager International Hostel, Edificio Di-Lido, Apt. 8, Calle Manuel Icaza, fax 507-223-3687, has air conditioning, Internet access, lounge with TV and stereo, self-service kitchen and laundry. The Voyager moved recently into conveniently located new quarters just down the street from the Hotel Continental. It's a bright and cheerful place with huge city-view windows and lovely outdoor terraces. The kitchen is large, new and shiny. This excellent value is popular with backpackers. Rates for a dorm bunk and shared bath start at $9.80. Private rooms are also available, and the complimentary continental breakfast adds a nice touch.

Residencial Turistica Volcan, Calle 29 and Av Peru, 24 rooms, ☎ 507-225-5263, cable TV, air conditioning, pay phone on premises, is next door to Hotel Covadonga. This place is a short on style and the rooms are dark, but it's in a good neighborhood, it's clean and secure and the beds are comfortable. Owner Daniel Gonzales' daughter owns the Hotel Covadonga next door, and guests can use the Covadonga's pool, parking and other facilities. Daniel also owns a taxi and provides reasonably priced sightseeing tours. Rates average $16 for a double. There's one tiny room with only a fan, which rents for $4.

I don't recommend any of the following, and caution you not to wander around outside at night if you stay at one of them. They're all in Casco Antiguo and should be considered only if it's all you can afford. Most offer nothing more than shared facilities without any services.

Hotel Herrera, Calle 9 at Parque Herrera, 44 rooms, ☎ 507-228-8994, has hot water showers. It's obvious that this was a splendid hotel – about a century ago. Unfortunately, the gigantic rooms have been divided into sleeping cells with lumpy beds covered in threadbare linens. A magnificent second floor, two-story circular front room opens onto a lovely balcony overlooking the park. Faded traces of once elegant painted ceilings and the carved mahogany banister along the wide stairways are enough to make you want to buy the place and restore it. It's secure and the manager's a nice guy. Doubles go for $12.

Pension Panamericana, Av A and Calle 10, ☎ 507-228-8759, fax 507-228-8923, has beds but little else for $7.70 to $8.80. There is also **Pension Tiza**, Av B, Santa Ana, ☎ 507-262-8826, $6 to $7; and **Pension El Parque**, Via Simón Bolívar, ☎ 507-225-4176, $10, which is a tad better.

Where to Eat

Panamá City has even more restaurants than hotels. Every imaginable cuisine is offered, and you'll also find all the familiar fast-food places – McDonald's, Subway, Burger King, KFC, Wendy's, Domino's Pizza, Popeye's, Pizza Hut, and more.

◆ Casco Antiguo

Manolo Caracol, Av Central and Calle 3, Casco Antiguo, ☎ 507-228-4640, $$$.

Elegant eclectic food is whisked from an open kitchen to antique dining tables surrounded by walls covered in modern art. No menus here; everything is prix fixe, according to Manolo's whim and freshest buy of the day. Nothing is frozen – Manolo won't allow a freezer in the place. Dinners are small servings of as many as a dozen different courses. One night, Manolo's Oriental/Mediterranean seafood purchase resulted in exquisite salmon carpaccio, *pulpo* (octopus) sautéed with garlic and tomatoes in wine and spices; tantalizing *corvina* in zucchini, onion, and carrot curry sauce; lobster spring rolls; grilled giant shrimp; and lemony grouper medallions with crisp salad, pineapple rice and sweet plantains. Desserts also vary, and there's an extensive wine list. Finish with a fine brandy or cappuccino. Call ahead to see what Manolo has dreamed up, and be sure to make a reservation.

Las Bovedas, Plaza de Francia, Casco Antiguo, ☎ 507-226-8058, $$$. This elegant French restaurant is actually in the dungeons under the Casco Antiguo seawall. (*Bovedas* means dungeon.) Fine meats and innovatively prepared grouper are standbys on a menu that includes delicious French comestibles with fine sauces and crisp-tender baby vegetables. There's an extensive wine list. Live jazz is featured on Friday nights.

Restaurante El Candelero, Calle 4, Plaza Bolívar, Casco Antiguo, ☎ 507-262-6598, $$. This wonderful new gathering place features tapas in a delightful fusion of the food and drink that influenced Panamanian history. Pleasure your tastebuds with Spanish, French, West Indian and Antillean specialties. Open for lunch and dinner and late on weekends.

Casablanca, Plaza Bolívar, Casco Antiguo, ☎ 507-262-7507, $$$. Sleekly modern with an intriguing black and white Bogart appeal, this sophisticated restaurant specializes in imported Black Angus beef and Mediterranean taste tempters. Be sure to sample the bouillabaisse Marsaillesa and save room for crème brûlée. Dine in candlelit air-conditioned comfort or outside on the plaza.

Café de Neri, Av 4A, two blocks from the bay, Casco Antiguo, ☎ 507-228-7568, $$. Start with luscious cream soup – broccoli or spinach are especially delicious. International specialties rely heavily on fresh seafood and chicken. Pastas are innovative and plenty of fresh veggies come with your entrée or à la carte. There's a full bar with a fine wine list and indoor or outdoor dining.

Café du Liban, Av Eloy Alfaro and Called de la Presidencia, Casco Antiguo, ☎ 507-212-1582, $$$-$$$$. Low lighting, comfortable seating and unobtrusive Middle-Eastern background music make dining here a delight. Try the curry shrimp, baba ganoush, or succulent garlicky lamb.

By the time your thick, dark coffee arrives, you'll be ready to sit back and watch the belly dancer.

◆ Downtown & Restaurant District

Sushi Ito has two locations, a sushi bar in Plaza Obarrio on Av Samuel Lewis, ☎ 507-265-1222, and a sushi bar and teppanyaki salon on Calle Miguel Brostella in front of the Do-It Center in El Dorado, ☎ 507-260-8897, $$. Stuff yourself from the buffet Monday through Thursday from noon until 3 pm at the Calle Miguel Brostella location.

Martin Fierro, Calle Eusebio A. Morales, #21, ☎ 507-264-1927, El Cangrejo, $$$$, is famed for its excellent imported steaks. The extensive à la carte menu includes less expensive local beef – tasty but chewier – and a variety of seafood dishes. This place is talked about in admiringly hushed tones and the service is impressive. The décor is typical steak house with Spanish overtones and lots of dark wood. Expect to pay around $25 for an imported steak – about $10 for local beef – and a skimpy salad bar. Add a potato or vegetable, wine and dessert and you'll see a hefty bill. They could do better.

XOKO, Calle Alberto Navarro, Casa 4, El Cangrejo, ☎ 507-302-3230, $$, one of the city's newest and best restaurants, features fine regional Spanish cuisine. Come for delicious authentic paella or perfect *corvina a la sal*, a house specialty. Delicious tapas, those wonderful "little" dishes of Spain, come in delightful variety, and steaks are grilled to perfection. For lunch, try the Spanish tortilla ($2.25) or escalibada ($3.95). Featured libations include a martini blue or a daiquiri XOKO and there's a daily Happy Hour. The service is attentive and XOKO is open for lunch and dinner seven days a week, until midnight Friday and Saturday.

El Patio Mexicano, Av Guatemala and Alberto Navarro (enter from Via Argentina), El Cangrejo, ☎ 507-263-5684, $$. Bright colors, hand-painted Mexican pottery and leather "esquipale" funishings highlight this authentic country-style restaurant run by the Uribe family from Guadalajara. Try the exceptional *cochinita pibil* (Yucatecan pork simmered in orange juice and achiote), *pollo molé poblano*, or overstuffed enchiladas with an ice-cold Carta Blanca.

Limoncillo, Calle 47 and Calle Uruguay, ☎ 507-253-5350, $$, is billed as a "New York Gourmet Bistro." The décor is bright and airy; the menu international, with Mediterranean, Italian and Greek influences predominating. Everything here is innovative and very, very good. Try the herb-crusted salmon over toasted bulghur and spinach with balsamic vinegar glaze.

Gaucho's Steak House, Calle Uruguay and Av 5A, ☎ 507-263-3369, $$$, has excellent beef imported from the US. In true Argentinean style, you select the steak or cut of beef before it's perfectly grilled to specifications. The house specialty is a delicious char-grilled rib eye. Other delicious entrées include superb T-bones, skirts, strips, and tasty beef sausage. They're all too good to smother in spicy red pepper sauce or

PANAMA PROVINCE

tantalizing chimichurri, but who can resist a dollop or two? Gaucho's offers an excellent wine list and attentive service.

Los Años Locos, Calle 76E, San Francisco, ☎ 507-226-6966, $$-$$$. This popular Argentinean steak house serves very good beef and fish specialties. Try the mixed grill, a selection of beef cuts grilled to perfection, or delicious *corvina a la plancha*. There's a salad bar or you can order an inventive seafood salad.

Parillada Jimmy, Via Israel and Via Porras, San Francisco, ☎ 507-226-1096, $-$$. Everything on the long menu is good. Special favorites are the *corvina al ajillo, pulpo* (octopus) baked in a garlic sauce, and tiny succulent clams in garlic sauce. Jimmy's owner is Greek, so you'll find souvlaki, moussaka and other tasty specialties. This popular place has dining indoors or outdoors on a recently enlarged covered and cooled terrace. Service can be slow when it's busy, but no one seems to care.

> **AUTHOR NOTE:** *Can't remember the translation for all these Spanish-language dishes? See the section about* Food & Drink, *which begins on page 27.*

Restaurant Sunly, Calle Miguel Brostella (in front of the Do-It Center), El Dorado, ☎ 507-260-1411, $$$. Perfectly prepared authentic Chinese food in an elegant setting. Try fragrant ginger steamed whole fish with scallions or crispy duck with a side of crunchy stir-fried vegetables. The service here is excellent. Reservations are recommended, as this place is deservedly popular.

El Trapiche, Via Argentina, El Cangrejo, ☎ 507-259-2453, $-$$. A *trapiche* is a wooden press used to squeeze the juice from sugarcane. There's one on display here in the traditionally decorated dining room. Generous portions of authentic typical country food include saucepan-sized bowls of steaming *sancocho, mondongo* (tripe) in a tasty tomato sauce, *pollo asado, tasajo,* and the house specialty, *tamal de ola.* The sandwiches are gargantuan and very good. Service is brisk but patient.

Las Tinajas, Calle 51, Bella Vista, ☎ 507-269-3840, $-$$. Painted festival masks, clay olas, and handcrafted wood and leather chairs are as traditional to Panamá as its lovely folkloric dances. Set your tastebuds singing with *corvina* ceviche or grilled giant prawns in garlic. If you prefer less spicy, order the *pastel de yuca* (chicken pie with yuca) or *tasajo.* There's a $5 cover charge for the excellent, authentic folkloric show on Tuesday, Thursday, Friday and Saturday nights at 9 pm. Don't miss this one. Get here early or reserve a balcony table for the best views.

Tambal, Via Porras ☎ 507-264-7133, across from Super 99, $-$$. Pastas and sauces are freshly made here every day, and they taste like it. Yum. The unpretentious red-and-white-checked tablecloths, posters of bella Italia along with the required plastic grapes and raffia covered wine bottle candle holders set the mood for fine casual dining. All the pizzas are good, sauces are imaginative, and the spinach ravioli with mushrooms, parmesan and cream is a winner. There are plenty of choices for vegetarians and service is fast, friendly and efficient.

Athens Pizza, Calle 59 and Calle Uruguay, ☎ 507-265-4637, $-$$, whips up excellent pizzas, strombolis and tasty Greek specialties. The Athens Special pizza is loaded with toppings and it is truly special. Indoor/outdoor casual dining. There's a second **Athens** at C1 San Miguel ☎ 507-223-1461. My only complaint is that they don't deliver.

La Papa, Calle 51, #25, across from Las Tinajas, Bella Vista, ☎ 507-265-5800, $$. This trendy eatery grills and spices meats and seafoods to perfection. Wide open spaces, glass walls, soaring ceilings, lots of stainless steel and oversize modern paintings enhance artfully prepared international cuisine with a hint of Colombian flair. Churrasco steaks, ribs and expertly seasoned skewered shrimp are favorites. You don't have to be a vegetarian to swoon over delicious pasta primavera or a creative salad. There's a unique bar and exceptional service.

Crêpes and Waffles, Calle 47 and Calle Aquilino de la Guardia, Bella Vista, ☎ 507-269-1574, $$. Crêpes stuffed and drenched in dozens of imaginative ways and gargantuan salads have made this place a hit. You can build your own entrée from an impressive list of ingredients or choose a menu favorite. Classic chicken, asparagus, and mushroom crêpes smothered in delicate creamy sauce and those stuffed with fresh spinach, mushroom and cheese are delicious. The crisp salads are large enough to share with a couple of friends. Soups and sandwiches are also very good, but the dessert crêpes don't measure up to the entrées. A second Crêpes and Waffles opened recently at Fort Amador Resort and Marina. Both offer a good selection of vegetarian choices.

Restaurante 1985, Av Eusebio A. Morales, ☎ 507-263-8541, $$$$, is renowned for fine French and seafood cuisines. Gleaming copper antiques reflect flickering candles in this excellent restaurant's softly lit interior, a creation of famed chef Willy Diggleman. Specialties include jumbo shrimp in cognac sauce, *corvina* with spinach, beef filet with morels, and a superb wine selection.

Rincon Suizo, Av Eusebio A Morales, ☎ 507-263-8310, $$$, is another of Chef Willy's fine dining creations, specializing in veal dishes and superb fondues. You'll find it ay the same location as 1985, above.

La Cascada, Av Balboa and Calle 25, ☎ 507-262-1927, $$. This kitschy place with a menu that rivals War and Peace in length has been here for about a gazillion years. You can dine indoors or out. Choose out – where colorful koi drift up and down a concrete canal cut through the dining terrace and tables are secluded in masses of flowering greenery. Butterflies flit, hummingbirds whir and life-size plastic cows, deer and burros peek from the green. You call a waitress by pushing a little button that lights a bulb next to the cash register inside. And then you wait. Since I suspect the light has been disconnected since 1967, this arrangement gives new meaning to the term, "wait staff." No matter, this place is so much fun that unless you're really starving, you won't care. Watch the fish, the birds, and butterflies and admire the flowers until your food eventually appears on a platter you'll swear was meant for King Kong. My order of grilled garlic shrimp included a dozen and a half whoppers

PANAMA PROVINCE

swimming in garlic-scented butter, patacones, steamed green beans, a baked potato with all the trimmings, French fries, green salad, a heap OF lemon wedges, a variety of cocktail sauces and garlic bread – all for about $10. This isn't gourmet dining, but it is good and a lot of fun. Stick to the seafood or chicken dishes as the beef tends to be overdone. After dark, the lighting provided by opaque globe lights and teensy clear Christmas bulbs strung through the foliage lend an oddball romantic atmosphere.

Alberto's Café, Fuerte Amador Resort and Marina, ☎ 507-314-4134, $$$. Sea breezes, good service and fresh green and beige umbrella tables highlight excellent Italian food. Ask for the fresh catch of the day and request a marina table to enjoy fantastic views of the Panamá City skyline. Glorious at night!

El Pavo Real, Calle 51 East, 19, Obarrio, ☎ 507-269-0504, $$, is Panamá's only British pub. Stick with tradition and order fish and chips, onion soup and roast beef, or opt for salmon mousse. There is always a fresh seafood dish and a pasta of the day. Wash it all down with hearty imported British ale.

Bucaneros, Fuerte Amador Resort and Marina, ☎ 507-314-0880, $$$. The casual open terrace restaurant and lounge offer views across the bay to the city skyline. Small, intimate rooms, candlelight, crisp white tablecloths, and fresh flowers add a touch of romance to indoor dining. The thick *corvina* fillet drenched in delicate herbed cream sauce and topped with lobster is to die for. Everything is good here, but quality of service is sporadic.

Manolo, Via Argentina and Av 2B Norte, ☎ 507-264-3965, $. Not to be confused with Manolo Caracol, this reasonably priced and casual old standby with red plastic booths offers a variety of Italian, typical and international dishes. It's very popular with locals and the service is efficient.

Crostini, in the Hotel Caesar Park, ☎ 507-274-0477, San Francisco, $$. This trendy little bistro overlooks the hotel's gorgeous pool and gardens. The featured item is pizza in an array of mind-boggling flavors. Order yours Hawaiian, Korean, Japanese, Mexican, German, Australian, Panamanian or even Italian. Save room for a strawberry one for dessert. If you're more in the mood for cool and crisp, choose from a selection of salads, both veggie and fruit.

Restaurante Mireya, Calle 50, diagonal to Hotel Marriott, $. Very good cafeteria-style vegetarian food in a pleasant simple atmosphere. The dozen or so hot entrées change every day. The dishes are imaginative and tasty. Vegetable lasagnas, *arroz* (rice) primavera and soyburgers are standbys and most cost $1.25. There's an excellent variety of crispy raw veggies, sprouts, fruits, cheeses and lettuces on the salad bar, but it's the desserts that really excel. Try luscious flans made with strawberry/cranberry or sweet-tart nance (a small, yellow-orange fruit), creamy rice puddings, or fruit-topped cheesecake. A delicious drink similar to *horchata* is made with liquified oats, natural brown sugar, milk and a dash of vanilla. Closed on Sundays.

Restaurante Mercado de Mariscos, west end of Av Balboa, upstairs from the city fish market, ☎ 507-212-0071, $$. This bustling, unpretentious place is for eating rather than dining. Although recently remodeled, it's a bit short in the décor department, but who cares, it boasts the "best and freshest fish in Panamá." The long menu includes *corvina*, jumbo shrimp and red snapper prepared a half-dozen ways, clams, mussels, octopus, seafood soups and plenty of hearty accompaniments. You can enjoy a full meal for less than $5.

◆ Best Dining on a Budget

Niko's Café, ☎ 507-270-2555 for nearest location, $. There are now six of these family-owned, cafeteria-style restaurants. All have immaculate light and bright interiors and surprisingly good food. Although up to a dozen entrées change every day, you can pretty much count on finding *chuletas de puerco* (pork chops), *arroz con pollo* (chicken and rice), chow mein, beefsteak milanesa, *corvina* or *pargo* (red snapper) and roast beef. There's a good selection of vegetable and side dishes. The gyro sandwich and burger bar is popular, and there are soup, dessert and beverage stations. Portions are generous and you can eat very well here for $4 to $5. Niko's restaurants are open 24 hours a day, every day of the year.

Entertainment

◆ Performing Arts

A performance of Panamá's beautiful traditional dances shouldn't be missed. To find out when and where performances will be held, call **Ballet Folklorico Panameno**, ☎ 507-317-9869, or go to Mi Pueblito (see page 70), where students in full dress hold performances on Thursday evenings.

English-language theater is performed at the **Ancón Theatre**, ☎ 507-212-0600. It isn't only in the US that the arts are falling by the wayside; this little theater, established 52 years ago to serve Panamá's English speaking community, is struggling to stay in business.

> **AUTHOR NOTE:** *John Aniston, father of actress Jennifer Aniston, was an Ancón Theatre actor in the 1950s.*

Panamá City's amateur theater groups perform in Spanish at **Teatro en Circulo**, ☎ 507-270-2418 and **Teatro Aba**, ☎ 507-236-3258. World-renowned international artists take the stage in the two **Atlapa Convention Center** theaters, Anayansi and Las Huacas, ☎ 507-270-1010.

Since **movies** are very popular here, you'll find first-run films from the US with Spanish subtitles or dubbed voice-overs. Two of the largest cineplexes are in the El Dorado Mall and new Los Pueblos II shopping center. Movie tickets cost from $1.50 to $3.90.

AUTHOR NOTE: La Prensa, *the capital's largest newspaper, publishes a Sunday arts supplement containing a calendar of cultural entertainment and movie listings. Events calendars are also featured in the free English-language tabloid* **The Visitor***, and the online* **Panamá News***, www.thepanamanews.com.*

◆ Bars & Nightlife

Panamá City's nightlife is sophisticated, trendy and late. And although downtown still rocks, many of the newest "in" spots are located in Casco Antiguo and the Fuerte Amador entertainment complex on Flamenco Island. Here are a few of the current favorites.

With its dark wood, live music, dartboards and pool tables, **El Pavo Real**, near the Marriott, ☎ 507-263-1510, is popular with the capital's 18 to 45 English-speaking crowd. Friday is rock night.

A cozy wine-cellar atmosphere, hundreds of fine wines to sample, good drinks and tasty snacks are featured at the **The Wine Bar**, Via Venetto, ☎ 507-265-4701, on the ground floor of the Las Vegas Hotel.

Sports fans rub shoulders at **Shula's Steak 2**, Calle Miguel Brustella, ☎ 507-260-265. **Liquid**, Plaza New York, Calle 50, ☎ 507-265-3110, caters to the young disco crowd with live bands, dancing and specially priced bottles of rum and seco on Friday nights.

Thursday is swing night at **Hotel Radisson Royal**, ☎ 507-265-3636, and, if you're in a romantic frame of mind, stop in on Friday, Bohemian night, for live romantic ballads and light classical.

Mangos has two locations, Calle Uruguay, ☎ 507-269-6846, and Edison Plaza, ☎ 507-236-2824. Both remain popular with Friday night disco dancing to live music. Friday is rhumba night at **S6IS**, Calle Uruguay, Bella Vista, ☎ 507-264-5237, and on Saturday nights, DJs play a selection of rock, salsa and disco music. Glug away at the **Rock Café**, Calle 53, Marbella, ☎ 507-264-5364. With a $5 cover charge, ladies receive unlimited drinks. The cover is $10 for men.

Jazz is featured Friday nights at lovely **Las Bovedas**, French Plaza, Casco Antiguo, ☎ 507-226-8058. The young and the beautiful flock to **Blu Room Martini Lounge**, Casco Antiguo, ☎ 507-228-9059. Live bands or DJs serve up hip-hop, rock and salsa to accompany house specialty martinis and other generous drinks.

Down 'em three-for-one during happy hour (5 pm to 9 pm) at **Bennigan's Extreme Planet**, Avenue Balboa, ☎ 507-214-7022.

The local business crowd, tourists and everyone else pack ever-popular **Fridays**, Amador, ☎ 507-269-4199. Happy hour is Friday from 5 to 8 pm. You can listen to live jazz at **Bar Take Five**, Calle 1, Casco Antiguo, on Friday and Saturday nights. **Barko**, ☎ 507-314-0010, and next-door **Bucaneros**, ☎ 507-314-0880, Fuerte Amador Plaza, Flamenco Island, draw a mixed crowd of revelers. Fridays and Saturdays are "Bar Nights," and feature a selection of specially priced drinks.

◆ Gay & Lesbian Clubs

Box Disco, Tumba Muerto, Urb. Industrial La Esperanza, ☎ 507-270-2978, e-mail boxpanama@cwpanama.net, is open Wednesday, Friday, Saturday, and Sunday from 11 pm until ? This cavernous club features progressive, techno-trance and Latin music.

G-Mart, Area Bancaria, next to El Pavo Real, ☎ 507-213-1768.

BLG Disco, Calle Uruguay and Calle 49, Bella Vista, ☎ 507-265-1624, www.farrurbana.com. Open Wednesday through Sunday, from 10 pm.

Space, Calle 70 Obarrio, in front of Baron's Boutique, plays Top 40, Latin and trance music. Drag shows are frequently held on Friday and Saturday nights. Open from 9 pm. (No phone available.)

D'Ross Disco, on the Trans-Isthmic Highway. (No phone available.)

Club 844, Casco Antiguo. Gays are welcomed at this "straight" club, one of the city's most popular. Patrons often join in to play or sing with live bands on the weekends. (No phone available.)

BLU Room, Casco Antiguo, ☎ 507-228-3503, two doors down from Club 844. The young and the beautiful (ages 18-45), both gay and straight, frequent this crowded club that plays the best trance and electronic pop around.

◆ Casinos

Casinos are everywhere in Panamá, and the biggest and glitziest are in the capital. The opposite of Vegas-style, they are rather low-key, and I've never seen one crowded. Most Panamanians would rather spend their money on their families, dancing and partying, than lose it. The best casinos are in the **Hotel El Panamá**, **Hotel Continental** and **Hotel Caesar Park**. For additional locations, call **Fiesta Casinos**, ☎ 507-269-0691; **Crown Casinos**, ☎ 507-264-2983; or **Gaming and Service**, ☎ 507-214-2690.

PANAMA PROVINCE

The Pacific Islands

Taboga Island

This enchanting 1,400-acre/560-hectare island lies in the Pacific, 11 miles/18 kilometers southwest of Panamá City. Known as the "Isle of Flowers," Taboga's serene beauty belies the centuries of history played out on its sandy shores and rugged hillsides. Balboa was arrested here while building the caravels Pizzaro later used to sack Peru's Inca empire. And it was from here that pirates Francis Drake and Henry Morgan launched attacks on the mainland. Taboga again saw action during Panamá's war for independence.

> **AUTHOR NOTE:** *In 1887, Paul Gauguin lived here for a time in a rented house. Disappointed that the $120 a month he earned as a Panama Canal laborer wouldn't afford him a home, he packed up and sailed off to Tahiti.*

Taboga's little colonial village curves around a calm horseshoe bay, back-dropped by steep, luxuriantly green **Cerro de las Cruces** (Hill of the Three Crosses). Faded *pangas* (flat-bottom dugout canoes), painted red, yellow, blue and green, add a splash of color to the golden-sand beaches. The island's peaceful demeanor is owed to a lack of motor vehicles; none other than a few small work trucks that double as taxis are permitted, and these stick to the few paved pathways wide enough to accommodate them.

A stroll around (or rather up and down) the quiet town's pathways takes you the Spanish Colonial **Church of San Pedro**, the Western Hemisphere's second oldest, still in use today.

> **AUTHOR NOTE:** *Look for famed red, pink and white **Taboga roses** among the hundreds of flowers that have given this island its nickname.*

You're sure to see blue morpho butterflies and tiny hummingbirds whirring among the flowers during a steep hike up and over the Cerro de las Cruces pathway to the **Taboga Island Wildlife Refuge**, a shorebird nesting area on the island's south side. A *mirador* (lookout) at the hill's summit offers incredible views of the sea and surrounding islands and, on a clear day, you can see all the way to Panamá City.

There isn't much shopping here. The few small stores and kiosks sell canned goods, fresh vegetables, soap and urgent necessities. Most eateries are tiny, family-operated affairs consisting of a few tables and chairs on someone's front porch.

Taboga is perfect for a day trip, but if you prefer to stay longer, 60-room **Hotel Taboga**, ☎ 507-260-1187/264-6096, htaboga@sinfo.net, is a good choice. Its extensive grounds, landscaped with exotic trees and flowers, cozy up to Restinga Beach, the island's best. Among the plentiful birds are the hotel's own preening peacocks that strut around in search of handouts. There is a swimming pool, volleyball and basketball courts and indoor billiards. The snorkeling is good and you can rent a water bike or kayak to paddle around the island. There's a cafeteria-style restaurant and bar or you can lug a cooler with fixings to char your lunch on one of the bohio-shaded barbeque grills. For $2, day-trippers can picnic, partake of all the facilities and the beach. Seasonal room rates average $60 for a double.

> **AUTHOR NOTE:** *If you want to dive, **ScubaPanama**, ☎ 507-261-3841 in Panamá City, maintains a small shop in Hotel Taboga. Call ahead to be sure it's open and that the divemaster is there.*

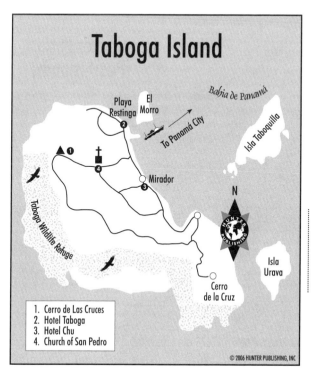

Taboga Island

Playa Restinga ❷
El Morro
Bahía de Panamá
To Panamá City
Isla Taboguilla
▲ ❶
✝ ❹
○ Mirador ❸
Taboga Wildlife Refuge
N HUNTER PUBLISHING
Isla Urava
○ Cerro de la Cruz

1. Cerro de Las Cruces
2. Hotel Taboga
3. Hotel Chu
4. Church of San Pedro

© 2006 HUNTER PUBLISHING, INC

New places to stay are opening faster than I can write this: **Hotel Vereda Tropical** is a 12-room bed and breakfast on a breezy hillside with air-conditioning, in-room TV, a lounge and restaurant. Seasonal rates are $50, doule. If your budget is limited, check out friendly **Uva's Guest Rooms** (☎ 507-240-2150, $8 per person, based on double occupancy). Optional meals are available. The new **Kool Youth Hostel**, ☎ 507-690-2545/696-3443, abdiel75@hotmail.com, $10 per person, is affiliated with Panamá City's low-budget standby, the Voyager (see page 97).

Taboga Island is a one-half to one-hour boat ride from Panamá City's Pier 18 at the Port of Balboa, in the city's Balboa neighborhood. Any tour operator can arrange your visit with convenient transfers, or you can buy your own ticket ($8-$12 depending on whether you choose express service) at the pier. **Expreso del Pacifico**, ☎ 507-261-0350, offers round-trips three times each day, and the *Calypso Queen*, ☎ 507-232-5736, operates once daily, Tuesday through Friday, with additional crossings on weekends and holidays. Note, however, that the *Calypso Queen's* ticket office at the pier was closed when I made a recent trip. Only Expreso del Pacifico was operating.

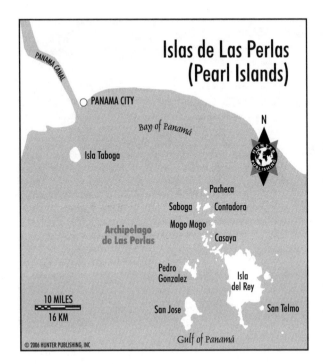

Islas de Las Perlas (Pearl Islands)

While trekking across the Darién to the "Southern Sea," Balboa learned from friendly natives that the pearls they traded for Spanish trinkets had come from a group of offshore islands. Historical accounts differ as to whether Balboa visited the islands, then ruled by hostile *caciques*, or if he claimed them for Spain without ever setting foot on one. Either way, he intended to return, defeat the Indians and reap the pearls. However, in 1515, Pedrarias sent Gaspar de Morales and Francisco Pizarro to the islands. As usual, the Indians were no match for the Spanish and many were killed before surrendering. By 1518, they had all perished and African slaves were brought to harvest the pearls. A counting house was established on **Isla Contadora** (contadora means "counting house" in Spanish) to record and store the pearls before they were shipped to Panamá City and on to Spain. After wiping out the oyster beds and, hence, the pearls, the Spaniards had little use for the islands, which soon became a haven for pirates. Iran's Shah Mohammed Reza Pahlavi chose to live on Contadora after the Ayatollah Khomeini's followers deposed him in 1979. A few Panamanians have vacation homes on Contadora and Isla del Rey, and there's a sprinkling of expats, but most of today's inhabitants are descendants of the slaves.

There are 90 named islands and 130 islets and cayes in Las Perlas group, which lies in an area of about 50 miles/80 kilometers to 70 miles/113 kilometers southeast of Panamá City. Very few are inhabited, and only little **Contadora** (.75 square miles/1.2 square kilometers) is developed for tourism. That may soon change, however, as the largest and most populated island, **Isla del Rey**, is now being developed. Check out Kingfisher Bay's Web site, www.kingfisherbay.net, for updated information on a spectacular new marina, housing development and five-star resort, none of which are yet completed. Nearby **Pacheca Island**, also called Isla de los Pajáros (Bird Island), is a marine bird sanctuary; **Mogo Mogo** is a pretty little island with lovely beaches; and a few pearl divers live in a small village on **Isla Casaya**. And yes, you can buy pearls, but none will compare with the 400-year-old, 31-carat Peregrine Pearl discovered here. It was once owned by the Queen of Spain; Elizabeth Taylor has it now.

> **AUTHOR NOTE:** *The Pearl Islands received a huge publicity boost when a recent series of the popular US version of the* Survivor *television show was filmed here.*

PANAMA PROVINCE

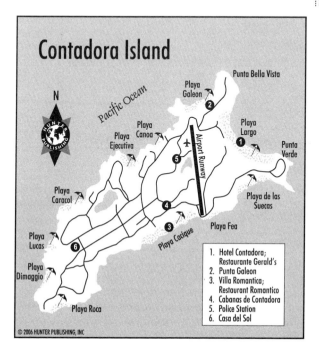

Contadora Island

N · Pacific Ocean

Punta Bella Vista

Playa Galeon

Playa Canoa
Playa Ejecutiva

Airport Runway

Playa Largo
Punta Verde

Playa Caracol

Playa de las Suecas

Playa Fea

Playa Lucas

Playa Cacique

Playa Dimaggio

Playa Roca

1. Hotel Contadora; Restaurante Gerald's
2. Punta Galeon
3. Villa Romantica; Restaurant Romantico
4. Cabanas de Contadora
5. Police Station
6. Casa del Sol

© 2006 HUNTER PUBLISHING, INC

◆ Getting Here

Aeroperlas, ☎ 507-315-7500, and **Aviatur**, ☎ 507-315-0311, fly twice daily to Contadora from Panamá City's Marcos A. Gelabart (Albrook) Municipal Airport. Round-trip fare for the 20-minute flight is about $60.

An **Expreso del Pacifico** ferry, ☎ 507-229-1539 or 229-1742, departs Panamá City at 7 am on Saturdays only and returns at 3 pm on Sundays. The ride takes about two hours and costs $46 round-trip.

◆ Adventures

On Water

Contadora's 13 lovely beaches invite sunbathers, and those who prefer their swimming and sunning in the buff will want to visit **Playa de las Suecas**. Angelfish, parrotfish, butterfly fish and more inhabit rich coral fields near the beaches. Deepwater denizens include white-tip sharks, sea turtles, eels, manta rays, and dolphins. July through October is the best time to watch for migrating humpback and pilot whales.

Salvatore Morello, ☎ 507-250-4109, offers scuba diving, glass-bottom boat tours ($15 per person), snorkeling trips, island tours, and deep-sea fishing from Hotel Contadora's marina.

If you're into terrifying sea life and annoying snorkelers and sunbathers, take a Jet Ski tour that costs $75 for two. **ScubaPanama**, ☎ 507-261-3841 or 507-261-4064, www.scubapanama.com, features a dive adventure from Panamá City with an overnight stay on Contadora.

> **AUTHOR NOTE:** *For an informative boat tour – in English, Spanish or German – that includes inland hikes, contact the Löfflers at* **Casa del Sol**, *☎ 507-250-4212, www.panama-isla-contadora.com (see details about their accommodations on the next page). They'll take you to the best snorkeling places or drop you off on a deserted island and come back for you later.*

On Wheels

Rent a four-wheeler ($25 an hour), a golf cart ($15 an hour) or a bike ($5 an hour) from **Hotel Contadora** and tootle around the tiny island to your heart's content.

◆ Where to Stay

Until Isla del Rey becomes more developed – and it's in the works – almost all services and facilities are on Contadora.

Hotel Contadora, ☎ 507-214-3719 or 507-214-3720, www.hotelcontadora.com, $$$, has air conditioning, cable TV, phones, in-room refrigerators, five restaurants/bars, a casino, pool and a mini nine-hole golf course, The 250-room all-inclusive resort is on gorgeous Playa Larga. After frequent management changes, it is now owned by a Colombian group. Recent reports have not been complimentary. Rates average $80 per person for a double room, unless you come with a group on a package deal, and include meals, use of all facilities, non-motorized sporting equipment, and local alcoholic beverages. There's a children's

❖ HOTEL PRICING	
Based on double occupancy	
No $	under $20
$	$20 to $39
$$	$40 to $79
$$$	$80 to $124
$$$$	$125 to $199
$$$$$	over $200

play area and a small zoo with caged wild animals that include monkeys and endangered macaws. If looking for an all-inclusive beach resort, you'll do much, much better at Decameron Playa Blanca (page 190) or Las Olas Resort in Chiriquí (page 254).

Punta Galeon, ☎ 507-214-3719/3720, www.puntagaleon.com, $$$, recently reopened after extensive renovations. It's on the northeast corner of the island, overlooking beautiful Playa Galeon, a five-minute walk from the north end of the airstrip. All 48 of its sleekly furnished, attractive rooms with sea views open to a lovely wooden deck. There's a freeform pool, a children's pool and a pleasant open-sided restaurant. Rates average $150 for a three-night stay in a double room. Contact the hotel for additional information or rates for shorter stays. Punta Galeon is operated by the same folks as Hotel Contadora.

Converted from a private home, **Villa Romantica**, ☎ 507-250-4067, www.villa-romantica.com, $$$, has five air-conditioned rooms and one suite on a bluff overlooking beautiful Playa Cacique. Some of the eclectic rooms have waterbeds, some breathtaking views. **Guesthouse Casa Charlito**, $$$, part of the Villa Romantica property, is a slightly less expensive alternative. A full breakfast comes with your stay at either.

Cabanas de Contadora, ☎ 507-250-4214, e-mail hcorrand@usa.net, are immaculate little studio apartments with one double bed, TV, and kitchen equipped with microwave and fridge. Breakfast, airport transportation, and the use of bicycles and snorkeling equipment are included. To get here, walk from the airstrip to the police station on the southwest side of the runway, and turn left (southwest) from in front of the station. Continue bearing left for about a quarter-mile (roughly 411.5 meters) until you come to the Cabanas.

◆ Where to Eat

Order your dinner from the prix fixe or à la carte menu at **Restaurante Gerald's**, ☎ 507-264-6772, on the hill above Hotel Contadora, $$$. Enjoy the day's fresh catch prepared with garlic butter and delicate herbs, with wine sauce or peppered. Carnivores can opt for grilled ten-

❖ RESTAURANT PRICING	
Entrée & non-alcoholic drink	
$	under $5
$$	$5 to $10
$$$	$11 to $20
$$$$	over $21

PANAMA PROVINCE

derloin with mushrooms, pork chops or a half-dozen other meats. Finish off the excellent meal with an imaginative dessert.

Restaurante Romantico, ☎ 507-250-4064, at Villa Romantica, $$$$, is a pretty place (with not so pretty prices) perched above the sea. The specialty here is "hot stone" cooking. A hot stone is delivered with your raw entrée so you can grill it to the desired doneness. If you don't feel like cooking yourself, order a ready-to-eat menu item.

Restaurante Sagitario, $, is a local hangout with the cheapest food around. The grilled chicken is tasty and the typical dishes are hearty. It's on the main street across from the Aeroperlas office, a three-minute walk from the north end of the airstrip.

Refresqueria Angelina, $, serves good pizza and sandwiches, a daily comida corriente, gelato and luscious fruit drinks. You'll find it just north of the police station.

Eastern
Panamá Province

The Panamá Canal divides Panamá Province – and the entire country for that matter – into eastern and western sections. Two highways run from Panamá City to the eastern part of the province. The **InterAmericana** leads to the town of **Yaviza**, where it ends at the beginning of a 54-mile/87-kilometer stretch of wilderness between Panamá and Colombia known as the **Darién Gap**. The **Trans-Isthmic Highway** (Transithmica) runs northwest across the isthmus to **Colón City** on the Caribbean. The new **Corridor Norte** expressway runs almost parallel to the the Trans-Isthmic, but hasn't yet been completed all the way to Colón. Two important national parks, **Soberanía** and **Chagres**, border the canal's east side, and both are watersheds providing fresh water for its operation and for Panamá City's water supply. Wildlife is abundant in the parks; a few Emberá villages lie in the jungles along the Chagres River.

Once outside of the capital's bustling suburbs, the InterAmericana slips through a vast region of lowland farms back-dropped on the left by **Cerro Azul Mountain** and the peaks of the **San Blas range**. Since the highway was paved from Panamá City beyond the little town of Chepo 60 miles/97 kilometers east, farmers and loggers have moved in and decimated the forests, leaving an aftermath of cleared land now devoted to rice farms and cattle ranches. This makes for a pretty monotonous cruise down the highway. Inland to the north, however, you'll find excellent nature trails, birding and adventure sports opportunities around Cerro Azul, less than an hour from downtown Panamá City.

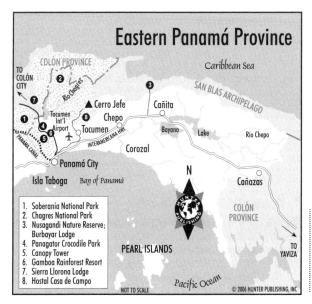

Sightseeing & Touring

◆ Nusagandi Nature Reserve

To protect their lands from an invasion of settlers, subsistence farmers and loggers, the Kuna established Nusagandi Nature Reserve, a 230-square mile/60,000-hectare mountainous rainforest wilderness within autonomous Comarca Kuna Yala. Smithsonian Institution scientists have rated it one of the world's top 10 in terms of its wealth of flora and fauna.

This is prime birding territory; trogons, tanagers, mot-mots, speckled antshrikes, veridian dacnis, pygmy tyrants and king vultures are some of the birds sighted here. The few trails that wind through these pristine primary forests lead to lovely waterfalls and crystal-clear pools that invite a refreshing dip. A knowledgeable guide will identify glorious butterflies, medicinal plants, unusual trees and flowers and, of course, the birds. Monkeys, sloths, agoutis, frogs and iguanas are often encountered along the trails and on the grounds of beautiful, ecological **Burbayar Lodge**, at the reserve's edge.

> **AUTHOR NOTE:** *Although it's confusing, you may also see Nusagandi Reserve called PEMASKY Reserve (Project for the Study and Management of Wilderness Areas of Kuna Yala).*

Nusagandi is approximately 47 miles/76 kilometers northeast of Panamá City. To get here, take the InterAmericana east from the city, and continue past the turnoff to the town of Chepo (37.2 miles/60 kilometers). The Nusagandi turnoff is to the north, 6.2 miles/10 kilometers past the Chepo turnoff. Only the first few kilometers of the turnoff road are paved, and it soon becomes dirt and rock, worsening steadily as it winds into the mountains. Fortunately, it's usually passable to Burbayar Lodge; however, on one visit, our high-clearance 4X4 couldn't get much farther and bogged down in the mud and potholes. All visits to the reserve require advance permission from the Kuna. You can't just show up here. Nevertheless, it's a magnificent experience in nature and shouldn't be missed. Contact **Ancon Expeditions**, ☎ 507-269-9414 or 9415, fax 507-264-3713, to make arrangements, including a stay at beautiful Burbayar Lodge.

◆ Panagator Crocodile Park

This park is a unique place to observe these powerful animals and learn about their habits, habitats and reproduction. Did you know humans and crocodiles benefit from each other's existence? Find out how and why by visiting this fascinating place dedicated to preservation and tropical ecology. You can see them in all of their life stages and feed them fresh meat. Or, if you're hungry, you can dine on one in Panagator's **Campestre Restaurant** – I know that doesn't sound very preservationist, but it is, and a portion of the farm's profits are donated to conservationist causes. You'll find the park at mile 16.5, just off the Trans-Isthmic Highway. For info, ☎ 507-216-6037, e-mail inavasa@sinfo.net. The entrance fee is $15 for adults, $7.50 for children under 12, and includes informative tours and a full lunch at the on-site restaurant. Plan to make this a day-trip.

Adventures

◆ On Foot

Soberanía National Park

Soberanía National Park is one of the hemisphere's most accessible tropical forests and a vital part of the Panama Canal watershed. Its rugged 54,597 acres/22,104 hectares of undulating landscape extend in a vertical strip across much of the isthmus along the canal's east side. Towering ceibas, royal palms, oaks and golden flowering guayacans are among the more than 200 tree species in this wilderness wonderland that harbors 105 mammal, 55 amphibian and 79 reptile species. Tamarin and howler monkeys, sloths, agoutis, coatis, frogs, toads and lizards are commonly seen, but birds are the biggest attraction, with 525 identified species.

AUTHOR NOTE: *Along famous **Pipeline Road/Camino del Oleo**ducto, the Panama Audubon Society established – and held for 19 years – the annual **Christmas Bird Count World Record** for the greatest number of species counted in a 24-hour period. Blue cotingas, collared aricaris, keel-billed toucans, crested owls, spotted antbirds, bay-headed tanagers and black-tailed trogons are frequently spotted. Come early in the morning when the birds are most active, and don't forget those binoculars!*

A section of the **Camino las Cruces/Crossroads**, the cobblestone road built by 16th-century conquistadors to transport goods and treasure across the isthmus, runs through the park. Some of the old stone trail is still visible and a small part has been restored. If you're in good shape, it'll take a little more than five hours to hike to the Chagres River, where you can camp, or about 1½ hours to the Plantation Road spur. Camino las Cruces is quite a distance from the park entrance. No problem if you're driving, but if coming on a Gamboa bound bus, ask to get off where the road forks to Gamboa and walk the remaining 3½ miles/six kilometers. Your best bet is to go with a guide from the city or take a taxi. To get to Plantation Road, turn right off the highway and follow the signs to Canopy Tower; the trail is to your left of the road leading to the tower.

Lovely **Sendero El Charco/Pond Trail** is an interpretive trail, sign-posted to identify the flora. It's an easy 1½-hour closed-circuit hike that loops around Río Sardinilla creek. Blue morpho butterflies abound near the clear pool below a small waterfall – a good place for a refreshing dip. There's a popular picnic area nearby.

The park entrance is just off Gaillard Highway beyond Summit Gardens. Buses bound for Gamboa will drop you, or, if you are driving from the city, look for the huge Parque Nacional Soberanía sign. The park office, ☎ 507-256-6370, is open 8 am to 4 pm, but since a few staffers live on the premises, there's usually someone around. You'll need a $3 permit to enter the park. **Camping** in the park is permitted, but there are no facilities. The fee to camp is $5, in addition to the $3 entrance fee.

Although privately owned, **Canopy Tower**, ☎ 507-264-5720, www.canopytower.com, and **Gamboa Rainforest Resort**, ☎ 877-800-1690 (US), 507-314-9000, www.gamboaresort.com, are inside the park, and both offer unique natural adventures. See *Where to Stay*, pages 117-120, for complete details about them.

Chagres National Park

Stretched across Panamá and Colón provinces on the canal's east side, this huge 318,600-acre/129,000-hectare park protects the Chagres River's hydrographic basin, which provides most of the water used to operate the Panama Canal locks and almost all of Panamá City's water supply. The US canal builders dammed the Chagres to create Gatún Lake and dammed it again in 1935 to create smaller Lake Alajuela. Rugged landscapes rise from 196.8 feet/60 meters above sea level to **Cerro**

Jefe's 3,303-foot/1,007-meter summit. Other important peaks include 3,195-foot/958.5-meter **Cerro Bruja** and 2,529-foot/771-meter **Cerro Azul**. The park's tropical rainforests, moist premontane and elfin forests protect a variety of animal species, including river otters, tapirs, crocodiles, caimans, two endemic salamander species, snakes, frogs, lizards, and all five of Panamá's cats. A few harpy eagles have been sighted within its boundaries, as has the rare, endemic Tacarcuna bush tanager, previously known only at Cerro Tacarcuna in Darién. Part of the Camino Real crosses the park, and there are a few small Emberá settlements along the Chagres River and on the banks above Lake Alajuela.

The park lies about 24 miles/40 kilometers from Panamá City, and is most easily accessed from its Cerro Azul entrance. To go there, take Av Domingo Diaz east from the city, heading toward Tocumen International Airport. Watch for the Riande Airport Hotel and turn left just before it. Continue up the winding mountain road while watching for signs to the park entrance.

There are also several launch sites for Lake Alajuela and the Chagres River within the park. For more information on how to access them, contact ANAM's headquarters in Panamá City, ☎ 507-229-7885. If you are not driving yourself – or even if you are – I recommend going from the capital with a local tour operator or guide. Finding your way around can be tricky, and one of the park's finest attractions is cruising upriver through the jungles while comfortably ensconced in a motorized hollow log!

Like all of Panamá's national parks, the entrance fee is $3, and an additional $5 if you wish to camp. Most visitors stay in Panamá City, but a preferred alternative is **Hostal Casa de Campo Country Inn and Spa** (see below) in Cerro Azul. There are few marked trails in this seldom-visited park, but there is a campsite next to the Cerrro Azul sdministrative branch office, where you will be allowed use of the facilities.

◆ On Water

Massive **Bayano Lake** was created in the mid-1970s when the Chepo River was dammed to produce hydroelectric power. The construction resulted in shortening the Chepo to about one-third of its original length and it has since been renamed the Bayano. I thought it interesting to learn that saltwater sharks are found in the lake, having made their way upriver from the sea – a journey of roughly 24 miles/40 kilometers. Although few anglers make it down this way, there is superb sportfishing for snook and giant tarpon near the river's mouth where it empties into Panamá Bay on the southern Pacific coast. If you're serious about catching some of the "big" ones, contact Captain Tony Herndon, ☎ 507-622-0212 in Panamá City, www.panamafishingandcatching.com. A full day's fishing for two anglers with an experienced guide in a 19-foot Triumph Bay boat costs $350, including transportation from the city, all the gear, bait and tackle you'll need, ice and cold drinks.

Where to Stay & Eat

Less than an hour from Panamá City, in the mountains near the Continental Divide, is **Hostal Casa de Campo Country Inn & Spa**, Las Nubes, Cerro Azul, ☎ 507-297-0067 or 507-270-0018, www.panamacasadecampo.com, $$. The former family manor house is operated by a delightful brother-and-sister team. After a day spent mountain biking,

❖ HOTEL PRICING
Based on double occupancy
No $ . . . . under $20
$ . . . . $20 to $39
$$ . . . . $40 to $79
$$$ . . . . $80 to $124
$$$$ . . . . . . $125 to $199
$$$$$ . . . . over $200

birding, bouldering, or rappelling in the cool cloud forest, relieve those aching muscles with a massage, sauna or dip in the pool. Hiking and birding, river rafting, special programs for seniors and even yoga are offered here. Or you might just want a day of pampering in the spa or swinging in a hammock. Each sumptuous room is named for a local flower – not surprising in a region boasting more than 420 flowering plant species. There are seven rooms in the main house and four in a newer building set between towering pines above the sloping lawn, some with flagstone floors and walls, a loft and Jacuzzi. Early morning mists often blanket the countryside to lend it an ethereal quality. Delicious meals are healthfully prepared and graciously served by the warm, obliging staff. Casa de Campo offers transportation service ($20). If you're driving, take Av Domingo Diaz from the city heading east toward the international airport. Make a left turn just before the Riande Airport Hotel and follow the signs to Las Nubes (The Clouds). Continue up into the mountains until Casa de Campo's directional signs appear.

I spent one night in the reserve's Nusagandi Lodge and can't recommend it. Of course, I didn't expect electricity or hot running water in the middle of the jungle, but neither did I expect to find both the kitchen and "outhouse" bathroom filthy. There was no food or drinking water (visitors are expected to bring their own, but my guide ignored that little detail). The only water here is rainwater collected in an open cistern. Birds cluster in overhanging branches and my "yuk" meter shot off the chart when the caretaker mentioned that he climbs up occasionally to fish out little forest creatures that have fallen in and drowned. I chose thirst. Most disheartening of all was the plight of the lodge's two starving dogs, one of which was crippled from an untreated injury. In the two days I was there, I saw them fed nothing but leftover rice.

Nusagandi Reserve and the surrounding wild lands comprise a rare microcosm of diversity, called by one scientist "the richest on Earth." Fortunately, since it shouldn't be missed, there is an alternative place to stay. Lovely **Burbayar Lodge**, set in its own 122 acres/49 hectares of mountainous rainforest, adjoins the reserve. Privately owned Burbayar features comfortable private rooms with full baths, solar powered electricity, superb cuisine and knowledgeable naturalist owners. Contact **Ancon Expeditions**, ☎ 507-259-9145, www.anconexpeditions.com.

Canopy Tower, ☎ 507-264-5720 or 507-263-2874, www. canopytower.com, $$$-$$$$ all-inclusive (breakfast, dinner, guided walk, park fees, taxes included), crowns the summit of Semaphore Hill in the heart of the park. Only half an hour from Panamá City, "Canopy" is one of the world's best bird-watching sites, and has earned its high rating as one of the world's best ecolodges as well. The only reminders of this lovely boutique hotel's former life as a US military radar tower are its elongated, beer-can shape and the 30-foot-high geotangent dome at its top. Paúl Arias de Para, Canopy's conservationist owner, calls it "the ultimate recycling project." The blue and yellow tower rises up from the jungle floor to a flat circular roof at the top; an ideal observation deck for looking down into the canopy. Each of its five floors offer an opportunity to observe at close range species encountered at each level of the forest. Bright Kuna *molas* and blooming orchids add a splash of color to serene, simply furnished rooms with gleaming hardwood floors, pristine white walls and bed covers, and wide, wide windows for watching the passing wildlife.

Panoramic windows enclose the top floor's open combination dining room/lounge/ library. There's an honor bar and menus for the delicious meals are planned by one of Panamá's leading chefs, famed for her cuisine and her cookbooks. She just happens to be Arias de Para's sister. Despite the cuisine par excellence, if someone gasps, "There's a rufous-crested cocquette," forks are dropped and binoculars grabbed up as diners make a mad dash to the windows.

Although birds are the featured attraction, you can expect to see (and hear) troops of passing howler monkeys. Other oft-sighted critters include capybaras, ocelots, armadillos, opossums, sloths, anteaters and coatimundis. Butterflies of blue and gold flit along pathways radiating from the tower and hummingbirds whir about its base. And who knows what you might see during a night excursion in the "Birdmobile," an open vehicle specially modified for viewing birds and wildlife.

Canopy Tower is a non-smoking property, and best enjoyed by adults and calm children over the age of 13. Younger children seldom enjoy the quiet and serenity of this haven for bird- and wildlife-watchers and, for that reason, are discouraged from visiting.

To get here, head east from downtown Panamá City to the Gaillard Highway. Pass the entrance to Miraflores Locks and continue past Pedro Miguel Locks and Paraiso Village. Soon after Paraiso, you'll come to a railroad bridge overpass. Make the first left turn immmediately after the bridge, and you'll see the entrance to Soberanía National Park on the right. Continue straight ahead for about one mile/1.6 kilometers and, after passing Summit Botanical Gardens, take the second road to the right and follow the signs to Canopy Tower. Expect the drive to take 40 minutes from downtown.

Gamboa Rainforest Resort, ☎ 877-800-1690 (US), 507-314-9000, www. gamboaresort.com, $$$-$$$$$, is a luxury complex that offers a whopping list of adventure and educational experiences. It's also in an enviable Soberanía National Park location on the Chagres River within sight of the Panama Canal's Gaillard Cut. The centerpiece of this 340-acre/137-hectare property is a gorgeous 107-room, five-star hotel with fine restaurants, lounges, a full spa, swimming pools, gift shops, library and every imaginable amenity. All the luxurious rooms have private balconies and huge bathrooms. The resort is handicap-accessible. For those who prefer the romantic days of yesteryear, Gamboa's 38 historic villas have soft pastel exteriors wrapping tropical Bogey and Bacall apartments. Built in the 1930s to house Panama Canal administrators, they've been freshly renovated without sacrificing any bygone charm. The resort features jogging trails, tennis courts, a marina, and educational exhibits staffed with naturalist guides. There are orchid and butterfly nurseries, a serpentarium, reptile house, plant nurseries and aquariums. A magnificent rainforest tram (*teleferico* in Spanish) glides silently up through the jungle canopy; where it stops, a graded ramp continues up to the summit of a hill. It's cool and breezy up here, and so high the giant ships passing through Culebra Cut below look like tiny toys.

> **AUTHOR NOTE:** *The one-of-a-kind rainforest tram has special cars built to accommodate wheelchairs, and the gently sloped ramp is easy to maneuver.*

Gamboa's Tour desk offers guided Chagres River and Gatún Lake sportfishing for snook, tarpon and peacock bass; Las Cruces trail hiking, an after-dark crocodile safari, and boat tours. Or take a helicopter tour to get a bird's-eye perspective of this beautiful country. Day visitor packages that include a room for the day and a host of resort facilities are sometimes available at a cost of $50 for up to four people. They're a great deal.

If you're day tripping to Soberanía from the city, you may want to bring a lunch or snack. Better yet, find your way to Gamboa Rainforest Resort's unique **Los Logartos Restaurant**, which serves lunch and dinner, $$-$$$, on the Chagres River within sight of the Panama Canal. The crocodiles for which the restaurant is named drift among the water lilies below the dining terrace, artfully disguised as floating logs. The food here, while not cheap, is imaginative and delicious. It's almost too pretty to eat. You can order a big juicy hamburger, ceviche, one of the innovative salads or an excellent seafood, beef or chicken entrée. Try one of the delicious fruit shakes – they can be prepared with or without alcohol – or a positively sinful gargantuan dessert.

To get here, take the Gaillard Highway past Summit Gardens and continue until you come to the railroad bridge over the Chagres River. Cross the bridge and make an immediate right turn. Follow the road to Gamboa Resort. There are plenty of signs.

Sierra Llorona Panamá Lodge, ☎ 507-442-8104, www.sierrallorona. com, is one of those places that, once you're there, you don't want to leave. Although it's technically in Colón Province, Sierra Llorona is easy to reach from both Panamá City and Colón City, and is included in this chapter because of its proximity to Soberanía and Chagres national parks. Sierra Llorona has comfortable rooms with private hot-water baths in the charming lodge for $55 double; three rooms with shared bath in the main building cost $48 double each. Delicious meals of local cuisine are served family style. Hearty breakfasts are $6, lunches $10, and dinners are bargain-priced at $12.

Sierra Llorona translates to "crying mountain" and, because it's on the eastern Caribbean slope, the skies drop a few tears here about 280 days a year, usually late at night or in the wee hours before dawn. At 985 feet/ 300 meters above sea level, mornings and evenings are usually cool, clear and breezy. Ida Herrera and her husband, Gonzalo, are dedicated to preserving the ecology of this 494-acre/200-hectare piece of paradise where Ida has lived for 30 years. To hear Gonzalo tell it, there are three ecosystems here, primary forest, secondary forest and the lawn. I couldn't help but notice that the lawn's native plants and trees have been carefully preserved although the grass around them was neatly trimmed. Two nature trails, La Poza and El Colibri, wind through forests lush with orchids, bromeliads, trailing vines, woody vines, bright red cashews, ferns, mosses, heliconias and scarlet hot lips flowers. Many small mammals, butterflies, amphibians and birds are visible. More than 160 bird species have been recorded here, including chacalacas, red-lored amazon parrots, blue headed parrots, eight hummingbird species, and three trogon species. There are observation stations, a lookout, shady thatch-roofed *bohios*, and a sparkling little waterfall beside the verdant trails. Visits can be arranged to nearby Caribbean slope bird watching sites, including Achiote Road, Coco Solo, Tiger Tail and Galeta Point's mangroves. A new butterfly farm here should be completed when you read this.

> ❖ **HOT LIPS**
>
> **Hot lips plants** produce bright red flowers shaped like a pair of very plump lips. They are quite common, and rural women use them superstitiously for contraceptives. One plant found at Sierra Llorona had several of the usual scarlet flowers and one that was a sunny golden yellow. This might be a first. How are they used for contraceptives? I'll leave that to your imagination.

Enjoy fantastic views to Limon Bay, the canal's Caribbean entrance and an expanse of azure sea from the lodge's eight guestrooms on a terraced mountainside. There's a lovely pool, tennis courts and an outdoor barbecue/wet bar.

From Panamá City, travel north on the Trans-Isthmic Highway for about 30 miles/48 kilometers, and start looking for a huge cement factory on the right. Continue past it and keep going until you've crossed four bridges, then watch for the turnoff to Santa Rita Arriba on the right. Head up this road and follow the posted signs to the lodge. If coming from Colón heading south on the Transithmica, the Santa Rita Arriba turnoff is just beyond

Sabanitas (about eight kilometers or 15 minutes south of Colón). Watch for the turnoff on your left. Sierra Llorona is 2.8 miles/4.5 kilometers farther up a steep mountain road. Note that the steep road has a few very rough patches. During the rainy season, call the lodge before setting out to get road conditions. You may need a four-wheel drive vehicle.

If coming by bus, get off at the El Rey supermarket in Sabanitas, where you can take a 4X4 pick-up truck taxi to the lodge for about $8. Ida and Gonzalo will also provide transportation from Colón City and Tocumen International Airport for parties of four or more. The per-person cost for this service is $5 from Colón City and $15 from Tocumen.

Western Panamá Province

The Panama Canal splits Panamá Province (and the entire country, for that matter) into two sectors – eastern and western, linked by the arching, mile-long **Puente de Las Americas** (Bridge of the Americas, also known as Thatcher Bridge), which soars over the canal's Pacific entrance. Western Panama Province's attractions are its lovely beaches; the country's first national park, **Parque Nacional Altos de Campana**; and a famed golf resort. As you travel west along the **InterAmericana Highway**, you'll notice the landscape becomes more agricultural – and flatter and dryer. This is the beginning of the region known as Arco Seco (dry arch), which continues west along the Pacific coast through Coclé and down the Azuero Peninsula. The beaches all lie south of the InterAmericana, and the largest towns you'll encounter are **Arraiján** and **Chorrera**; since neither town holds much of interest, they are not covered here.

Adventures

◆ On Foot

Altos de Campana National Park

The turnoff to 11,888-acre/4,813-hectare Altos de Campana is three miles west of the little town of Capira. Watch for the small sign on the right indicating the turnoff road. The tiny ranger station at the park entrance is 2.85 miles/4.6 kilometers from the turnoff. Stop to pay the $3 entrance fee and the lonely ranger will invite you inside to see park maps, a small assortment of animal skulls, fossils and pickled reptiles. Beyond the station, the lookout point at Cerro Campana's wind-whipped summit offers dramatic views of craggy peaks and deep valleys stretching all the way to the Pacific. Formed of basaltic rock, Campana's rugged terrain hosts four distinct forest types. The drier, deforested mountains on the Pacific side are an amazing contrast to the lush rainforests of the Atlantic slopes. Sloths, crab-eating raccoons, vampire bats, black-eared opossums and Geoffrey's tamarins are a few of the 39 mammal species found here; to date, 267 bird species have been identified. There are 86 reptile and 62 amphibian species, including Panamá's largest frog species, fabled golden frogs, poison dart frogs, and spiny toads.

There's more than flora and fauna to see when hiking Campana's rugged trails. Its high peaks offer spectacular vistas of craggy cliffs, volcanic tors and plunging valleys. Altitudes range from 1,968 to 3,280 feet/600 to 1,000 meters above sea level; it gets cool and windy here, so take a windbreaker. Nature lovers will note the vast differences in the woodlands, from premontane tropical forest to premontane rainforest. Expect to spend several hours if hiking beyond the continental divide to the Atlantic rainforests. You may want to call ANAM's administrative office in Coclé, ☎ 507-997-7638, or the Smithsonian's Tupper Center in Panamá City, ☎ 507-212-8000, e-mail smitham@tivoli.si.edu, for a copy of the park's interpretive trail guide compiled by University of Panamá students and faculty.

> **AUTHOR NOTE:** *Only 47 of the park's 267 recorded species are migratory. Even if you're not a birdwatcher, take binoculars to zoom in on flowering trees, distant plants and the wild beings that inhabit them. Almost certainly an orange-bellied trogon, violet-headed hummingbird or scaled pygmy tyrant will come in view. Emerald and yellow-eared toucanettes, spotted barbtails and white-ruffed manikins frequent the park, and spotting a few of these lovely avians will add spice to your hike. Dedicated birders will, of course, already have their targets in mind.*

◆ On Water

The Beaches

Two beautiful beaches, **Playa Kobbe** and **Playa Veracruz**, lie south of Veracruz village, only minutes west of Panamá City. White-sand Kobbe is operated by a concession that charges a $7 fee to visit. Don't despair; your $7 is exchanged for tickets you can use to "purchase" food and drinks from small concession stands on the beach. Ranchos (shady open-sided thatch-roof huts) and beach umbrellas are available to rent.

Calm, robin's-egg-blue waters wash the wide golden beaches of nearby Playa Veracruz. There is no fee here, and food and drink are not permitted on the beach. You will, however, find plenty of comestibles in Veracruz village. There's a mini-market and several small restaurants where you can get fresh fish, barbeques, coconut rice, and fried plantains. If you prefer fine dining, Spanish-style **Rincón de Filo**, ☎ 507-290-0985, $$$, specializes in paellas and a variety of superb lobster and *langostino* (giant shrimp) dishes, served with cold sangria and huge loaves of freshly baked garlic bread.

Playas Kobbe and Veracruz are less than 4.3 miles/seven kilometers from downtown Panamá City. Watch for the turnoff to sign to Veracruz on the south side of the InterAmericana. There are no hotels here.

Playa Punta Chame is a black-sand beach at the end of a small peninsula. It's popular with windsurfers and nesting sea turtles, but can be

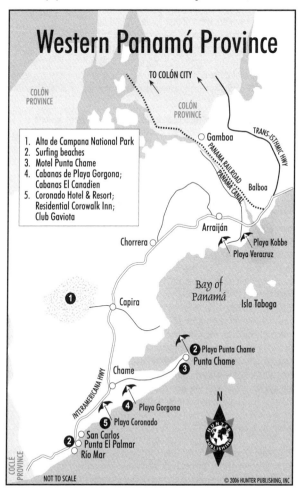

Western Panamá Province

TO COLÓN CITY

COLÓN
PROVINCE

COLÓN
PROVINCE

TRANS-ISTHMIC HWY

○ Gamboa

PANAMA RAILROAD

PANAMA CANAL

1. Alta de Campana National Park
2. Surfing beaches
3. Motel Punta Chame
4. Cabanas de Playa Gorgona;
   Cabanas El Canadien
5. Coronado Hotel & Resort;
   Residential Corowalk Inn;
   Club Gaviota

Balboa

Arraiján

Chorrera ○

Playa Kobbe
Playa Veracruz

Bay of
Panamá

Isla Taboga

1 Capira

2 Playa Punta Chame
Punta Chame

3

INTERAMERICANA HWY

Chame

N

4 Playa Gorgona

5 Playa Coronado

2 ○ San Carlos
○ Punta El Palmar
○ Río Mar

COCLÉ
PROVINCE

NOT TO SCALE

© 2006 HUNTER PUBLISHING, INC

overrun with stingrays. A sting from one of these critters is terribly painful and, in some cases, life-threatening. Obviously, swimming here is not recommended. Unless you're an avid windsurfer or want to visit the peninsula's shrimp farms, I suggest you continue west, where you'll find much better beaches. The Punta Chame turnoff is 29.75 miles/48 kilometers west of Panamá City, and the beach is another 17.3 miles/28 kilometers down the turnoff road.

With views of Coronado's high rises to the west, pretty **Playa Gorgona** curves around a small bay. Its mixed black and white sand can get hot enough to singe your tootsies, so wear flip-flops or booties. The turnoff to Playa Gorgona is 49.6 miles/80 kilometers west of Panamá City (2.5 miles/four kilometers west of the Punta Chame turnoff).

Playa Coronado is a vanilla-fudge swirl of mixed black and white sand, lined with luxury vacation homes, high-rise condominiums and apartments. To get to the beach, you will have to pass through the snazzy Coronado development. There's a guard house at the entrance, so be sure to have identification (passport, driver's license or similar) as the guard will ask to see it.

> **AUTHOR WARNING:** *Riptides at the beaches pose serious danger, but there are ways to protect yourself. Should you get caught in one, don't try to swim to shore; instead, swim parallel to it until you've made it past the rip current. If you want to swim long distances, swim parallel to the shore rather than away from it. There are no lifeguards at most beaches.*

Windsurfing & Surfing

If you don't have your own windsurfer, you can rent one at **Punta Chame Windsurf**, ☎ 507-612-7940, next to Motel Punta Chame. They also offer courses in this exhilarating sport. Those staying at **Coronado Hotel and Resort** have use of kayaks, Sunfish and windsurfers – or, if you're into disturbing the peace, rent a Jet Ski.

Surfers will find plenty of waves along the coast in a cluster of good **surfing** beaches. Near Coronado, **Playa Serena's** waves average six feet (1.8 meters) with a good swell. Waves break right with excellent tubes. **Playa Teta**, west of Coronado in Punta Barco, is a favorite local surfing beach. It has a rock bottom point break with lefts and rights that vary with weather conditions. The seven- to eight-foot waves (2.1-2.4 meters) at **Punta el Palmar**, south of San Carlos, are powerful, yet smooth enough for beginners. Popular **Río Mar** usually has decent right break waves. This one is also good for beginners.

◆ On Wheels

The steep winding road that leads through Altos de Campana National Park all the way up to the continental divide is a great workout if you have the stamina. You'll need your own wheels and a way to transport them, as cycling here via the highway isn't wise. Some dedicated bikers do, but speeding traffic and the frequent lack of shoulders make it very, very dangerous. **Panamá City Tours**, ☎ 507-263-8918, www.panamacitytours. com, offers a variety of cycling tours both in the city and throughout the countryside. **Panamá Explorer Club (PEX)**, ☎ 507-983-6939 in El Valle, or ☎ 507-215-2330 in Panamá City, features tours both in El Valle and mountain biking in the mountainous areas around the town.

If you are staying at **Coronado Resort** and want to wheel around this huge development area, you can rent bicycles from the resort's office.

Where to Stay & Eat

◆ Playa Gorgona

Attractive **Cabanas de Playa Gorgona**, ☎ 507-240-6160, $$-$$$, has 44 rooms and cabanas (cabins), all with air conditioning, living room, and kitchenette furnished with refrigerator, stove and basic cooking utensils. Each has a private terrace with a hammock, and there's a communal barbeque area.

Cabanas El Canadien, ☎ 507-240-6066, fax 507-240-6397, $$, has eight spotless, two-bedroom air-conditioned cabins on the beach that accommodate up to five people and have full kitchens. Each has a private veranda and hammock. There's a bar, laundry and separate swimming pools for adults and children.

You'll find several restaurants nearby, along the InterAmericana. **Restaurante Mi Posada** is good and inexpensive. Busy **Malibu Restaurante** is in the small shopping center next to the Coronado turnoff (Av Roberto Eisenman). Also inexpensive, it's known for serving generous portions of delicious Panamanian specialties.

◆ Punta Chame

The only lodging here is the overpriced **Motel Punta Chame**, ☎ 507-223-1747. There are much better places to stay at Playa Gorgona or Coronado.

◆ Coronado Beach

Coronado Hotel and Resort, ☎ 800-267-6465 (US), 507-264-2724 or 507-214-3164, fax 507-213-4380, www.coronadoresort.com, $$$$. This expansive resort has 77 suites and features an 18-hole golf course designed by George and Tom Fazio. A full range of other goodies includes a spa, four lighted tennis courts, pools, hot tubs, golf pro shop, restaurants, bars and nightclubs. Even the smallest of its lovely, luxe suites is as large as many studio apartments. A gaily painted open-sided bus shuttles to

PANAMA PROVINCE

and from the beach club where you can sun and swim, kayak and windsurf. The waters here aren't usually good for snorkeling.

Even if you are not staying at the Coronado, I recommend dining at one of the resort's fine restaurants, which include popular, open-air **La Terraza Restaurant** ($$-$$$), known for its weekend buffets; gourmet **Le Club** ($$$-$$$$), on the mezzanine overlooking the golf course, featuring fine dining and international specialties. You can order hot dogs, steaks, cool salads and ceviches while relaxing outdoors by the pool under the shady, thatch-roofed ranchos at **Parillada El Fogon** ($-$$$). Guests are welcome to attend the horse shows that are held frequently at the resort's **Club Equestrienne**, a private membership club. If you're here during one of these events, you'll see a notice posted in the main lobby. During the shows, the club's restaurant, **Estibos de Plata**, offers diners a view of the perfectly outfitted Colombian and Peruvian Paso Finos performing their cadenced paces.

Residential Corowalk Inn, on the InterAmericana at the intersection of Av Roberto Eisenman (the turnoff and main road through Coronado), ☎ 507-240-1516, $$, offers 14 attractive rooms with air conditioning, cable TV, and phones.

Club Gaviota, ☎ 507-224-9053 or 507-224-9056, is a less expensive option, with five air-conditioned cabanas, TV, an adult pool and a kiddie pool on attractive grounds; $$. There's a pleasant restaurant ($$). Reservations are recommended, as this place fills up fast on weekends. Ask at the guardhouse for directions.

◆ Camping

Panamá Campsites, ☎ 507-236-1261, recognized the country's need for quality campgrounds and set out to fill it. Their **Los Panamas Beach Camp** is 61.5 miles/99 kilometers west of Panamá City. It's a 15-minute walk down the beach from the Coronado resort complex. If you don't have your own tent, you can rent one, and an air mattress, too. There is a swimming pool, his and hers bathrooms, a communal kitchen, and shady *bohios* on the beach. Tent rental is $15 per night for a double tent; if you bring your own, the camping fee is $5.

Colón Province

Culturally rich and rife with history, Colón curves along the Caribbean coast from Darién west to Veraguas, bordered by Panamá and Coclé provinces to the south. Its largest city and provincial capital, also named Colón, lies at the Panama Canal's Caribbean terminus, a scant 48 miles/77 kilometers northwest of Panamá City by road.

The area beckons eco-adventurers, watersports enthusiasts, birders and sightseers with Spanish forts; scuba diving and snorkeling; river journeys and nature treks through virtually undisturbed forests teeming with rare trees, plants and wildlife; festive, offshore Isla Grande; indigenous Emberá communities; and sleepy coastal villages with more past than present. The complex topography of **Portobelo National Park** rises dramatically from the coral reefs, mangrove swamps, beaches and lagoons of its beautiful bay to a rugged mountainous jungle landscape with winding rivers and lovely waterfalls. Threatened avifauna, all five of Panamá's cat species and indigenous Emberá people live in the wilderness of **Chagres National Park**, which spreads across Colón and Panamá provinces (see *Panamá Province*, page 115, for information about the park).

Testifying to the province's Spanish Colonial history are **Portobelo's** massive forts, cobbled streets and restored "counting house," well-preserved **Fuerte San Lorenzo** on a jungle-enclosed promontory above the Chagres River, vestiges of the cobblestone treasure route, **Camino Real**, and the ghostly skeletons of sunken galleons – one of them perhaps Columbus's long-lost *Vizcaina*. More recent additions that you won't want to miss are massive **Gatún Dam**, the impressive **Gatún Locks**, and one of the country's most beautiful resorts, **Meliá Panamá Canal Hotel**, in a building that once housed the infamous US School of the Americas.

Colón's predominant **Afro-Caribbean culture** dates back to the 16th- and 17th-century **Cimmarones**, slaves escaped from the Spanish who founded settlements here. Construction of the Panama Railroad and Panamá Canal between the mid-19th and early 20th centuries brought waves of immigrant workers from Barbados and Jamaica, and the ill-fated French canal project drew laborers from Martinique and Guadaloupe. Descendants of the Cimmarones, called **Congos**, are a festive people, known for their colorful costumed dances and rhythmic music.

History

◆ Timeline

1501:	Rodrigo de Bastidas arrives on Colón Province's shore.
1510:	Nombre de Dios is founded on the Caribbean coast.
1544:	First Portobelo Fair. The annual fairs that attracted merchants and trade goods from around the globe made Portobelo the world's most important commercial center. The fairs last almost two centuries, until 1731.
1595:	Privateer Francis Drake destroys Nombre de Dios.
1586:	Construction of Portobelo's massive forts begins.
1597:	Ft. San Lorenzo is built above the mouth of the Chagres River. Portobelo is officially founded.
1671:	Buccaneer Henry Morgan destroys Fort San Lorenzo.
1739:	British Admiral William Vernon destroys Portobelo.
1740:	Vernon returns and destroys Fort San Lorenzo.
1848:	As the California Gold Rush gets underway, forty-niners begin to arrive near the shores of present day Colon City to cross the isthmus on their way to the gold fields. By the time the rush was over, tens of thousands had swarmed across Panamá.
1850:	Construction of the Panamá Railroad begins. The town of Aspinwall is founded.
1881-1888:	Fedinand de Lesseps' French canal builders attempt to build a sea-level trans-isthmian canal.
1904:	The US canal builders arrive to build the Panama Canal.
1948:	The Colón Free Zone is established.
1949:	The US School of the Americas opens near Colón City.

Getting Here & Getting Around

Many of Colón's adventures and attractions are within easy driving distance of Panama City, making it possible to visit them during day-trips. However, since Colón offers a great variety of adventures and many places of interest, I recommend spending a few days in one of the one of the hotels or resorts listed in this chapter. Some are quite extraordinary, and you'll save the time it takes to commute.

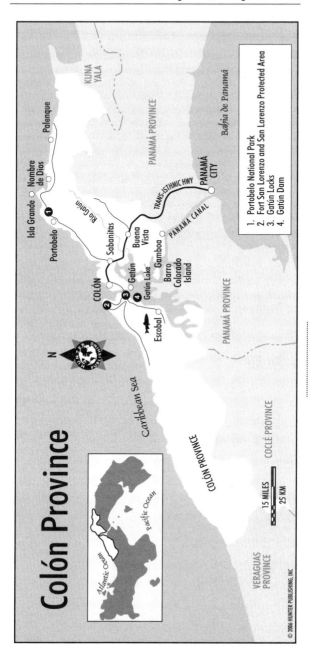

Colón Province

1. Portobelo National Park
2. Fort San Lorenzo and San Lorenzo Protected Area
3. Gatún Locks
4. Gatún Dam

COLON PROVINCE

© 2006 HUNTER PUBLISHING, INC.

◆ By Car

The congested 48-mile/77-kilometer **Trans-Isthmic Highway** – also known as the **Boyd-Roosevelt Highway** and, in local jargon, the Trans-ithmica – is the only road between the capital and Colón. Crowded with buses, local traffic, Panamá City residents commuting to and from work in Colón's Free Zone, and truckers hauling shipping containers from port to port, it runs across the isthmus through the heavily populated urban corridor. Try to avoid traveling this highway during rush hours, when a pleasant 1½- to two-hour journey can dissolve into a three-hour (or more) ordeal of stalled traffic and blaring horns. An alternative route – or part of one – is the **Corridor Norte**, the expressway starting from Panamá City. Construction on the expressway stalled when it was completed about halfway to Colón City, and isn't expected to resume anytime soon. It isn't as scenic and will cost about $2 in tolls, but it does avoid some of the Transithmica's worst congestion.

◆ By Train

Since its resurrection a couple of years ago, the **Panama Railroad** has been a boon to commuters and visitors alike, providing early morning service from the capital to Colón City and return service in the late afternoon. Adult tickets cost $20 one-way, $35 round-trip, and half that amount for children under 12 (see *Panama Railroad*, page 81).

◆ By Air

If you prefer air travel, **Aeroperlas**, ☎ 507-430-1038 (Colón), 507-315-7500 (Panamá City), www.aeroperlas.com, offers two daily flights each way, in the early morning and in the afternoon. A one-way ticket for the 15-minute flight costs approximately $38.

Car rental in Colón City is available from **Budget**, ☎ 507-263-8777 (central reservations), ☎ 507-441-7151 in Colón City; and **Hertz**, ☎ 507-441-3272 in Colón, ☎ 507-238-4081 (Tocumen International Airport).

◆ By Bus

Buses direct to Colón City leave Panamá City's Albrook terminal every 20 minutes, with good connections along the route. An express bus takes about two hours and costs $2.

Colón City

History

Construction of the Panama Railroad brought Colón into existence. It all started on a chunk of coral rock in Limón Bay called Manzanillo Island. Separated from the mainland by a narrow inlet, Manzanillo was an uninhabitable morass of swamps and rank vegetation. So bad, in fact, that the first railway engineers lived on an old sailing ship in the bay. When construction began on the railroad a few shacks began to appear in the swamps but the town didn't begin to grow until 1851 when a storm prevented two New York ships from making port at the Chagres River's mouth and instead discharged their passengers at Colón. The railroad's track had been laid as far as Gatún, and the delayed passengers – forty-niners on their way to California – convinced railroad officials to transport them there. This proved to be easier and faster than the old Chagres route across the isthmus, and soon more ships began to dock in Colón.

The town mushroomed, but still didn't have an official name; Panamá City residents called it *Otro Lado* (Other Side), some called it **Colón**, and others, **Aspinwall**, in honor of the railroad's founder. In 1852, the railway celebrated the laying of its passenger station cornerstone by ceremoniously naming it Aspinwall. There were no sewage or water systems; refuse was dumped into the streets and disease flourished. Robberies and murders became a nightly occurrence. The large numbers of railroad workers and stranded forty-niners attracted prostitutes and pimps who brought new diseases. Aspinwall came to be called the "Pesthole of the Universe" and the "Wickedest city in the Americas."

The arrival of De Lesseps' French railroad company in 1879 brought a short-lived prosperity and a few classic French-style buildings, including de Lesseps' "palace" to the town's Cristobal neighborhood. After fires destroyed most of the city in 1884, the French rebuilt its center with graceful late 19th-century buildings, broad avenues and lovely parks. But it was the American canal builders who arrived in the first decades of the 20th century that installed sewers and water systems, and paved the streets.

Colón City Today

After years of poverty and neglect, the city is shabby, crowded, and littered with trash. Its wealthy residents live along the curving seafront, behind barred windows and high fences topped with rolled barbed wire.

Poorer residents crowd into decrepit apartment buildings and tumbling wooden shacks. Poverty and unemployment (about 40%) are higher than anywhere else in the country.

❖ THE NAME GAME

The isthmus was a forgotten Columbian backwater when the American Railroad company arrived in 1852 and rechristened the town Aspinwall, after the railroad's founder. The name didn't sit well with Columbian officials in Bogota, who demanded the name be changed back to Colón. The Americans refused, saying they built the town and could name it whatever they pleased. Not so, replied Bogota, it's under our sovereignty and its name is Colón. Confusion reigned for years, as mail arrived addressed to Colón-Aspinwall, Aspinwall-Colón or simply to either Colón or Aspinwall. The debate finally ended in 1890 when the Columbian government ordered its post office not to deliver any mail addressed to Aspinwall. Rather than interrupt mail delivery, the railroad conceded, and it has been Colón ever since.

Amid much fanfare in October 2000, the **Colón 2000** mega-complex cruise port opened with a duty-free shopping mall, marina and tour bus terminal. It isn't as grand as had been expected and hasn't provided as many jobs for city residents as had been hoped for. Disembarking cruise passengers can shop in the heavily guarded duty-free complex or hop aboard a tour bus and be whisked off on a "three-hour tour" or to a swank resort without ever setting foot in the city. Colón's most important industries are the huge cargo container ports at Manzanillo and the **Colón Free Zone**, the Western Hemisphere's largest free trade zone.

Wandering around this city isn't a good idea; there's a reason for all those high fences, barbed wire and barred windows. If you absolutely must see it, take a guided day tour or hire a taxi. If driving, keep your doors locked. The city is dangerous – even more so if you look like a tourist. Nowhere else in the country is the poverty or the separation of the rich from the poor more obvious. The few interesting things to see include the old Washington Hotel, the Colón 2000 shopping complex, and the once elegant main street, which hints at the city's short-lived prosperity. Shopping in the Colón Free Zone may sound tempting, but few shops sell individual items. Most merchandise is sold by the ship's container load. The few that do sell single items don't have much of a selection. After buying a gray-market camera here, a friend learned she could have gotten it for the same price in Panamá City or on sale in the US with a manufacturer's warranty. If you still want to go, take a taxi to the guarded entrance and present your passport for a four-day pass.

To see what one woman's hard work and determination can accomplish, pay a visit to **Centro Mujeres Colónesia**, a combination women's shelter and skill center with a nursery and educational day school for older children. This extraordinary place, started by a woman who prefers to remain anonymous, helps some of the city's poorest and most abused women rise from poverty to independence. Nutritious lunches and snacks are provided for those who might otherwise go hungry. Children's clothing, quilts, decorative pillow covers and pottery are some of the items made by the women that you can purchase from the gift shop. If you'd like to visit it, call the Colón IPAT office, ☎ 507-441-9644, and they'll arrange it for you.

West of the Canal

Fuerte San Lorenzo, **Gatún Locks** and **Gatún Dam**, and the fishing village of **Escobal** on Gatún Lake are "don't miss" places of interest west of the Canal, and all are within easy distance from Colón City and the Transithmica. Called *Costa Abajo* (Lower Coast), this region is largely covered by dense forests sweeping from the Caribbean coast into the rugged Cordillera Central. One short coastal road connects a few small villages, running only 22 miles/35 kilometers before ending at the village of Río Indio. Beyond Río Indio, transportation is via rivers and trails through the jungle. There are no services for travelers along this coast, which has unattractive beaches and dangerous riptides.

COLÓN PROVINCE

Sightseeing & Tours

◆ Gatún Locks

Gatún Locks, the only Panamá Canal locks on the Caribbean side, provide the best close-up views of ships passing through. While Miraflores on the Pacific side has two lock chambers, and Pedro Miguel, also on the Pacific has one, the gargantuan Gatún has three pairs stretching almost one mile/ 1.5 kilometers in length. According to David McCullough in his bestseller, *The Path Between the Seas,* each chamber is large enough to have accommodated the *Titanic,* with room to spare. There's an observation platform opposite the control tower where you can watch giant southbound ships, guided by locomotives called *mulas* (mules), enter the lower chambers and rise to the level of Gatún Lake. You won't find a fancy visitor center like the one at Miraflores, but there is a scale model of the canal here and you'll get a very impressive show. Brochures in English and Spanish are available. The observation area is open every day from 9 am until 4 pm, and there is no fee to visit.

The locks are 6.2 miles/10 kilometers southwest of Colón City. After entering the city, turn left at the fourth stop sign and continue on the good, paved road until you come to the signposted detour on the right that leads to the locks. Buses run every hour from Colón City's terminal. The fare is $1.25 each way for the 20-minute ride, or you can take a taxi.

◆ Gatún Dam

Massive Gatún Dam, built to create Gatún Lake, was the world's largest earthen dam when the Panama Canal first opened in 1914. The dam controls the flow of the Chagres River, and supplies sufficient power to operate all of the canal's electrical equipment. Like Gatún Locks, it's pretty impressive, even more so when the spillway opens to let millions of gallons of water rush through. You can get an excellent view from the road and from the small bridge to the right of the spillway. The dam is .75 mile/ 1.2 kilometers beyond Gatún Locks. To get here, cross the swing bridge over the locks and take the first left. If you hire a taxi in Colón to visit both the locks and the dam, expect to pay $15-$20. Be sure to agree on the cost before heading out.

◆ Fort San Lorenzo

About 19 miles/30 km north of Gatún locks, imposing Fort San Lorenzo, officially named El Castillo de San Lorenzo el Real de Chagres, and often called El Castillo (the castle), crowns a promontory cliff affording spectacular views of the coast, the surrounding rainforest and far out to sea. Built of wood in 1595 to guard the river's entrance from pirates, San Lorenzo had already suffered numerous attacks and was deteriorating when attacked and burned by Francis Drake only a year later, in 1596. The rebuilt fort was attacked twice by Henry Morgan who burned it again after destroying Panamá in 1671. Rebuilt of masonry in1680, it survived until BEING destroyed by British Admiral Vernon in 1740. But the Spanish regained control and, using massive coral blocks, resurrected it one last time. Soon after, Spain lost its grip on the isthmus and the need for the fort vanished. The British again took control, occupying San Lorenzo until its abandonment in 1844.

Designated a UNESCO World Heritage Site 1981, San Lorenzo is one of the best-preserved forts in the Americas. Located in the 30,000-acre/ 12,000-hectare San Lorenzo Protected Area, which includes 12 miles/19 km of Caribbean coastline, famed Achiote Road for bird and wildlife watching, and the former US Fort Sherman military base's Jungle Training Center. The protected area's four ecosystems are a vital part of the Mesoamerican Biological Corridor, formerly called Paseo de Pantera

(Path of the Panther), that stretches north from South America through Central America and Mexico. Since the US Military's departure, loggers, hunters and slash and burn farmers have invaded the area, and there is talk that a mega-resort might be built here. For more information about its preservation, contact CEASPA, ☎ 507-4330-1675 or ☎ 507-225-0602, www.sanlorenzo.org.pa.

❖ TOURING SAN LORENZO PROTECTED AREA

Although it is an on-again, off-again policy, only approved organized tour groups are permitted into the protected area. Contact any of the tour operators listed on page 52.

Adventures

◆ On Water

If fishing strikes your fancy and you have your own tackle, cross the swing bridge at Gatún Locks and turn left. Continue southwest 12.4 miles/20 km on the dirt road that skirts Gatún Lake (overpopulated with delicious-to-eat peacock bass) to Escobal village. You can rent a fishing boat here for about $4 an hour or a kayak for $5. There are no hotels in Escobal yet, but if you want to stay overnight, contact Bill Eversley, ☎ 507-434-6020, to arrange a homestay with friendly locals.

Where to Stay & Eat

I don't recommend staying in the city since it's foolhardy to venture out after sunset. Much better options are the luxurious Melia Resort or lovely ecological Sierra Llorona Panamá Lodge (see page 119). If you do opt for city digs, historic Hotel Washington is the best choice.

When first opened in 1913, magnificent **Hotel Washington**, Av del Frente, 84 rooms, ☎ 507-441-7133, fax 507-441-7397, $-$$, was the epitome of elegance. It built and operated by the Panamá Railroad Company for the US government. Its huge rooms with vast balconies overlooking the sea, gourmet restaurants, magnificent ballroom and what was then the world's largest swimming pool, drew well-heeled guests from around the globe. The railroad leased it out in 1954, and it's since passed on to an Arab consortium and is now operated mainly as a casino. A bit down at heel, this grand old dowager is still something to see.

Melia Panamá Canal Resort and Casino, ☎ 507-470-1000, fax 507-470-1925, www.solmelia.com, 280 rooms, 7 suites, $$-$$$$. A mere eight minutes by road from Colón City on the former US Fort Gulick Military base, this luxurious five-star resort on a lush Chagres River penin-

COLON PROVINCE

sula offers every imaginable amenity, and with rates far less than one would expect. Spanish Majolica ware, carved indigenous ceremonial Cayucos, and Iberian artworks accent the main lobby and hallways. Two superb restaurants offer casual international and fine gourmet dining. Wide windows and French doors provide sweeping views of the resort's grounds, its three tiered cascading pools – Panamá's largest, with a swim-up bar — and the jungle-enclosed river. Other amenities include a full spa, casino, tennis courts and shady trails through beautifully land-scaped grounds, a nearby private Caribbean beach and a complete business center. Melia, as it's called by locals, offers optional visits to many of the area's finest attractions. This wonderful resort is more than a place to stay – it's a destination.

East of the Canal

The **Costa Arriba** (Upper Coast), as the region east of the canal is called, is famed for its long stretches of beach, excellent scuba diving, snorkeling, the ruins of historical **Portobelo town** and **Portobelo National Park**. It's also the jumping off point to laid-back **Isla Grande**, favored by Panamá City "weekenders." Getting here from either Panamá City or Colón is easy via the Transithmica and a good paved road that runs along the coast. Buses from both cities and from the town of Sabanitas on the Transithmica ply this road every 20 to 30 minutes.

Portobelo

History

According to legend, Portobelo was named in 1502 when **Columbus** sailed into its bay and exclaimed "Puerto Bello" (beautiful port). The town wasn't founded until 1597, after pirate **Francis Drake** burned Nombre de Dios in 1596. A seriously ill Drake then sailed to Portobelo, where he died and was buried at sea. His lead casket is said to lie at the bottom of the bay that bears his name. The destruction of Nombre de Dios convinced the Spanish government that more fortifications were needed to safeguard its ports and in 1597, when the royal treasure house was moved to Portobelo, engineers were sent to build its forts. Fort San Felipe, at the harbor entrance, was equipped with 35 cannons. Fort San Geronimo was built on the east, and Fort Santiago de la Gloria, on the west. Their coral rock walls are as hard as granite. In 1602, less than a year after the forts were completed, pirate **William Parker** sacked the town. Mercifully, he didn't destroy it.

Portobelo soon became the New World's most important port and the scene of the great **Portobelo Fairs**, which lasted almost a century. In 1666, infamous **Henry Morgan** sacked and burned the town; the cannons he was unable to haul away were spiked so they couldn't be used again. In 1679 the city was again sacked by British **Bartholomew Sharp** and French pirate **La Sound**, and a 1744 attack spared the city but destroyed the customs house. Admiral **Edward Vernon** was the last to sack Portobelo in 1789.

Portobelo Today

Portobelo today is an impoverished fishing village of about 500 inhabitants living around and on top of the ruins. Most are the mixed descendants of African slaves, and are known as **Congos**. The kids here are especially charming. Giggly little girls will try to sell you plastic bracelets or beads and tiny boys, not to be outdone, will find a rock or piece of driftwood they're sure will entrance you. Despite the obvious poverty, these children don't beg and they don't plead for a sale..

Rusting cannons still guard the harbor from Forts Santiago and San Geronimo, their wooden carriages long since rotted away. Some of the original cobblestone streets are still here, the forts are remarkably well preserved and the customs house that has been destroyed and rebuilt several times was restored in 1989. It now houses a small museum. The village's Church of San Felipe, dating from 1814, is next to the ruins of the much older Iglesia de San Juan de Dios, built in 1599. Inside San Felipe, you'll notice the many gold watches, charms, bracelets, necklaces and doodads pinned to the Black Christ of Portobelo's velvet garments. Thousands of worshipers and onlookers flock here every October 21 to celebrate the **Festival of the Black Christ**.

There are more ruins secluded on a jungle hillside across the road, and on an island in the bay. Get information from the helpful staff at the **IPAT office**, ☎ 507-448-2073, west of the customs house.

COLON PROVINCE

❖ CRISTO NEGRO DE PORTOBELO

No one remembers now how the Black Christ statue came to Portobelo, but several legends attempt to explain the mystery. According to the first, the statue was aboard a Columbian ship in Portobelo's harbor and whenever the ship attempted to leave, sudden raging storms forced it back. Finally, during a horrendous gale, the desperate and superstitious sailors tossed the box containing the Christ into the sea. Instantly, the storm abated and the ship sailed away.

The box containing the Christ floated to Portobelo's shore where it was discovered by the townspeople.

A second tale relates that Portobelo's townsfolk who found the Christ washed onto the shore had no idea how it had gotten there and assumed its arrival miraculous.

The third and most logical story(since the Christ is carved from a dense hardwood too heavy to float) is that Portobelo's church ordered a statue of Santo Domingo at the same time and from the same supplier in Spain as the Church on Taboga Island ordered one of a Black Christ. Somehow, there was a mix-up and Santo Domingo went to Taboga, the Black Christ to Portobelo. Attempts made over the years to swap the statues always ended in a mishap that prevented the Christ from leaving Portobelo. Eventually, both churches agreed that the Christ had chosen to remain here.

On October 21, 1821, as a cholera epidemic swept across the isthmus, Portobelo's frantic townspeople gathered in the church and prayed to the Christ to spare them. Apparently their prayers were answered; not a single resident became ill. Another twist to this tale recounts that villagers already stricken by the disease miraculously recovered after praying to the statue. Every year, on October 21, the village honors its mysterious benefactor. Supplicants from throughout the country converge to give thanks for answered prayers or plead for them to be answered. The most devout travel the last miles on their knees, don royal purple robes or wear crowns of thorns and lug heavy wooden crosses.

Getting Here

From Panamá City, take the Corridor Norte or Translsthmic Highway to the town of Sabanitas and turn right immediately past Supermarket El Rey. Continue on the well-paved road until you come to Portobelo on your left, 62 miles/100 kilometers from Panamá City. If coming from Colón, turn left at the afore-mentioned market. If coming by bus from Panamá City, ask the driver to let you off in front of the Sabanitas El Rey, and then take a bus bound for Portobelo.

Sightseeing & Touring

◆ Nombre de Dios

Ancient trees shade this pleasant little town's few quiet streets, friendly residents, snoozing dogs and two charming policemen. The town boasts vast stretches of golden sand beach, but no post office, no bank and only one pay phone. Since it was destroyed by pirate Francis Drake more than four centuries ago (1596), Nombre de Dios slumbered under the tropical sun. Nothing of note happened until 1997, when former Floridian Warren White discovered a sunken galleon while diving. According to Columbus's log of his last voyage, one of his ships, the *Viscaina*, was lost somewhere near Portobelo in 1502. Although not yet proven, recovered artifacts indicate that White had found the *Viscaina*.

> **❖ HOW NOMBRE DE DIOS (NAME OF GOD) GOT ITS NAME**
>
> In 1510, the Spanish Crown sent Conquistador Diego de Nicuesa from Hispanola to found a colony in Castilla de Oro, as the isthmus was then known. Nicuesa's fleet, carrying 700 colonists and crew, encountered a fierce storm off the Caribbean coast, between the Rio Belén and the Gulf of Urabá. More than 400 men were lost as the gale battered and tossed Nicuesa's ships onto the reef. When the storm finally abated, Nicuesa gathered the survivors on the shore and exclaimed, "In the name of God, we will stay here."

COLON PROVINCE

There isn't much to do here other than slurp fresh green coconut water (*agua de pipa*), lounge on the beach, and, if you speak Spanish – or want to try – chat up the friendly locals. Of course, you can always dive in search of treasure, but not near the galleon that in all probability is *Viscaina*. That archaeological treasure is off-limits.

To get here, travel 5.1 miles/8.3 km past Portobelo to the signposted turnoff that branches to the right. Continue 10 miles/16 km to the town. If coming by bus from Colón or Panamá city, get off in front of the El Rey Supermarket in Sabanitas and transfer to a Nombre de Dios or Palenque bus. The fare from Sabanitas is about $1.

If you want to hang around soaking up sun and tranquility, there is one very simple guesthouse, appropriately called, **Guesthouse**. Rooms with private or shared bath and fan cost $5 per person. Call the mayor's office ☎ 507-448-2063, to make a reservation. If you show up without an advance booking, walk over to the police station and they'll find someone with a key.

AUTHOR NOTE: *Columbus lost nine ships during his four voyages to the New World, two of them on the isthmus: The Vizcaina off Portobelo's shores and the Gallega in River Belén.*

◆ Palenque

If your choice of adventure is to escape the madding crowd, continue past Nombre de Dios to even smaller Palenque. This little village offers peace, quiet, lovely beaches and not much more to do than sling a hammock and sway. There are two small restaurants, no hotels – although rumor has it that an eco-resort is planned – but the town's ex-mayor, Señor Fermin, has two nice rooms to rent for about $15 each. Call him at ☎ 507-448-2188, the town's only phone (as of this writing). Between Palenque and the road's end, there are three even smaller villages and a few deserted beaches, but no facilities for visitors.

Adventures

◆ On Foot

The town of Portobelo lies within the complex topography of the 88,744-acre/35,929-hectare **Portobelo National Park**, which includes Portobelo Bay, a series of lagoons, coral reefs, mangrove forests and sea turtle nesting beaches. Several important rivers rise in its lush mountainous rainforests where precipitation averages 189 inches/480 centimeters annually. River otters, crab-eating raccoons and iguanas are found in large numbers and there are many bird species. You can see a few more of Portobelo's ruins hidden in the foliage across the road from the present town. Rough trails lead from there into the dense jungles. However, only the very adventurous should hike far from the roadway without a guide. There is a $3 entrance free to the park that is easily accessed from an entrance across the road from the town. However, it isn't wise to wander far without a guide as it's easy to get lost, the terrain is rugged and there are some dangerous denizens.

The local **IPAT** office, ☎ 507-448-2073, on the main street, has an exceptionally friendly staff who delight in sharing historical information and can recommend a local guide. Or you can contact **Selvaventuras**, selvaventuras@hotmail.com, a local tour company that specializes in hikes through the park's rugged wilderness. It's operated by three delightful young men, all named José. If you're already here, ask for them at the Selvaventuras Cultural Café on the main street.

◆ On Water

Diving

You'll see a few decent beaches west of Portobelo and kids splashing around in front of Fort Santiago, but the water doesn't look all that clean. Portobelo is best known for offshore diving. **Buena Ventura Island** has both shallow and deep diving and an interesting drop-off. The remains of wooden galleons rest on the sea floor near **Salmadina Reef**; 75 feet down you can explore a sunken C-45 aircraft.

Twin Oceans Dive Center, ☎ 507-448-2067, www.twinoceans.com, offers a full range of options – from one day of diving to a one-week package that includes accommodations at lovely **Cocoplum Resort**, six days of meals, and five days of three-tank diving, including the tanks and weights. They also run dive trips to the virtually untouched reefs around Coiba Island, and PADI instructors teach classes from beginner all the way up to divemaster. Twin Oceans can also arrange jungle treks, horseback riding and other activities. Contact them for prices.

Contact **ScubaPortobelo**, ☎ 507-448-2147, for a one-day resort course here; or, for all certifications, try **ScubaPanama**, ☎ 507-261-3841, www. scubapanama.com, in Panamá City.

Where to Stay

The few places to stay along the coast are before you reach Portobelo; there are none in the town.

ScubaPortobelo Dive Resort, ☎ 507-261-3841, www.scubapanama.com, $-$$, built specifically to accommodate divers, has six air-conditioned cabins with private baths and showers. It's owned by ScubaPanama, the country's foremost dive operator, has its own beach, offers certification courses, and rents scuba and snorkeling equipment. Rates range from $30 per night during the week to $50 per night on weekends and holidays.

Nautilus Dive Resort, ☎ 507-448-2035 or 507-613-6557 (cell), $, six miles/10 kilometers west of Portobelo town, has added 10 sparkling new rooms, all with air conditioning and private bath. There's a good restaurant and bar. Dive certification is offered here as well and, although the resort caters to divers, it's a good place to stay even if you don't dive.

Buzo Aquatic Park, ☎ 507-448-2175, $, has a few rooms and an open-air restaurant/bar on a well-used stretch of grayish beach. You'll see it soon after passing Happy Lobster and Nautilus Resort.

COLON PROVINCE

Where to Eat

The few restaurants along this coast specialize in seafood. **Nautilus Dive Resort** (see above) is a good choice, as is **Los Canoñes**, ☎ 507-448-2032, which offers excellent seafood Caribbean style with lots of coconut and coconut milk. The whole deep-fried snapper is perfect; moist and delicate. You might prefer *corvina al ajillo* (with garlic) or a fresh grilled lobster. Complete meals average about $10. Sea breezes cool the outdoor dining terrace overlooking the property's extensive gardens and beautiful Portobelo Bay. The last time I visited, Los Canoñes was for sale; if it's been sold, I hope the new owners haven't made many changes. **Happy Lobster** was always closed when I traveled this coast, but you can't miss the huge building with an overhanging balcony on the left a couple of miles before Portobelo village. Friends who dined here told me the food is good and portions generous. Dinners run about $10.

Isla Grande

This laid-back Caribbean island, popular with weekenders, is a 10-minute boat ride from the mainland. Its pleasant little village spreads along the western seafront, back-dropped by a steep, jungle hillside. Stationed in the sea in front of the village pier, the Christ of Isla Grande watches over the town; a gift from a man whose son regained the use of his legs here. The main – and only – drag is the wide sand pathway that runs almost the village's length, but everyone gets around on foot since the island is only three miles long and less than a mile wide. Most of the 1000 or so inhabitants of African descent make their living from fishing, coconut production or tourism. Reggae is very popular and Congo bands often perform on weekends. The action is concentrated around the main pier and nearby outdoor restaurants that specialize in fresh fish, shrimp and crab, lavishly prepared with locally grown coconut products. Don't pass up delicious coconut rice.

Getting Here

Continue southeast on the road from Portobelo to the hamlet of La Guira, where you'll see a large parking area in front of the docks to your left. You can park in the open lot for $1 a day (hire one of the local kids to watch your car for an additional $1) or in the secure fenced lot just left of the dock for $5 per day. A waiting water taxi will take you to the island's village pier for $5-10 one-way, depending on the number of passengers.

Adventures

◆ On Foot

A stroll along the wide sand "main" street is a people-watchers delight of interesting characters and sights: fisherman heaving their catches onto the pier, a few surfers "biting the wet" in front of Sister Moon; and, on weekends, a steady stream of revelers arriving by boat from the mainland. Although somewhat strenuous, the jungle-enclosed pathway from the village, up to the top of the hill and down to Bananas Resort on the other side, is a beautiful hike. Stop at the hill's summit, where someone has thoughtfully placed a couple of benches, to watch birds and butterflies and drink in the spectacular sea views. Take a bottle of water because it's a hot and sweaty trek.

◆ On Water

There are only two good **swimming beaches** on the island. Hotel Isla Grande's white-sand crescent beach is the best, and on the other side of the island, the one at Bananas Village Resort is smaller and far from the madding crowd.

You can hire a boatman at the pier to take you to a nearby uninhabited island where you can swim, snorkel and sun on white-sand beaches. You can go on a tour or be dropped off on a deserted island and picked up later. A three- to four-hour tour costs about $30.

Isla Grande Dive Center (no phone, open only on weekends) is the only dive center. **ScubaPanama**, ☎ 507-261-3841, offers dive trips from Portobelo. You'll need your own gear if you want to fish. If you're staying at Bananas Village Resort, they'll arrange an excursion. If not, ask around the pier for an experienced guide or boatman. There aren't any surf shops, so you'll need your own board to surf in front of Sister Moon. The waves get raves and the bottom's mostly coral, so bring booties, too.

Where to Stay

Most of the one-story lodgings along main "street" are similar in price and dreary décor. Those with air conditioning and hot water bathrooms cost a bit more, but are well worth it. During the week, you'll have your pick, so check out a few before deciding. If coming on a weekend or holiday when the island is

❖ HOTEL PRICING	
Based on double occupancy	
No $	under $20
$	$20 to $39
$$	$40 to $79
$$$	$80 to $124
$$$$	$125 to $199
$$$$$	over $200

packed, make an advance reservation. Only two of the lodgings (Bananas and Hotel Isla Grande) are resorts and they vary dramatically in style and quality.

Candy Rose Cabins, ☎ 507-448-2200 reservations, $, faces the sea and is two houses left of the pier. The 10 rooms (seven with air conditioning) are spotlessly kept, with good beds, private baths and linoleum floors.

Cabanas Jackson, ☎ 507-448-2311, $, has six rooms with private bath, A/C and fan. All are immaculate, with good beds and tile floors, but vary in size. Discounts are available for stays longer than two nights.

Cabanas Villa Ensueño, ☎ 507-338-2064, $-$$, offers 16 rooms all with A/C, restaurant, bar, pool and laundry. The rooms, arranged around a central courtyard, are nicer than most others along the main street. You can camp on the grounds here, with use of toilet and shower, for $10.

Hotel Isla Grande, ☎ 507-448-6722, fax 507-448-6721, $-$$, 52 rooms, some with A/C, others with fan only. There's a restaurant, a bar and pool tables. This hotel's setting on the island's best crescent-shaped beach that curves around a beautiful bay, back-dropped by towering green jungle makes you expect more than you get! The popular cabana rooms along the bay are small, musty and dreary with worn, hard beds. A second, newer and much larger two-story building set back from the beach in an unkempt weedy lot was closed "for remodeling" each time I visited. I never saw signs of work in progress and locals said that it had been shuttered for more than a year. Perhaps it's finished by now. The so-so restaurant serves all three meals and snacks, including hot dogs and hamburgers. A dinner of fish or shrimp costs about $8.

Secluded on a terraced hillside above the sea, **Sister Moon**, ☎ 507-448-2182 or ☎ 507-226-2257 (Panamá City), $$-$$$, is a charming, eclectic place. Some of its 14 simple and comfortable thatch-roof cottages that accommodate two to five people have balconies and lovely views. There is also a dorm, popular with surfers, that accommodates up to eight ($15 per person). If it's not taken, ask to see the cottage built around a huge boulder that was too big to dig out. Stairs are carved into one side of the rock to access the top that was lopped off and hollowed out to accommodate a king mattress. It is unique. Sister Moon's small restaurant specializes in excellent Spanish/Columbian cuisine, there is a bar and a delightful breezy veranda extends out above the cliff. You can arrange for a room only, bed and breakfast package or an all-inclusive stay.

Bananas Village Resort, ☎ 507-263-9510 or 263-9766, fax 507-264-7556, www.bananaresort.com, $$$$, 28 rooms with private balcony, A/C, ceiling fans, cable TV, safes, restaurant, bar, pool. This is the island's best, a secluded tropical getaway with eight Caribbean-flavored cottages snuggled into a jungle hillside above the sea. Each two-level cottage has two rooms on the first level and one on the second furnished with one king or two queen beds. The outdoor dining/bar area hugs the seafront for breezes and views; the food is excellent, the atmosphere relaxed. There is a sparkling pool, a basketball court, game room, a dock and small private beach. Use of all non-motorized sports equipment and watercraft is included with your stay. On weekends, there is an outdoor Caribbean-style barbeque with entertainment by local Congo bands. Bananas arranges fishing and snorkeling tours and visits to small, deserted islands.

> **AUTHOR NOTE:** *If you've reserved a stay at Bananas on the island's opposite side, let them know what time you will get here and they'll send a bright yellow "Bananas" boat to pick you up. If one isn't waiting, take a water taxi and when you arrive, go with the boatman to Bananas outdoor bar and the bartender will pay him for your transport.*

Where to Eat

Several restaurants along the seafront serve mostly uninspired Caribbean-style seafood, although a few are quite good. I've listed a few, but you can stroll main street to find one that appeals.

❖ RESTAURANT PRICING
Entrée & non-alcoholic drink
$ . . . . under $5
$$ . . . . $5 to $10
$$$ . . . . $11 to $20
$$$$ . . . . over $21

Candy Rose, ☎ 507-448-2947, $-$$. Dine on the front porch or on a seafront terrace across the street. Good seafood and chicken dishes cost $3.50 to $8.

Restaurant Don Teleton, $, on the village shore, offers a variety of fish, chicken, beef or pork chop meals for about $5.

Jah rules at **Club PuntaProa**, $-$$, the bright red, yellow and blue outdoor place with an oversize Bob Marley likeness dominating an outer wall. Enjoy a *corvina*, snapper or seafood combination plate while listening to the tinkling coconut and seashell wind chimes — if the Wailers aren't drowning them out.

If you are able to negotiate the steep rocky path to **Sister Moon**, ☎ 507-448-2182, you'll find delicious Spanish and Columbian seafood specialties served in breezy ambiance. Dinner prices average $9 and reservations are necessary.

If staying at **Bananas Resort**, plan to enjoy dinner there and grab lunch while exploring the village. You might want to try the French fare at **La Turquesa**, $$-$$$. Unfortunately, I missed it, but heard it is superb.

COLON PROVINCE

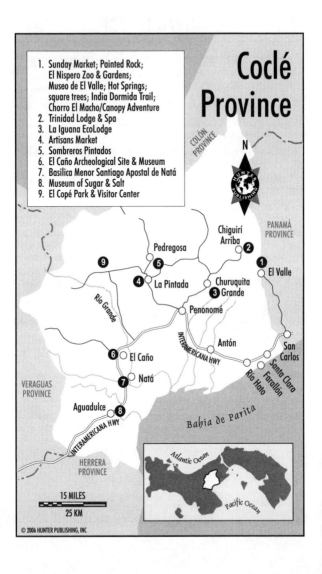

1. Sunday Market; Painted Rock;
   El Nispero Zoo & Gardens;
   Museo de El Valle; Hot Springs;
   square trees; India Dormida Trail;
   Chorro El Macho/Canopy Adventure
2. Trinidad Lodge & Spa
3. La Iguana EcoLodge
4. Artisans Market
5. Sombreros Pintados
6. El Caño Archeological Site & Museum
7. Basilica Menor Santiago Apostal de Natá
8. Museum of Sugar & Salt
9. El Copé Park & Visitor Center

Coclé
Province

N

COLÓN PROVINCE

PANAMÁ
PROVINCE

Chiguirí
Arriba

Pedregosa

9

5

El Valle

4   La Pintada

Churuquita
Grande

3

Peñonomé

Río Grande

Antón

San
Carlos

INTERAMERICANA HWY

Santa Clara
Farallón
Río Hato

6   El Caño

VERAGUAS
PROVINCE

7   Natá

Aguadulce   8

INTERAMERICANA HWY

Bahía de Parita

HERRERA
PROVINCE

15 MILES

25 KM

Atlantic Ocean

Pacific Ocean

© 2006 HUNTER PUBLISHING, INC

Coclé Province

Coclé lies immediately west of Panamá Province. It's the easternmost of the country's Central Provinces "heartland" region that includes Veraguas, Herrera and

Los Santos. Dry coastal plains slope inland from Coclé's white-sand beaches to sudden, abrupt mountains and soaring cloud forests, replete with rushing rivers and dancing waterfalls. This diversity of landscapes offers something for every adventure traveler. There are challenging cliffs and waterfalls for rappelling, rivers to raft and kayak, jungles to trek, trails for biking and horseback riding, and an ingenious rainforest adventure ride to swoop you through the forest canopy.

Encompassing 6,968 square miles/11,239 square kilometers, Coclé stretches north from the magnificent beaches of the Pacific coast, across rolling agricultural foothills, to the forested peaks of the Cordillera Central. Although a large province, it's sparsely populated, and most of its 202,000 friendly inhabitants live in small rural villages. Coclé's two largest cities are **Penonomé**, the provincial capital, with a population of 16,000, and **Aguadulce**, with about 8,000.

Sugarcane and rice grow in the lowlands, coffee and fruit thrive on cool mountain slopes and Panamá's national flower, the waxy white orchid Flor del Espiritú Santo, grows wild in the rainforests. More salt and sugar are produced in Coclé than anywhere else in the country – and more presidents. There are pre-conquest archaeological sites, mystifying carved petroglyphs, bubbling hot springs and a lovely mountain resort town in the crater of an extinct volcano. You'll also find golden frogs, square trees, handmade hats, Panamá's largest Sunday market, its only RV park, and the oldest church in the Americas still in use today.

History

The central region's gold brought Spanish colonization early to Coclé, the domain of fierce indigenous warriors. Starting in 1520, more than 20,000 conquistadors battled armies led by caciques (chiefs) Chirú, París, Natá, Estibir and Urraca – whose likeness is immortalized on Panamá's one-cent coin. In 1522, the town of Natá de Caballeros was founded as a Spanish outpost for the wars that lasted more than 30 years. By 1556, the great caciques had been defeated, their surviving subjects scattered into the mountains of the Cordillera Central or enslaved to work the mines

COCLÉ PROVINCE

along with imported African slaves. By the end of the 16th century, the gold played out and Coclé became the center of the Spanish *cacicazgos,* fiefdoms ruled by local political bosses.

The Province Today

The gold mines and the fiefdoms are long gone. The treasures you'll find instead are friendly locals who reflect their blended Spanish, indigenous and African heritage; the dazzling white beaches of Santa Clara, Farallón and Playa Blanca; El Copé's magnificent wilderness cloud forests; colonial Natá, virtually untouched by the passing centuries; the pre-Columbian archaeological site of El Caño, and El Valle de Antón's refreshing climate and challenging adventure sports. Fine handicrafts produced in Coclé include Panamá's famed **sombreros pintados** (spotted hats), **soapstone carvings** made by Ngöbe-Buglé people, exquisite **hardwood carvings**, **dolls** dressed in finely stitched miniature *polleras,* and **drums** made of wood and leather.

> **AUTHOR NOTE:** *Panamá hats are actually made in Ecuador. The true hats of Panamá are called* somberos pintadas *(or* pintaos) *and* sombreros ocueños, *named for the towns where they are made.*

Getting Here

There are no commercial airports in Coclé; access is via the **Inter-Americana Highway**, which runs east/west through the province. Penonomé lies alongside the InterAmericana, 92.3 miles/149 kilometers (about two hours) west of Panamá City, and is a major connecting point for bus travelers.

El Valle

Although its full name is **El Valle de Antón**, the town is most often called simply El Valle. This lovely mountain town nestles in the crater of an extinct volcano 2,000 feet/606 meters above sea level. The crater was formed millions of years ago when the volcano literally blew its top to create the five-mile-long by 3½-mile-/5.6 kilometer-wide crater. The crater eventually filled with water and became a lake. Sometime between 20,000 and 10,000 years ago a fissure opened in its side, and the lake slowly drained away. Lush vegetation and a profusion of flowering trees and plants testify to El Valle's rich volcanic soils. Its refreshing springlike climate that averages between 68 and 78 degrees year-round has made it a tranquil weekend retreat for Panamá City residents, evidenced by lovely homes set back from quiet streets and country lanes. Famed for its colorful Sunday Market, golden frogs and square trees, this picturesque village is fast becoming an adventure and extreme sports center.

El Vallé is 77.5 miles/125 kilometers west of Panamá City, a drive that will take less than two hours. Head west on the InterAmericana from Panamá City and, after 58.2 miles/94 kilometers, watch for the San Carlos village sign on the right. The turnoff to El Valle is on the north (right) side of the InterAmericana, about 2.5 miles/four kilometers past the sign. Make the turn and proceed up the winding mountain road another 17.3 miles/28 kilometers to El Valle. The road becomes Av Central when you enter the village.

Sightseeing & Touring

◆ Sunday Market

It isn't on the scale of Guatemala's Chichicastenango market but El Valle's famed Sunday market is Panamá's biggest and best. Artisans and craftspeople from all over the country converge here to sell handicrafts, artworks, produce and flowers. Once confined to the town's covered marketplace, the event has grown to spread along the main street and down side streets. A few vendors in the covered market stay open all week, but you won't find the variety, crowds, excitement or festive atmosphere that prevails on Sundays.

> ### ❖ SHOPPING AT THE MARKET
>
> A vast array of items includes finely stitched *molas* hawked by traditionally dressed Kuna women; Ngöbe-Buglé soapstone and wood **carvings**, and lovely chacara **bags**; exquisite Emberá **baskets**; appealing little painted clay **figurines** depicting traditional scenes; reproduction pre-Columbian **pottery** painted boldly in red, black, green and cobalt geometric designs; bamboo **birdcages**, clever wooden **plant stands**, **birds** of carved and painted wood, and "**Panamá**" **hats** made in Ecuador. Beautiful hand-carved hardwood **serving trays** are either highly polished or painted in the bright colors in the style called "batea." The latter, especially if painted by a well-known artist, are rare and highly desirable.

COCLE PROVINCE

The **Panamá Explorer Club** (PEX) offers a fascinating behind-the-scenes tour that takes you to meet rural artisans at work in their homes and workshops. Contact PEX at ☎ 507-215-2330 in Panamá City; ☎ 507-983-6939 in El Valle.

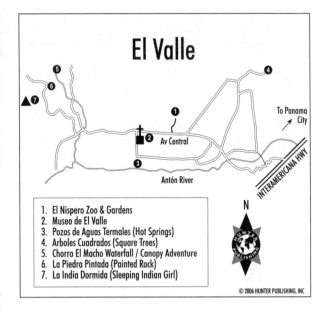

1. El Nispero Zoo & Gardens
2. Museo de El Valle
3. Pozos de Aguas Termales (Hot Springs)
4. Arboles Cuadrados (Square Trees)
5. Chorro El Macho Waterfall / Canopy Adventure
6. La Piedra Pintada (Painted Rock)
7. La India Dormida (Sleeping Indian Girl)

© 2006 HUNTER PUBLISHING, INC

◆ La Piedra Pintada (Painted Rock)

Indigenous people that lived in this valley long ago – no one knows for sure how long ago – carved curving lines, circles and geometric shapes into the rocks. One of the rocks, a massive boulder called La Piedra Pintada, is in a lovely forest setting beside a cascading stream. There is a parking area nearby and usually a few Guaymí or Cholo kids wait here to serve as guides. Pick one of the kids and, for about $1, he or she will lead along the rocky forest path to the rock. Once there, your little guide, using a long stick as a pointer, will explain the carved squiggles. The explanations are fanciful and varied, but since archaeologists haven't deciphered these markings, the kids' stories are as good as any. I'd like to think the information had passed down through the generations to them– but perhaps that's a tad too fanciful. Best to consider it entertainment.

To get here, head northwest from the market on Central Av and turn right after the bridge, then left at the next crossroad. A few cars have been broken into here, so if driving, hire a second kid to watch your wheels. Pay your "guard" the same as your "guide." From the market, take any bus marked "Pintada." The fare is 35 cents. Should you prefer to walk, it will take a little more than a half-hour each way from the town center.

◆ El Nispero Zoo & Gardens

Privately owned El Nispero's beautifully landscaped grounds, glorious flowers and shady pathways aren't enough to detract from the pitifully small cages in which some of this zoo's animals are confined. If you want to see the orchids, and it's your only chance to get a look at golden frogs (these guys have ample quarters), go ahead and pay the $2 entrance fee. It's open from 7 am until 5 pm daily. El Nispero is less than one mile/1.6 kilometers from the town center. To get here, walk or drive west from the market on Av Central and stay to the left when the road forks. Continue on the left fork until you come to the zoo and gardens on the right. A taxi from the market will cost about $1.50 each way.

◆ Museo de El Valle

This charming little museum, owned and maintained by the town's Catholic church, started with historic and religious items donated by townspeople, and with pottery shards discovered by the parish priest during his hikes around the countryside. The collection has grown to include religious art, traditional antiques, original polleras made of fine bark cloth, and a few good pre-Columbian vessels. A lot of hard work and love went into the displays, one of which traces El Valle's geological history. The museum's 25¢ entrance fee is a bargain, but it's open only from 10 am until 2 pm on Saturdays and Sundays. You'll find it behind the Church on Av Central, the main street.

◆ Pozos de Aguas Termales (Hot Springs)

These thermal springs are a 15-minute walk from town. If you're interested in a soak or the scientific aspect of springs, head west from the market and turn north onto Calle del Macho to the second road to the left (Calle la Pintada) and continue on to the springs. There are several pools here, some attractively shaped like little freeform swimming pools although the murky water doesn't look all that inviting. On weekends it's packed with families and splashing, squealing kids. Included with your 25 cents admission is a truly fascinating 10-minute recitation detailing El Valle's geological history and formation.

COCLE PROVINCE

Adventures

◆ On Foot

Square Trees Trail

The trunks of these odd *arboles* are almost, but not quite perfectly, square – their corners are slightly rounded. If here with a guide, you can be sure he/she will whip out a ruler to prove their "squareness." If *sans* guide or ruler, you can judge just by looking. The **square trees trail** brims with birds in the forest behind Hotel Campestre (see page 155).

El Valle

El Valle's quiet streets and shady rambling lanes invite on-foot explora-tion, as do the many trails radiating from town up into the mountains – they are the "highways" used by local and indigenous people. Kept clear by the foot traffic, these trails invite a leisurely walk, a long hike or a birding adventure. Contact **Panamá Explorer Club**, ☎ 507-215-2330 in Panamá City, ☎ 507-984-6969 in El Valle, www.pexclub.com, for the best guided hikes that include the India Dormida Trail through the rainforest to the top of the El Valle crater and to Cerro Gaital's wind-whipped summit where the views stretch out below as far as the eye can see. Clear moun-tain streams, waterfalls, ancient petroglyphs and burial grounds, and an abandoned sugar mill hidden in the jungle are a few highlights of these hikes that can be enjoyed by those aged six to 60.

❖ LA INDIA DORMIDA (THE LEGEND OF FLOR DE AIRE)

Spend a day or two here and you're sure to hear this soap-opera-sloppy tale at least once, but here it is anyway: Flor de Aire (Air Flower) was the beautiful daughter of the mighty Indian cacique, Urráca. Although many suitors vied for her attentions, she had chosen to marry the young warrior, Yaraby, who loved her with all of his heart. One day, as Flor de Aire walked alone in the forest, she met a handsome conquistador. Their meetings soon became clandestine trysts but after a few weeks, the conquistador told Flor de Aire that his regiment was leaving. She begged him to take her with him but he merely laughed and rode away. Meanwhile, Yaraby had learned of his beloved's betrayal and, with a broken heart, took his own life. Too late, Flor de Aire realized that it was Yaraby she truly loved. Desolated by the pain she had caused, she fled into the mountains and sobbed until she fell asleep. To this very day Flor de Aire's sleeping form is seen as the mountain named *La India Dormida*, the Sleeping Indian Girl.

Chorro El Macho (Canopy Adventure Trails)

The protected area around Chorro El Macho offers an opportunity to see forest wildlife and birds as well as this beautiful cascading waterfall and the clear pool beneath it. Swimming is permitted during weekdays, but not on weekends when the preserve is too crowded. A $2 entrance fee goes to maintain the preserve's trails and pristine cloud forest lands. See *In the Air* below for more information.

> **❖ BIRD-WATCHING**
>
> In this country, there are simply so many spectacular, interesting and unusual avians everywhere one looks, it's impossible not to notice and mention a few. In an hour's walk around El Valle, I saw white-shouldered tanagers, spectacled parrotlets, a black guan, a smoky brown woodpecker, a black-crested jay, social and Panamá flycatchers, scale-crested pygmy tyrants, a blue-crowned motmot and a crested oropendola.

◆ On Wheels

Bikes can be rented by the hour or the day from **Hotel Residencial**, the big yellow building on the right at the town's entrance. You can also rent bicycles from **Hotel Los Capitanes Eco-Resort** (see page 156), and **Park Eden Bed and Breakfast**, ☎ 507-983-6167, offers rental bicycles to guests. Explore beautiful El Valle's peaceful side streets or gear up for some serious mountain biking. Whichever you choose, **Panamá Explorer Club (PEX)**, ☎ 507-214-2330 in Panamá City, ☎ 507-983-6939 in El Valle, uses only the best Alpine mountain bikes. You'll get the rides, the guides, and refreshments for what most places charge just for bikes.

◆ On Water

Rafting the Río Grande, Coclé's longest river – its entire 12.4-mile/20-kilometer length is a single rock bed – is an exhilarating journey that begins in the highlands and ends in the sea. Beginners, bird watchers and nature lovers will want to peacefully raft the Chame River's marshlands through Pacific mangroves rich with local and migratory bird life.

Wet rappelling is fast becoming one of the coolest hot new sports, and sparkling Chorro Escondido (Lost Waterfall) presents an unforgettable challenge.

A Río Farallón **kayak** journey takes you through unusual geological formations and magnificent rainforests filled with exotic wildlife. All of these adventures are available from **Panamá Explorer Club (PEX)**, ☎ 507-214-2330 (Panamá City), ☎ 507-983-6939 (El Valle). Their guides are excellent, itineraries carefully planned, and they'll custom tailor adventures for you as well.

COCLE PROVINCE

Panamá's white-water pioneer, respected **Chiriquí River Rafting**, ☎ 507-720-1505, fax 507-720-1506, www.panama-rafting.com, also offers classes II-III and III-IV runs through awesome Río Grande gorges.

◆ On Horseback

Senor Muñoz rents horses for $3 an hour. He doesn't have a phone, but you'll find him by following the signs to Crater Valley. His establishment is on right side of the road past Crater Valley's driveway. You can't miss the bright blue building with a big horse painted on the front. Most El Valle hotels can arrange horseback adventures with or without a guide.

◆ In the Air

You start this thrilling ride above the rainforest canopy and swoop down through it while securely harnessed to steel cables. The adventure begins with a walk up through pristine cloud forest to your take-off point at the top of a ridge. After you're securely ensconced in a specially designed harness, the decent begins, lasting five stages as you go from one platform to the next. There's time to admire the surrounding forest, orchids and bromeliads while waiting for your guide to arrive and re-harness you for the next descent. Speed is controlled by gently applying hand pressure, so you will need at least average strength in your hands. Keep your eyes peeled for Sam, the resident sloth who will probably be laughing himself silly watching you expend your energy. The view above Chorro el Macho waterfall, 180 ft/54 meters above the valley floor, is the high point of this adrenaline-pumping glide. According to local legend, the pool at the waterfall's base is enchanted, but I've never seen any elves or fairies. Locals, however, do come to swim. The cost for this one-of-a-kind adventure is $40 per person; advance reservations are not required but it is first-come-first served. A good option if you won't be staying overnight in El Valle combines the ride with a day tour from Panamá City that includes transportation, a tour of El Valle's highlights and lunch for $95. Contact **Canopy Adventure**, ☎ 507-264-2720, fax 507-263-2784 in Panamá City or ☎ 507-612-9176 (cell); English and Spanish are spoken, or ☎ 507-983-6547 in El Valle, Spanish only.

Shopping

The handicrafts market isn't the only place to find artesans or souvenirs. **David's Shop** (on the left as you enter the town) has an exceptional inventory of Panamanian handicrafts and folk art, and some from throughout Central America and Ecuador. There are gourmet food items, postcards and T-shirts. Souvenirs, high-quality arts and crafts, and locally made clothing is also available in the row of little shops across from the market.

Where to Stay

Residencial el Valle, Av Central, ☎ 507-983-6536, e-mail residenti-alelvalle@hotmail.com, $, has pleasant, comfortable rooms decorated with lovely handcrafted furniture and artworks. Everything is tasteful and immaculate. The beds are orthopedic quality, and double-paned windows ensure quiet, peaceful rest. Some of the rooms have breezy verandas overlooking the main street. Owner Enrique Tiban speaks perfect English and fairly bursts with information to share. This is an excellent value.

❖ HOTEL PRICING	
Based on double occupancy	
No $	under $20
$	$20 to $39
$$	$40 to $79
$$$	$80 to $124
$$$$	$125 to $199
$$$$$	over $200

   Hotel Don Pepe, ☎ 507-983-6425, $, is right next door to Residencial el Valle and also above an attractive gift shop. Rooms here are similar and equally appealing and the rates are about the same. There's a convenient self-service laundry and the second-floor outdoor veranda in back of the hotel offers magnificent views of Cariguana and El Gaital Mountains. Another good value.

   Restaurante Santa Librada, Av Central, ☎ 507-983-6376, has four dismal rooms with private bath and cold-water showers in back of the restaurant. It's run by a couple of lovely older women. Although the rooms are clean and cheap ($10), they're decidedly unattractive and the beds have seen better days.

   Hotel Campestre, ☎ 507-983-6146 (El Valle), 507-233-4179 (Panamá City), e-mail explorer@sinfo.net, $$. This lovely old hotel, set on the crest of a hill above vast green lawns and spreading shade trees, resembles a grand hunting lodge transported from rural Spain. It was built in 1923 and showing its age until recent renovations brightened up the atmospheric existing rooms and a wing with new rooms was added. An aura of decadent grandeur pervades the cavernous lobby with its stone fireplace large enough to roast a steer. The "square trees" trail begins in the forest in back of the hotel's extensive lawns and freshwater swimming pool. Birding is excellent along this trail and in the Cara Coral hill forests.

   Hotel Rincon Vallero, Via Espave, ☎ 507-983-6175, fax 507-983-6968 (El Valle), or ☎ 507-264-9119 (Panamá City), www.rinconvallero.com, $$-$$$. Flowers and flowering trees of every imaginable color and scent surround this gorgeous one-story hacienda-style hotel. All of its 14 charming rooms and suites are different and all have comfortable beds, private bath, cable TV and air conditioning. There's a magnificent flag-stone-floored honeymoon suite with a sunken stone whirlpool – in a bathroom larger than many hotel rooms I've seen – and unique touches throughout. A sparkling waterfall tumbles into a stream stocked with koi that meanders through the lovely open-air, flagstone-floored lobby and romantic dining rooms. Fish and duck ponds, birdhouses, a children's pool and playground nestle among flowers in the back garden.

Hotel Los Capitanes Eco-Resort, ☎ 507-983-6080, fax 507-983-6505, www.panamainfo.com/loscapitanes, $$. This immaculate resort in a lovely garden setting with fruit and flowering trees is run by a delightful retired sea captain. All of its appealingly decorated large rooms and suites, most in two-story sparkling white roundhouses with red-tile roofs, have comfortable beds and spacious bathrooms, TVs and VCRs. The beautiful suites with charming lofts and balconies are equipped with refrigerators. There are handicap-accessible rooms and public areas. This peaceful haven with stunning mountain views, has a playground and pool for children and a laundry. The restaurant here serves creative, international specialties in a classy, casual atmosphere.

Park Eden Bed & Breakfast, ☎ 507-983-6167 El Valle or 226-8858 Panamá City, www.parkeden.com, $$-$$$. This delightful find offers storybook charm in a park-like setting. There are two lovely suites in the gracious main house, both with refrigerators, microwaves and coffee makers, and a lovely room with a private balcony and coffee maker. Separate from the main house, an enchanting European-style two-story cottage features a fully equipped kitchen, living room with DirecTV and VCR, front porch and private outdoor terrace on the first floor. There are two full bathrooms and each of the two upstairs bedrooms – one with a four-poster queen bed and the other with two twin beds – has its own balcony. All are air conditioned. A simpler, cozy room at the rear of the cottage has bunk beds. The beautiful grounds invite a quiet read, a stroll or bird watching. Delicious full breakfasts are included with all of the rooms.

Crater Valley Adventure Spa, Calle Ranita de Oro, ☎ 507-215-2326, fax 507-215-2319, www.crater-valley.com, $$. Lavish gardens surround this oasis of serenity and its eight luxurious rooms, sprawling outdoor terraces, crystal-blue pools and calming ponds. Everything here is top quality and every huge room is unlike any other. One features a private enclosed outdoor garden, another a charming sitting area. Some open to mountain-view verandas, some have skylights. All are luxuriously appointed with ceiling fans, telephones, oversize bathrooms, pure cotton linens, plump comforters, and louvered native hardwood shutters to let in the refreshing mountain air. Continental breakfasts, included with the room, feature selections of tropical fruits and fresh juices, freshly roasted organic coffee and herbal teas, natural yogurts and cheeses, granolas, homemade fruit preserves, and pan del valle – delicious bread baked in wood-fired ovens unique to this valley. Equally healthful and delicious New Panamanian-style lunches and dinners are reasonably priced, special menus are available upon request, and there is a fully stocked bar and a gift shop. Together with its sister company Panama Explorer Club, Crater Valley combines wellness with natural adventure by offering a full range of spa services from a relaxing massage to yoga classes. This is my absolute favorite place to stay in El Valle.

◆ Camping

Panama Campsites, ☎ 507-236-1261, cell ☎ 507-613-5006, is Panamá's first outfitter to fill the country's need for quality campsites. Their **Cariguana Campsites** ($15) include his and hers bathrooms, hot-water showers, outdoor public grill and campfire areas, and shady *bohios*. If you didn't bring your own tent, you can rent one and an air mattress when you get here. Guides are available and there are rental bicycles and four-wheelers.

Where to Eat

Restaurante Santa Librada, on the main street at the town entrance, offers good typical food at very reasonable prices. Hearty *sancocho* is always available for $2; most other meals are less than $4.

❖ RESTAURANT PRICING
Entrée & non-alcoholic drink
$. . . . . under $5
$$ . . . . $5 to $10
$$$ . . . . $11 to $20
$$$$ . . . . over $21

Restaurante Mar de Plata is in the two-story, Residencial El Valle building on the left as you enter town. It's a cheery place, with handcrafted dining chairs painted bright red and vases of fresh flowers on the lavender table covers. Very good typical fish, beef and chicken dishes are $5-$7. The sancocho is excellent and the *corvina* is fresh and delicious; daily specials are also offered.

Restaurante Don Pepe is at the opposite end of the same building as Mar de Plata, and almost identical to it in décor, with blue-and-white-checked table covers. The menu and prices are similar as well, with typical fish, shellfish, beef and chicken. Ditto on the *comida corriente*.

Hotel and Restaurante Los Capitanes (see details under *Where to Stay*, $$, serves prideful German and local specialties in a lovely round-house restaurant set in beautiful gardens. Crisp linens, comfortable hand-crafted wood and leather chairs, ceiling fans and a wood-burning fireplace add to the welcoming décor. Fine wines and liquors are available but, if the mangoes are ripe, go for a mango shake, maybe with a splash of vodka. Yum.

COCLE PROVINCE

Santa Clara & Farallón

The white-sand beaches of Santa Clara and Farallón lie along the Pacific, just off the InterAmericana (Interamerican Highway). The first one you'll come to is Santa Clara, 68 miles/110 kilometers from the capital and eight miles/11 kilometers southwest of the El Valle turnoff. Prominent signs posted on the highway's south side will direct you to these beach resort areas. Santa Clara's beaches begin 1.1 miles/1.8 kilometers south of the highway. The turnoff to Farallón and Playa Blanca is 170 miles/115 kilometers west of Panamá City. If coming by bus, ask to be dropped at the Santa Clara turnoff, where there are usually taxis waiting. Buses run to Farallón from the InterAmericana turnoff intersection.

Sightseeing & Touring

◆ Antón

West of the turnoff to Farallón, the InterAmericana bends inland to the north, away from the beaches into the beginning of Panamá's cultural heartland. The first town you'll come to along this stretch of highway is Antón – not to be confused with El Valle de Antón – with its center south of the highway.

It's a quaint and quiet place, known best for the riotous **Toro Guapo Festival** ("handsome bull") held every October. If you've plenty of time, it's worth a stop to visit the museum in the town's old cathedral, built in 1692. There's a cross here that was found in the sea in 1711, a few fine *polleras*, historical artworks, Spanish Colonial items and a smattering of pre-Columbian Churu culture artifacts, festival masks and the Toro Guapo costume. The $1 admission is a small price to pay to see the pride on its caretaker's faces.

Adventures

◆ On Water

Balneario Santa Clara, on Santa Clara Beach, ☎ 507-993-2133 rents small boats at very reasonable rates. **Kayak Panamá**, ☎ 507-993-3069, www.kayakpanama.com, specializes in river and ocean kayaking. You can take a day-trip on the Río Chame, Río Santa Maria or along the Pacific, or a longer (and possibly extreme) three- , four- , or six-day adventure all the way to the Caribbean. Owner Dennis Parsick, who's as good as one gets at this, and his experienced guides also teach and coach this exhilarating sport. Take in some breathtaking scenery along the way. You'll see the Kayak Panamá/XS Memories signs on the right-hand side of the highway in Santa Clara.

◆ On Wheels

Cabanas Las Veraneras, ☎ 507-230-1415, on Santa Clara Beach, offers a few sturdy bikes, and **XS Memories** (see next page), which has some excellent bike trails, rents bicycles to guests only.

◆ On Horseback

Balneario Santa Clara, ☎ 507-993-2123, and **Cabañas Las Veraneras** (see *Where to Stay & Eat*, below) will arrange horseback adventures, with or without a guide, along the beach, quiet dirt roads and pathways. This pleasant and inexpensive way to take in some sweeping sea views from the bluffs above Santa Clara beach will run you $2 to $3 an hour.

Where to Stay & Eat

In Antón, two acceptable hotels straddle the InterAmericana. **Pension Panamá** rents rooms with cold-water bathrooms for $10. The more comfortable **Hotel Riviera** has $20 rooms have air conditioning and TV.

XS Memories, Santa Clara, ☎ 507-993-3096, fax 507-993-3069, www.kayakpanama.com, e-mail xsmemories@

❖ HOTEL PRICING	
Based on double occupancy	
No $	under $20
$	$20 to $39
$$	$40 to $79
$$$	$80 to $124
$$$$	$125 to $199
$$$$$	over $200

COCLE PROVINCE

hotmail.com, is Panamá's first and only RV park. It's also the home of **Kayak Panamá**, and the place local expats gather to swap stories with RVers in the sports bar/restaurant or on the shady patio. There are full-service hook-ups for 18 campers, five spotless air-conditioned cabins ($-$$ with one to three double beds), tile floors, and a shady camping area. Sports bars are catching on in Panamá, and the one here, with its giant satellite TV, might have been transplanted from the US. It's a place to watch the game, enjoy a juicy steak or thick burger, and an ice-cold beer. You'll find restful hammocks shaded beneath thatched ranchos, an inviting swimming pool and a small zoo with a few lovingly tended critters. Owners Sheila and Dennis Parsick have thoughtfully created this little piece of paradise to be wheelchair-accessible.

Serendipitous **Cabañas Las Veraneras**, Santa Clara Beach, ☎ 507-230-1415, fax 507-230-5397, $-$$, has second-story thatched-roof bungalows at the edge of sea and cabanas on a bluff above it, all with sweeping views of wide white beach, calm azure waters and small fishing boats bobbing near green offshore islands. Lofts and balconies add a touch of charm to the three rustic cabanas. These favorites are cooled by sea breezes. Similar cabanas with air conditioning and fully equipped outdoor kitchens are set back on the bluff and nine newer ones nestle in a gorgeous garden setting. The bungalow and cabanas accommodate up to five persons, and one less charming little house accommodates up to 10. The two-story bungalows have shared bathroom facilities – all the rest have private baths. Some cabañas have international cable TV and some don't. You'll have to ask. Flaming bougainvillea and tropical greenery drape the open-air, beachfront restaurant that serves good seafood, chicken and beef dishes at surprisingly reasonable prices. The mango shakes are to die for. There's a full bar, live entertainment on weekends and holidays, and a beach barbecue. A lovely new adult swimming pool and one for children, on a terraced hillside above the beach, should be completed when you read this. Whenever possible, the eco-conscious owners used recycled or sustainable natural materials to create this rustic, delightful place.

Las Sirenas Resort, Santa Clara Beach, ☎ 507-253-8771/223-5370, fax 507-263-7860, pesantez@sinfo.net, $$. This lovely resort's six air-conditioned beachfront cabanas with white walls and red Spanish tile roofs connect like townhomes. They're unusually spacious, with fully equipped kitchens, tile floors, a first-floor master bedroom, sitting room with futon, and sleeping lofts. There are hammocks on the shaded verandas, barbecues and shady thatched ranchos on the gorgeous beach. This is beach living at its best. Five more cabanas, one with soaring ceilings that accommodates seven, perch on a terrace above a hillside massed with blooming red bougainvillea. Strolling peacocks and miniature chickens looking more fluffy than feathered complete the picture-postcard scene. The only drawback is that the nearest restaurant is at Cabañas Las Veraneras (above). Transportation to Las Sirenas can be provided from Panamá City's airports or from downtown at additional cost. Ask when making your reservations.

Royal Decameron Costa Blanca y Playa Blanca, Via Principal, Farallón, ☎ 507-214-3535, fax 507-214-3539 (Panamá City), ☎ 507-993-2255, fax 507-993-2415 (Farallón), www.decameron.com. It would take a chapter or more to list the amenities you'll find at this all-inclusive mega-resort on a vast white-sand beach. Exceptionally friendly staff members go out of their way to be helpful. Since the resort first opened two years ago it has received rave reviews. The biggest decision you'll need to make here is whether to swim in the sea, one of the six beachfront pools – two of them for kids – or in one on a terrace above the sea. Very comfortable rooms have gleaming tile floors, either a king or two double beds, matching tropical print drapes and bedspreads, furnished balconies overlooking the sea and lushly landscaped grounds, individually controlled air conditioning, and hair dryers in the large bathrooms.

All meals, snacks, alcoholic and non-alcoholic drinks – even cigarettes – are included. For breakfast, two buffet-style restaurants offer dozens of taste-tempting comestible choices, or have your eggs and omelets whipped up to order. For dinners, choose from Thai, Italian, Japanese, Mediterranean, steak, and seafood specialty restaurants – each with a different décor, atmosphere and menu. Snack bars, open all-day, are sprinkled conveniently throughout the property, and there are beach bars, pool bars and indoor bars that serve generous drinks. Professionally choreographed and screamingly hilarious stage shows take place every night in the outdoor amphitheater. The casino is open day and night and the disco every night.

Golfers, take note – the 18-hole golf course will soon be expanded to 27 holes. Beach chairs and towels and all non-motorized water sports equipment – snorkeling gear, wind sailers, kayaks and paddleboats – are included, and you can rent a fishing boat or banana boat, learn to scuba dive, or, if certified, arrange a scuba adventure. There is a Kids Club with planned activities for children; babysitting service can be provided. The resort offers a variety of off-site tours. To get here, take the left turn after the airfield and drive down the road to the resort. You'll see an **IPAT** office (☎ 507-993-3141) on your right almost immediately past the turn. The resort also arranges transportation from Panamá City and the international airport. Advance reservations are required.

❖ PLAYA BLANCA'S AIRFIELD

A little more than one mile/.62 kilometer past the Santa Clara turnoff, you'll notice a wide open field on the left. During Noriega's time, the Panamá Defense Force's Río Hato military base was located nearby. If you look closely, you'll notice the field is paved down the middle. At precisely 1 am on December 20, 1989, zero hour for the start of "Operation Just Cause," two US F-117 stealth bombers zoomed in and bombed Río Hato. It was the first flight for the swift, black-as-midnight planes that had flown direct from Nevada. The bombs, however, were not intended to strike the barracks filled with sleeping soldiers, but merely to frighten them into surrender. It did. The field is now used occasionally by charter planes. You won't see them from the road, but there are some excruciatingly wealthy homes along beautiful Playa Blanca. One of these was Noriega's vacation home. Its bullet-riddled walls were falling down when I visited, but you might find it still standing down a narrow road to the left of the entrance to Decameron Resort. Plans to tear it down were put on hold when superstitious workmen refused to go near it.

COCLE PROVINCE

◆ Camping

Balneario Santa Clara, Santa Clara Beach, ☎ 507-993-2123, is a bargain for beach lovers. For a $1 admission and $2 a night for the campsite, you can pitch a tent on the gorgeous white-sand beach or back from the sea in a shady spot surrounded with flowers and tropical foliage. Either way, drift off to the sound of waves gently lapping the shore. There are clean bathrooms and showers and a restaurant/bar kiosk next to the beach where you can get a burger and fries, fresh fish, a steak, snacks, beer, wine and mixed drinks. Shady *bohios*, hammocks and beach chairs are available to rent.

Cabañas las Veraneras, ☎ 507-230-1415, offers camping with use of all facilities (see *Where to Stay*, page 160).

Palms and mango trees shade the pleasant campground at **XS Memories**, ☎ 507-993-3096, fax 507-993-3069, about a mile from the beach on the highway's opposite side (see *Where to Stay*, page 159).

Penonomé

Coclé's provincial capital borders the InterAmericana 92 miles/149 km west of Panamá City. Founded in 1581, Penonomé served briefly as the isthmus's capital after Panamá City was sacked and destroyed by Henry Morgan in 1671. Today this bustling commercial town of about 67,000 inhabitants is worth a stopover to visit its small surviving colonial neighborhood, excellent Museum of History and Tradition (Calle Simon Quiroz, $1 entrance fee), artisan's market (Mercado de Artesanías) (to the left of the highway just before the turnoff to downtown Penonomé) and its interesting central market west of the highway. If you would like to stand in Panamá's **exact center**, it's in a clearly marked little kiosk across from the central park on Av Juan Demostenes Arosemena, the city's main street that forks north from the InterAmericana. Although it seems a long way to cart a bunch of rocks, the low fence around the park was built of stones salvaged from the ruins of Panamá la Vieja. If you're wondering why there are so many benches in the park, well, those who donate one get his/her their name carved on it.

Held in March or early April, the city's festive **Carnival Aquatico** begins when the carnival princess and her attendants arrive on a raft floated down nearby River Zaraté.

Penenomé's main bus terminal is on InterAmericana's the south side at the intersection of Av Juan de Arosemena.

Sightseeing & Touring

◆ La Pintada

A smooth blacktop road undulates northwest from Penonomé, through rolling hills and cattle pastures to the little town of La Pintada. The few tourists that make their way here come to buy a *sombrero pintado* – the traditional black and white hat of Panamá – and handicrafts from the **Mercado de Artesanias La Pintada**, the artisans market. You'll find it on Av Central – a continuation of the road from Penonomé – across from the baseball field. Prices for the beautiful, handwoven hats average $75 here; the same hat in a Panamá City shop will cost at least $140. Other handicrafts include brightly colored woven wool rugs, dolls dressed in exquisitely stitched traditional polleras, drums made of wood and hide, baskets, pottery, embroidered *montuño* (men's) shirts, seco bottle covers, palm-frond brooms, local honey and candies, and miniature *sombreros pintados*. The market is open every day until 5 pm.

To promote sustainable tourism locally, La Pintada's mayor and a group of townspeople have initiated natural and cultural adventure opportunities that include trail hiking, horse trekking, mountain biking, visits to ancient petroglyphs and to an artisan town to see the region's famous hats crafted. The group also plans to hack a trail through the jungle foothills of the Cordillera's to remote Farallon Mountain. This sheer rock jutting above the forest canopy is ideal for extreme rappelling. An information kiosk at the town's central park should be built by the time you read this and IPAT, the country's tourism bureau, had promised assistance in training local guides. Whether or not this has all been accomplished, there are knowledgeable locals to provide assistance and services

> **AUTHOR NOTE:** *Rural people from distant mountain areas form processions as early as November to work their way down to La Pintada's central park for its major celebration, the **Festival El Topon**, held every year on December 25th. Some carry statues of saints, others arrive early to visit with friends and pray in the town's lovely old church, Iglesia de la Santisima.*

COCLE PROVINCE

◆ El Pedregosa

This little settlement strewn through mountain forest, 3.75 miles/six km up a steep dirt road from La Pintada, offers a unique cultural adventure and an opportunity to see how Panamá's famed *sombreros pintados* (painted hats) are made. All 35 of the community's families earn their livings as hat makers, and some of the children begin learning the craft when only three or four years old.

Elicerio Soto's lovely family welcomes visitors and gladly demonstrates the painstaking process that results in one of these beautiful black and white hats. Elicerio's mother, Maria Liboria, will show you their outdoor kitchen with an ancient clay stove (called a *fogon*) on which the plant fibers used in the hats — and the family's meals – are prepared. The Sotos occasionally have available for purchase one or two of these hats that will last a lifetime. If so, this is the best place to buy yours. These hardworking people earn an average of $80 for each hat, a little more for the fanciest. The Sotos speak only Spanish, so if you don't, it's best to visit with a guide. Bilingual **Juan Cedao** can provide one or take you there himself. You'll find Juan at La Quinta Bed and Breakfast, facing the park on the corner of Central Av and Calle 5.

If driving yourself, turn east onto the dirt road from Central Av in La Pintada and continue up into the mountains. You'll need four-wheel-drive. Or you can take a *collectivo* – usually a 4X4 pick-up – from Av Central. The fare is 35 cents each way. The Sotos had not yet set a fee for their time and courtesy when I visited, but the stop might now be included in a local cultural tour. In either case, please leave a few dollars tip.

❖ SOMBREROS PINTADOS

Two fibers, called junco and chisna, obtained from a plant called bellota, are used to make the beautiful black and white sombreros pintados. The first steps in the long process are to locate the bellota plants, cut their leaves and strip them of the fibers. The long fibers are boiled together until pliable and then left to dry in the sun until bleached white. To make black fibers, the junco and chisna are boiled with a few handfuls of dirt until they are a reddish color that will turn black when dried. When completely dry, the thin fibers are braided into strips of white and black. Finally, the braided fibers are woven together to make the design and shaped around a hat form. One person working alone can make an "average" pintado in about four weeks; a hat with a more complicated design might take three or four people as long as three weeks to complete. If buying one, first do the math and please don't haggle about the price.

AUTHOR NOTE: *The most intricately designed sombrero pintado that costs $80 when bought from its maker in El Pedrigosa will sell for $300 in Panamá City.*

◆ El Caño Archaeological Site & Museum

Records indicate that when the Spanish arrived in the early 1500s, between 20,000 and 40,000 indigenous people occupied this region. El Caño, Panamá's best archaeological site that is open to the public, can be explored in an hour or so. Its fine small museum features pottery displays, stone tools and carvings, unearthed burials and other artifacts, along with explanations and descriptions. Pictorial recreations show how the site looked in its heyday. A ceremonial center and burial ground from about 500 until 1500 AD, El Caño's 19.75-acre/eight-hectare grounds contain a dozen burial mounds, an excavated burial pit with skeletons in situ, and rows of baffling stone stelae that had once been topped with carvings. It's unclear as to when the carvings were removed, although unauthorized excavations were carried out here in 1924 and 1925.

None of the several classes of people interred here is thought to have been royalty. The different types of burials include skeletons found folded individually into large earthenware jars, others tossed together like heaps of chicken bones, some with missing skulls, and those thought to be of higher classes are stretched out in natural poses. Most of the burial mounds have not been excavated, but agate jewelry and 270 pieces of earthenware pottery were discovered in one excavated in 1975-1979 by a team supervised by Panamá's first woman archaeologist, Reina Torres de Araúz. The capital's National Archaeology Museum is named for this extraordinary woman.

To get here from the InterAmericana, take the sign-posted turnoff 19 miles/27 km west of Penonomé. At a second sign, bear to left and continue on the good dirt road another 1.9 miles/three km to the site. Admission is $1 for adults and 25 cents for children.

◆ Natá

Natá de los Caballeros was built on the site of an Indian village governed by a powerful cacique named Natá. In 1517, after Natá's defeat, Gaspar de Espinosa founded the town as an outpost settlement to pursue París, another of the great caciques, and to forge territories further west. The town's first settlers were conquistadors who agreed to remain after Pedrarias divided among them the town, the lands around it and the defeated Indians as slaves. Despite its awful history, much of Natá's lovely colonial architecture and its exquisite church have been well preserved.

Basilica Menor Santiago Apostal de Natá, founded May 20, 1522, is the oldest church still in use anywhere in the Americas. Although recently restored, only its choir platform, a few wooden supports and the interior ceiling are reproductions – everything else, including the beautiful altars and artworks, are original. If familiar with Mesoamerica's mythical feathered serpents, you'll immediately notice the two that jut from between the flowers and fruits of the Altar of the Virgin's carved columns. Look closely at the little faces (and unhappy expressions) of the cherubs – they are definitely Indian, an indication that the altar was carved by slaves. The angels carved at its base are another uncommon feature. During the restoration, the remains of three people were discovered buried under the floor to the right of the altar. There is nothing to indicate who they might have been or when they were placed there. More are believed to be interred here but no one knows for sure. One of the tunnels found under the church floor runs to the nearby *cabildo* (government house), but others have collapsed and it isn't known where they might have led. This wonderful church guards many ancient mysteries.

COCLE PROVINCE

To get here, take the Natá turnoff from the InterAmericana, 4.5 miles/seven km west of El Caño and 19.2 miles/31 km west of Penonomé.

◆ Aguadulce

West of Natá, the highway curves back toward the coast and the landscape becomes flatter and drier. The next town you'll come to is Aguadulce, named, according to legend, by thirsty conquistadors when they discovered freshwater wells here. Aguadulce is known as the "town of salt and sugar," but, when it doesn't rain for a while, the most noticeable feature is the dust that settles onto and into everything.

Commercial Aguadulce doesn't offer much for tourists other than its fine **Museum of Sugar and Salt**, ☎ 507-997-4280, in front of 19 October Park. The museum's small rooms are called salons, and several are dedicated to exhibits of Panamá's pre-Columbian people, the civil war with Colombia, and historical displays of salt and sugar production. Sugar is still produced here – you'll see fields and fields of sugarcane growing in the countryside – but salt is no longer produced commercially. Shrimp, however, are cultivated on a grand scale.

Adventures

◆ On Foot & On Wheels

La Pintada

Four good hiking trails, some suitable for mountain biking, radiate from La Pintada into the surrounding forests and mountains. If there's no kiosk at the park, walk over to La Quinta Bed and Breakfast on the west side of the park (see page 170), and ask Juan Cedaño to point you in the right direction. Juan rents mountain bikes for $3 a day and can arrange for you to rent a horse and/or a guide. An hour's walk or ride up hilly dirt roads will take you to a cow pasture filled with ancient **petroglyphs** carved into flat volcanic rocks, and you can visit the nearby iguana farm to observe the mini-dinosaurs.

◆ El Copé

The full name of this lush park is Parque General de Division Omar Torrijos Herrera, but it's most often called simply El Copé, after a tree that grows abundantly here and for a local village of the same name. Torrijos adopted the village and provided much assistance to its residents. Sadly, but fittingly, Torrijos died when his small plane crashed into a remote mountainside here. The park's magnificent 62,419-acre/25,275-hectare wilderness begins in the Cordillera Central of Coclé and spreads over the continental divide before spilling down through Colón Province all the way to the Caribbean. From the lookout at its visitor center 4,756 feet/1,450 meters above sea level, it's possible on a clear day to see both the Caribbean and the Pacific oceans. Rainfall is heavy, with most precipitation on the Caribbean side. The jungles never dry completely and hot, humid days combined with chilly nights produce frequent fog and mists. El Copé's pristine primary forests consist of four biological zones that harbor a wealth of flora and fauna, including all five of Panamá's cat species, white and collared peccaries, whitetail deer and tapirs. Among its 2,604 identified plant species are 375 orchids, and a staggering variety of ferns, epiphytes, heliconias and bromeliads. The country's largest numbers of rare golden frogs are among the 135 frog species, and rare avians include bare-necked umbrella birds, red-fronted parrotlets, golden-olive woodpeckers and several endemic hummingbird species. Four well-defined trails of varying length and difficulty start from the visitor center. The shortest and easiest Interpretive Trail can be covered in an hour, and the longest trek will take you through the mountains over the continental divide and all the way down to the Caribbean.

Since few visitors are willing to brave the abominable road to the park, its new Alto del Calvario Visitor Center with glass viewing walls and sophisticated, informative displays is an unexpected surprise. There is always a naturalist guide on hand to provide information (though usually only in Spanish). If you want to overnight, camping is permitted but a better choice is the newly remodeled cabin. Equipped with a full kitchen and bath, sitting and dining area, it will sleep up to 12 persons in two sets of bunk beds downstairs and in sleeping bags in the loft. The park entrance fee is $3 (paid at the ranger station on the left as you enter the park). Add $5 if you plan to camp or stay in the cabin. In either case, you'll need to bring your own food and bedding. Trails are open 8 am to 4 pm, and the visitor center from 8 am to 5 pm, seven days a week.

The El Copé turnoff from the InterAmericana is on the right 12.5 miles/ 20 km west of Penonomé. Watch for the sign next to the Accel gas station in La Candelaria village. The road is paved for the first 20 miles/33 km, but dissolves to dirt (or mud), worsening steadily as it inclines steeply into the mountains. You'll need a 4X4 vehicle at any time of year; the road can become impassible when rains are heavy. If coming by bus, transfer in El Copé village to one bound for Barregon and ride to the end of the road. You can hike the rest of the way up the mountain – it takes about an hour – or call ahead to the Navas family (☎ 507-983-9130) to arrange a 4X4 lift from the bus turnaround. The Navases also rent horses for about $3 an hour. To check on weather or road conditions beforehand, call the park ranger station, ☎ 507-997-4562. Additional information is available from the National Parks Office, ☎ 507-997-9086 in Coclé, or from ANAM, ☎ 507-997-7538. ANAM also provides excellent guides (Spanish-speaking only) for about $8 per day.

Where to Stay & Eat

◆ In Penonomé

Pension Los Pinos, on the InterAmericana, ☎ 507-997-9518, has small rooms with air conditioning and TV for $10, and there's a laundry on the premises.

The 40 rooms at **Hotel Dos Continentes**, InterAmericana, ☎ 507-997-9325, fax 507-997-9390 $-$$, offer comfortable beds, air conditioning, cable TV, and telephones.

A best bet is **Hotel Las Fuentes**, InterAmericana, ☎ 507-991-0508, $, the first hotel on the right as you enter Penonomé. Its spotless, quiet rooms, set back from the public areas and the highway, have comfortable beds, A/C and cable TV; four are equipped with Jacuzzis. The restaurant serves very good local and international food. The $2.25 featured lunch special changes daily and might include a roast beef, pork or chicken entrée with salad, vegetable, rice and drink. There is also a pleasant bar/lounge.

Parillada El Gigante, on the north side of the highway, just west of the Esso gas station, serves huge and delicious portions of typical food, pizzas, and a few Middle-Eastern specialties like falafel, lamb shanks and tabouli. Prices are very reasonable and the waitresses just can't seem to do enough to make you feel welcome.

You'll find good, inexpensive typical food at nearby cafeteria-style **Restaurante Las Tinajas.** The more expensive restaurant at **Dos Continente** is popular with the local business community.

◆ Outside the City

Albergue Ecológica la Iguana (Iguana Ecolodge), Churuquita Grande, ☎ 507-983-8056, or 507-224-9737 in Panamá City, $. Perfect for outdoorsy types who enjoy country walks and communing with nature, this lovely place in the Cordillera foothills has trails through semi-deciduous forests and reforested areas. One trail ends at a stone stairway leading down to the river for swimming or quiet contemplation while listening to the waterfall or watching for birds. Pre-Columbian motifs highlight the attractive public areas and airy, quiet rooms (some with lofts) with comfortable beds that are set apart in the forest. Very good international or typical-style meals, prepared with fresh, natural ingredients, are served in a lovely thatch-roof circular restaurant or the stone-paved outdoor dining terrace. But most appealing are the crystal-clear circular swimming pools set deep in a shady forest glade. Children are welcomed and La Iguana's charming owner will provide a nature or birding guide, a horseback trek or you can wander the forests on your own.

The ecolodge is nine miles/14 km northeast of Penonomé. To get here from the InterAmericana, turn north (right as you head west) onto the road immediately past Hotel Dos Continentes. Travel two blocks and turn right again onto the road to Churuquita Grande. If coming by bus, take one headed to either Chruquita Grande or Chiguiri Arriba from the Penonomé station and ask the driver to let you off at the lodge. The bus fare is 75 cents.

La Posada del Cerro la Vieja/Trinidad Lodge and Spa, Chiguiri Arriba, ☎ 507-983-8900, 507-264-5378 in Panamá City, www.posadaecologica.com, or Ecocuircitos, ☎ 507-314-1586, or 708-810-9350 US fax, annie@ecocircuitos.com. This magical mountain retreat lies in its own 660 acres/227 hectares of forests, high in the Cordillera Central. The main lodge, rooms and cabins – 23 at last count – are set in gardens awash with flowers and fruit, birds and butterflies. Wreathed in morning mists, the dramatic jagged peak of rugged Cerro la Vieja (Old Lady Mountain) rises from the nearby forest to provide a breathtaking backdrop. With its beautiful forests, abundant birds and wildlife, ancient petroglyphs, streams and waterfalls – including 100-ft/ 30-meter La Tavidá falls with an icy-cold pool at its base – and little communities of friendly locals, this region is a wanderer's delight. The lodge can provide a guide and arrange a horse trek with or without one.

Accommodations include rooms in the main lodge and separate cabins simply furnished in tasteful country style with comfortable beds, hot water bathrooms, a desk and good reading lamps. With sliding glass doors that open to balconies on two sides, the upper rooms of the two-story cabins called Chicibali and El Turega offer the best views of Cerro La Vieja. The delicious meals are prepared with only fresh, organic products and when served with a fine wine… ahhhh. There is a small bar and the restaurant's windowed walls open to fresh mountain breezes, views of Cerro La Vieja and, after the splendid sunsets, a chorus of singing lizards. If there is Heaven on Earth, this may be it.

Seven varieties of clay and mud found on the property contain high concentrations of minerals, including the copper touted by exclusive cosmetics firms as an ingredient in their skin care products. The muds and clays are mixed with organic herbs grown on the property and applied for therapeutic and beauty purposes. During my last visit, the full Trinidad Spa and a freshwater swimming pool were still under construction. Now complete, they are a wonderful bonus.

From the InterAmericana, take the first right immediately past Hotel Dos Continentes in Penonomé (94 miles/151 km west of Panamá City). Turn right again after two blocks at the sign pointing to Churuquita Grande and Chiguiri Arriba. The road is paved part of the way before becoming steep and rugged as you drive higher into the mountains. The lodge is 18 miles/28 km from the Penonomé turnoff. During the rainy season, you

COCLE PROVINCE

will need a high clearance 4X4 vehicle. If coming by bus, take one marked Chiguiri Arriba from the Penonomé station. The fare is $1.50.

◆ Aguadulce

Hotel Sarita, Calle José Maria Calvo and Pablo Arosemena, ☎ 507-997-4437, $, a simple friendly place with air conditioning, and **Hotel Interamericano**, on the InterAmericana Highway, ☎ 507-997-4363, $, with cable TV, pool, gym and the works. There is no restaurant at Hotel Sarita but, three doors down, on the same block, a tiny local eatery serves huge typical breakfasts and lunches for $1.75 to $2.

Hotel Interamericano's restaurant specializes in jumbo local shrimp (about $8) prepared in a variety of different ways, and they also have very good beef dishes. It's currently Aguadulce's most popular place for lunch, offering a complete meal for $2.50.

The large indoor/outdoor restaurant at **Turiscentro El Gallo** also specializes in seafood, most notably a heaping plate of succulent garlic shrimp. Order *concha negra* if you're feeling adventurous and like shellfish. Chicken and beef dishes as well as hamburgers and pizza are available. Lunches cost $2 to $4; dinners $4 to $8.

◆ La Pintada

When last I visited, there was only one place to stay in La Pintada, but more B&Bs and guesthouses were expected to open. Facing the park on the corner of Av Central and Calle 5, Juan and Meri Cedaño's home, **La Quinta Bed and Breakfast**, ☎ 507-983-0289, funsalap@cwp.net.pa, $12 single, $15 double, has two comfortable rooms, one with a double bed and one with two twins. There is a pleasant garden-view lounge with cable TV, stereo, VCR, movies, magazines and books. Juan speaks perfect English and Spanish, arranges or guides sightseeing excursions and serves as the town's unofficial greeter. You'll find a couple of inexpensive small and similar restaurants along Central Av, and more choices in Penonomé, less than eight miles/12 km away.

Azuero Peninsula

The central provinces of **Herrera** and **Los Santos** and a strip of **Veraguas** lie on the Azuero Peninsula, which juts into the Pacific south of Coclé and Herrera. For the sake of continuity, only Herrera and Los Santos are covered in this chapter. The little strip of Veraguas is covered in the next chapter, along with the rest of that province.

Called "Cuña del Folkloric Traditions" (Cradle of Folkloric Traditions), the peninsula is small, only 55 miles/90

kilometers long by 60 miles/100 kilometers wide, and is famed for its many spirited festivals and traditional religious celebrations – some dating from medieval Spain. Panamá's beautiful national women's dress, *la pollera*, and its "typical" music are said to have originated here, where musical instruments and *polleras* are still made painstakingly by hand.

Modernization came late to the Azuero, and today it's an appealing, oxymoronic blend of the old and the new. Typical music, more popular than salsa, rock or pop, plays on the radio, echoing the sounds of the *repicador*, *mejorana*, and the *tambores*. Cowboys on horseback round up cattle, oxen-powered plows till rural fields, but soccer moms drive SUVs.

> ### ❖ MEJORANA
>
> The **mejorana** is a traditional four-stringed musical instrument, similar to a guitar. **Cajas**, **repicadors** and **pujas** are three different types of **tambores** (drums). All three are made of wood and hide, and each has a different sound.

Less appealing, however, is the land devastation caused by deforestation and slash-and-burn farming. The **Arco Seco** (dry arch) climate stretches from Panamá Province westward along the Pacific and extends down the semi-arid peninsula's agricultural landscape of grassy rolling hills, vast fields of sugarcane, and cattle pastures. It seldom rains from December to the end of May. How dry is it? I stopped to ask a farmer who was lugging pails of water from a nearby creek to pour onto his cornfield. He said he hadn't seen a drop of rain in more than five months.

> **AUTHOR NOTE:** *In the Central Provinces, a* **junta de embarra** *is a gathering of friends and neighbors that work together to build a house, a barn, or bring in a harvest. Junta means "to work," and* embarra *to "cover with mud."*

Heavily populated since prehistoric times, this is the country's richest archaeological region. Excavations have yielded remains more than 11,000 years old, the earliest yet found in Central America. Some of the recovered pottery, gold effigies, tools and other artifacts are on display in the fine Museum of Herrera (see page 175) in **Chitré**, the peninsula's largest city. Ceramics first appeared on the peninsula about 3,000 years ago, and today's Azuero artisans re-create these ancient styles along with pottery to suit more modern tastes.

Charming colonial villages, perfectly preserved 17th- and 18th-century churches, wildlife reserves, mangrove sanctuaries, excellent museums, and the country's only desert are a few of the attractions you'll find in this historic region, where folktales pass down through generations and ancient superstitions are still regarded as gospel. For a fascinating glimpse into the true soul of Panamá, be sure to visit Herrera and Los Santos.

History

Indigenous people who had lived on the peninsula for thousands of years were organized into chiefdoms led by powerful *caciques* when conquistadors led by Gaspar de Espinosa and Gonzalo de Badajoz arrived early in the 16th century. The chiefdoms met the Spanish with armed resistance that lasted several years until the defeat of the great *cacique* Antatara. One by one, the others fell to the Spaniards' superior forces. Those who survived and managed to escape capture into slavery retreated into the mountains. After stripping the region of its wealth and its people, the Spanish retreated to conquer new territories elsewhere. As was customary at the time, many of the Azuero's Spanish towns and villages were named for the defeated *caciques* who had ruled here.

❖   **LOCAL LORE: "THE SILAMPA"**

A beautiful child named Tepesa lived in the Central Provinces during colonial times. Tepesa loved to sing and dance but most of all she loved parties. When she was of age, her father arranged her marriage to one of his friends – a man as old as himself – hoping it would calm her and keep her at home. It did nothing of the sort – her elderly husband was a merchant who traveled, and whenever he was away Tepesa behaved with wanton abandon. Rumors condemning her virtue swept through the village.

Hoping to restore the family's honor after the embarrassment of hearing her grandchildren called bastards, Tepesa's mother came to stay and keep her at home when her husband was away. This worked for a time, until Tepesa heard about a fiesta on the other side of the mountains and couldn't resist. She prepared to leave even as her mother protested and her baby wailed. Nothing would stop her, not even her mother's anguished curse, "Damn you. I hope you die for what you are doing to your children. I hope your horse falls on you but if you live, you will live miserable in the ground. From this night you will drag yourself, forever looking for your children. You will be so disgustingly horrible that no one will help you or even look at you." Tepesa laughed and went anyway. As she rode home from the party, her horse stumbled and fell in the middle of a forest, breaking her back. She dragged herself to a cave, where she lived like a wild animal, changed from a beautiful girl into a horrible, misshapen creature – a half-human monster called a *silampa*.

True to her mother's curse, the *silampa* lives on, and every night her baby's cries draw her from the cave to search for her lost children. Of course she can't find them; they lived centuries ago. And so she steals other children. No one has seen her for many years, but she is often heard scratching the walls of village houses, wailing pitifully, "Me pesa, Me pesa" (I'm sorry, I'm sorry).

AUTHOR NOTE: *Babies were often dressed in red during colonial times to protect them from the* **Mal de Ojo** *(Evil Eye).*

Getting Here

◆ By Car

Chitré, Herrera's provincial capital, is the peninsula's largest city and commercial hub. It's a 3½- to four-hour drive from Panamá City (157 miles/242 kilometers) via the **InterAmericana Highway** and the **Carretera** Nacional (National Highway). Many of the peninsula's attractions are nearby, making it a good base for exploring, as most of the peninsula's attractions can be visited from there as day-trips.

The Carretera Nacional forks southeast off the InterAmericana at the hamlet of **Divisa**, 133 miles/215 kilometers west of Panamá City, and continues southeast down the Peninsula – with typical Panamanian name changes along the way – linking most principal towns and villages. You can't miss the fork in Divisa, just before a huge Delta gas station, and prominent, clearly marked signs point the way to Chitré, 24 miles/38 kilometers south.

◆ By Bus

The bus fare from Panamá City to Chitré is about $7. Once you've arrived, it's relatively easy to get around, as buses run here, there and everywhere on the peninsula, and the Carretera Nacional passes through most of the towns and villages.

AZUERO PENINSULA

◆ By Air

Chitré has the peninsula's only commercial airport. **Aeroperlas**, ☎ 507-315-7500 in Panamá City, 507-996-4021 in Chitré, www.aeroperlas.com, offers a morning flight from Panamá City's Marcos A. Gelabart (Albrook) domestic airport every day of the week, and an afternoon flight every day except Sunday. Airfare each way is about $37.

If you arrive by air and want to rent a car, there is a **Thrifty Car Rental**, ☎ 507-996-9565 in Chitré, 507-264-2613 in Panamá City, near the Chitré airport on Paseo Enrique Geenzier – as the Carretera Nacional is called when it runs through the city.

Getting Around

Taxis are plentiful on Chitré's main streets, and in-town fares are only a dollar or two. You can also hire a taxi to take you to nearby attractions that are not served by local buses. Note, however, that the chance of finding a driver who speaks anything other than Spanish is slim to none.

Herrera Province

This smallest of Panamá's provinces – and its most densely populated – lies at the top of the Azuero Peninsula, bordered by the provinces of Coclé on the northeast, Veraguas to the west and northwest and Los Santos to the south. Many of the province's finest attractions are along or nearby the Carretera Nacional. Be sure to visit **Sarigua National Park**, the artisan town of **La Arena**, **Playa El Aguillito's** hordes of migrating birds, the mysterious crater-like springs of **Los Pozos**, and the **Refugio de Vida Silveste Cenegon del Mangle**, a mangrove refuge with thousands of nesting herons.

Herrera's capital, **Chitré**, is the Azuero's largest city, with a population fast approaching 50,000, and its plentiful hotels, restaurants, banks and services make it a good base for exploring the peninsula's towns and nature sites. Tourism has barely touched the Azuero, and its people are some of the world's friendliest. However, few speak anything but Spanish.

The **IPAT office**, ☎ 507-966-8040, in nearby Los Santos opposite Simón Bolívar Park, can provide information and, since they see so few visitors, you'll be doing them a favor to stop by.

Other than the cathedral and museum, about all that's interesting in the city is the bargain shopping. This stuff isn't Tommy Hilfiger or Ralph Lauren, but it is cheap. And there are plenty of places to stay unless there's a festival somewhere in the area. If that's the case, there won't be an available room anywhere. Reservations for festival times are booked months and sometimes a year or more in advance.

> **LOCAL LORE:** *According to legend, Herrera's people descended from the passengers and crew of a Spanish ship that foundered on the shore centuries ago. Colonial culture is deeply rooted in these people, who have fair complexions, blue and hazel eyes, and light brown or blonde hair, some of whom eventually intermarried with African and Indigenous peoples. Their combined backgrounds produced Panamá's traditional culture.*

Sightseeing & Touring

◆ Chitré

Museo de Herrera (Herrera Museum)

The lovely old building housing this fascinating anthropology and natural history museum has recently undergone a much-needed interior face-lift – one that included new air-conditioning units. This excellent museum contains a fine collection of pre-Columbian artifacts and pottery dating from 5000 BC; much of it was collected and later donated to the museum by a local resident and amateur archaeologist. There are exquisitely detailed Monagrillo and Macaracas culture ceramics, collections of prehistoric remains from Sarigua (see below) and a life-size replica of *cacique* Parita's burial in 1517, complete with gold effigies known as *huacas* (the *huacas* on display here are replicas). There's an ecological display, a lovely exhibit of authentic folkloric costumes, religious artifacts and much, much more. This excellent museum, ☎ 507-996-0077, is a must-see. It's on Chitré's main street, Manuel Maria Correa, at the corner of Av Julio Arjona. Hours are 9 am until noon and 1pm until 4 pm, Tuesday through Saturday, and 9 am until noon on Sunday. Admission is $1 for adults, 25¢ for children 12 and under.

Iglesia San Juan Bautista (Saint John the Baptist Church)

Magnificent stained-glass windows highlight the elegant simplicity of this 18th-century church's interior. The ceilings are of gleaming teak and its walls are lined with statues of saints. It's at Union Park, the city's central square.

AZUERO PENINSULA

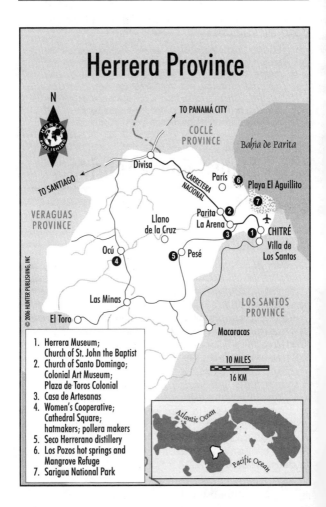

Herrera Province

N

TO PANAMÁ CITY

COCLÉ
PROVINCE

Bahía de Parita

Divisa

TO SANTIAGO

CARRETERA
NACIONAL

París 6 Playa El Aguillito

VERAGUAS
PROVINCE

Parita 2
La Arena 7
3
1 CHITRÉ

Llano
de la Cruz

Villa de
Los Santos

Ocú 4

5 Pesé

LOS SANTOS
PROVINCE

Las Minas

El Toro

Macaracas

© 2006 HUNTER PUBLISHING, INC

1. Herrera Museum;
   Church of St. John the Baptist
2. Church of Santo Domingo;
   Colonial Art Museum;
   Plaza de Toros Colonial
3. Casa de Artesanas
4. Women's Cooperative;
   Cathedral Square;
   hatmakers; pollera makers
5. Seco Herrerano distillery
6. Los Pozos hot springs and
   Mangrove Refuge
7. Sarigua National Park

10 MILES
16 KM

Atlantic Ocean

Pacific Ocean

◆ Parita

Parita is six miles/10 kilometers northwest of Chitré, just off the Carretera Nacional. If coming by bus from Chitré, the fare is 50¢. There are no accommodations for visitors, but it's an easy day-trip from Chitré.

Colonial Parita's main attraction is its 18th-century church, **Iglesia de Santo Domingo de Guzmán**, and the **Colonial Art Museum** housed in its chapel. This is the country's only church with a bell tower directly over the front door. Its lovely baroque wooden altars and sculptures, elaborately carved with flowers and fruit, survive from the 18th century. The serpents carved into the church's central altar indicate that it was made by indigenous artisans. The museum's fine collection of 17th- and 18th-century artifacts include woodcarvings, elaborate silver candelabra and a lovely statue of the Madonna.

In colonial times, bloody bullfights were once held in the **Plaza de Toros Colonial**, a wide, open field next to the church. Bullfights are still held here today, but now the bulls are only heckled and no blood is shed. Across from the plaza, the row of original 18th-century colonial apartments with wide front verandas were used for viewing the event. Today they're owned mostly by wealthy Panamanians who visit only during Carnaval or other major celebrations. It's worth a stroll around this little town to see its many other equally old, lovingly kept homes.

❖ THE MASKMAKER

Darido Lopez began making **folkloric festival masks** and satin *diáblicos sucios* costumes when he was a child, and passed the art to his nine children. They're young adults now, with other occupations, and some have children of their own, yet all nine continue to make these traditional fantasies. Darido has become so well known that most of his masks are now exported and sold in exclusive shops. You can visit him to see works in progress and perhaps buy one of these wonderful creations. His house is on the Carretera Nacional in Parita, just beyond the gas station on the opposite side of the road. Look for the sign in front.

◆ La Arena

La Arena is on the Carretera Nacional, 3.75 miles/six kilometers northeast of Chitré. You can take a taxi here from Union Park (Chitré's central park) for $2. By bus, the ride takes less than 10 minutes and costs 25¢. There are no hotels in this little "suburban" village.

Dizzying displays of **handcrafted pottery** spill from tiny shops onto even tinier front yards in this little artisan town. La Arena is famed throughout the country for pottery that has been made in the same way for centuries. Look for exquisite reproduction glazed and painted pre-Columbian earthenware that stands out among cavorting green iguanas and bright red parrots made of clay.

Painted carnival masks and serving trays, handcrafted wood and leather furniture, embroidered lace napkins and tablecloths are only a few of the items for sale in the **Casa de Artesanias**, the large white building on the corner past the clustering shops. Visitors are welcome to watch potters and leather crafters at work. The little restaurant across the street is a good place for a quick lunch or dinner. Complete meals run about $2 and a cup of coffee is 25¢.

AZUERO PENINSULA

AUTHOR NOTE: *There's an excellent bakery squeezed in between the pottery shops where you can buy delicious* **chicheme**, *a hearty drink made from toasted ground corn, milk, sugar and cinnamon, by the gallon.*

◆ Ocú

Ocu's large **cathedral** faces the square in the center of this little town. After church on Sundays, the square becomes an event packed with farmers and townspeople who gather to socialize. One Sunday, gracious Matty Nunez materialized from the crowd, introduced herself and offered to share with me information and a tour of her lovely Spanish colonial home. Matty is the town's unofficial historian and a treasure trove of fact and folklore. She told me "Panamá's First Cry of Independence" had actually issued from Ocú, rather than Los Santos as the history books claim, adding, "Here they screamed, but nobody listened." Built around a central courtyard, Matty's home has huge rooms and the soaring ceilings typical to the Azuero. She's been thinking about converting an unused wing of the house into guest quarters since there are no hotels in town. With its 20-ft ceilings, generations-old photographs, furnishings, paintings and family treasures, the wing is a glimpse into the gracious past. If you're visiting Ocú and would like to learn more about the region, stop by to see Matty. Hers is the big house on the right as you face the cathedral.

❖ LA POLLERA

Considered the world's most beautiful national dress, the *pollera* is reminiscent of Spain, particularly the provinces of Galacia, Andalusia and Valencia. The two-tiered skirt of a "gala" *pollera* requires 10 yards of delicate white handkerchief linen embroidered in one color of cross-stitch or applique in floral designs. The matching blouse, with two flounces embroidered like the skirt, and edged with lace, is worn off the shoulders. Wool threads woven through the lace of the blouse end in two large pompoms (*motas*) in the front and two in the back. Ribbons worn around the waist and flat, ballet-style shoes match the color of the threads that contrast with the embroidery. Traditional jewelry includes a delicate filigree gold and pearl brooch (*mosqueta*) pinned to the ribbon or the pompom at the neck of the blouse, three to seven long gold chains, gold or gold and pearl earrings, and one or two gold bracelets. Hair ornaments – a large gold comb (*peinetón*), two to four small gold combs called balcony combs (*peinetas de balcón*) – and *trembleques* – delicate ornaments made of fine wires, pearls, crystals and beads – complete the costume. It can take up to one year to make an exquisite gala *pollera* that will be passed from mother to daughter for generations. The average cost of a gala *pollera* is $2,000, but can be much higher. When the jewelry and ornaments are added, the cost can top $10,000.

While not as elaborate as the gala, the ***pollera montuña*** is very pretty and feminine. Less jewelry is worn with the *montuña*, usually only a flat gold chain and dangling pendent earrings. The blouse is white, with one flounce instead of two and the skirt is a solid color with no embroidery. Balcony combs, a straw hat, flowers or lace are worn in the hair. A ***pollera basqiña*** differs from the montuña only in that a fitted white jacket with a small collar and tiny pleats from the shoulder to the flared hem is worn instead of the blouse.

Bridal *polleras* are completely white – even the embroidery. Brides from wealthy Central Province families still wear these beautiful creations, especially near the traditional town of Ocú.

Traditional **men's dress** (*montuño*) consists of an embroidered shirt with short pants, an Ocueño straw hat and a chacara bag woven of vegetable fibers.

Ocú is 31miles/50 kilometers west of Chitré. Head north from Chitré on the Carretera Nacional to Parita, and turn west (left) at the intersection just north of the village. This takes you onto the curving rural road that winds to the one and only intersection in Llano de la Cruz. Turn north (right) at the intersection and continue west to Ocú. If planning to visit the Seco Herrerano seco distillery in Pesé (see below) on the way back to Chitré, a turn to the south at the Llano de la Cruz intersection will get you onto the road that loops into Pesé and back to the Carretera Nacional just north of Chitré. Buses run from Chitré to Ocú every hour during the day. The ride takes about an hour and costs $2.

There are no hotels in Ocú, but you can get something to eat in one of the two or three small restaurants on the main street. Only typical food is available.

> ❖ **EATING LIKE A LOCAL**
>
> Among the Azuero Peninsula's typical foods are **chiricanos**, which are said to be of pre-Columbian origin. They are made by mixing roughly ground corn and shredded fresh coconut, sweetened with sugarcane juice and honey, into a coarse dough. The dough is wrapped in a banana leaf or cornhusk and roasted over a wood fire. The resulting flavor is deliciously smoky sweet.

◆ Pesé

This little farming town's only place of interest is the seco factory, **Seco Herrerano**. Seco, like rum, is an alcoholic distillation made from sugarcane, and this is the nation's largest distillery. The factory's mill operates only during harvest season from mid-January to mid-March. Visits must be requested in writing a week or so in advance; fax your request to ☎ 507-974-9793.

AUTHOR NOTE: *Pesé's big party, the **Festival of Cane and Sugar**, is held in March to "exalt the cane and its derivatives." Sounds like fun. Check with IPAT, ☎ 507-966-8040, for exact dates.*

Pesé is 15.5 miles/25 kilometers southwest of Chitré. The turnoff road from the Carretera Nacional to Pesé is in La Arena, 3.75miles/six kilometers north of downtown Chitré. If you're driving, you'll find it easy to visit both Ocú and Pesé during the same trip as the road loops around. See directions to Ocú, above. Buses run from Chitré to Pesé every 20 minutes. The fare is $1 each way.

There are no hotels in the village, but there is a supermarket, a gas station and a pharmacy.

Adventures

◆ On Foot

Parque National Sarigua (Sarigua National Park)

Sarigua is a harsh example of the destruction caused by land over-use and slash-and-burn agriculture. Deforestation began thousands of years ago when indigenous people first cleared the land for farming and continues today. Although the 19,760-acre/8,000-hectare park was created in 1984, a section near the entrance was used as a garbage dump until recently, and you'll see bits of trash poking up through the ground. Sarigua is called a desert, but in reality this barren, Mad Max landscape receives up to 468 inches/1,200 mm of rainfall annually – a true desert receives only about 400. High concentrations of magnesium and iron lend a reddish cast to its sun-baked landscape interrupted by a few scrubby bushes and midden heaps left by indigenous people thousands of years ago. In fact, Panamá's oldest archaeological sites, dating back 11,000 years, were discovered here. Some of the recovered remains of early civilizations are on display in Chitré's Museó de Herrera.

Not all of Sarigua is barren; there are a few small areas of deciduous tropical dry forest along the Santa Maria and Parita rivers and the Bay of Parita, where there are also five species of mangroves. A surprising number of animals include green and black iguanas, armadillos, caimans, boa constrictors, margays and false coral snakes. Eight heron species are among the many birds here, which include rare savanna hawks, frigate birds and bat falcons. It was also a surprise to find commercial shrimp farms in the park and that visitors can tour them. The park entrance is six miles/10 kilometers northeast of Chitré, where a large sign marks the turnoff from the Carretera. Admission is $3, parking $1. Camping ($5) is permitted and there are bathrooms and showers in the building that houses the ANAM ranger station.

You will need a guide to visit this park. If you haven't come with one, you can call **Grupo Ecologico Paris**, ☎ 507-974-2165. The **ANAM** rangers, ☎ 507-996-8216 (ANAM's Herrera office), serve as guides, but there may be only one on duty, so call ahead to let them know you're coming. They're exceptionally knowledgeable and can rattle off the names of all the animal and bird species at the drop of a hat. There's no charge for their services, but a tip will be appreciated.

◆ Playa El Aguillito

Migrating birds are the attraction here and, despite the name, these mud flats can't be called a beach, although when the tide is in a few daring souls splash around. When it's out, thousands of birds swoop down to scour the flats for edibles; when it's in, they congregate around nearby salt ponds. Local people also come here at low tide to poke in the mud, looking for clam-like shellfish called *concha negra*.

The nondescript building across from the beach is the **Alejandro von Humboldt Ecological Station**, where scientists study bird migrations. By banding some of these birds, they have learned the same ones return to this exact spot year after year. Although this isn't a well-known birding site, anyone with an interest in seeing huge congregations of migratory birds or learning about the work carried out by the station will find it an interesting place indeed. There are seven species of mangroves nearby that host both local and migrant birds. Francisco Delgado heads the station, speaks English and Spanish, and knows all about these birds and their habits. There's no phone at the station, but if you'd like to visit, e-mail Francisco at delgado_francisco@hotmail.com. There is no charge, but a donation would be a nice gesture. There's a pleasant walkway above the muddy shore, a children's playground and a little restaurant where you can buy fresh fried fish and *patacones* for $2. The *concha negra* hunters are pretty interesting, too.

Los Pozos & Refugio de Vida Silveste Cenegon del Mangle

With its flat gray mud surface and little craters of bubbling water, Los Pozos looks like a fantastic science fiction moonscape. The mysterious little craters appear suddenly and, although you would expect them to be the result of underground volcanic activity, the water has no sulphuric odor and is cold and sweet like spring water. It is believed to be curative; if you visit here on a weekend, you'll see people dipping it out in cups to drink, dribble over their faces, or carry home in glass jars.

Past the mud flats, raised wooden walkways lead into a mangrove refuge and heron breeding ground at the mouth of Río Santa Maria. These regal white birds are so populous that some are taken as chicks to live on the grounds of the Heron's Palace, the Presidential Palace in Casco Antiguo.

AZUERO PENINSULA

There are no buses to this refuge, which is just north of Parita in París, 4.5 miles/seven kilometers northeast of the Carretera Nacional. If you're not driving, check with IPAT, ☎ 507-966-8013, in Los Santos, to see if they can supply you with a guide or recommend one. If you come by taxi ($3) there is usually someone at the entrance to Los Pozos who will guide you. Note that visitors are forbidden to enter the mangroves without a guide.

> ❖ **PRETTY IN PINK**
>
> The herons inhabiting the Mangrove Refuge are stately, snow-white birds. Recently, some of these birds have appeared with pink feathers. They are the same species, identical in every way except for their color. It isn't yet known what might have caused the genetic aberration.

Where to Stay

Chitré offers the widest range of hotels, restaurants and services on the peninsula. Because most of the Azuero's towns and attractions are within easy distance of it, it's also the best choice for lodging.

> ❖ **HOTEL PRICING**
> Based on double occupancy
> No $ . . . . under $20
> $ . . . . $20 to $39
> $$ . . . . $40 to $79
> $$$ . . . . $80 to $124
> $$$$ . . . . . . $125 to $199
> $$$$$ . . . . over $200

Pension Chitré, Av Herrera, ☎/fax 507-996-0059, $8-$10, is the cheapest place in town. Its six rooms have private cold-water bathrooms. Some are more comfortable than others.

Pension Central, Av Raul Burgos Avila, ☎ 507-996-0059, $15 to $17, has 21 clean comfortable rooms, most with air conditioning.

Hotel Santa Rita, Calle Manuel Maria Correa at Avenida Herrera, ☎ 507-996-4610, fax 507-996-2404, air conditioning, telephones, cable TV, $18. This is an old hotel, but clean and well-maintained.

Hotel Hawaii, Calle San Pedro, near Paseo Enrique Geenzier, ☎ 507-996-3542, fax 507-996-2090, $, has 33 neat and tidy air-conditioned rooms with cable TV and phones, and there's a swimming pool.

Hotel El Prado, Av Herrera, south of Calle Manuel Maria Correa, ☎ 507-996-4620, $. This older property's 28 air-conditioned rooms have cable TV and in-room phones.

Hotel Versailles, Paseo Enrique Geenzier, ☎ 507-996-4422, fax 507-996-2090, $, with air conditioning, cable TV, in-room phones, room service, swimming pool, gift shop, restaurant and lounge, is an excellent value. This attractive hotel has 61 pleasant, well-furnished rooms that overlook a pretty central courtyard garden. Suites are priced only $5 more than double rooms.

Until Hotel Guayacanes opened, 28-room **Hotel Hong Kong** was the best in town. It's on Avenida Carmelo Espadafora (also called Circunvalacion), ☎ 507-996-4483, fax 507-996-5229, $, and offers air conditioning, cable TV, room service, pool, restaurant and bar. It is wheelchair-accessible. Rooms are spacious, comfortable and attractively furnished.

Beautiful **Barceló Guayacanes**, ☎ 800-227-2356 (toll-free from the US, Canada and Latin America), ☎ 507-206-3100 in Panamá, www.barcelo.com, $$$$, is more resort than hotel. Spacious rooms, painted in restful pastels, have individually controlled air conditioning, cable TV, a desk, well-placed reading lights and comfortable beds. Rooms are separated from the public areas in three two-story buildings surrounding lovely grounds and a small lake. Each has its own lakeview terrace or balcony. The restaurant here is the best in town, with an outdoor terrace on a breezy hilltop or air-conditioned indoor dining. There's also a casino, disco, bar/lounge, swimming pools for adults and children, gym and spa. All-inclusive rates start at $150.

Pension La Amistad, Calle Jose A. Corro, ☎ 507-996-9338, $. There's nothing remarkable about this property with only 13 rooms, but there is a restaurant and bar, and the rooms have air conditioning and cable TV.

Where to Eat

Hotel Barcelo Guayacane's restaurant, $-$$$, is Chitre's best. Built of beautiful native hardwoods, the lovely open-walled dining room atop a breezy hill offers superb comestibles and fine views. Delicious international entrées in-

❖ RESTAURANT PRICING	
Entrée & non-alcoholic drink	
$	under $5
$$	$5 to $10
$$$	$11 to $20
$$$$	over $21

clude fork-tender filets, superb grilled breast of chicken in light, lemony mushroom sauce, corvina in garlic sauce and plump, succulent shrimp prepared in endless variety. Salads are crisp, vegetables tender and desserts sinful. The views are good, the wine list and service excellent.

Chinese food is popular here, and **Hotel Hong Kong's restaurant** ($5 to $6) serves the best – but don't expect anything to be spicy-hot. The restaurant is open from 7 am until 10 pm, serving breakfast, lunch and dinner.

Inexpensive **Restaurante y Parillada Vincente**, two blocks south of Union Park, offers hearty, complete meals of soup, entrée, dessert and beverage for about $5.

Restaurante Yully, a block east of Union Park, is a cafeteria-style eatery offering a variety of local dishes, including roast beef or pork ($1) and chicken and fish ($1.50-$2) prepared in a number of ways, and plenty of starch and vegetable sides (30¢-75¢). Breakfast is available from 5 am.

AZUERO PENINSULA

Las Tejitas, **Popular**, and **La Estrella** serve full meals of typical Panamanian food (beef, chicken or pork, rice and beans, plantains) at a cost of $3 to $5. All are downtown, within easy walking distance from the park.

Los Santos Province

P anamá's most festive province is famed for its spirited folkloric festivals, which haven't changed much since the time of the conquistadors. Los Santos' proud people also display the physical characteristics of their Spanish heritage. Like Herrera's, they're generally taller than most Panamanians, with fine fair features. You'll notice some with blue or hazel eyes and blonde or light brown hair.

The provincial capital of Los Santos is **Las Tablas**, a quiet pastoral town 15 miles/24 kilometers south of Chitré.

The country's most elaborate *polleras* are made in the towns of Las Tablas and **Guararé**, and homes in the rural countryside are still built in the colonial style using whitewashed mud bricks. Fine saddlery and gold work are also produced here.

The **IPAT** office, ☎ 507-966-8040 in Villa de Los Santos, serves the entire peninsula. You'll find it in the little row of shops across from the cathedral, next to the Museum of Nationality. Only one or two helpful employees speak a smattering of English.

Sightseeing & Touring

◆ Villa de Los Santos

Head south from Chitré on the Carretera Nacional and within minutes you'll cross the bridge over the **Río la Villa**, which separates Herrera Province from Los Santos. Once on the other side, you're in Los Santos Province and Chitré's sister town, Villa de los Santos.

Panamá's first "Cry of Independence" issued from this picturesque colonial town on November 10, 1821. Much of its old colonial architecture has survived; including the **Museo de la Nacionalidad** (Museum of Nationality), ☎ 507-966-8192, building where the country's Declaration of Independence was signed in 1821. Except for the pre-Columbian artifacts, I didn't find the displays – historical documents and artifacts, colonial religious art and paintings – as interesting as the graceful building housing them. Its open, airy rooms with high ceilings of bark-stripped saplings and handmade clay tile floors open to a beautiful back courtyard and gardens. The curator is an archaeologist, which may account for the fine pre-Columbian display. The museum is open Tuesday through Saturday,

9 am to 4:30 pm, and Sunday, 9 am to 1 pm. Admission is $1 for adults, 25¢ for children under 12. It faces Parque Simón Bolívar, the central park, adjacent to the church on Calle Jose Vallareno.

First opened in 1782, **Iglesia de San Atanacio** (Church of Saint Atanacio) received national monument status in 1938, and underwent restoration in 2003. Almost everything in this magnificently baroque-style church is original. The arch in front of the stunning carved and gold leafed rosewood and mahogany alter is signed and dated 1733, and the retablo of the Immaculate Conception is dated 1721. The intricately detailed woodcarvings of flowers and fruit, saints, pink-cheeked blonde angels and cherubs, some with garments adorned in gold leaf, are exquisitely beautiful. There is an almost life-size Christ in a glass case and a smaller black Christ set into a niche in one of the altars. Notice the thick stone floor pavers that have held up through the centuries and the large stone plaques embedded in the church walls. They're the gravestones of former priests interred behind them. If you visit only one of Azuero's churches, make it this one. San Atanacio is next to the central park, adjacent to the museum. The main entrance to the church is kept open for visitors during daylight hours.

Los Santos offers little in the way of accommodations and dining, and most visitors stay in Chitré. If you decide to stay here, check out **Hotel La Villa**, Barriada Don Marcel, ☎ 507-996-9321, fax 507-996-8201, $24 double. Its 38 comfortable rooms have air conditioning, cable TV and telephones. There's a restaurant, a bar and pool. **Hotel Kevin**, on the Carretera Nacional, ☎ 507-996-8726, fax 507-966-8391, with 20 rooms, is a good option. The rooms are shiny and quite new, with air conditioning, satellite TV and phones, but there is no pool. The restaurant here is good and there's a small bar.

◆ Guararé

Surrounded by a pastoral "cattle country" landscape of low rolling hills and thickets of graceful oaks, tiny Guararé straddles the Carretera Nacional (it's called Via Nacional here) 13 miles/21 kilometers south of Chitré. The monument at the town's entrance displays a huge *mejorana*.

Musicians and dancers from throughout the country descend on this quiet town every September to entertain and compete in the annual *Festival Nacional de la Mejorana* (National Festival of the Mejorana). Panamá's largest folkloric festival includes an oxcart parade, crowning of a festival queen and fireworks, but most important are the music and dance presentations.

AZUERO PENINSULA

❖   **FOLK TRADITION**

The burning of Judas is an Easter Sunday folk tradition in Guararé. After the morning's mass and religious processions, townspeople and musicians gather in the plaza for Judas' "wake" and a lively reading of his will. The will relates the previous year's scandals and is read aloud – much to the embarrassment of some of the townspeople. The spoofs, partying and wake end when Judas is burned.

Devoted to folkloric costume, **Casa Museo Manuel F. Zárate**, Calle 21 Enero, displays some of the country's oldest and finest *polleras*, *diáblicos sucios* costumes, masks and musical instruments.

❖   **DIÁBLICOS SUCIOS**

Dancers disguised in whirling red satin capes, red and black striped body suits, and fearsomely grotesque red and black masks stomp to the cadence of pagan drumbeats. These are the *diáblicos sucios* – the "dirty devils." *Diáblicos* represent the hosts of Satan during Corpus Christi, a pagan religious festivity dating back to the Middle Ages, when the Catholic Church used costumed dancers to represent the life of Christ. Held 60 days after Easter Sunday, the tradition arrived here during colonial times and is celebrated in Los Santos with the same fervor today as four centuries ago. These exciting masked dancers appear at folkloric festivals and costumed events throughout the country.

◆ Las Tablas

This charming, traditional town of about 8,000 people is 16 miles/26 kilometers south of Chitré and only minutes south of Guararé on the Carretera Nacional. The capital of Los Santos Province is best known for hosting the country's most authentic **Carnaval** celebrations and for its combined patron saint and *pollera* festival.

Women here and in Guararé sew the country's beautiful national dress, the *pollera*; it's an art passed down through generations of mothers and daughters. **Sra. Astevia Belen C. de Sanchez** is one of the town's foremost *pollera* makers. Sra. de Sanchez began stitching *polleras* with her mother when she was a young girl. She's in her 60s now, and the two women still work together. To visit her or one of the town's other *pollera* makers, call the Los Santos **IPAT office**, ☎ 507-966-8040, and they'll make the arrangements.

History buffs and political mavens may want to visit the **Museo Belisario Porras** (Belisario Porras Museum), housed in the colonial former home of this three-time President. Porras, who was president when the Panama Canal opened, established much of the country's infrastructure, including its public hospitals. His country estate, **El Pausilipo**, is located outside the town. It's open to visitors from 9 am to 4 pm, Tuesday through Saturday, and 9 am until noon on Sunday. The baroque-style **Iglesia Santa Librada**, on the town's central square, dates from 1789. In 1950, it was damaged by fire, so some of its interior is reproduction.

◆ Pedasí

Pedasí is a quiet little fishing village, 46 miles/74 kilometers south of Chitré (28 miles/45 kilometers south of Las Tablas), on the peninsula's southeastern tip. It may not remain quiet for long, though. A 75-room Decameron resort resort will soon be under construction, and an airstrip is planned to push tourism down this way. Pedasí is the hometown of Panamá's former president, Mireya Moscoso, who recently renovated a former US military installation on nearby Punta Mala beach into a lavish personal "retreat" with a private aircraft runway.

There's a good white-sand beach here, and you can rent a boat (about $100 for the day) to go snorkeling or fishing. There are no taxis as yet, but with all the activity, this may soon change. Beyond Pedasí, the road curves west to **Tonosí**, a small town in a green mountain valley once occupied by a sophisticated pre-Columbian civilization. This frontier town offers little of interest to visitors.

Adventures

◆ On Water

Surfing

You'll need your own transportation – or better yet, go with a guide – to reach the excellent surfing beaches near Pedasí. Adjoining **Playa Lagarto** and **Playa El Toro** are down a dirt road about 10 minutes east of town. Sections of El Toro are usually safe for swimming, but the muddy brown sand and opaque water isn't very inviting. **Playa Los Destiladeros** has silvery-gray sand that is far more appealing. It's roughly six miles/10 kilometers south of town.

Continue southwest along the Carretera Nacional and you'll find excellent, virtually deserted, surfing beaches – most have waves too powerful for bathing – strung all along the coast. Some are fairly close to the highway, but you may have a long hike over rough terrain or through cow pastures to reach others. The only facilities along here are at **Playa Venao**, about 30 minutes west of Pedasí, where international surfing events that include the Billabong Pro are held. Your best bet for surfing this region is to contact the experts, **Panamá Surf Tours**, ☎ 507-236-8303 or 507-236-7069 (in Panamá City), www.panamasurftours.com.

Snorkeling

Twenty Eastern Pacific coral species are found in the 35 acres/14 hectares of coral reefs near **Isla Iguana**, a wildlife refuge and a wonderful place for snorkeling. More than 200 fish species and endangered whales ply these waters. Isla Iguana is accessible by boat from Pedasí (about $160 for up to eight people).

Wildlife Watching

Isla de Cañas, a few miles offshore between Pedasí and Tonosí, is a wildlife refuge and Panamá's primary Pacific sea turtle nesting site. Thousands of olive ridley, loggerhead, Pacific green, hawksbill and gigantic, lumbering leatherbacks come ashore each year to lay their eggs on its beaches. During the months of August and September, as many as 200 are here in a single night.

If your visit is timed right, you'll see the adults and perhaps thousands of tiny hatchlings as they pop from the sand and struggle to the sea.

Isla de Cañas is 38 miles/49 kilometers southwest of Pedasí. Take the Carretera Nacional west from town and stay on it past the turnoff to Cañas (village). The turnoff to the island is roughly four miles/6.4 kilometers farther on the left (south) side of the road. Drive down the rocky dirt turnoff road for 1.5 miles/2.5 kilometers to its end. During daylight hours, you'll find boatmen here to take you on the three-minute crossing to the island. The round-trip cost is $1 per person.

> **AUTHOR NOTE:** *Although not always enforced, there's a rule that all visitors to Isla de Cañas must be accompanied by a guide, so you may be approached when you land on the island. The cost for a guide is $10, but most speak only Spanish.*

Buses run several times a day between Chitré and Tonosí during daylight hours. Ask to be dropped at the turnoff road and hike the rest of the way to the mangroves. The cost is $3.50.

To get the most from your visit and avoid the hassle, I suggest you go with an environmentally sensitive specialist tour company. **Iguana Tours**, ☎ 507-226-4516 or 226-1329 (in Panamá City), www.nvmundo.com/iguanatours, offers an excellent package. Some of the tour companies listed on page 52 also offer trips here.

Laboratorio Achotines (Tuna Laboratory), a tuna research laboratory and hatchery dedicated to the study and conservation of yellowfin tuna and other threatened fish species, is at the edge of a beautiful bay 18.5 miles/30 kilometers southwest of Pedasí. Although it isn't open to the general public, you can arrange a visit with Iguana Tours (see above).

Where to Stay

Hotel la Mejorana, Via Nacional, Guararé, ☎ 507-994-5794, fax 507-994-5796, $, offers traditional appeal in a beautiful setting, although rooms vary in quality and size.

❖ HOTEL PRICING	
Based on double occupancy	
No $	under $20
$	$20 to $39
$$	$40 to $79
$$$	$80 to $124
$$$$	$125 to $199
$$$$$	over $200

Hotel Manolo, Av Belasario Porras, Las Tablas, ☎ 507-994-6372, $, has nine comfortable air-conditioned rooms, a pleasant restaurant with good typical food and a small bar.

If visiting nearby Isla Cañas or Isla Iguana, it makes sense to stay in one of Pedasí's three lodgings – all of which are on the main street.

Best bet is **Dim's Hostal**, ☎ 507-995-2303, e-mail mirely@iname.com, $, with six rooms. It's a lovely bed and breakfast with air conditioning and a pool. Mirna Batista, one of the area's top naturalist guides, operates it. Mirna employs a contingent of locals who serve as guides (but only Mirna speaks English). A full day's tour of the region costs about $20.

Residencial Moscoso, ☎/fax 507-995-2203, $, has 19 rooms, air conditioning, cable TV and telephones.

Residencial Pedasí, ☎ 507-993-2322, $, has 17 rooms, air conditioning and a restaurant.

If you're not staying in Pedasí, there are only two options near the beaches. **Resort La Playita**, ☎ 507-996-2225 (in Chitré), $$, features a duplex with two lovely rooms in a gorgeous garden setting next to a beautiful beach. There are no dining or cooking facilities here, so bring your own food and the caretaker will prepare it for you. Watch for the marked turnoff 1.25 miles/two kilometers east of Playa Venao. The other option is **Jardin Vista Hermosa**, on the beach at Playa Venao, ☎ 507-995-8107, which offers two (very) rustic cabins for $16 each. There's a good seafood restaurant and, if you eat here the owner will let you camp on the premises.

Where to Eat

AZUERO PENINSULA

Restaurante Los Portales, on the corner across from Hotel Manolo in Las Tablas, offers rural, open-air ambiance and a tasty *comida corriente* with soup, entrée, vegetable or salad and a drink for a bargain $2. Around the cor-

❖ RESTAURANT PRICING	
Entrée & non-alcoholic drink	
$	under $5
$$	$5 to $10
$$$	$11 to $20
$$$$	over $21

ner, **Bakery Rico Pan** sells delicious pastries. Try the cheese empanadas and coconut cookies.

There are only a few restaurants in Pedasí. You'll find hearty, inexpensive ($3-$5) local food at **Restaurante Angela** and **Restaurante Las Delicias**. French food is the specialty at tiny **Restaurante JR** ($10-$14) on the main street, in the home of a retired Canadian who worked as a chef in Canada and France, and was also Executive Chef at Hotel El Panamá in Panamá City. This is Pedasí's best. Call ahead for reservations, ☎ 507-995-2116.

❖ TYPICAL COOKING

When making your way south on the Carretera Nacional in Guararé, you might notice the nameless, open-sided eateries that seem to spring up in the oddest places. They're little more than a gaggle of plastic chairs and tables – or mismatched wooden ones – propped in the dirt under a vast rickety roof supported by a few columns. If the fragrance of roasting meats compels you to stop, and you don't mind a few chickens pecking around your feet, you'll get a taste of genuine traditional fare: smoky beef or pork ribs, tamales, empañadas, roasted sweet corn, or *pollo guisado*, a richly flavored local chicken stew. Do try it. It's delicious, even if the chicken is tough as rubber (the birds develop a lot of muscle dodging kicks).

Veraguas Province

Bordered by two oceans, Panamá's third-largest province is one of its least populated. Wedged between Coclé to the east and Chiriquí to the west, Veraguas feels like the wide-open spaces after the densely populated Azuero Peninsula that borders

its southeast corner. Its capital, **Santiago**, with a population of slightly less than 33,000, is the largest town in this mainly agricultural province.

Veraguas is generally considered a region to pass through on the way to somewhere else – and that's a shame, as it has much to offer. There are colonial villages, lush jungles, rugged mountains and rolling cattle ranches complete with cowboys and entertaining rodeos. Surfing beaches include famed Santa Catalina's 20-foot/six-meter waves; and only a few fortunate divers and sportfishers have discovered Veraguas' Pacific waters, which teem with marine life and fantastic coral formations. The landscape dazzles, with white-sand beaches overshadowed by green mountains and hidden waterfalls pouring into crystal pools. You can find extraordinary bird watching in the forests and in coastal marshes; pan for gold; or climb to the summit of a cliff where uplifting winds are so strong you couldn't plummet off even if you wanted to. Pacific **Coiba Island's** jungle wilderness and the deep-sea trenches surrounding it teem with magnificent wild land and sea creatures. Inland treasures include delightful **San Francisco village**, with its exquisite, recently restored 18th-century church; and, in the forests around **Santa Fé**, a remote town high in the magnificent Cordillera Central, you can seek out elusive orchid and abounding bird species, revel in spectacular scenery and trek mountain trails on foot or on horseback. If you want a beach all to yourself, you'll find one along a little strip of land that dips down onto the **Azuero Peninsula**. What more could you ask for? Veraguas has all this and more – you just might have to look a little harder to find it all.

History

During his last New World voyage in 1502-1503, Columbus sailed Central America's Caribbean coast in search of gold and a westward passage to the Orient. While trading trinkets for the precious metal, he learned that natives who lived alongside Río Belén obtained it from mines deep in the jungle. Hoping to locate the mines, he sailed up the river and moored his fleet. This maneuver didn't sit well with the local Indians who planned a raid to rid themselves of Spaniards. Word of the imminent attack reached the Spaniards and they began moving the fleet out of the river to the safety of the sea. Before completing their escape, a few of his men were killed and one of his ships, the *Gallego*, foundered on a sandbar and sunk to the bottom of Rio Belén. All later attempts to subdue the region's Indians ended in failure until 1555, when they were at last defeated and the mines located. A settlement was established and African slaves were brought to work the mines which produced for about 30 years. Most of the gold is gone now, but prospectors still straggle in every so often. Some just talk, others go so far as to survey, and a few have dug some pretty big holes, but today, the jungles around Río Belén are as wild as when Columbus ventured here more than five centuries ago. There are no roads into this region of torrential rainfall. Its few native inhabitants travel by river.

Santiago Area

L ying about halfway between Panamá City and the Costa Rica border, the provincial capital, Santiago, is a commercial farming town that doesn't offer much of interest. However, its variety of hotels, restaurants and services make it a good base for exploring the countryside.

Access to Santiago is by the **InterAmericana** (Inter-American Highway) – it's 154.3 miles/249 kilometers west of Panamá City (a 3½- to four-hour drive) and 36 miles/58 kilometers west of Divisa. Although still open to private aircraft, no commercial flights land at Santiago's airport. Aeroperlas used to offer a once daily-flight from Panamá City, with a stop in Chitré, but it has been discontinued. However, you can connect to anywhere in the country from Santiago's busy **bus terminal** on the city's southwest side, or catch an eastbound or westbound bus in front of Hotel Piramidal on the InterAmericana. SANPASA and Expreso Veraguense buses run from Panamá City's Gran Terminal de Transporte (Albrook) every hour and the fare is $6. If coming from the Azuero Peninsula, the fare from Chitré to the bus stop at the Delta Station in Divisa is $1. You won't have to wait more than half an hour for a connection on to Santiago ($3).

Budget Rent A Car, ☎ 507-998-1731, has an office at the intersection of the InterAmericana and Av Hector Santacolom in Santiago.

> **AUTHOR NOTE:** *For more information about the province, contact the regional **IPAT** office in Santiago, ☎ 507-998-3929. You'll find it on the northwest side of Av Central, about a block from the InterAmericana intersection. Note that the helpful, friendly staff members speak only a smattering of English.*

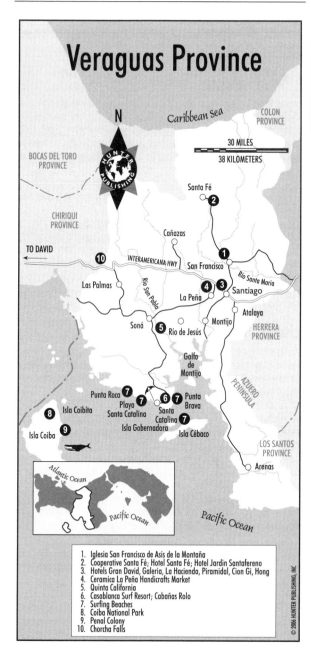

Veraguas Province

1. Iglesia San Francisco de Asis de la Montaña
2. Cooperative Santa Fé; Hotel Santa Fé; Hotel Jardin Santafereno
3. Hotels Gran David, Galeria, La Hacienda, Piramidal, Cion Gi, Hong
4. Ceramica La Peña Handicrafts Market
5. Quinta California
6. Casablanca Surf Resort; Cabañas Rolo
7. Surfing Beaches
8. Coiba National Park
9. Penal Colony
10. Chorcha Falls

Sightseeing & Touring

◆ San Francisco

Famed for its lovely adobe church, this pretty and very friendly little town, officially named San Francisco de la Montaña, is about 10 miles/16 kilometers northwest of Santiago. Established by a Dominican friar in 1671, the picturesque town's population then consisted solely of 30 indigenous people. By 1756, it had grown to 2,277 souls, including two priests, seven "notables" and their families, slaves, indigenous peoples and some individuals of mixed blood. It isn't much larger now, and many of its current residents commute to work in Santiago, making it a quaint and quiet "bedroom" community.

To get here, take the InterAmericana west through Santiago, pass the Hotel Gran David and continue to the first intersection with a traffic light. Turn right (north) at the intersection (a sign here points to San Francisco) and continue on the well-paved road to the town. Buses run to San Francisco from Santiago's terminal on the city's southwest side every 15-20 minutes. If you are heading into the mountains and Santa Fé, you can make San Francisco a stop on your way.

Iglesia San Francisco de Asis de la Montaña

This lovely little church in San Francisco village is one of the finest examples of 18th-century Baroque religious art and architecture anywhere in the Americas. The gold leafing so prominent in churches of this period is absent from its magnificent carved wood altar, and there are statues that still retain their original vegetable paints mixed with gesso and earth. Among the expected statues of the crucifixion, saints and the Virgin, you'll see many obvious Native American elements, including angels and cherubs with Indian faces and an eagle piercing its own heart. A carved cedar statue of John baptizing Christ is exceptionally lovely, and a heavy carved stone baptismal font is inscribed "Ano Dei 1727." This wonderful church, in a green pastoral setting, was undergoing restoration that should be completed when you read this. It's open to visitors from 8 am until 2 pm, Monday through Saturday. Historian Ricardirr (that's how he spells it) Rodriguez is usually on hand to provide information.

> **AUTHOR TIP:** *Nearby,* **Panaderia San Roqué** *sells delicious* pan dulce *(sweet bread) and* chicheme *(see page 30). To cool off, you can swim in the pool at the base of nearby* **Chorro del Spiritú Santo** *(Waterfall of the Holy Ghost).*

◆ Santa Fé de Veraguas

Santa Fé is 35.3 miles/57 kilometers northwest of Santiago and, since the road to this pleasant little mountain town at the brink of the continental divide passes through San Francisco, it is convenient to stop there to visit the church on your way. The excellent blacktop road serving as San Francisco's main street runs directly north to Santa Fé, roller-coasting into lush farming country in the Cordillera Central foothills before winding steeply upward through a kaleidoscope forest landscape, replete with sparkling streams and breathtaking views. The trip from Santiago or San Francisco takes a little more than an hour by passenger car or 1½ hours by bus. The lovely mountain town of Santa Fé perches perched on a peaceful mountainside above deep green valleys at the road's end.

Although founded in 1557 to garrison soldiers and supplies for Spanish gold mines, Santa Fé isn't laid out in typical grid pattern. Its curving unnamed lanes run every which way, but it's small and everyone knows everyone else, so you won't have any difficulty finding your way around. Take a stroll in the clear, refreshing mountain air and be greeted with a shy "buenos" from everyone you pass.

Cooperativa Santa Fé market and restaurant is a good place to buy chacara bags and hats made by local Ngöbe-Buglé people and freshly roasted Café el Tuté organic coffee. A few of the other interesting items for sale include hand-stitched clothing, simple pottery, carved wooden birds and homemade pastries, picante, jams and jellies, fresh herbs and a variety of locally grown fruits, vegetables and grains. Two golden ripe bananas sell for 5¢, and you can get a huge meal of fish or meat with rice and vegetables for $5.

◆ West of Santiago

Heading west from Santiago, the few small towns shrink away from the highway into a pastoral landscape overshadowed by the looming Cordillera Central. Tractor-trailers roar past smatterings of slapped-together roadside stands, their wake fluttering colorful dresses made by Ngöbe-Buglé women. Indigenous families in single file and farmers in high rubber boots, bent under burdens of coconuts or corn stuffed into huge chacara bags, trudge the well-worn path beside the highway. There isn't much else to see other than the advancing and receding mountains to the north, or herds of brahma and sembrah cattle grazing on rolling pasturelands between the few surviving forests to the south.

Pottery and masks from the Azuero, baskets and wood carvings made by Emberá and Wounaan from Darién, woven chacara bags and soapstone figurines made by local Ngöbe-Buglé people are a few of the fine handicrafts for sale at **Ceramica la Peña Handicrafts Market**. Watch for it on the highway about five miles/eight kilometers past Santiago, near the turnoff to tiny La Peña village. The market is open weekdays, 9 am until 4:30 pm.

The eastern border of **Chiriquí Province** is 60 miles/96.5 kilometers west of Santiago. If you are continuing a road-trip west, you'll see a huge sign erected by proud Chiricanos to welcome you to their province. Watch on the right for **Chorcha Falls**, which looks like a long silvery ribbon cascading from the mountainside's dense green forest into the Chorcha River, hidden in the jungles below. To visit the pool at the waterfall's base, turn right off the InterAmericana onto the next road after the falls and follow the signs. It will take about 45 minutes over the dirt road to reach the pool. Attractions along this stretch of highway between Santiago and David, Chiriquí's provincial capital, include **La Casa de Artesenal**, one of the country's best and least-expensive places to buy Ngöbe-Buglé handicrafts; **Playa las Lajas**, a magnificent golden sand beach; and a remarkable adventure into the rugged Cordillera Central to visit the indigenous peoples of **Comarca Ngöbe-Buglé**. See pages 211-213 in the Chiriquí Province chapter for detailed information on these three interesting excursions.

Adventures

◆ On Foot

Santa Fé

Berta de Castrellón, ☎ 507-954-0910, is one of Panamá's best **birding**, **hiking**, and **trekking guides**. Based in Santa Fé, she leads expeditions over the Continental Divide into the lush Caribbean slope jungles that for so long defeated gold-greedy conquistadors, and to looming Cerro Tute's summit, where strong upward winds prevent you from toppling over the cliffs. If you trust in nature's oddities, go ahead and stand on the edge of the cliff at the summit, where you'll be buffeted upright by the winds, but, if not, the dazzling panoramic views from this high aerie are sufficiently heart-stopping.

Berta's other favorite treks are to lovely rivers and waterfalls hidden in the jungles, to Río Santa Maria, and trips to look for rare orchids. Other destinations include an abandoned gold mine that was operated by a Canadian company from 1900 until the gold played out in 1939. Small amounts of the precious metal can still be found in nearby streams and, if "gold fever" strikes, Berta will find a guide to take you panning.

> ❖ **THE ORCHID LADY**
>
> Around town, Berta's known as the orchid lady. If you're an enthusiast, she'll show you her wonderful collection, which is made up of 95% native species. She doesn't charge for her kindness, but a donation for the time spent would be a courtesy. The best months to see orchids blooming, here or

in the forest, are June, July and September. Santa Fé's annual **Orchid Fair** is generally held from July 31-August 3, but dates are subject to change. Call the Santiago **IPAT** office, ☎ 507-998-3929, to be sure.

North of Santiago, the forests around Santa Fé harbor an incredible variety of visible wildlife. For birders, this is the best place in the entire country to see rare **lattice-tailed trogons**. Other frequently spotted species include emerald and yellow-eared toucanets, mot-mots, honeycreepers, keel-billed and chestnut mandibled toucans, tanagers in an array of colors, vireos, and dozens more.

◆ On Water

Surfing

Playa Santa Catalina, Panamá's premier surfing beach, is 68.5 miles/ 110 kilometers south of Santiago. To get here, take the Soná Road southwest from Santiago, bypass Soná and continue through the rural countryside's pastureland and rice fields. Expect the drive to take about two hours over the good paved road that diminishes to dirt the last 6.3 miles/ 10 kilometers before it ends in Santa Catalina village. Buses run every half-hour from Santiago to Soná (the fare is about $2), where you'll have to change to another bound for Santa Catalina. Note that only three buses run daily from Soná to Santa Catalina (about $3) – at 5 am, noon and 4 pm. There are no local buses or taxis in tiny Santa Catalina village, and most visitors are serious surfers. But bring your own board, as there weren't any available to rent when I visited.

Santa Catalina's waves promise a consistently good ride year-round and frequently top 20 feet/six meters during February, March and April. The rocky volcanic bottom here produces some perfect tubes. Waves at Santa Catalina break both left and right but, because of hazardous submerged rocks, this isn't a place for beginners.

Powerful **Punta Brava**, a 25-minute walk southeast of Santa Catalina, breaks both left and right over a sharp rock bottom with a point break at low tide. Its left break is even higher than Santa Catalina's. Punta Brava is difficult to get to, fickle, and *muy peligroso* because of lava rocks.

Also a reef break, **Punta Roca**, a half-hour walk northwest from Santa Catalina, breaks left with a good, short tube.

Isla Cébaco, with both beach and point breaks, is about 1½ hours from Santa Catalina by boat.

The only services in the area are in Santa Catalina village or at nearby surf resorts. There are more remote surfing beaches along this coast, most accessible only from the sea or by a difficult trek through an extreme landscape. Don't go without a knowledgeable guide.

Fishing

Casablanca Surf Resort (page 201) offers charter-fishing trips in covered *pangas*, flat-bottom boats designed for stability when hauling in the big ones. One is a 20-footer and the other is 24 feet. Casablanca's owner, Ricardo Icaza, supplies the captain and deckhand for sportfishing, but you'll need to bring your own gear. The fishing here is good all year, with December to June the best months for hooking black marlin, wahoo, and dorado. Ricardo can also take you sightseeing and birding along the coast and to offshore islands to snorkel or dive. For more information or to make a reservation, contact Ricardo at Casablanca Surf Resort, ☎/fax 507-226-3786. (See also deep-sea fishing in the *Panamá Province* chapter, page 85.)

> **AUTHOR NOTE:** *The western hemisphere's largest Pacific reef system lies just off Coiba Island, and singing humpback whales can often be observed – and heard – in these waters during winter months.*

Beaches

If you are staying in Santiago, want to chill out for the day and have a 4X4 vehicle, you'll find some beautiful beaches along the **Montijo Gulf coast**, the little strip of Veraguas that dips down onto the Azuero Peninsula's west side. To get to them, take the Atalaya turnoff from Santiago, bypass the town and continue down the dirt road skirting the sea. There are no hotels or services on this coast, only a few picturesque little villages and *fondas* selling snacks, lunches and cold drinks.

If you are traveling from Santiago on to Chiriquí Province, consider a visit to **Playa Las Lajas**, one of Panamá's most beautiful golden-sand beaches; it's a great place to break your road-trip. For more detailed information, see page 211 in the *Chiriquí Province* chapter.

Coiba National Park

Coiba Island is the focal point of this huge park (675,000 acres/270,125 hectares), which has the largest reef system in all Central America. Coiba protects three distinct habitats; reef, island and sea life. Two species of dolphin, migrating sperm, orca and humpback whales, rays, tuna, sailfish, and blue and black marlin inhabit Coiba's species-rich waters. Coiba Island is the largest island in the Panamanian Pacific, with a surface area of 124,000 acres/50,315 hectares. Tropical forests still cover 80% of this beautiful, rugged island, which is part wildlife sanctuary – Panamá's largest remaining colony of scarlet macaws make their home here – and part penal colony. Because of its distance from land, a prison was established here in 1910, and it's been operating ever since. Rumors that it may be closed down circulate from time to time, but nothing has yet come of them. Escaped prisoners sometimes roam the island before they're recaptured or learn they don't have Robinson Crusoe survival skills and give themselves up. Coiba is about three hours by boat from mainland Veraguas' southern tip.

Visits to the park are permitted only if authorized by **ANAM**, ☎ 507-998-3829 in Santiago. Because of Coiba's remote location and the time-consuming red tape involved, you should visit only with an approved tour operator who will handle the headaches and make sure the one place to stay (at the ranger station) is fit for habitation. Go only if you don't mind heavily armed guards surrounding your quarters, a necessity to ward off escaped prisoners who sometimes roam the island. This excursion isn't recommended for those with limited time. The speediest craft might get you here in about two hours, but expect it to take three to four from the southern tip of mainland Veraguas, the jumping-off point to Coiba. **Ancon Expeditions**, ☎ 507-269-9415, www.anconexpeditions.com, offers custom-tailored Coiba expeditions.

Scuba Diving

A Smithsonian Marine Institution scientist described the diving experience in **Coiba National Park's** virgin waters as a mixture between the Galapagos Islands and Costa Rica's Cocos Islands. Most of the diving here takes place around jagged undersea volcanic pinnacles that swarm with marine life. Some of the pinnacles rise all the way to the sea's surface, while others top out at a depth of 120 feet/36 meters below it. These incredibly rich waters contain hammerhead, tiger, bull, black tip, giant nurse and white tip reef sharks; dolphins; and spotted eagle, mobola, devil and giant mantra rays. Other sea creatures range in size from tiny rainbow shrimp, seahorses, butterfly fish and sergeant majors to massive humpback, pilot and sperm whales that migrate through these waters. At certain times of year, orcas (the killer whales of *Free Willy* fame) and whale sharks have been observed.

Twin Oceans Dive Center, ☎ 507-654-1224, www.twinoceans.com, offers three-, four-, and 10-day all-inclusive land-based (Coiba Island) dive adventures.

Scubapanama, ☎ 507-261-3841, fax 507-261-9586, www.scubapanama.com, offers a three-day diving adventure that includes a stay aboard the 115-foot/34.5-meter luxury M/V *Coral Star*, transportation from Panamá City, all meals, tanks and weights for about $500 per person.

◆ On Horseback

In Santa Fé, many trails too long or rough for a comfortable hike can be explored on horseback, or you can just ride around town, drinking in Santa Fé's rural ambiance, fresh mountain air, and spectacular mountain views. Several hours' use of a local steed will set you back only $15... a bargain. Better yet, give **Berta de Castrellón** (see page 196) a few days' notice and she'll arrange an amazing horse-trekking expedition into the jungles.

Where to Stay

◆ Santiago

Santiago has plenty of acceptable and a few very good hotels conveniently located along the InterAmericana. Inexpensive in-town lodgings include **Pension San José**, ☎ 507-998-4057, and **Pension Central**, ☎ 507-998-1831. Both offer cheap rooms without air conditioning and shared cold-water bathrooms for $8 a night. All of the places listed below are located along the InterAmericana.

❖   HOTEL PRICING
Based on double occupancy
No $ . . . . under $20
$ . . . . $20 to $39
$$ . . . . $40 to $79
$$$ . . . . $80 to $124
$$$$ . . . . $125 to $199
$$$$$ . . . . over $200

Hotel Gran David, ☎ 507-998-4510, fax 507-998-1866, $, has air conditioning, cable TV, telephone, and good-sized rooms along quiet outside corridors set back from the highway. They tend to be a bit dark and the décor is somewhat dated, but they're very clean and well kept, and the beds are comfortable. There's a pleasant swimming pool and a restaurant with decent food and deplorable service. Check the supplies in the public restrooms before using them. When I visited, there was no toilet paper in any of the stalls and no hand soap or paper towels.

Hotel Galeria, ☎ 507-958-7950/51, fax 507-958-7954, $, with air conditioning, cable TV, room service, and telephone, was Santiago's best until a new hotel opened farther west on the highway. There's nothing remarkable about the rooms with comfortable double beds or the small bathrooms, but I appreciated the consistently hot water and international cable TV with plenty of English channels. Service throughout is outstandingly efficient and friendly, and its restaurant serves very good, inexpensive typical and international specialties. There's a small bar, a pool, sauna and a gym. Even if you don't stay here, it's a good place to stop for lunch or dinner.

Hotel La Hacienda, at Santiago's western edge, ☎ 507-958-8580, fax 507-988-5477, $$-$$$, offers air conditioning, cable TV, telephone, business office with Internet access, copy machine and fax service, restaurant, bar, pool, gym, and room service. It's handicap-accessible. Santiago's best hotel is a gorgeous recreation of a Guadalajara hacienda from a century ago. When owner Alex Botasio returned from living in Mexico, he brought with him the idea to build a hotel exactly like the old haciendas he admired there. Authentic handcrafted Mexican furnishings and accessories grace the bright, cheerful rooms and oversize suites arranged around a quiet central courtyard. Every detail, right down to the fountain splashing merrily from a lobby wall, has been carefully planned and executed. A windowed wall in the attractive bar/lounge overlooks a second courtyard with an adult pool, one for children and a children's play area.

Hotel Piramidal, at the Av Central intersection in back of a shopping arcade, ☎ 507-998-4483, fax 507-998-4411, $, offers air conditioning, cable TV, and telephone. This is an okay hotel, with nothing remarkable about its cafeteria-style restaurant, bar or pool. It's a couple of dollars cheaper than the Galeria and Gran David. The rooms are small and unappealing and, because there's a casino here, it can be noisy.

Hotel Hong, ☎ 507-998-4059, air conditioning, TV, telephone, isn't fancy, but it does have clean rooms, decent beds and a restaurant, bar and pool. Rates range from $14 to $16.

◆ Santa Fé

Hotel Santa Fé, ☎ 507-954-0941, $, has 20 simple rooms that straddle a mountain ridge above a deep valley. All are well kept, have private baths and are in a lovely garden setting with awesome views. Fifteen of the rooms have fan only and five in a newer wing have A/C and televisions. Good typical meals ($2-$3, breakfast, lunch or dinner) are served in the small restaurant and there is an even smaller bar. Delightful proprietress Eudocia Rodriguez will do her best to ensure you a comfortable stay.

The four cabins at **Hotel Jardin Santafereno** ($10) are rundown and seedy, but serviceable if the Santa Fé is full or your budget shot.

◆ Playa Santa Catalina

Casablanca Surf Resort, ☎/fax 507-226-3786, $-$$, is on a magnificent 14.8-acre/six-hectare bluff overlooking Santa Catalina's beach, a few minutes from the village. Accommodations include comfortable, stand-alone cabins with fans; an air-conditioned duplex house; a single house with air conditioning and a full kitchen, perfect for families or groups; and a camping area ($4, including the tent). There are two restaurants, one an inexpensive barbecue-style spot, the other offering more sophisticated food. Owner Ricardo Icaza is Panamá's surfing pioneer, and has surfed in California (where he lived for a time) and other parts of the world. He returned home to Panamá in search of the perfect wave and the perfect homesite, and found both on this remote bluff. Ricardo offers boat excursions along the coast, and can also arrange a stay at Coiba Island's ANAM ranger station (see page 198). To get here, just before entering Santa Catalina village, take the (only) left turn up the steep hill and continue to where the road forks. Stay on the right fork, and follow the signs pointing the way to Casablanca.

Cabañas Rolo, ☎ 507-998-8600, e-mail cabinasrolo@yahoo.com, $ and under, is the only place to stay right in Santa Catalina village. Up to 14 guests can be accommodated in the six simple, spotless rooms on a lovely bluff above the beach. Each room, with shared bath facilities, is furnished with one to three comfortable beds, ceiling and portable fans, and a reading light. Home-cooked breakfasts, lunches and dinners ($2-$3) are available in the small restaurant on a pleasant outdoor covered terrace. Owner Rolando ("Rolo") Ortega, who speaks some English, and his lovely wife, Vielta, are a warm and welcoming young couple. Rolo can also take you sightseeing by boat along the coast, fishing, snorkeling and to other nearby surfing beaches. To get here, drive straight into the village and look for the Cabañas Rolo sign on the left. Although I previously mentioned that there were no surfboards to rent in Santa Catalina, Rolo was considering offering a few. If you'll be staying here, e-mail him ahead to ask about rentals. For more sportfishing outfitters, see *Panamá Province*, page 82, and *Chiriquí*, page 215.

Where to Eat

◆ Santiago

Charlie Shop, $, looks like a truck stop but the food is good, cheap and authentic. Steaks and hamburgers are as popular as typical food in this unpretentious little place just inside the city limits on the south side of the highway.

❖ RESTAURANT PRICING
Entrée & non-alcoholic drink
$ . . . . under $5
$$ . . . . $5 to $10
$$$ . . . . $11 to $20
$$$$ . . . . over $21

Mar del Sur, $$$, on the south side of the InterAmericana at the Av Central intersection, is famous for delicious Peruvian specialties, superb seafood dishes and an excellent wine list.

Hotel Galeria's restaurant, $, on the north side of the InterAmericana, serves good, reasonably priced international and typical food. Try the chicken breast sautéed and drenched in light, lemony sauce with crisp steamed veggies.

> **AUTHOR NOTE:** *Many of Santiago's restaurants do not have telephone numbers.*

The lovely restaurant at new **Hotel la Hacienda**, $, on the south side of the InterAmericana on Santiago's west side, features Mexican food as authentic as the décor. You'll find a variety of seafood dishes along with chimichangas, flautas, fajitas and pollo in mole sauce.

For fast foodies, there's a **KFC** next door to Hotel Galeria, a **McDonalds**, and a **McPato**, Panamá's home-grown version of McDonalds. (Since *pato* is Spanish for duck, the name translates to McDucks.) All three are on the InterAmericana.

◆ South of Santiago

Restaurant Mi Ranchito, ☎ 507-954-3957, $$, about an hour's drive southwest of Santiago, between Soná and Santa Catalina, is a real find. Bolívar and Marlenes Gonzalez serve hefty portions of super-size perfectly grilled shrimp enhanced with zesty garlic sauce, juicy steaks or roast pork with all the trimmings. Local handicrafts, musical instruments, saddlery and massed sheaves of local corn and rice authentic to the region decorate the interior of this charming restaurant, an unexpected treat in a rural landscape. On your way to or from Santa Catalina – better yet, both ways – make this a lunch or dinner stop.

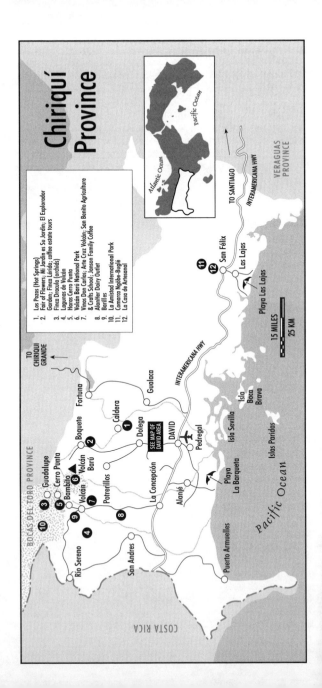

Chiriquí Province

1. Los Pozos (Hot Springs)
2. Fair of Flowers; Mi Jardín es Su Jardín; El Explorador Garden; Finca Lérida; coffee estate tours
3. Finca Dracula (orchids)
4. Lagunas de Volcán
5. Haras Cerro Punta
6. Volcán Barú National Park
7. Vinos Don Carlos; Arte Cruz Volcán; San Benito Agriculture & Crafts School; Janson Family Coffee
8. Alanfter Dairy Outlet
9. Barillas
10. La Amistad International Park
11. Comarca Ngöbe-Buglé
12. La Casa de Artesaní

BOCAS DEL TORO PROVINCE

VERAGUAS PROVINCE

COSTA RICA

Pacific Ocean

Atlantic Ocean

Pacific Ocean

TO SANTIAGO

INTERAMERICANA HWY

TO CHIRIQUÍ GRANDE

INTERAMERICANA HWY

San Félix
Las Lajas
Playa Las Lajas

Isla Boca Brava
Isla Sevilla
Islas Paridas

Fortuna
Gualaca
Caldera
Boquete
Dolega
DAVID
SEE MAP OF DAVID AREA
Pedregal
Playa La Barqueta
Alanjé
La Concepción
Potrerillos
Volcán Barú
Volcán
Bambito
Cerro Punta
Guadalupe
Río Sereno
San Andres
Puerto Armuelles

15 MILES
25 KM

Chiriquí Province

The pre-Columbian peoples of Panamá's southwestern region called their homeland *Chiriquí*, a word that translates to "valley of the moon." The name stuck, and when the moon casts silvery light over jagged mountain peaks and deep valleys, it's easy to see why. Nature's cataclysms have bequeathed this province, bordered by the Pacific on the south and Costa Rica on the west, with stunning beauty, rich soils and an unmatched biodiversity.

Chiricanos like to say their province "has it all," and perhaps it does. Some of the tropical Pacific's most highly developed coral banks lie in its offshore waters abundant with fish. White and black sand beaches alternate with mangrove island mazes along its low-lying tropical coastline. Massive **Volcán Barú's** 11,401-foot/3,420-meter summit, Panamá's highest peak, dominates cool highland cloud forests of the Talamanca's towering mountains. Thecountry's white-water rafting and kayaking originated on the wild rivers that rush through Chiriquí's jungle-clad rock canyons. Sparkling streams burst with trout waiting to be hooked, and clear pools beneath dancing waterfalls invite a cooling dip. **La Amistad (Friendship) International Park**, a biosphere reserve and UNESCO World Heritage Site shared with Costa Rica, harbors some of Central America's last remaining old-growth forests and the region's greatest numbers of large animal species. Clustering orchids and bromeliads cling to the mossy branches of ancient trees, and all five of Central America's cat species, including the endangered jaguar, roam the chilly forests of the "Altas Tierras de Chiriquí." Rugged trails twist through varied landscapes populated with more than 400 bird species, among them the largest known numbers of resplendent quetzals, one of the world's most elusive and beautiful birds.

As if to disguise its wilder nature, Chiriquí's stately pine forests and steep cultivated fields lend it an outwardly pastoral demeanor. Placid cattle and sleek thoroughbred horses dot lush green pastures splashed with golden flowering guaycan trees. Sweet strawberries, famed Boquete naval oranges, excellent coffee and infinite vegetable varieties thrive here in the cool, moist climate of Panamá's "bread basket."

History

In the early 16th century when the Spanish arrived to conquer and convert, the region was populated with as many as 60 separate indigenous groups sharing no common language or customs. Constantly at war among themselves, they soon forged alliances against the invaders, attacking and destroying Spanish missions and towns until well into the 17th century. As if this wasn't enough to occupy the Spanish, pirates plundered the region throughout the 17th and 18th centuries, lured by the gold mined and looted from pre-Columbian graves. English pirates Sharp and Sawkins attacked the town of Remedios in 1679 and again in 1685. John Cockburn's forces recruited local indigenous warriors to sack and destroy Alanje. David survived until destroyed by Miskito warriors from Nicaragua in 1732. A handful of towns, including Alanje and David, were rebuilt but tragically, only one indigenous group, the Ngöbe, survived the wars, slavery and diseases brought by the Europeans.

AUTHOR NOTE: *The Ngöbe-Buglé people are called* **Guaymí** *in Chiriquí.*

Gold fever eventually played out, along with the remaining mines, until the mid-1800s when archaeological excavations near Volcán Barú turned up artifacts and gold effigies (*huacas*) in pre-Columbian graves. When word of the finds leaked out, opportunists and adventurers, many of them forty-niners on their way to California's gold fields, detoured into Chiriquí to rob the sites. Finding the cool, exuberant climate to their liking, a few remained to settle and farm.

❖ THE MYSTERY OF LA ESTRELLA

Records filed in Seville, Spain during the late 1700s list prodigious quantities of gold shipped from the region to Spain. Most of it was recorded to have come from a mine called La Estrella (The Star), near the Pacific coast of what is now Costa Rica. The mine was reportedly so rich in ore that thousands of natives were enslaved to work it, and cargo ships laden with bullion sailed regularly from the docks of a small coastal village to Spain. According to legend, when the ships returned to load up one year, La Estrella had vanished. Despite frantic searches, not a trace of the village, docks, the mine or its Spanish overseers and guards could be found. After more than 300 years, legends of the mysterious lost mine live on – revived in 1906 when a group of indigenous people appeared in David with crude gold bars to exchange for currency. The Indians refused to explain how the gold had come into their possession. Many a Chiricano will tell you the Indians still guard the secret of La Estrella.

During the late 1800s, farmers came from Europe and North America, attracted by the region's pleasant climate and rich volcanic soils, to establish vegetable farms and coffee plantations. Banana cultivation began along Chiriquí's tropical Pacific slopes early in the 20th century, displacing the remaining Guaymí, who retreated deeper into the mountains. A second wave of immigrants arrived from Switzerland and Yugoslavia in the 1930s and settled in higher elevations near Costa Rica's border – a region now known as "Little Switzerland" for its green mountain landscapes and chalet-style architecture. Finally, as the 20th century drew to a close, yet another wave of foreigners began to arrive – North American and European retirees who had "discovered" Chiriquí's healthful climate, high quality of life and reasonable cost of living. This migration continues to gain momentum as mostly North American investors build and promote retirement communities here.

CHIRIQUI PROVINCE

Getting Here & Around

◆ By Air

The city of David, a one-hour flight from Panamá City, is the jump-off point for Chiriquí. **Aeroperlas**, ☎ 507-315-7500, www.aeroperlas.com (about $61.50 one way, no round-trip discount), and **Aero Mapiex**, ☎ 507-315-0888 (similar fare) offer daily flights from the capital's Marcos a Gelabart Municipal Airport (Albrook) to David's Enrique Malek Airport.

Car rental agencies with airport locations include **Thrifty**, ☎ 507-721-2477; **Budget**, ☎ 507-775-1677; and **National**, ☎ 507-721-0974. **Avis**, ☎ 507-774-7046, and **Hillary**, ☎ 507-775-5459, have in-town locations. Expect to pay about $30 per day for a compact, $60 to $70 for a larger 4X4.

> **AUTHOR NOTE:** *If you plan to rent a four-wheel-drive vehicle or SUV, be sure to reserve in advance. They're in great demand here.*

◆ By Car

David is on the InterAmericana Highway, halfway between Panamá City and San José, Costa Rica. If you're driving straight from Panamá City, the trip will take about seven hours, factoring in a couple of rest stops.

◆ By Bus

The trip from Panamá City by bus ($10-$15) is almost nine hours with stops along the way, unless you opt for an express that will take about seven, the same as a passenger car. **Padafont** and **Transchiri** buses depart Panamá City's Albrook Terminal every daylight hour.

Local buses **Transbusa**, ☎ 507-720-1064, and **Sertabusa**, ☎ 507-720-1120, leave David's bus terminal every half-hour to the highland towns of Boquete (one hour), Volcán (1½ hours) and Cerro Punta (1¼ hours), making stops along the way. Fares range from $1.50 to $3.

David & Environs

Plunked into a sea of cattle ranches, sugarcane and rice fields, Chiriquí's low-lying provincial capital, a commercial city of about 78,000 inhabitants, combines a hint of city sophistication with a dash of rural Wild West. Parque Cervantes, its central park, attracts young and not-so-young lovers, chatting mothers, whooping children, shop girls on break, and pushcart vendors hawking pastries, flowers, balloons, sugarcane juice and green coconut water called *agua de pipa*. Ancient trees shaded the entire park until recently when those on one side were cut down. It seems that many who enjoy the park's ambiance weren't quite as joyful about fallout from the hundreds of birds congregated in overhanging branches. Oh, and the coconut water is deliciously refreshing, but try the sugarcane juice only if you like sticky sweet drinks.

> **AUTHOR NOTE:** *Chiriquí's capital city, David, is pronounced Dah-VEED.*

Sightseeing & Touring

◆ David

Most of the David's colonial architecture succumbed long-ago to the humid climate, replaced now with a conglomeration of modern and semi-modern buildings. Facing the central park and restored a few years ago, its colonial **Iglesia de San José** (Church of Saint Joseph), while not as remarkable as many of the country's old churches, is still worth a visit.

David's residents think of its one surviving colonial neighborhood, **Barrio Bolivar**, as their own small-scale version of Casco Antiguo. Other than age and the varying degrees of decrepitude, I couldn't make the comparison. However, it does have a seedy charm and some of the best-preserved buildings are (or are scheduled to be) under restoration. Among them, the former home of Chiriquí's founder, José de Obaldia Orejuela, is now the **Museo de Historia and Arte José de Obaldia** (Jose de Obaldia Museum of History and Art), Calle 8, ☎ 507-775-7839, open Tuesday through Saturday, 8:30 am to 4 pm. Its fine collections include ceramics and artifacts from local pre-Columbian Barilles and Bugaba cultures, 18th-Century religious art, colonial period historical documents and artifacts, and the home's original furnishings. It's an easy four-block walk from the park; a taxi will cost about $1.

Held in mid-March, David's annual fair, **Feria de San José**, is one of Central America's biggest and best. This 10-day event attracts exhibitors and visitors from throughout Central America. Food, rodeos, bullfights, horse shows, traditional music and dance are featured, along with the livestock, horticultural and technology exhibits. Contact IPAT's David office, ☎ 507-775-4120, for information. If visiting during the fair, be sure to make reservations well in advance.

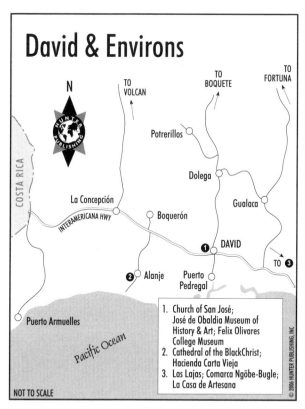

David & Environs

N

TO VOLCAN

TO BOQUETE

TO FORTUNA

Potrerillos

Dolega

La Concepción

Gualaca

INTERAMERICANA HWY

Boquerón

DAVID ❶

TO ❸

❷ Alanje

Puerto Pedregal

Puerto Armuelles

COSTA RICA

Pacific Ocean

1. Church of San José;
   José de Obaldia Museum of History & Art; Felix Olivares College Museum
2. Cathedral of the BlackChrist;
   Hacienda Carta Vieja
3. Las Lajas; Comarca Ngöbe-Bugle;
   La Casa de Artesana

NOT TO SCALE

© 2006 HUNTER PUBLISHING, INC.

CHIRIQUI PROVINCE

◆ Alanje

This pleasant little town makes an interesting detour on the way to the Western Highlands or can be included in a day tour if you're staying in or near David. Founded in 1591 as Santiago de Alanje, its main attractions are the famed **Cathedral of the Black Christ** and nearby **Hacienda Carta Vieja**, ☎ 507-770-7073, Panamá's largest rum distillery. The distillery, with an interesting museum, offers free weekday tours. Rum and souvenirs can be purchased and there's a good typical restaurant for lunch.

Destroyed in 1686 by pirates allied with local Indians, Alanje was rebuilt in the early 1700s and later served as the provincial capital until replaced by David in 1831. It's a quiet little farming town where nothing of note happens until Holy Week each year when thousands of pilgrims descend to pay their debts to the mysterious Black Christ. Believers arrive in a motley assortment of motorized and non-motorized vehicles, on horseback, on foot or on bloodied knees. Watch for the Alanje sign on the highway's left about 10 miles/16 kilometers west of David.

❖   **THE BLACK CHRIST OF ALANJE**

Folk tales recount the legend of a humble "foreigner" who suddenly appeared in Alanje during the turbulent early 1600s. When the townspeople asked where he had come from, the foreigner replied that it didn't matter, he had come to make them a gift and would need a place to carry out his work. This pleased the townspeople who gave him a little house and agreed to bring him food every day. He then asked if he might cut a neighbor's orange tree to make the gift. Again the townspeople agreed. The tree was carried into his house and soon the townspeople heard him sawing away. They kept their promise, and every evening brought food, leaving it on the doorstep. One day the sawing stopped. Expecting to hear him pounding nails, the townspeople listened but all was silent. The next day they found his food untouched. Thinking him preoccupied, they carried it away and left fresh food. Again the next day they found the food as they had left it and the house was still silent. After a few days of this, the townspeople began to worry that an accident might have befallen the foreigner. There was no answer when they knocked and when they peeked through the windows, it was too dark inside to see anything. When they finally pushed open the door, sunlight streamed in to reveal the Black Christ statue in all its splendor. But search as they might, they could find no trace of the foreigner. There was no sawdust on the floors, no tools, nothing. It was as if he had never existed. And to this day Alanje's townspeople wonder if he ever really had.

Over the years many attempts have been made to move the Black Christ statue from Alanje to a larger cathedral more befitting its status. Each attempt ended in failure when accident or mishap intervened. If the Christ was placed in a wagon, the wheels would fall off, the horses would bolt, or the wagon would become mired in mud. As the mysterious foreigner intended, the Black Christ still watches over Alanje's townspeople.

◆ La Concepción

Gateway to Chiriquí's Western Highlands, this dusty commercial sugar and cattle town is famed for the fine handcrafted saddles made here. Other than a colorful weekend market, there isn't much to interest visitors. On Saturdays and Sundays, the streets and sidewalks surrounding its pretty central park are packed with friendly farmers selling fresh produce from the backs of loaded pick-up trucks; fishermen hawking their catch from ice chests; fresh-cut flowers and plants; and artisans and craftspeople displaying their works. The town is also called Bugaba, after a pre-Columbian people who once lived here (and now also the name of the district). It is only minutes north of the InterAmericana, about 34 kilometers west from David. If heading to the Western Highlands, exit the InterAmericana at the marked turnoff to La Concepción and drive straight through town until you come to the signposted (you can't miss the sign, it looms smack in front of you) road to Bambito. Turn onto the Bambito road and continue north into the mountainous rural countryside.

◆ East of David

From the InterAmericana's San Felix turnoff, 43 miles/69 kilometers east of David, you can access **Playa Las Lajas**, one of Panamá's most beautiful golden sand beaches; the semi-autonomous lands of **Comarca Ngöbe-Buglé**; and **La Casa de Artesenal**, the best place in the country to buy Ngobe-Bugle handicrafts. If you're coming to Chiriquí Province by road, and haven't already visited these interesting places that are a little more than halfway between Santiago and David, consider visiting all three during a day-trip from David. If you leave David early, there will be plenty of time.

Playa Las Lajas

Playa Las Lajas is one of Panamá's a most beautiful golden-sand beaches and is a great place to break your road-trip. Although there are no hotels nearby, the **Carrizal Country Club** next to the beach has covered parking ($5 per day weekends and $3 on weekdays), bars, a restaurant with typical food, and well-maintained showers and changing rooms (25¢ weekends/10¢ weekdays). There are a few small shops and restaurants and a public phone in nearby Las Lajas town and a beachfront restaurant that's open only on weekends. Playa Las Lajas is 73 miles/118 kilometers west of Santiago. Take the Cruce San Félix turnoff from the InterAmericana and continue 9.5 miles/15 kilometers south through Las Lajas village to the beach. Expect the drive from Santiago to take about 1½ hours.

Comarca Ngöbe-Buglé

Collectively called Ngöbe-Buglé, or sometimes Guaymí, Panamá's most numerous indigenous peoples, the Ngöbé and the Buglé are similar, but separate ethno-linguistic groups. The Buglé once inhabited much of today's Veraguas, Herrera, Los Santos, Cocle and Panamá provinces but after their defeat by the Spanish, fled to the mountains of Veraguas and Chiriquí. The Ngöbe suffered invaders from the time of the Spanish into the late 1930s, when they were driven from their lands along the Caribbean and Northern Pacific plains by cattle ranchers and transnational banana companies. After almost 100 years of struggle, Panamá's government awarded both groups autonomous status and a combined homeland in the mountainous regions of Chirquí, Veraguas and Bocas del Toro. Today, about 180,000 Ngöbe and 10,000 Buglé inhabit Comarca Ngöbe-Buglé, land so poor that almost half the men must migrate from their homes to labor on coffee, rice, sugarcane and vegetable farms. Their territories still suffer invasion by foreign mining companies, landless peasant farmers and cattle ranchers.

These proud people will welcome you to their 45,240-sq mile/116,000-sq kilometer homeland (*comarca*) high in the Cordillera Central. Little girls in traditional long dresses and little boys, sometimes three or four astride a single nag, smile shyly or wave exuberantly in greeting. Outsiders are rare in this rugged land, abundant with birds and wildlife, although community leaders hope to promote tourism here – a difficult task as these traditional people live scattered through the mountains in small family groups rather than in village communities. The closest thing to a village is little **Quebrada de Quabo**, with a school and a market where you can buy traditional handicrafts, artworks and cold drinks. Although the soil is poor, it's well suited for growing the excellent organic coffee produced here. To learn more about how these stately people are working to preserve their cultural identity and their lands, or to buy the delicious coffee, contact Asociacion de Professionales Agropecuarios Ngöbe/Buglé, apanb@hotmail.com (English and Spanish). To get here from the InterAmericana, take the San Félix turnoff (62 miles/100 kilometers west of Santiago). After passing through San Félix village, continue straight ahead for about 45 minutes to the Comarca's boundary. You'll need a 4x4 vehicle to maneuver the steep, potholed dirt road. It's best to visit during a day trip from Santiago or David with **Panamá City Tours**, ☎ 507-263-8918, www.panamacitytours.com, or **Ecocircuitos**, ☎ 507-314-1586, www.ecocircuitos.com.

La Casa de Artesanal

In my opinion, this cooperative is the country's best place to buy Ngöbe-Buglé handicrafts. Almost a hundred of the nearby *comarca's* women contribute to its dazzling collection of handmade clothing, appliquéd linens, woven hats, soapstone carvings, beaded jewelry – and those beautiful *chacara* bags in every imaginable size and color combination. (see shopping, page XX for a description of *chacaras*).You'll find the cooperative signposted beside the highway, 63 miles/100 kilometers west of Santiago. If traveling by bus, ask the driver to let you off at the "artesanal" driveway or at the Cruce San Félix bus stop, where someone will point you the way. The cooperative is open Monday through Saturday, 9 am-5 pm. If coming on Sunday, phone Yanileth Rodriguez, ☎ 507-727-0717, for an appointment. There's a 24- hour restaurant, a gas station and bus stop in nearby Cruce San Félix town.

Where to Stay

Gran Hotel Nacional, Av 1ra and Calle Central, ☎ 507-775-2221, fax 507-775-7729, $$, is a favorite. It has 75 rooms and suites, air conditioning, cable TV, telephone, safe, pool, restaurant, bar, disco, and casino. This lovely, immaculate hotel is the best in town. All of the comfortable, attractively decorated rooms, suites and junior suites are big

❖ HOTEL PRICING
Based on double occupancy
No $ . . . . under $20
$ . . . . $20 to $39
$$ . . . . $40 to $79
$$$ . . . . $80 to $124
$$$$ . . . . . . $125 to $199
$$$$$ . . . . over $200

and airy. There's a large swimming pool and recreation area, an outdoor barbecue terrace on the beautiful grounds, and secure parking.

Hotel Puerta del Sol, Calle 3 Este and Av Central, ☎ 507-774-8422, fax 507-775-1622, $$, has 86 rooms and offers air conditioning, international cable TV, telephone, safe, pool, restaurant, cafeteria, bar, gym, and parking. This is a newer hotel with attractive, comfortable, but somewhat small rooms, two blocks from Parque Cervantes.

Hotel Iris, Calla A Norte, opposite Parque Cervantes, ☎ 507-775-2251, fax 507-775-7233, $, has 66 rooms, air conditioning, TV, and restaurant. It is an okay place to stay, but nothing fancy. An average double goes for $20.

Hotel Fiesta, InterAmericana Highway, eastern city limits, ☎ 507-775-5454, fax 507-774-5484, $, 64 rooms, air conditioning, international cable TV, telephone, pool, restaurant, bar, $. Small, clean rooms and small bathrooms are built around a large pool terrace. Most of the rooms have been recently upgraded; ask to see one or two before deciding. Hotel Fiesta is a good choice if you don't want to stay in town, and the restaurant here is good and very friendly. The average price of a double room is $30.

Hotel Occidental, Av 3 de Noviembre, opposite Parque Cervantes, ☎ 507-775-4695, fax 507-775-7424, $, has 64 rooms and air conditioning, cable TV, telephone, restaurant. It's nothing fancy, but the beds are good and it's clean and friendly.

Pension Clark, Av Francisco Clark, ☎ 507-774-3452, has eight rooms, some with private bath. It's a no-frills place; just clean and friendly budget accommodations. Rates average $8-$9.

Best bet if you're budgeting, sociable, or crave a home-like atmosphere is the handicap-accessible **Purple House Hostel**, Calle C Sur and Av 6, ☎ 507-774-4059, www.purplehousehostel.com. Purple House, which opened in March, 2002, is on a quiet street within walking distance of the bus terminal, the town market, a 24-hour supermarket, restaurants and those familiar fast-food places. Dorm accommodations with shared bath cost $6.60 per person. A private double room with A/C and private bath is only $20.60 (taxes included). Continental breakfast is complimentary, the communal kitchen is supplied with condiments and free coffee, tea and orange juice (and fresh fruit in season) available all day, every day. The comfortable lounge has cable TV, stereo, a lending library, reference books, board games and a variety of tourist information. There's a pleasant dining terrace and sun worshippers can cool down in lounge chairs equipped with personal "shower/misters." Closets and storage areas have locks and Purple House will store your luggage you might not want to lug to the beach or on highland treks. Fluent English and Spanish are spoken and the personable hosts have arranged useful discounts from local businesses for their guests.

Where to Eat

While David isn't known for its culinary adventures, **Gran Hotel Nacional's** restaurant is an exception. Some of the delicious fare is European-inspired; there are traditional and pasta dishes, and pastries and desserts are to die for. Service too, is excellent. You'll find it on

❖ RESTAURANT PRICING
Entrée & non-alcoholic drink
$ . . . . under $5
$$ . . . . $5 to $10
$$$ . . . . $11 to $20
$$$$ . . . . over $21

the corner of Av Central and Calle 1. Also good is the hotel's pizza place across the street.

Restaurante Churrasco's Place, Av 2 Este ($2-$4) near Parque Cervantes, serves generous servings of typical food, with good grilled meats and *arroz con pollo*.

The restaurant at **Hotel Occidental**, Av 3 de Noviembre opposite the park, has breakfast and sandwiches for less than $2.

If you're hankering for pizza or spaghetti, stop by **Mio Bello Pizzeria** on Calle 8 and Av 3 de Noviembre.

For good international food and local specialties, the **Hotel Fiesta** restaurant is a fine choice. Dinners here average $5 to $6 and the service is friendly and efficient.

CHIRIQUI PROVINCE

AUTHOR NOTE: *If you're staying downtown near the park, you'll find many small eating establishments with good typical food and a few Chinese restaurants with long menus and huge portions for $3-$4. There's a McPato's among the well-known fast-food places and a new Subway Sandwiches next to the Super 99 market.*

A few other fast food places scattered around town include a new Subway Sandwiches near the Super 99 market, a McPato's, a McDonald's.

If you're hankering for hard-to-find specialty foods or imported wines and cheeses, stop at **Super Barú**, the huge supermarket on the corner of Av Francisco Clark and 3 de Noviembre, a block from the InterAmericana on David's east side. Some very unusual items turn up on the shelves and there's an excellent bakery, a pharmacy, a deli and a little indoor café. You'll find a **Price-Costco** on the highway west of the city, next to the large shopping mall with six movie theaters.

The Pacific Lowlands

Most visitors to Chiriquí's lowlands come to dive or sport fish the almost virgin waters. Black marlin, sailfish, dolphin, wahoo, yellowfin tuna, cubera snapper and more are plentiful. Scuba divers will enter a virtually unexplored underwater world of rare, abundant sea life, magnificent reefs, deep drops and pinnacles.

Adventures

◆ On Water

Diving & Sportfishing

The luxury 115-ft/34.5 meter **M/V Coral Star**, ☎ 866-924-2837 (toll-free in the US), www.coralstar.com, offers both live-aboard and day-long fishing and deep-sea diving tours. All-inclusive packages include two nights' hotel in Panamá City (on departure and arrival) and air transportation to/from David from the capital. The ship departs from Puerto Pedregal, a few minutes south of David.

The **Panamá Big Game Fishing Club**, Isla Boca Brava, about one hour from David, ☎ 866-281-1225 (toll-free in the US), fax 305-653-2331, www.panama-sportfishing.com, offers all-inclusive packages for two or more days that include land-based accommodation in the club's lovely cottages, all in-country transportation and transfers, all meals and beverages.

Las Olas Resort, Barqueta Beach, ☎ 507-772-3000, fax 507-772-3619 in Panamá, ☎ 800-346-1329 (toll-free in the US), offers a full day of sportfishing from $550 (up to three anglers) to $1200 (up to five) per day, depending on destination waters.

Where to Stay & Eat

Facing the sea, elegant Mediterranean-style **Las Olas Resort**, Barqueta Beach, ☎ 507-772-3000, fax 507-772-3619 in Panamá, ☎ 800-346-1329 (toll-free in the US), www.lasolasresort.com, is part of a 5,000-acre property, bordered by a 15-mile/24-kilometer stretch of glittering black sand beach. All 48 lovely air-conditioned rooms and suites in the two-story complex have mini-bars and private terraces or balconies for enjoying sea views, breezes and glorious sunsets. The food and service are superb, and you can dine indoors at **La Abigail**, an elegant gourmet restaurant, or on the shady outdoor dining terrace. There's a full spa, gym, weight room and saunas, games room, pub bar, outdoor wet bars, two pools and more. If you've always wanted to gallop along a tropical beach, you can – astride one of the resort's own magnificent steeds. All-inclusive packages that include accommodation, all meals, snacks, bar and soft drinks, use of non-motorized sports equipment (kayaks, canoes) and more, average $165 daily for two (depending on the season). Room-only rates are about $120 for two. The resort offers a "Day Pass," but I recommend a longer stay. My own ended much too soon. Las Olas is a half-hour drive from David – and they'll provide transportation if needed. The resort also offers a wealth of optional sightseeing and adventure opportunities throughout the region.

The Eastern Highlands

Boquete

It takes slightly less than an hour to drive the smoothly escalating black-top road from David's lowland humidity to this charming agricultural town in the green foothills of the Cordillera Central. Immediately before the town limits, atop a promontory to the right, you'll see a two-story yellow house that would look at home on a Kansas farm. No, Auntie Em doesn't live there – it's one of the tourism bureaus ridiculously expensive CEFATI (Centros Felicidades Touristicas y Interpretacion de Panamá – or, for simplicity's sake, tourist welcome centers). Stop here to pick up brochures, maps and information, or to get help making reservations, then order a delicious cappuccino or shake from the on-premise Café Ruiz Coffee Shop and step outside for an awesome view of the town below.

Divided by the Caldera River, Boquete lies in a peaceful valley surrounded by cloud-capped mountain forests dwarfed by majestic Volcán Barú looming in the distance. If a rainbow isn't straddling the valley – and one often is – you just might conjure up the Jolly Green Giant. The into-town road descends through hillsides planted with orange trees, shaded coffee plants and multi-hued fields of flowers grown commercially or for export. Not to be outdone, Boquete's residents have turned every tiny yard and spare patch of ground into blooming gardens, and almost everyone has a few orange trees and coffee plants. All this "lushness" results from the pleasantly cool climate, rich volcanic soils and, as residents are quick to point out, frequent mists of afternoon rain called *bajareques*. Year-round temperatures average 80°F/26°C during the day and 60°F/16°C at night.

Many of Boquete's early European and North American settlers arrived during the late 1880s and early 1900s. Some came to retire, others to establish coffee or vegetable farms. In 1816, the town's first hotel was founded by retired British steamship captain, Henry J. Watson. American Frank Tedman brought from California the first navel oranges, forerunners of today's famed Boquete oranges. More recently, an exodus of North American retirees has produced a spate of new construction – including some of those divisive "gated" communities.

◆ Sightseeing & Touring

The road from David dips into town to become **Central Avenue**, Boquete's main street that runs parallel to the river on the east. An hour's stroll around town – it's impossible to get lost – will familiarize you with the "downtown" area; the nearby residential neighborhoods spread from its central park, **Parque Dominico Medica**. Among the established shops and restaurants is combined Gringo's Bike and Scooter Rental, Estate Coffee Shop, Café Internet, a gift shop and small Museum Las Huacas ($1 admission). Stop by and Patricia, who manages the entire conglomeration, will whip you up a delicious fruit shake, help you arrange a tour, provide directions or rent you some wheels.

Walk a couple of blocks northeast from Central Avenue to **Parque de las Madres** (Mother's Park), a delightful garden spot with a lovely statue of a mother and child and a sparkling fountain centerpiece. Nearby, a tiny railroad car sits frozen in time on a slice of track – all that's left of the rail-

CHIRIQUI PROVINCE

way built in 1912 by President Belisario Porras to link Boquete to the Pacific coast. Cross the rickety suspension bridge to the **Fair of Flowers**. Sharing the spotlight with flowers of every size and hue are orchids and famed carmine red, port wine-scented Black Prince roses. The river and singing birds supply sound effects, while benches painted to resemble jungle critters and chairs shaped like blossoms add a touch of whimsy.

On a lovely hillside a few minutes walk north from the town center, **Mi Jardin es Su Jardin** (My Garden is Your Garden) is on the private estate of a gracious retired couple who keep it open for visitors. The manicured grounds, rare posies, flowering trees, little streams and fountains are gorgeous, but you might find the miniature windmills, elves and almost life-size bovines painted with bright yellow sunflowers or red roses a tad distracting. There is no admission but since this is the family's home, please time your visit between 10 am and 4 pm.

You'll wonder if a frenetic Holly Hobby and wacky Austin Powers design team added the final touches to Sra. Deyanira de Miranda's extraordinary five-acre/two-hectare **El Explorador gardens** high above the town. Cypress trees trimmed and shaped to resemble comic book characters, massed roses and lilies, bonsai displays, orchids, singing birds, wild rabbits, fruit trees and clumps of daisies planted in old shoes share awesome mountain views with Punch and Judy and the Wicked Witch of the West posed in tubeless TV sets. Sra. de Miranda's love of all things beautiful is obvious – and so is her humor. Visit the gardens in the morning and have lunch at her charming little restaurant at the entrance. The chicken dishes are excellent and the fruit shakes scrumptious. Plan to spend at least an hour or two exploring the gardens. Admission to the gardens is $2.

❖ COFFEE ESTATE TOURS

During harvest season, Guaymí Indians gathering bright red coffee cherries flood hillside coffee plantations. Several of the plantations offer tours that might end with a tasting session called "cupping."

Famed **Café Ruiz** offers a free short tour of its roasting and packing plant, a few minutes from the town center and a three-hour plantation tour ($14) to see how coffee is grown and processed. ☎ 507-720-1392 (Spanish only) or you can send an e-mail in English, Spanish, Dutch or German through their website, www.caferuiz.com.

Coffee grown on lovely **Finca Lerida**, ☎ 507-720-1324, panamont@cwpanama.com, is rated among Central America's top five. Tours of varying length are offered to this cloud forest estate.

Established in 1918, **Café Kotowa**, ☎ 507-270-1430, kotowa@chiriqui.com, has set aside 500 of its pristine cloud forest acres as a wildlife sanctuary. Tours include a visit to its historic coffee mill.

AUTHOR NOTE: *The coffee fruit that most of us think of as a bean is called a cherry.*

Adventures

◆ On Foot

Birding

Quetzals, bellbirds and volcano juncos are only a few of the rare birds inhabiting Finca Lérida's cloud forests, part of the coffee estate owned by the Collins family of historic **Hotel Panamonte**, ☎ 507-720-1324, fax 507-720-2055, www.hotelpanamonte.com. More than 800 species have been recorded in these primary and secondary forests that rise to 9,800 feet/3,000 meters above sea level. All-day birding tours with an experienced guide start at $75 per person for a minimum of three people. To get here, head west on Calle Central until it forks; continue on the right fork to the hotel, on the outskirts of Boquete. Guided visits to private **Finca Lérida** (see *Coffee Estate Tours*, above) can be arranged at the hotel. See *Where to Stay*, below, for directions to Hotel Panamonte.

One of the most popular and easy birding hikes is the **Sendero de los Quetzales** (Quetzal Trail). This well-marked trail starts at the Fair of Flowers grounds and skirts part-way around the volcano to the little town of Cerro Punta. Expect to spend six to seven hours on this interesting trail, even if birding isn't your passion. There's some wonderful scenery and plenty of other wildlife. To get here, walk two blocks east from the central park and cross the suspension bridge. You can't miss the lovely Fair of Flowers on the left at the end of the bridge. Local tour operators provide guided hikes, or you might want to contact birding specialist guide **Abdiel Baules** (☎ 507-649-6223, e-mail abaules@hotmail.com).

Hiking & Trekking

If you're physically fit and have the time, consider hiking the Summit Trail to the top of **Volcán Barú**. It will take about seven hours up and another five to get back down over the steep, rough trail that gets downright hairy at times. The trail ascends through several biological zones as cloud forests give way to sub-alpine scrub and rocky canyons and, at the summit, cold barren rock populated with a jumble of radio and TV towers. There's a rudimentary campground about halfway up or you can spend the night on the summit to watch the sunrise. It's said that watching a sunrise from up here is a life-changing experience. The best views are early in the morning before the clouds roll in and if the day is clear, you can see both the Atlantic and Pacific coasts. Take plenty of water, food, a flashlight, sunscreen and warm clothing; the higher you climb, the colder and windier it gets. Temperatures near the summit can drop to below freezing after sunset, making hypothermia a possibility. During the day, sunburn is a risk, so lather those exposed parts with plenty of sunscreen. Amateur hikers should go with a guide and never, ever attempt this trek after dark. You won't find a better guide than **Rodrigo Marciacq**, ☎ 507-720-2165, a horticulturist with deep knowledge and an abiding respect for Barú, its wild inhabitants and ecosystems. Rodrigo and his wife, Priscilla, own lovely Villa Marita Cabins. To get to the volcano's summit road from Boquete, turn west on Calla 2a Norte and continue 455 yards/500 meters to the gravel road on the right. Turn right and stay on the gravel road that dissipates to rock and potholes as it escalates steeply up through the forests

> **AUTHOR NOTE:** *The drive to the summit of Volcán Barú can be made only in a high-clearance 4X4 vehicle during the dry season. It's a difficult drive when dry, and you would be foolhardy to attempt it during the rainy season.*

Good trails into the protected Palo Alto Cloud forest north of Boquete include Bajo Mono, which roughly translated can mean either "pretty short" or "low monkey."

Los Pozos de Caldera (hot springs) are great for soaking those aching tootsies after a long hike. The four pools, all with different temperatures, are near the village of Caldera, south of Boquete. To get here, backtrack from Boquete on the David-Boquete road and turn onto the signposted road to Caldera. Several dirt roads run from Caldera, so ask a local which one is to the springs that are another 8.7 miles/14 kilometers distant. Buses run from Boquete to Caldera but none passES the springs, which are a 45-minute hike from the village. The springs are on land owned by the Collins family of Hotel Panamonte, ☎ 507-720-1320, in Boquete, so please ask permission before visiting. It's best to go with a local guide.

> **AUTHOR NOTE:** *When hiking or camping, please pack out anything that you pack in.*

If you're heading to Bocas del Toro's islands, consider hiking the **Puma Trail** with **Nolo Picota**, ☎ 507-644-2377, masucato@hotmail.com. This four-day excursion includes about six hours each day hiking along a scenic route that climbs to 885 feet/2,952 meters through the mountains of Comarca Ngöbe-Buglé. The trail crosses rivers and streams with time out for swimming, fishing or relaxing. One night is spent camping, and two are in local *fincas*. The $100 per-person, per-day rate includes meals, guides, all equipment and water taxi transportation from Almirante to Bocas. Add $30 if a pack horse is required. If you wish, Nolo will arrange your accommodations in Bocas.

◆ On Wheels

You'll need a sturdy mountain bike and sturdy legs to navigate Boquete's steep side streets and country lanes. The reward is some awesome scenery. Rent your wheels for $12 a day from **Gringo's Bike and Scooter Rental** (☎ 507-720-2720) on Av Central in the center of town. Scooters are $29 for the day and you'll need to show your driver's license and insurance card.

Personable **Feliciano Gonzalez**, ☎ 507-624-9940 or 507-632-8645, e-mail felicianogonzalez255@hotmail.com) can take you just about anywhere in his high-clearance 4X4 – to the top of the volcano, the thermal springs, and other interesting spots, and even arrange to pick you up in David. Feliciano is a delightful character who includes an hour of free Spanish lessons with his tours.

Franklin, ☎ 507-720-2284/659-9841, who speaks English, Spanish and Italian, will take you on a delightful five-hour cultural tour to the Río Caldera and hot springs to meet local people, enjoy a typical lunch and to watch as sugarcane is pressed through a *trapiche* (sugarcane press). If you have a high-clearance 4X4, you can drive up the horribly rough, seldom-used maintainance road to the volcano's summit. During the rainy season between mid-May to mid-December, both the road and the trail can turn into rivers of slippery, dangerous mud. It's wiser and more fun to go with a local tour operator.

CHIRIQUÍ PROVINCE

◆ On Horseback

If you prefer to explore on someone else's four feet rather than your own two, **Eduardo Cano**, ☎ 507-720-1750, will take you touring aboard one of his sturdy steeds for an average of $15 per hour, depending on how many hours you want to ride and how many are in your party. Although Eduardo speaks only Spanish, he's been at this long enough to communicate with just about anyone.

Nolo Picota, ☎ 507-644-2377, e-mail masucato@hotmail.com, rents horses with a guide for $7 per hour. Nolo speaks English and Spanish.

Pension Marilos, **Pension Topas** and **Hotel Panamonte** also arrange horse rentals or horseback tours (see *Where to Stay*, below, for contact information).

◆ On Water

Family-owned **Chiriquí River Rafting**, ☎ 507-720-1505, fax 507-720-1506, www.panama-rafting.com, pioneered Panamá's white-water rafting on the **Chiriquí** and **Chiriquí Viejo** rivers only a few years ago. Both of these fast-running rivers descend through beautiful scenery and are run during the rainy season from May until about mid-December. During the dry season, water levels drop. Río Chiriquí's Bajo Mendez section is a three- to five-hour class III or IV run, depending on rainfall. This awesome journey rushes you over several waterfalls, including one called "The Hammer." The river's Barrigona section is a milder, class II and III version of Bajo Mendez over calmer waters. Barrigona is perfect for beginners, bird watchers or those looking for an adventurous way to take in the scenery.

Getting to Río Chiriquí Viejo isn't quite as easy. There's more drive time involved through virgin primary rainforests and views of spectacular Volcán Barú. Chiriquí Viejo's Palon (big stick) section consists of classes III+ and IV runs with non-stop excitement through pristine tropical forests and deep canyons. The magnificent scenery includes a lovely 30-foot waterfall. It's a 3½- to four-hour run that drops at a fast speed and requires quick, tight maneuverings through many rock gardens and around huge boulders. The Sabo section is ranked class II, with several class III rapids. Because of the many birds inhabiting the area, the Sabo section is perfect to combine with birding and easy enough for beginners. You can also arrange a two-day trip that includes rafting both sections of Chiriquí Viejo with one night of camping between the runs.

Highly regarded Chiriquí River Rafting also offers **kayaking** trips on both rivers or, if you're experienced and want to go it alone, they'll rent you a kayak and gear.

Where to Stay

La Montaña y el Valle, **The** Coffee Estate Inn, ☎ 507-720-2011, www.coffeeestateinn.com, $$. Secluded on a lush mountain hillside, three luxury bungalows, each with a private balcony, overlook Boquete valley and looming Volcán Barú in the distance. These spacious, delightfully appointed quarters have gracious living/dining areas with

❖ HOTEL PRICING
Based on double occupancy
No $ . . . . under $20
$ . . . . $20 to $39
$$ . . . . $40 to $79
$$$ . . . . $80 to $124
$$$$ . . . . . $125 to $199
$$$$$ . . . . over $200

wide windows for the view, bedrooms with comfortable orthopedic beds, and kitchens fully equipped with everything you'll need, including a supply of freshly roasted estate-grown coffee. There's a vast library of reference books and novels. Trails populated with myriad bird and butterfly species run through the forested hillside property, which is rife with fragrant coffee, banana and orange trees. Attentive Canadian hosts Jane Walker and Barry Robbins, both gourmet cooks, offer an optional menu of delicious specialties served by candlelight or on your private balcony. La Montaña is .75 mile/1.2 kilometers northwest of Boquete's town center. To get here, head north on Av Central, pass the church, and follow the signs.

The six lovely roundhouses at **Isla Verde**, on Calle 5A Sur two blocks west of Av Central, ☎ 507-720-2533, $$, are based on a modern concept of ancient Indian design with high, domed ceilings, cheery kitchens and magically suspended sleeping lofts. Smaller roundhouses will accommodate from two to four and the larger ones comfortably sleep up to six. All have tile floors, white-walled interiors and large bathrooms. Three are fully handicap-accessible. Two more architecturally conventional new suites are equally lovely, with well-designed appointments, charming interiors and breezy balconies. This pleasing property in lushly blooming gardens is a pleasant three-minute walk from town.

Built in 1816, **Hotel Panamonte**, ☎ 507-720-1324 or 1327, fax 507-720-2055, www.hotelpanamonte.com, $$, is Boquete's grand dowager. This wonderful old hotel, owned by the Elliot-Collins family since 1928, retains all of its original country charm. Fresh flowers and art treasures collected from around the world highlight public rooms and a cheerful log fire blazes in the lounge's fireplace on chilly evenings. Lavishly decorated rooms in jewel-tone floral fabrics wrap a courtyard equally lavish with flowering plants and trees. Rife with history, Panamonte has entertained more than its share of celebrity guests. Greta Garbo stayed here, as did Teddy Roosevelt and Charles Lindbergh. Admiral Byrd chose it to complete his South Pole expedition book, and Ingrid Bergman visited so frequently her favorite room was kept on reserve. The same staff stays on year after year to provide the best in personalized service. There are single, double and triple rooms, apartments that accommodate up to four and a little house with three bedrooms and two baths as charming as the hotel. To get to the Hotel Panamonte, walk or drive north on Av Central and, after passing the church, you'll come to a fork in the road. Take the one on the right to the hotel, which is at the edge of town.

Villa Marita Lodge, ☎ 507-720-2165, www.panamainfo.com/marita, $, is 2.4 miles/four kilometers from Boquete's center. French-style windows, warm hardwood interiors and comfortable furnishings enhance seven spacious cabins with separate sitting rooms and bedrooms perched on a terraced bluff above Boquete Valley. The cabins and welcoming main lodge share stunning volcano, mountain and valley views. Delicious meals are served in the attractive lounge or on the outdoor balcony in the refreshing eucalyptus- and bellflower-scented mountain air. Host Rodrigo Marciacq is an expert on the volcano and an agriculturist with Panamá's only hydroponic gardens. You can tour the gardens and pick fresh lettuce or tomatoes from vines that often grow 30 feet tall. Rodrigo and his lovely wife Priscilla speak English and Spanish. Children are welcomed, and Rodrigo tailors personalized tours. To get here, head north from the central park on the road marked "To Alto Lino," and turn at the arrow marking the way to the lodge.

English, Spanish and German are spoken at **Pension Topas**, on Av Belisario Porras three blocks south of the central park, ☎ 507-720-1005, e-mail schoeb@chiriqui.com, $. It's a pleasant, charming place in a shady flowering grove. There are six large, comfortable and well-decorated rooms with private bath, and two smaller rooms with shared bath around a beautiful flagstone terrace and swimming pool. Guests are welcome to help themselves to produce from the organic garden, and delicious home-cooked breakfasts are available.

Momentum Luxury Cabins, ☎ 507-720-4385, www.momentum-panama.com, $ B&B rooms, $$ cabins, offer a paradisiacal escape from the ordinary. Pathways curve through shady landscaped gardens to the delightful spacious cabins with shiny full kitchens, dining alcoves, large comfy living rooms and separate bedrooms with orthopedic queen beds. Or you can choose to stay in a bed and breakfast room. There are spectacular mountain views from the expansive pool terrace, plenty of shaded hammocks for an afternoon siesta, and a fully equipped gym, also with a view. Momentum is east of Boquete. Watch for the signs on the right just past the town of Dolega on the David-Boquete road. Reservations are suggested, and Momentum will supply a detailed map.

Villa Lorena, ☎ 507-720-1848, e-mail jrhydro@sinfo.net, $, nudges up to the Caldera River across from the Fair of Flowers gardens. Its three spacious and comfortable two-story townhouse apartments have fully equipped kitchens, two attractive bathrooms and loft bedrooms. The closets are amazingly big and laundry service is available. The reasonable rates and convenient location are definite assets.

Highland Hostal Mozart, ☎ 507-720-3764, $, is a charming little place, creatively decorated by its artist owner. Three guestrooms, separate from the main house, are not fancy, but they are comfortable, inexpensive and situated in lovely gardens on a mountainside with awesome views. The owner is also an accomplished baker and gourmet cook and wonderful meals are available. You'll find Mozart in Volcancito, a left turn from the David Road just before IPAT's big yellow CEFATI building.

Hotel Rebequet, ☎ 507-720-1365, $, has nine spiffy rooms with cable TV and convenient refrigerators built around a central courtyard. There's a very pleasant lounge and guests are welcome to use the kitchen. It's on Av A Este at the corner of Belisario Porras, a few minutes walk from the central park.

Kalima Suites Aparthotel, Av A Este, across the street from Pension Marilos, ☎ 507-720-2884, e-mail diprch@latinmail.com, $, has seven spacious suites with large airy rooms, fully equipped kitchens, a beautifully decorated living/dining room and bedrooms with cable TV. Each of the bedrooms has two double orthopedic beds and one single, and an extra bunk can be brought in if needed. The charming managers will help you make 25¢ calls to the US or Canada, and the internet café here is the cheapest in town. I paid a $1 for an hour's use. Checking my e-mail took only 15 minutes, and they insisted on giving me 75¢ change!

Pension Virginia, ☎ 507-720-1260, is an older hotel with worn, welcoming appeal. Its 23 rooms of varying size and décor are spotlessly clean. Some are cheery and bright, some are a tad drab and some have shared bathrooms. Look a few over before deciding. There's a pleasant balcony overlooking a back garden and a nostalgic second-floor lounge accented with books, souvenirs, 78RPM records, and an old record player dating from the 1940s. Rates average $17 for a large double room with private bath. This place is popular with budget travelers and backpackers. You'll find it downtown facing the central park.

Pension Marilos, Av A Este, across the street from Hotel Rebiquet, ☎ 507-720-1380, offers the best value in Boquete – perhaps in the entire country – for budget travelers or anyone who prefers a convenient, homey atmosphere. Gorgeous Ecuadorean blankets highlight the simple, tasteful guestrooms with comfortable beds, well-placed reading lamps and ample closets. Guests are welcome to cook in the huge kitchen that has a professional-size stove, and the pleasant dining room offers a choice of seating arrangements. There's a cozy lounge with cable TV, a book "trading" library and oodles of printed travel information available. Guests who stay longer than two nights can use the laundry facilities at no charge. Fluent English and Spanish are spoken at this immaculate, family-operated hostel. Rates, including tax, start at $6.60 for a single with shared bath and top out at $15.40 for a spacious double with private bath.

Hotel Los Establos Bed and Breakfast, ☎ 507-720-2685, $$$, is intimate, exquisitely decorated, and expensive. It's a few minutes from town on a lovely hillside with commanding views of the mountains and valleys. The six luxurious rooms have private balconies, TV and DVD, queen beds and marble bathrooms. There are two suites with lovely glass-enclosed sitting rooms. An exceptional collection of South and Central American artworks adorns the walls and accents the guestrooms, hallways and a delightful bar/lounge with billiards. Everything comes with a view, including the outdoor dining terrace, glass-enclosed Jacuzzi, putting green, PGA bent grass golf green with four chipping areas, and pathways winding through the coffee plantation. Los Establos is slightly less than one mile/1.5 kilometers northeast of the town center.

Camping

For $5 you can pitch your tent on **Highland Hostal Mozart's** lovely grounds or at **Pension Topas** for the same price. Pension Topas will also rent you a tent and both offer shared bathroom facilities. **La Montaña y el Valle, the Coffee Estate**, will rent you space amidst the coffee and orange trees for $7. (See *Where to Stay*, above, for details.) You can also camp in Parque Nacional Volcán Barú. The $5 cost is payable at the **ANAM ranger station** in Las Nubes, ☎ 507-774-6671.

Where to Eat

Santa Fé Bar and Grill, opposite the Fair of Flowers, $, is a delightful place to hunker down and enjoy some real Tex-Mex food. Start off with jalapeño poppers, stuffed potato skins or buffalo wings and move on to hot Texas chili. The burritos are huge, delicious and

❖ RESTAURANT PRICING
Entrée & non-alcoholic drink
$ . . . . under $5
$$ . . . . $5 to $10
$$$ . . . . $11 to $20
$$$$ . . . . over $21

served piping hot, or you can order a steak, fish fillet sandwich or cooling chef salad. Most entrées are $4 to $6 and soft drinks and ice-cold beer come with frosty mugs, perfect after an afternoon hike. Pleasant casual dining indoors, or outside on a covered terrace next to the soothing Caldera River. There are two bars – the larger one with a pool table, and a big satellite TV that draws in the sports fans. Reggae or salsa bands often play here on weekends.

La Casona Mexicana, Av Central, in the town center, ☎ 507-685-1120, $. This charming restaurant in an antique wooden house with slightly tipsy floors and walls painted in old México's sun-faded pastels. It serves delicious, authentic Mexican food. Candlelight and fresh flowers accent the series of small, atmospheric dining rooms with one to five tables each. The salsa is fresh and homemade, the tortilla chips light and crispy. *Pechuga a la Michoacán* (chicken breast Micoacan style) is perfectly seasoned and drenched in an exquisite sauce. My dining companion's chicken fajitas also scored a 10. The glass of house wine was so good, I ordered a second. Most menu items are from $4 to $6 – a steal.

> **AUTHOR NOTE:** *If your sweet tooth needs a fix or you'd just like a loaf of fresh baked bread,* **King's House Panaderia y Dulceria** *is opposite Parque de las Madres. Both* **Pasteleria Alemana**, *known for delicious pastries, and* **Panaderia Victoria** *are on Avenue Central.* **Fresas Mary** *specializes in delicious homemade fresh strawberry ice cream. You'll find it on the Volcancito road just off the David-Boquete road.*

Hotel Panamonte, ☎ 507-720-1324 or 1327, www.hotelpanamonte. com, $$-$$$, has a quietly elegant restaurant that is renowned for superb cuisine. Antique framed oil paintings, sparkling crystal, fresh flowers, and fine linens complement its country manor house style and excellent service. Everything is freshly prepared and served to perfection, including fork-tender filet mignon and fresh trout smothered in buttery almandine sauce. Thick and hearty seafood soup brims with *fruits de mer*, tiny yellow potatoes swim in butter and parsley, and crisp vegetables and salad greens taste just picked. Entrées come complete with soup or salad, vegetables, dessert and coffee or tea, or you can order à la carte. Vegetarians rejoice – the wild mushroom polenta is delicious. Panamonte is open seven days for breakfast, lunch and dinner.

Restaurant Lourdes, Av Central, $, is a spotless little place near the Central Park in the same complex as Chiriquí River Rafting. A breakfast of steak or pork chops with eggs, tortillas and coffee costs $1.50 to $2.50. Prices for a tasty and complete lunch or dinner that includes rice and beans, choice of meat or chicken, salad or potato average $3. Fruit shakes and pastries are very good and only fresh, natural juices are served. Try delicious papaya or nance.

El Sabrason, Av Central, $, is the cheapest place in town to eat. For $2, you can stuff yourself silly with decent typical food in this popular, no frills cafeteria-style restaurant.

Pizzeria La Volcanica, Av Central, $-$$, a couple of doors up from Gringo's, is a bit expensive for so-so pizza, but if you've a craving, pizzas and other Italian specialties cost around $5.

Restaurante Viñedo, across from King's Bakery, ☎ 507-720-1739, $, serves very good and nicely presented *comida tipica* in a pleasant café-style atmosphere. Lunch and dinner specials range from $2.25 to $3.50 and change every day. Get here early – delicious *pollo guisado* and *bistec picado* go fast.

Restaurante Pension Virginia, facing the central park, ☎ 507-720-1260, $, has two large attractive dining rooms, both with garden views and one with a lovely fireplace. There's also a small café-style eatery next to the street. Chicken in Creole sauce and beefsteak with rice and vegetables were the $2 daily specials when I visited. Tasajo with vegetables and spaghetti dinners go for $3, and there is a wide selection of full breakfast choices for $2. Sandwiches and hamburgers are always on the lunch menu.

Café Punto de Encuentro, Calle 6 Este, $, a block and a half from Pension Marilos, is a delightful little eatery open only for breakfast from 7 am until noon. The best breakfasts in town are served in a backyard garden or on an outdoor terrace. Olga whips up yummy omelets, French toast or pancakes and keeps your cup filled with excellent hot coffee – all for about $3.

I didn't have an opportunity to visit Hans and Jackie Collins's new restaurant, **Palo Alto**, but friends whose culinary judgment can be trusted described it as "absolutely wonderful" and "out of this world." I'm sorry to have missed it. The restaurant is on the east side of the Caldera River, a few minutes north of town. Reservations are a must; ☎ 507-720-1076.

The Western Highlands

Separating Chiriqui's Eastern and Western Highland regions, massive, mist-crowned 11,401-foot/3,420-meter **Volcán Barú** soars above the peaks of the surrounding Talamancas. The volcano lies within the perimeter of Barú Volcano National Park, roughly defined by its base and forest-clad lower slopes. To get to the Western Highlands from Boquete, you'll need to backtrack to the outskirts of David and head west on the InterAmericana to the town of La Concepcion, where the Bambito turnoff will take you north into the mountains. You can't miss the turnoff; a huge sign at the intersection points to Bambito.

If you have time, it's also possible to hike (about seven hours each way) from one region to the other via the long-distance footpath, Sendero de los Quetzales (Quetzal Trail) that skirts around the volcano's lower slopes

CHIRIQUI PROVINCE

– or by climbing up and down over the volcano – an arduous, grueling trip that takes two days. If traveling from the eastern region to the western by bus, connect in David's terminal to one headed for Volcán, Cerro Punta or Guadalupe.

If you plan to camp or rent a cottage – or if you have an urge to shop – stock up on supplies at the new Super Barú market, Price-Costco store or the newish shopping center alongside the highway on David's western outskirts. Once past this shopping glut, tall sugarcane and cattle ranches dominate the lowland rural landscape and, after leaving La Concepcion, you'll be on the well-paved road that curves steadily upward into the Cordillera, a beautiful scenic drive.

Sightseeing and Touring

The Bambito road winds steadily upward into dairy country – a landscape of tidy farms and steep emerald pastures dotted with black and white Holstein cattle. About half an hour's drive beyond La Concepcion, you'll come to AlanHer Dairy Outlet on the left. Make this a rest stop and sample famed homemade cheeses, delicious pastries and *huevos de leche* (milk egg) candies. Add a cup of hot chocolate or my favorite, *chicheme*, a tasty drink made of milk, toasted ground corn, vanilla and cinnamon, then mosey to the outdoor *mirador* (lookout) terrace to enjoy your treats with breathtaking views of the spectacular mountain countryside. As you continue on toward Bambito, you'll see little produce stands alongside the road. Don't pass up an opportunity to sample sweet juicy strawberries or luscious oranges if they're in season.

◆ Hato de Volcán

Just before Hato de Volcán (called Volcán), the first real town on this road, watch for the little wooden sign "Viños Don Carlos" staked in front of a small house on the right. Stop and be welcomed in to sample extraordinary peach and blackberry wines pressed from fruit grown in the owner's back yard. For $4 or $5 you can cart off a bottle of the delicious elixir. A little further along on the left you'll see the woodworking shop of José de la Cruz Gonzales, Arte Cruz Volcán. Exceptionally talented de la Cruz and his apprentices create signs, plaques, carved doors, furniture and anything else one can imagine that can be made from wood. Multi-talented de la Cruz studied glass engraving in Murano, Italy, and will etch a requested design into glass or crystal of any size or shape. Small, personalized items can be made in minutes or, if choosing a complicated or large item, you can pick it up on your return trip or have it shipped anywhere in the world.

About 20 miles/32 kilometers north of La Concepcion, Hato de Volcán is the largest of the Western Highland towns. It's main street is the road from La Concepcion. With   plenty of fine accommodations in town or nearby, Volcán is a good base for exploring the region's many attractions. Like Boquete during the 1880s and early 1900s, the lands here attracted European farmer settlers and today, it's fast becoming another retirement haven for North American and European expats.

The in-town **San Benito Agriculture and Crafts School** features a large gift shop where you can buy crafts made by students. The school holds an outdoor market every weekend. If staying in a cabin or cottage with cooking facilities, or to pick up snacks and picnic supplies, head for Berard's spotless market where you'll find a variety of Swiss-style foods and international specialties.

◆ Barilles

Barilles is the site of a culture that flourished until about 600 AD when an eruption of Volcán Barú buried it beneath layers of lava and ash. Since Barilles is the Spanish word for "barrels", and the first huge carved stones discovered here were barrel-shaped, the name stuck. Later excavations uncovered pottery, intriguing massive stone statues and metates (carved stone tables on which corn was ground) so large they may have been ceremonial. The statues and metates have been carted off to museums, but there's still plenty to see, including boulders carved with undeciphered markings, stone grinding tools, altars, a burial site with ancient pottery encrusted in its walls, and a baffling recent excavation that, although as yet unstudied, is surmised to have been the center of a baby sacrifice cult. Barilles is on private land, a farm owned by the welcoming Landau family. The Landaus have put together a photographic display of the archeological work carried out here, along with copies of *National Geographic* and other magazine/newspaper articles about the site. Speaking in English or Spanish, gracious Edna Landau will guide you around and explain what little is known about this "lost" culture. While there is currently no fee for visitors, it is appropriate to leave a donation to help maintain the site and to show appreciation for Mrs. Landau's time and courtesy.

I recommend combining your Barilles visit with an eco-agro tourism farm experience that adults enjoy and children adore. The Landau's is a working farm and here you can pick juicy blackberries as big as golf balls, snack on guavas, bananas and oranges, sip homemade blueberry or blackberry wine and learn how to milk a cow the old-fashioned way. Edna Landau will demonstrate how she makes fresh cheese and offer a sample of her delicious blackberry marmalade. You can buy fruit, berries and cheese, as well as the wine and marmalade. To get here from Volcán's main road, turn left at the crossroad alongside Panaderia Hermanos Ortega and stay on the well-paved turnoff road for 15-20 minutes until you see the Barilles sign at the Landau's driveway on the right. As a courtesy, please time your visit between 9:30 am and 4:30 pm. At the time of this writing, there was no fee for the farm experience but if there is now, it will be reasonable and a great value.

CHIRIQUI PROVINCE

A visit to **Janson Family Coffee** is an absolute must for connoisseurs and eco-agro buffs. The 100% organic Arabica coffee grown on this beautiful farm 4,500 feet/1,350 meters above sea level is picked, processed and micro-roasted daily in small batches to exacting standards. Janson's café-style coffeehouse atop a steep hill affords sweeping views of the pastoral countryside and majestic Volcán Barú. Whether served unadulterated, hot or iced, or as a delicious cappuccino or latte, I can honestly say this is the best coffee I have ever tasted. Combine it with those fantastic views, the fresh mountain air and a delicious pastry – heaven. Preservationist adventurers will appreciate that Janson adheres to the strict ecological standards of wildlife conservation, reforestation and waste reduction set by the Rainforest Alliance. Buy your coffee while you're here or they'll ship it almost anywhere in the world. Check their website, www.jansoncoffee.com, for more information. To get here from Volcán, turn left from the main street at Mercadito (Mini-super) Liam, and stay on the blacktop road to its end, then turn right and continue 1.5 miles/2.4 kilometers to the rarely (if ever) used airport runway. Make another right and continue down the runway for a half-mile/.8 kilometers to the Janson Family Coffee sign on the right.

◆ Cerro Punta

Terraced vegetable fields crazy-quilt the steep mountainsides around Cerro Punta, a small town in the collapsed crater of an extinct volcano. Although it's only 4.5 miles/seven kilometers north of Bambito, Cerro Punta is noticeably cooler at an altitude of 5,904 feet/1,800 meters. Chiriquí is Panamá's breadbasket, and Cerro Punta is its very heart, with almost 80% of Panamá's vegetables grown in this area.

Visitors are welcomed at **Fresas Manolo**, and **Fresas Cerro Punta** strawberry farms and at **Plantas y Flores**, a commercial flower farm. People come here mostly during the dry season (mid-January to May) to tour **Volcán Barú National Park** and **La Amistad International Park**, and to view the beautiful resplendent quetzal.

January to May is also foaling season at **Haras Cerro Punta**, ☎ 507-227-3371 in Panamá City, ☎ 507-771-2057 in Cerro Punta, which is a must-see for equine addicts. In 1945, Panamá's horse racing pioneers, Carlos and Fernando Eleta, brought the first thoroughbreds to Cerro Punta's rolling green pastures. Haras Cerro Punta (Haras means "horses with wings," or unicorns) was founded in 1977. In 1985, the stable's Proud Truth, Panamá's most valuable racehorse, won the coveted Breeder's Cup Classic World Thoroughbred Championship. Now 21 years old and retired, he may no longer have wings, but he still has the "look of eagles." I was enraptured by the farm's giant percherons, especially a coal-black stallion fittingly named Centurion. What a magnificent animal!

AUTHOR NOTE: *While visiting Haras Cerro Punta, be sure to stop in at **Café de Eleta Coffee and Gift Shop** to enjoy a delicious cup of the Eletas' home-grown brew. Most of the charming crafts and gift items sold here are made by the farm's employees and their families – another way this pioneering family helps provide income to people that might otherwise practice slash-and-burn farming or hunt endangered animals.*

A complete tour of the farm (about $7 adults) includes meeting Proud Truth, the newest up-and-coming stallion Slaughter Beach, brood mares, foals and the magnificent percherons. Riding is available.

> ❖ **LOCAL LORE**
>
> According to local legend, Western Chiriquí's wild cloud forests conceal a lost city of gold. The city prospered until the late 16th or early 17th century when it was discovered by marauding European pirates in search of gold. The pirates committed such horrible atrocities on the city's residents that it was abandoned and cursed by local priests. The legend lives on and it is said that even today, Europeans venturing into the wilderness might hear an irresistibly lovely, melodious voice calling. Drawn to search for its source, they forge deeper into the forest and become lost forever. Note: Try as I might, I couldn't find one person who actually knew of anyone who had been lost forever here. Perhaps this legend is somehow connected to lost Estrella mines story and the gold bars that turned up in David centuries later.

◆ Guadalupe

Continue north from Cerro Punta and in a few minutes you'll be in the heart of tiny, flower-festooned Guadalupe village. If visiting Haras Cerro Punta, Guadalupe is only a stone's throw away – about three minutes uphill by car or bus. Roses, white calla lilies, orange and tiger lilies, sunflowers, gladiolas, portulacas, geraniums and every other blooming thing imaginable burst from resident's yards, sway from porches, pop from flowerpots and drape fences.

Finca Dracula, ☎ 507-771-2223, isn't a medieval vampire hangout but an orchid nursery named for the rare vampire orchids (*Telipogon vampirus*) discovered in the cloud forest. Dedicated conservationist Andres (Andrew) Maduro started Finca Dracula in 1970 to rescue and propagate rare orchids in danger of extinction. Today, the finca is recognized as one of the world's finest and largest cool species (orchids that thrive in a cool climate) orchid nurseries, with 2,200 types on display. Maduro has discovered a dozen previously unknown species in Panamá and Costa Rica and created world renowned hybrids. You don't have to be an enthusiast to be enchanted by these beautiful plants, which may produce one glorious flower, or two, three, a dozen or a hundred, all at one time. Some are pure white or golden yellow, lavender, green, pink, red, orange or almost black. Some are striped or spotted like jungle cats and some are rainbow-hued. Finca Dracula is an easy 15-minute uphill walk from Los Quetzales (see *Where to Stay* on page 237); it's open from 8 am until 5 pm, seven days a week. The $7 admission includes a guided tour (in English or Spanish) of the nurseries and lovely cloud forest grounds with small lakes, streams, clinging orchids, quetzals and butterflies.

Adventures

◆ On Foot

Parque Nacional Volcán Barú

This park's 35,000 acres/14,325 hectares follow roughly the contours of massive 11,401-foot/3,475-meter Volcán Barú, Panamá's highest peak with towering massifs that loom above the surrounding Talamanca Mountains. Hot springs and frequent seismic activity attest that the volcano is only dormant, not extinct. It last erupted about 600 years ago. Forests dominated by several species of towering oaks and grassy plains (*llanos*) spread over the arid soils of old lava flows blanket Barú's lower slopes. Higher elevation elfin and cloud forests are brightened by orchids and epiphytes but near its cold, barren rock summit, only scrub and a few hardy wildflowers can survive.

> **❖ WORTHY WILDLIFE**
>
> Resplendent quetzals, great currasows, black and white hawk eagles, and black-bellied and colibri hummingbirds are among the park's more than 250 bird species. Although all five of Panamá's cat species have been recorded here, pumas are the most common. Other mammals include red brocket deer, collared peccary, porcupine, paca, several bat species and a rare, endangered little mouse.

The park's trails offer opportunities for hiking, mountain climbing, bird watching and camping. The **Sendero Las Tres Rocas** (The Three Rocks Trail) is a pleasant three-hour hike to huge rock formations and, from a high lookout, spectacular views.

The **Sendero de los Quetzales** (Quetzal Trail) skirts around the volcano's lower slopes between Boquete in the Eastern Highlands and Cerro Punto in the Western Highlands. To hike this beautiful trail, famed for the quetzals spotted along the route, watch for the Los Quetzales Lodge signs posted between Cerro Punta and Guadalupe villages. Pass through the village to the painted sign that marks the trailhead. Expect the hike to the Fair of Flowers in Boquete to take about six hours, although serious birders and wildlife watchers tend to tarry. If hiking from east to west, see page XX.

> **AUTHOR NOTE:** *The trail from Cerro Punta to Boquete is easier hiking it in reverse as there is less "uphill."*

The western side of the **Summit Trail** up, over and down the volcano to Boquete starts at Paso Ancho, two miles/3.25 kilometers north of Volcán. See page 219, *Hiking &Trekking, Eastern Highlands*, for a description.

La Amistad International Park

This is the country's second-largest park (Darién is bigger), extending over 850 square miles/207,000 hectares into Chiriquí and Bocas del Toro provinces. Although more than 90% of the park is within Bocas del Toro, it is more easily accessed from Chiriquí. Declared a UNESCO World Heritage site in 1990, La Amistad is the world's first bi-national reserve with an additional 193,929 hectares lying in neighboring Costa Rica.

One of Central America's most ecologically diverse regions, the park encompasses nine of Panamá's 12 Holdridge life zones. Its soaring massifs, spectacular cliffs and deep valleys, lush with dense, dripping cloud forests, are of volcanic origin, the country's oldest replete with orchids, ferns, bromeliads, vines and countless mosses. Sub-Alpine scrub covers higher mountain ranges while lower elevations that slope toward the Caribbean support tropical rainforests. More than 400 bird species have been identified, including rare bare-necked umbrella birds, quetzals, bellbirds, harpy and crested eagles. Among the 100 mammal species are peccaries, tapirs, all five of Panamá's cats, howler, black-handed spider, capuchin, and night (lemurine) monkeys. Expect to see as many as 100 bird species, some amphibians, butterflies and while may not see any large mammals, you will see evidence that they have been around. Several Amerindian groups live in this park and, as usual, the biggest threat to the ecology is of human origin. Poaching, illegal logging, slash and burn farming and even cattle grazing have increased since the completion of the now defunct Chirquí-Bocas del Toro pipeline and an adjacent highway.

The park's main entrance is in Las Nubes (The Clouds), 4.5 miles/seven kilometers west of Cerro Punta. Stop at the ANAM ranger station at the entrance to pay the $3 visitor fee, ask if trail maps are available, and to see the small display of some of the park's inhabitants. Two excellent trails start from the station. **Sendero La Cascada** (Cascade Path) is an uphill hike, roughly two miles/3.5 kilometers to La Cascada waterfall. If the day is clear, there will be panoramic views from the *miradors* (lookouts) along the way. Shorter and easier **Sendero El Retoño**, about one mile (two kilometers) long, loops through lovely forests and across wooden bridges spanning clear streams.

❖ **TOUR GUIDES**

Volcán's attractions are spread out over a wide area and, even if you're driving, you should consider hiring a local guide. Those listed below are great guys who know every inch of the territory, and they're all conservationists.

Gonzalo and Nariño Aizpurúa's **Highlands Adventures**, ☎ 507-771-4413/685-1682 (cell), e-mail ecoaizpurua@ hotmail.com, offers a long list of naturalist adventures, all reasonably priced. The Aizpurúas have been in business more than seven years, and now employ eight naturalist and adventure specialist guides, some of whom speak English. A smattering of German is also spoken. They'll take you over the volcano while explaining the different ecological zones, birding, cloud forest trekking, on a fascinating agrotour, or to ancient unrecorded archaeological sites. You'll find their office, Highlands Adventures/Turismo Ecologico, in town next to the Shell station.

Personable and fully bi-lingual **Manolo Morales**, ☎ 507-771-5762, e-mail sealion31@yahoo.com, grew up in Volcán and, after serving five years as a tour manager/ administrative officer for a major cruise line, returned home to help develop tourism in his community. Following in the footsteps of his brother Rick, one of ANCON Expeditions's exceptional guides, Manolo specializes in naturalist and hiking tours.

◆ On Horseback

You can explore Guadalupe and the surrounding cloud forests with or without a guide by renting a horse from **Los Quetzales** for about $7 an hour. See *Where to Stay*, below, for contact information. Check also with **Haras Cerro Punta**, ☎ 507-771-2057. When I last spoke with them they were planning to have horses available for rent.

◆ On Water

Lagunas de Volcán

These three interconnected lakes are part of Panamá's highest wetlands, 3,937 feet/1,200 meters above sea level. Tall native forests surround these beautiful lakes and lagoons, where you'll find excellent bird-watching. Jacanas, several species of tanagers, flycatchers and ducks as well as the rare rose-throated becard inhabit the marshlands and forests of this 350-acre/140-hectare protected area. You can rent a canoe in Volcán to fish for the largemouth bass that are plentiful in the lakes. Swimming here is dangerous and discouraged. Superstitious locals believe the lakes haunted as several drownings have occurred. The cause isn't ghosts or evil spirits, but underwater weeds in which swimmers become entangled. The lakes are about 20 minutes from town. To get here, turn left just after the fork to Cerro Punta and follow the somewhat confusing signs. You'll need a four-wheel-drive vehicle and, during the rainy season, the awful road is even worse. Your best bet is to come with a guide.

Trout Fishing

Chiriquí's rivers and streams brim with rainbow trout, a non-native fish first introduced into the Chiriquí Viejo River in 1925. This delicious fish thrived and soon became so popular with local residents that it was introduced it into other cold mountain streams and is now farmed in the region. You can fly-fish for them in any number of rivers or streams, buy one fresh-caught, or fish one from Hotel Bambito's trout ponds. (See *Where to Stay.*)

Where to Stay

◆ Volcán

Hotel y Restaurante Don Tavo has 16 rooms, on Volcán's main street; ☎ 507-771-5144, www.volcanbaru.com/turismo/dontavo, $ ($33 for a double room). It is a pleasant, in-town, two-story hotel with 16 attractive, quiet rooms with TVs set around a beautiful courtyard. Laundry service is offered, and the adjoining Cybercafé Volcán charges only $1 per hour.

❖ HOTEL PRICING	
Based on double occupancy	
No $	under $20
$	$20 to $39
$$	$40 to $79
$$$	$80 to $124
$$$$	$125 to $199
$$$$$	over $200

Hotel Dos Rios, 16 rooms, two casitas, ☎ 507-771-5555 or 771-4271, fax 507-771-5794, e-mail hdosrios@cwpanama.com, $$, is a beautiful hotel on the main road 1.5 miles/2.4 kilometers outside of Volcán. Built entirely of wood, its two stories overlook the mountains and lush landscaped gardens with a babbling brook. There is a large, attractive restaurant, an outdoor dining terrace and pleasant bar. The rooms are small but simply and attractively decorated, and the bathrooms large. The only drawbacks are the wood floors that carry every sound, and poor lighting in the bathrooms.

Cabañas Finca La Providencia, ☎ 507-771-4162, e-mail laprovi@hotmail.com, $, has three large and lovely two-story Swiss-style cabins in a delightful garden setting just a few miles outside of Volcán. They have complete kitchens, living rooms, second floor balconies, cable TV and telephones. The larger ones will comfortably sleep up to eight. Long-term rentals are available. Accommodations are set on four hectares of beautiful grounds with tall oaks and pines. Hosts George and Elizabeth Bubos, proprietors of in-town **Café Acropolis** (see *Where to Eat*) also offer La Providencia's guests customized meal plans.

Hostal Cielito Sur Bed and Breakfast, ☎ 507-771-2038, www.cielitosur.com, $$, is a gorgeous B&B in a magnificent garden setting. Two of the four lovely rooms, named for Panamá's indigenous groups, have sinks, refrigerators, microwaves and coffee makers. There are two rooms on each side of the cozy, delightful lounge with comfy sofas and chairs, a cheering field stone fireplace, plenty of reading material, reference books and local information. The rooms and lounge open onto a wide mountain view verandah buzzing with tiny hummingbirds. You'll find plenty of hammocks in a shady *bohío* and the indoor Jacuzzi in its own little house is a wonderful place to unwind tired muscles after a day on the trails. Superb full breakfasts are served in the café-style dining room. Welcoming hosts Janet and Glenn Lee, who are fully bi-lingual, offer a variety of tours in the area. You'll find Cielito Sur just beyond Volcán on the road to Cerro Punta.

AUTHOR NOTE: *Be sure to make advance reservations at Hostal Cielito Sur, as it is a favorite with naturalists and birders.*

◆ Bambito

There is no Bambito town to speak of, but there are good countryside accommodations with restaurants in this area between Volcán and Cerro Punta.

Four-star-rated **Hotel Bambito**, 45 rooms, 10 suites, ☎ 507-771-4265 or 507-772-4219, 507-223-1660 in Panamá City, www.chiriqui.com/bambito, $$$, has all the features one expects in a fine resort. Large, recently redecorated rooms are exceptionally comfortable with huge picture windows overlooking lushly landscaped grounds and the Bambito trout ponds. There's an indoor landscaped pool, sauna and hot tub, masseuse, lighted tennis courts, business center, gift shop, restaurant and relaxing bar/lounge. Hotel Bambito's **Las Truchas Restaurant** is famed for delicious, just-caught trout prepared in a dozen different ways. The food here is imaginative, beautifully presented and the service is superior. I've eaten here several times and each meal seems better than the one before. The resort offers a variety of tours or you can rent a horse or a mountain bike.

Unrelated to Hotel Bambito, **Bambito Forest Resort**, e-mail eproject@ chiriqui.com, $$$$, is an upscale adventure lodge nestled up to the Chiriquí Viejo River in a forest setting. This is a beautiful place – as well it should be for the price. Lovely, but slightly over-decorated, individual one- and two-bedroom suite cabanas have excellent beds, hair dryers in the bathrooms, good lighting and mirrors, and satellite TV. There's also a huge three-bedroom, three-bath house and a $10 per-person, per-night barracks cabin with shared bath facilities. Kayaking and canoeing are offered, and you can camp in the resort's private 420-acre/170-hectare forest reserve. Camping is $10 if you bring your own gear, or $40 for a two-person tent, sleeping bags, lantern, etc., if you rent from the resort. Mountain bikes, fishing equipment and horses are available to rent. Very good international specialties are served in the lovely wooden alpine lodge-style restaurant, and there's a cozy, relaxing bar/lounge.

Cabanas Kucikas, ☎ 507-771-4245; in the US, call 512-396-0769, www.cabanaskucikas.com, $$. Eighteen mostly A-frame cabins border the Chiriquí Viejo River. They're not as fancy as Bambito Forest Resort's, but they're not as expensive either, and they have fully equipped kitchens. This pleasant, kid-friendly place has a large playground, barbeque areas and lovely gardens. Bring your own gear and fish your dinner from the river.

◆ Cerro Punta

Hotel Cerro Punta, ☎ 507-771-2020, fax 507-775-7233, $27, is a recently remodeled, pleasant hotel near Haras Cerro Punta. All rooms have comfortable beds, cable TV and telephones and there is a pool. Very good Panamanian and international specialties are served in the hotel's restaurant. Desserts and shakes are scrumptious.

◆ Guadalupe & La Amistad

Hotel y Cabanas Los Quetzales, ☎ 507-771-2291/771-2182, fax 507-771-2226, www.losquetzales.com, in Guadalupe village, offers a choice accommodations in its main hotel's two chalet-style lodges that include hotel rooms, $$, apartment suites, $$$, and dorm accommodations ($12 per person). Or you can choose a rustic chalet in La Amistad's ethereal cloud forest, 6,800 feet/2,060 meters above sea level. Tall trees draped with orchids, mosses, bromeliads and vines enclose the chalets where only birdsong and the rustlings and chatterings of little forest creatures interrupt the quiet. Each comfortably furnished chalet with a full kitchen, hot water bathroom and fireplace is slightly different from the others. Kerosene lamps are provided as only one chalet has electricity. If you don't want to go out to eat, you can cook your own meals, order them ready made from Los Quetzales excellent restaurant, or the lodge will provide a cook. Once-a-day round-trip transportation to the lodge in Guadalupe is an included perk.

The full-service spa at the main lodge offers everything from facials and manicures to shiatsu, deep muscle massage and weight loss therapies. Los Quetzales proprietor, Carlos Alfaro, is an ardent protector of the natural environment who hires and trains local people to earn their livings as hotel workers, naturalist guides, gardeners and caretakers. The resort's excellent restaurant serves only organically grown fruits, vegetables and herbs, most grown in its own gardens, and fresh trout from its ponds.

Los Quetzales offers a range of adventures and two daily hikes with a naturalist or birding specialist guide are included with your stay here. The excellent guides know intimately the cloud forest trails and they know where the quetzals nest. Many of the cloud-forested acres, roads and trails around tiny Guadalupe village can be explored on horseback. The lodge offers horses to both guests and non-guests for about $6 an hour. You can trundle about the village and steep hillside trails on a bicycle for about the same price. Whether you choose your adventure on wheels, two or four feet, a guide is available at no additional fee, although reasonable tips are customary and appreciated. Los Quetzales also offers its guests one or two-day whitewater rafting excursions, up to class IV, at a discounted rate with Panama Rafters. Haras Cerro Punta offers adults and children horseback riding through its beautiful lanes and rolling green pasturelands.

❖ EXTREME ADVENTURES

Los Quetzales offers an eight-day extreme overland adventure from Cerro Punta to the Caribbean Coast. This highly rewarding, physically challenging trek takes you up (and down) steep mountains through rugged cloud forests and steaming jungles. Overnights are spent in tents and two days of travel through Teribe Indian country are on rivers aboard *cayucos* (canoes). You'll need your own equipment, including tent and sleeping bag, waterproof ground cloth, etc. This incredible journey is outrageously underpriced at $20 per-person, per day. Bring a few small gifts for the friendly folk you'll meet along the way. Stock up on waterproof plastic bags to keep your cameras dry because without photographic proof, friends back in Dayton, Birmingham or Syracuse won't believe this one!

◆ Camping

Camping is permitted in La Amistad for the usual $5 fee, payable at the ANAM ranger station at the main entrance in Las Nubes. A much better option is to stay in the dormitory at the station for the same price. You'll have less chance of getting soaked or chilled here. The dorm rooms have bunk beds, there's a fireplace and a kitchen. You will need to bring your own sleeping bag or bedding. To make arrangements in advance, call ANAM's regional office in David, ☎ 507-775-2055 or 507-775-3163.

Where to Eat

◆ Volcán

Don't pass up an opportunity to enjoy exquisite, light-as-air moussaka, stuffed grape leaves, pastitsio, or one of the other delicious Greek specialties at **Café Acropolis** (no phone), $$. Host George Bubos owns Finca La

❖ RESTAURANT PRICING
Entrée & non-alcoholic drink
$ . . . . under $5
$$ . . . . $5 to $10
$$$ . . . . $11 to $20
$$$$ . . . . over $21

Providencia, where he grows organic spices that are used fresh to flavor this wonderful food. His wife, Elizabeth, is the "chef extraordinare." The menu also includes typical dishes, spaghetti, and roast chicken. A juicy hamburger with cheese and bacon is $1.75 and there is always a daily special. Dinner prices range from $3.50 to the most expensive, a $7.50 beef filet. Finish up with yummy baklava and a cup of George's home-grown coffee. To get here, turn left from the main street at the crossroad by Berard's Market. Drive about two blocks and watch for the café's sign on the left.

Restaurante y Pizzeria La Biga (no phone), $$, on the main street across from the Accel gas station, garners rave reviews. As one friend put it, "imagine finding world-class Italian food in such a small town." In addition to superb pizzas and pastas, you'll find some wonderful salads. Most menu items are from $3 to $6.50.

Dining choices at inexpensive **Hotel y Restaurante Don Tavo**, in town on the main street, ☎ 507-771-4258, $-$$, include tasty typical beef and chicken dishes, soups, salads and sandwiches.

Order from the menu at **La Luna** Chinese restaurant in Paso Ancho, 1.4 miles/2.3 kilometers south of the town center (no phone), $. Ask the chef/owner what he recommends, or he'll prepare a dish to your order. This simple, inexpensive place serves very good Chinese food.

The most formal place around is the restaurant at **Hotel Dos Rios**, ☎ 507-771-5555, $$, owned by the same folks who own Panamá City's excellent Tambal Italian restaurants. I expected Dos Rios' food to be better than it was. It was nicely presented and served, but I rated it only average. Perhaps I should have opted for the trout. My dining companion said it was excellent. There are great views of the mountains and the volcano from the Barilles Bar.

> **AUTHOR NOTE:** *During my last visit to Volcán, I heard about a wonderful new restaurant called* **Cerro Bruja** *(Witch Hill) outside of town. Unfortunately I was scheduled to leave and didn't have time to check it out or get a phone number. The reviews were so good you may want to ask in town for its location. I was told it is very small and will actually accept reservations.*

If you plan to camp or stay in a cabin with cooking facilities, stock up on supplies at the new **Super Barú** west of David on the InterAmericana, or in Volcán at **Berard's** wonderful market.

◆ Bambito, Cerro Punta & Guadalupe

Bambito isn't actually a village, just a few houses sprinkled along the roadside with huge Hotel Bambito Resort beaming down from a rise. You might find it odd that this huge resort, perched all by itself in a rural forested area, is known throughout Panamá, not only for it host of amenities, but even more so for its superb restaurant, **Las Truchus** (The Trouts), $$-$$$, ☎ 507-771-4265. Make it a point to stop here for a delightfully unexpected dining experience. As the name indicates, fresh trout prepared in a dozen different ways reigns supreme, or you can choose from a vast menu of international specialties. Hotel Bambito has its own trout farm and, if you wish, you can pull your own, flopping fresh, from the clear, cold water. The superlatively prepared meals here look almost too pretty to eat – and taste even better. Wide picture window views, sparkling crystal, fresh flowers, gleaming chandeliers and friendly tuxedoed waiters make this a delightful choice. There is also a full bar and a quiet, relaxing lounge.

Set in a forest glade, **La Campagnola**, the lodge-style restaurant at Bambito Forest Resort, ☎ 507-771-5125, $$$, is accented by warm hardwood walls and floors. There's a crackling fireplace in the lobby lounge, and the bar is a great place to relax and chat up sports enthusiasts and naturalist adventurers. The menu is international and dining casual. Attractively served meals include lightly sauced grilled chicken with a palette of colorful veggies, grilled meats and, of course, fresh trout.

In Cerro Punta, **Hotel y Restaurante Cerro Punta**, ☎ 507-771-2020, $, just past Haras Cerro Punta Thoroughbred Farm, serves very good, inexpensive typical food, exquisite desserts, healthful fruit juices, and shakes made with fresh local fruits and berries – the strawberry shakes are especially yummy.

Guadalupe's welcoming **Los Quetzales Lodge Restaurant**, ☎ 507-771-2291, $$, is perfect for purist foodies to enjoy freshly caught trout from the lodge's own ponds and imaginatively prepared vegetables and fresh fruit grown in its organic gardens and orchards. Delicious wholegrain breads and pastries are made on the premises; fresh herbs are used for cooking; and a true pizza oven produces tasty pies made, of course, with fresh, organic tomatoes. The varied selection of regional and international dining choices includes plenty of vegetarian dishes, and there is a fine wine list. Cheery wood-burning fireplaces add an extra measure of warmth to the alpine lodge-style ambiance of the restaurant and adjoining bar/lounge. If you're a birder, hiker, or simply love nature in its unadorned wilderness state, plan to relax in the lounge where folks with similar interests gather before and after dinner.

Bocas del Toro Province

Bocas del Toro flaunts all of the country's complex geographical and topographical features. Its lowland tropical rainforests, as pristine as before Columbus ventured here in 1502, slope upward to the cool cloud forests of the rugged Talamanca

Mountains (Cordillera Central). Offshore coral reefs teem with marine life around an archipelago of white sand and mangrove-fringed tropical islands. Tucked into Panamá's northwestern most corner, "Bocas" is bordered by the Caribbean on the north, Costa Rica on the west, Chiriquí on the south and Veraguas on the east. Only about 90,000 people live in its 1,684 square miles/4,632 square kilometers and there are only three principal towns; **Changuinola**, in the heart of banana country, the port town of **Almirate**, and **Bocas del Toro** town, the offshore provincial capital on 23. 5-square mile/60-square kilometer **Isla Colon**. Only Bocas town is developed for tourism. Unless you're fascinated by banana production, you'll head straight for the laid-back Caribbean islands and their wealth of natural and sporting adventures.

Rainforests still cover about 92% of the archipelago's six large islands and cays, inhabited by 75 mammal species, more than 200 bird species and a variety of rare amphibians, including two species of tiny, neonbright poison dart frogs that exist nowhere else on earth. At last count, fully 74 of the Caribbean's 79 known coral species have been identified in Bocas del Toro's offshore reefs.

Visits to deserted island beaches, rainforest trekking, scuba and snorkeling, birding, wildlife watching, surfing, fishing and sea kayaking are popular pastimes here. Ride a rental bike through funky Bocas town or to a nearby beach, get close up and personal with a bat colony, watch nesting sea turtles, and bend elbows with a parade of foreign transients and friendly, offbeat locals in a seafront bar.

Until a few years ago, these paradisiacal islands were virtually unknown outside of Panamá. Nothing of note happened from day to day here, except for the few wandering expats that happened by and stayed to put down roots. The scant tourism industry relied on backpackers busing down from Costa Rica and a few naturalist adventurers. Almost over-night a rush of settlers from Europe and the US arrived and began to establish hotels, resorts and restaurants. Investors and entrepreneurs, mostly North American, flocked in to cheaply buy up island property to develop or to plant with teak. Property values skyrocketed.

Fortunately, this wave of expats hasn't diluted Bocas' core culture of English-speaking Blacks whose forefathers arrived generations ago; Spanish-speaking Mestizos; Guaymí and Teribé Indians; the few descendants of long-ago European settlers and mixtures of any or all of these. Despite the rush to buy it up, Bocas is still laid-back: English is still spoken in honeyed Caribbean accents or lilting Guari-Guari (WAh-ree-WAh-ree), a local patois derived from Caribbean English, Old Spanish, and Indian dialects spiced with a hint of French; the ginger-breaded wooden houses look as weathered as ever; pony-tailed Jimmy Buffet look-alikes still sit around sucking up cold beers; calypso and reggae blasts from the bars at night, and the guy who builds giant model airplanes still hauls his latest four-footer up and down the main drag. There's just more of everything lately – more hotels and resorts, more restaurants (some of them extraordinary), more tourists, more transient yachtsmen, and more Gucci-shod entrepreneurs with cell phones stuck in their ears.

History

Columbus explored the bay and some of the islands while still searching for gold and a westward passage to the Orient. He found neither. Only lush forests, white sand beaches and bays so beautiful, he attached his name to some of them: **Isla Colón** (Columbus Island), **Bahia de Almirante** (Admiral Bay) and **Isla Cristobal** (Christopher Island). Since no gold was found here, he sailed away. The Spanish continued to ignore the region and by the 17th century, its islets, cayes and lagoons had become a haven for pirates. Rumors of buried treasure still exist, but none has ever been found. During the 17th and 18th centuries, inter-tribal wars, Spain's convert-or-die policies, and European diseases decimated the local indigenous population. It was also during the 18th century that a small group of **French Huguenots**, in search of religious freedom, settled near the coast. The Spanish discovered them and in 1725 most were killed. By the mid-1700s, a handful of **British** immigrants had established poultry and cattle farms on the north side of Isla Colón. By the early 19th century, British ships were arriving with goods to trade for mahogany, turtles and turtle shells, coconuts and sarsaparilla and Bocas del Toro town had developed. About the same time, wealthy English and Scottish immigrants arrived from the United States and Columbia's Providencia and San Andrés islands, bringing with them their Black slaves who stayed on after slavery was abolished in 1830.

In 1890, the **Snyder Banana Company** established the first banana plantations along the lagoon. In 1899, the **United Fruit Company** moved in, bought out the Snyders, and built its headquarters in Bocas town. United Fruit established most of the island's infrastructure of roads, bridges and a nine-mile/15-kilometer canal connecting to Changinola on the mainland. French-speaking Blacks from Martinique and Guadalupe who had worked on the French canal and West Indians Blacks from Jamaica, Barbados and Antigua, who worked on the railroad and US canal, moved to Bocas to work on the banana plantations. Trade flourished until between 1914 and 1934, when a banana pest called "Panamá disease" wiped out the plantations. United Fruit moved its headquarters to mainland Changuinola and Bocas town began to decay. A few years ago tourists began to recognize Bocas for the gem it is. Word spread, more visitors arrived, and this unique, historical little town is flourishing again.

❖   YES, WE HAVE BANANAS...

Gros Michel, the species of banana grown by United Fruit, was susceptible to Panamá Disease. The disease swept periodically through the plantations, destroying the trees and wiping out the crops. By the early 1960s, United Fruit's competitor, Standard Fruit, was growing Cavendish bananas – a species resistant to the disease. United Fruit soon followed suit and began producing only the Cavendish variety. In 1970, United Fruit merged with Morrell, a major food producer, and the company's name changed to United Brands. A few years later the name was changed to Chiquita Brands. By 1990, Chiquita was producing 33% of the world's bananas. Today, banana plantations stretch along Bocas del Toro's northwestern coastal plains from the islands to the Costa Rica border.

Getting Here

◆ By Car or Bus

The province's one north-south road begins east of David in Chiriquí Province. Called the **Fortuna Road**, it runs north over the Continental Divide to connect with the (newer) road west to Almirante and Changuinola. If coming from the Chiriquí Highlands, backtrack to David and drive east on the InterAmericana (Inter-American Highway) for 7.4 miles/12 kilometers to the Gualaca turnoff. Turn north onto the Gualaca Road (also called Fortuna) and continue north past the massive La Fortuna Hydroelectric project and the eastern corner of protected Palo Seco Forest reserve to Punta Peña – a 57-mile/92-kilometer haul over the Continental Divide through some of Panamá's most spectacular scenery. The recently resurfaced road is in good condition, but the drive through the mountains can get a bit hairy for anyone with a fear of heights. At the Punta Peña intersection, turn northeast to continue to Chiriquí Grande, or west to reach Almirante and Changuinola. Almirante is 39 miles/63 kilometers west of the turnoff and Changuinola 13 miles/21 kilometers farther. Water taxis and ferries run from Chiriquí Grande and Almirante to Bocas del Toro town on Isla Colón. See *By Water*, below, for details. If coming from Panamá City, take the InterAmericana west to the Gualaca crossroad – a distance of 263 miles/424 kilometers – and continue north as above.

Taking the bus is infinitely easier than driving, and is also cheaper. Buses run from Panamá City's main terminal at Albrook to Almirante, a 10-hour trip that costs $28 one-way. Buses from David's terminal take roughly three hours and cost about $8.

> **AUTHOR NOTE:** *Getting to Bocas town on Isla Colón is more easily accomplished – and cheaper – from Almirante than from Chiriquí Grande.*

◆ By Air

Aeroperlas, ☎ 507-315-7500 in Panamá City, 507-757-9341 in Bocas town, offers two flights each day (morning or afternoon) from the capital's Marcos A Gelabart Municipal Airport (Albrook) to Bocas town. The fare is $62 each way for the one-hour journey. There is no round-trip discount. **Mapiex Aero**, ☎ 507-315-0888 in Panamá City, 507-757-9371 in Bocas, provides one morning flight (weekdays only) for a similar fare.

From David, **Aeroperlas**, ☎ 507-721-1195, provides an 8 am (weekdays only) flight that makes a stop in Changuinola before continuing to Bocas town. The fare between David and Bocas town is $38 each way. The little airport in Bocas is roughly four blocks from the town center, an easy walk if you're not overburdened with luggage. If you are, or would prefer a lift, there are always a couple taxis waiting.

◆ By Water

Water taxis operate from Chiriquí Grande to Bocas town three times each day (usually). The one-hour boat ride costs $10 per person. There is no set schedule, as time and frequency of service depends on the number of people waiting for transport. Speedy **launches** leave Almirante for Bocas town about every half-hour during daylight hours. The 25- to 30-minute boat ride costs $3 per person.

Although there is a car ferry service, called **Palanga**, to Bocas town, it's best to leave your car in a secure parking lot in Almirante or Chiriquí Grande – you won't get much use from it on the island. The very slow ferry between Almirante and Chiriquí Grande stops in Bocas town. As of this writing, it operates only on Wednesday, Friday, Saturday and Sunday. Schedules often change with little or no notice, and the cost to transport a vehicle is between $30 and $40. Bear in mind that tourism to the islands is steadily increasing, and additional service may be added. To check cur-

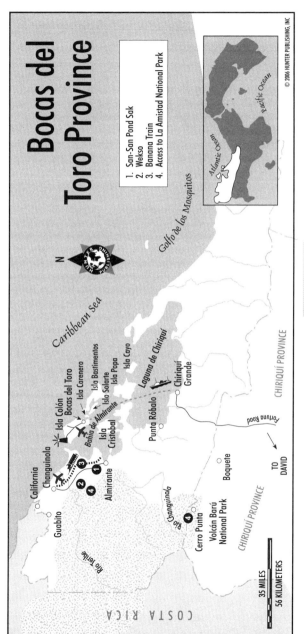

Bocas del Toro Province

1. San-San Pond Sak
2. Wekso
3. Banana Train
4. Access to La Amistad National Park

Golfo de los Mosquitos

Caribbean Sea

Isla Bastimentos
Isla Carenero
Isla Colón   Bocas del Toro
Isla Solarte
Isla Popa
Isla Cayo
Bahía de Almirante
Isla Cristobal
Laguna de Chiriquí
Punta Róbalo
Chiriquí Grande

Changuinola
California
Almirante
Guabito
CHIRIQUÍ PROVINCE
Fortuna Road
TO DAVID
Boquete

Río Teribe
Río Changuinola
Cerro Punta
Volcán Barú National Park
CHIRIQUÍ PROVINCE

COSTA RICA

35 MILES
56 KILOMETERS

© 2006 HUNTER PUBLISHING, INC
Pacific Ocean
Atlantic Ocean

rent schedules, call the ferry office in Chiriquí Grande, ☎ 507-757-9691, 507-757-9260 in Bocas del Toro town, and hope the phones are working and someone will bother to answer!

Mainland Bocas del Toro

The mainland's lowland jungles, black-as-night swamps and hauntingly lovely forest-clad mountains remain remote, wild, magnificent and dangerous. Prowling jaguars, herds of peccary, solitary tapirs, chattering and roaring monkeys, rare birds and insects, and nightmarishly huge snakes thrive within its H. Ryder Haggard landscapes. The majority of its human inhabitants are indigenous peoples– about 35% **Ngöbe** (Guaymí), with a few isolated communities of **Buglé** (also called Bokata), **Bri-Bri** and **Naso** (Teribe). There are no roads and, with only rivers for transportation, those in the most remote regions have been spared cultural exchange with the outside world.

Although 90% of the Panamanian portion of **Parque Internacional La Amistad** (International Friendship Park) lies within the province, buffered on the north and east by the protected Palo Seco Forest, access is more easily accomplished from **Las Nubes**, Cerro Punta in Chiriquí (see page 233). To enter the park from Bocas del Toro's Caribbean side, see *Adventures On Foot*, below. The mainland's only marginally developed region lies on its northern Caribbean coastal plains and slopes, a vast empire of banana plantations that spread outward from the towns of Almirante and Changuinola.

Almirante

If you are traveling by road, chances are you'll head for Almirante and hop on a water taxi to Isla Colón. There isn't much to see or do around this port town, which has about 13,000 residents – mostly impoverished banana plantation laborers. Train buffs might get a kick out of the many trains pulling in to disgorge loads of bananas at the docks or find interest in the swarm of railroad tracks criss-crossing the town. Note that there are only three hotels and no decent restaurants or services for tourists. If you get stuck here, three places (none with phone) – hotels **Hong Kong**, **San**

Francisco and Cristóbal Colón – offer rooms for about $8 a night. Don't expect such luxuries as hot water, air conditioning, or a comfortable bed – although 12-room hotel Cristóbal Colón boasts a bar.

Changuinola

Changuinola, 40 minutes northwest of Almirante, is a larger "banana town" and doesn't offer much of interest. However, it is a jumping-off point for two extraordinary adventures – the wetland forests of **San-San Pond Sak**, and **Wekso**, an indigenous Teribe (also called Naso) community in the jungles at the edge of La Amistad International Park. Most businesses and hotels are along Changuinola's main street, **Avenue 17 de Abril** (also called Av Central – no surprise there).

If you do want to overnight here, attractive **Hotel Atlantic Suites and Resort**, Av 17 de Abril, ☎ 507-758-9999, $$, has air conditioning, cable TV, a restaurant, bar and pool. **Hotel Semira-Mis**, also on Av 17 de Abril, ☎ 507-758-9034, $, is a good value with air conditioning, cable TV, a restaurant and bar. Worn **Hotel Changuinola**, Baseline (at the town's north end near the airport), $, air conditioning, is a tad less expensive, as is **Golden Sahara** (don't ask me where they got the name) on Baseline, ☎ 507-758-7908, offers cable TV, but no air conditioning. You'll find more bars than restaurants, but **Restaurant and Bar Chiquita Banana** serves pretty good, inexpensive food.

BOCAS DEL TORO

❖   THE BANANA TRAIN

The train chuffs between Changuinola and Almirante, stopping frequently to pick up bananas and often a few plantation workers. Although it wasn't designed for passengers and isn't very comfortable, it can be a fun way to see the banana fields and how the fruits are transported. If you have plenty of time and don't mind a little discomfort, the ride between towns will cost $3 to $4. Schedules vary, and locals in either town can point your way to the station.

Adventures

◆ San-San Pond Sak

Expect to get your feet wet – jungle boots and mosquito repellent necessary – when visiting San-San Pond Sak's wetlands, which begin 2.8 miles/4.5 kilometers north of town. Crowds of exotic wildlife frequent the area around an approximately one-mile/1.6-kilometer-long boardwalk, which passes through magnificent jungle sprouting from the swamp's inky waters. There are plenty of birds to be observed and you'll most likely spot a few staring iguanas, sloths and whiteface monkeys peering from the trees. The boardwalk ends on a deserted Caribbean beach where, between the months of April and August, hawksbill, green, loggerhead and extremely endangered leatherback turtles come ashore to lay their eggs.

AUTHOR NOTE: *Locals swear by an insect repellent made by Burt's Bees. It's sold in Bocas town shops (and throughout the US, too; check the company's Web site at www.burtsbees.com for locations).*

If you bring food and gear, you can spend a night at the ANAM ranger station (no phone) at the boardwalk's north end for $5. **Servitur**, ☎ 507-264-3029 (in Panamá City), e-mail tropict@cwpanama.com, provides guides in Changuinola (no phone), so call or e-mail to see if they can provide one for this adventure. If not, or if you prefer to go by yourself, hire a taxi in town to take you to the edge of the wetlands and arrange for the driver to come back for you at a designated time. Ask to be let out at the edge of the wetlands. You'll have to walk across a muddy area to the start of the area's elevated, and sometimes sodden, boardwalk.

◆ Wekso Indigenous Adventure

This indigenous **Naso** (Teribe) community project at the edge of La Amistad International Park offers visitors a rare cultural and naturalist adventure. In the midst of rainforest sloping up to the magnificent Talamanca Mountains, the community has transformed the former US-Panamanian military jungle survival training facility, Pana-Jungla, into a peaceful retreat. The Naso, who create beautiful wood carvings, handwoven baskets and hammocks, will introduce you to their way of life and to their king (Pru), take you on a dugout canoe river journey to other remote villages, and guide you on jungle pathways to observe birds, wildlife and the rich vegetation. Day-trips are offered, but you'll see much more by staying a night or two in one of the comfortable rustic bungalows.

Wekso is about 1½ hours from Changuinola: 30 minutes by road to the village of El Silencio, and an additional 45 minutes by boat up the Changuinola and Teribe rivers. If you wish to come on your own, contact any of the following to make arrangements: **Adolfo Villagra**, ☎ 507-757-7350; **Leonardo Aguilar**, ☎ 507- 759-7241; **Nilka Vargas**, ☎ 507-759-7355, e-mail odesen@hotmail.com. The day rate, including transportation from/to El Silencio, lunch and a guided jungle walk, is about $50 for two. For longer stays, add $20 for each night's accommodations for two, and $16 per person for three meals daily. If trekking into La Amistad, there is a $3 park entrance fee. Additional tours are available at costs for $5 and up per person. Highly respected eco-cultural tour operator **Ecocircuitos**, ☎ 507-314-1586 in Panamá City, fax 708-810-9350 in the US, www.ecocircuitos.com, has recently added Wekso to their itineraries. Contact them for convenient package rates that include all transfers, lodging, meals, tours and hikes from the village.

◆ La Amistad International Park

Bocas del Toro's only entrance to La Amistad's rainforests and spectacular mountain cloud forests lies beyond the remote Wekso community, making it a simple matter to combine the Wekso Indigenous Adventure detailed above with a trek into the park's awesome wilderness. You can also come here on your own and hire a knowledgeable guide from the community for a few dollars. There is a ranger station and a camping area at the park entrance. The rangers also serve as guides; there is no fee for their services, but tips are welcomed and recommended. Be aware that both the people in the Wekso community and the park rangers speak only the Naso dialect or Spanish. Although birding and wildlife watching are extraordinary here, under no circumstances should you attempt to wander into the park without a guide. There are no trails into this rugged landscape beyond the immediate vicinity of the ranger station. The park entrance fee is $3 per person; camping is an additional $5.

Bocas Town & Environs

More Caribbean than Spanish in flavor, casual Bocas town on the southern shores of Isla Colón is laid out in a typical grid pattern around its central park, **Parque Simón Bolívar**. It's the only place in the islands with services for visitors – other than a few outlying self-contained resorts. The town is small, and all the *calles* (streets) are numbered and *avenidas* (avenues) are lettered, making it easy to find your way around. Most businesses, hotels, restaurants and shops spread from the park on Calle 3, the town's main drag, or along Calle 1 on the seafront. Walk around for half an hour or so and you can familiarize yourself with the entire town. Foot traffic is more common than vehicle, so take your time – everyone else seems to – and amble down quiet residential side streets, where fences draped with sun-drenched flowering vines enclose small weathered wooden houses. Some of the more elegant homes are charming gingerbreaded Victorian or stately Colonial pretensions.

In town and throughout the islands, the predominant language is softly spoken, lyrical Caribbean English. Spanish is also widely spoken in this

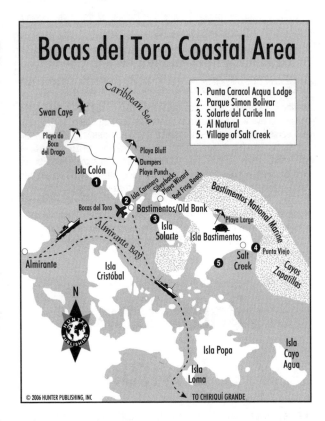

Bocas del Toro Coastal Area

Caribbean Sea

Swan Caye

Playa de
Boca
del Drago

Playa Bluff
Dumpers
Playa Punch

Isla Colón ①

Isla Carenero
Silverbacks
Playa Wizard
Red Frog Beach

Bastimentos National Marine

Bocas del Toro

② Bastimentos/Old Bank
③ Isla
Solarte

Playa Larga

Almirante Bay

Isla Bastimentos ④ Punta Viejo

Almirante

Isla
Cristóbal

Salt
⑤ Creek

Cayos
Zapatillas

N

HUNTER PUBLISHING

Isla Popa

Isla
Cayo
Agua

Isla
Loma

TO CHIRIQUÍ GRANDE

© 2006 HUNTER PUBLISHING, INC

1. Punta Caracol Acqua Lodge
2. Parque Simon Bolivar
3. Solarte del Caribe Inn
4. Al Natural
5. Village of Salt Creek

town of 4,100, as is Italian. Don't be surprised to hear local Indian dialects, Caribbean patois or lilting local Guari-Guari.

Getting Around

You'll probably walk everywhere in Bocas town because it's so small. In fact, just observing the colorful local and transient characters can be classified as an adventure!

◆ On Wheels

The one road from town runs across the island's midsection – with a branch that skirts the sea – to the little community of **Boca del Drago** (Mouth of the Dragon, or Dragon's Mouth) on the opposite side. The is-land's few taxis, mostly 4X4 pick-ups, will run you around town or can be hired to take you on a tour of the island. They'll also drop you at a distant beach or the edge of a forest path and come back for you at a pre-arranged time. The few *collectivo* **mini-buses** you'll see are used to transport locals who work in town.

◆ On Water

Based in Bocas town, water taxis and private boat hires provide transport throughout the islands. Despite the name, **Galapagos Tours**, on Calle 3, ☎ 507-757-9073, provides only water taxi service, sans guide. Fares range from $4 to $20, depending on distance. Most local boat tour operators and independent boat hires can be easily located on the seafront behind Calle 1. Although independents will take you almost anywhere within reason, the tour operators offer set and similar itineraries – such as to gorgeous **Isla Bastimentos National Marine Park** and the **Cayos Zapatillos** (Zapatillo Cayes); to snorkeling adventures around **Isla Solarte** (Solarte Island), also known as Nancy Caye and other offshore reefs; **Swan Caye** (also called Isla Pajaros, or Bird Island); a trip up the historic **Changuinola Canal**; on fishing trips, and more. Most have itineraries that combine from two to four flexible adventures. Contact Cristian at **Bocas Best Boat Tours**, ☎ 507-638-2220, who offers good rates. Cristian's boats depart from El Limbo Hotel's dock on Calle 1, a few steps left from where it forms a Y to intersect with Calle 3.

Both **J&J Boat Tours** and **Transparente Boat Tours**, ☎ 507-757-9915 (same phone number), www.bocas.com/operaciones/transparente/transparent.htm, depart from Restaurante El Pirate's docks on Calle 3, a few steps south of the Calle 1 intersection, and both enjoy fine reputations. Day tour prices range from $7 to $20 per person, with a minimum of six to eight.

Gallardo Livingston, ☎ 507-757-9388, is an expert boatman who knows every nook and cranny of these islands and every inch of the waters around them. He's a character who says he'll "go anywhere" and prefers to be called Livingson. If he doesn't answer his phone, look for him at the Bocas Inn on Calle 1 or leave a message there for him. His rates start at about $8 per person, based on a minimum of six, with snorkeling gear and an ice chest to keep drinks cold. If traveling solo or in tandem, you may want to rustle up other visitors to share the cost.

BOCAS DEL TORO

Sightseeing & Touring

◆ Bastimentos Island

A vast belt of national park rainforest separates this island's two culturally different communities, both of which are worth a visit. **Bastimentos town**, also known as **Old Bank**, is a 10-minute boat ride from Bocas town. Bastimentos town's residents speak **Guari-Guari** (WAH-ree WAH-ree), a lilting combination of words and accents drawn from Caribbean English, old Spanish, and Indian dialects, spiced with a hint of French. The people here support themselves mostly by fishing and subsistence farming, and the obvious poverty can be off-putting. The forest wilderness behind the town begs to be explored, but don't go by yourself. It's too easy to get lost and there are plenty of locals who will guide you for a couple of dollars. **Playa Wizard** is a long, lovely beach with powerful surf, but it sometimes has strong undertows.

Salt Creek, on the island's southeastern side – go by boat, you can't walk there – is a friendly Guaymí community of a few thatch homes, a little store and a blue-and-white-painted cement block elementary school on a hilltop overlooking it all. Some of the school children must have heard our boat's engine. As we clambered onto the rickety wood dock, a flood of little blue-and-white-clad bodies poured from the school and down the hill to greet us. Every child wore navy blue and white school uniforms – but not one had a pair of shoes. Strangers are a novelty to these beaming children. The equally welcoming adults are a bit more reserved and less exuberant. The community's men eke out meager livings from subsistence farming and fishing and the women make and sell chacara bags and beaded chaquira collars. The Salt Creek ladies will demonstrate how **chaquira bags** are made without the use of needles. If you tote groceries, beach items or books around in canvas or plastic bags, consider buying a few of the large bags from the little hut that serves as a cooperative gift shop. These incredibly strong bags, used routinely to carry babies, farm produce and other heavy loads are attractive, eco-friendly and almost never wear out. The smaller ones can be used as stylish, unusual handbags.

> **AUTHOR NOTE:** *Bastimentos town's two bands both play traditional Caribbean Calypso music. Both have six members and both are called the "Bastimentos Beach Boys." Check with local bars in Bocas town to find out if either group has managed to land a gig.*

The tiny critters that gave **Playa Rana Rojo** (Red Frog Beach) its name live nearby in a slice of shady jungle. The wide curving expanse of beautiful beach is good for surfing, but usually too rough for swimming. It is also too rough to anchor the small boats that tie up to a rickety dock on the island's opposite side. Expect to pay $1 per person to the Guaymí family at the edge of the forest path leading to the beach. It's a beautiful walk through the jungle, and will take anywhere from 15 minutes, depending on how much time you spend playing with the frogs.

> **AUTHOR NOTE:** *Before leaving the docks, make sure the boat you've hired has life jackets on board. Check them over, as some may be of such poor quality as to render them useless.*

Adventures

◆ On Foot

Follow Hospital Street north and you'll come to the dirt road that crosses the island through lovely forests, rolling pasturelands, and up steep hills that offer lovely views of the sea and other islands. Bring your binoculars to observe birds or stop at some of the beaches. Go with a guide to **Playa Bluff** during turtle nesting season, which runs from about May through August. Nature trails on other islands are listed below (see *Birding*, page 257).

❖ COUNTING SLOTHS

Mangrove stands at the far northwest end of Isla Colón harbor black hawks, kingfishers, great patoos and dozens more birds, but the real fun here is counting sloths. Both the two-toed and three-toed varieties can be observed from a slow-moving boat wending through the narrow mangrove enclosed channels. These cute little guys have been isolated on the islands for so many generations they've evolved into smaller, lighter-furred versions of their mainland cousins. They move faster, too, scurrying quickly (quickly for sloths, anyway) up their trees when we came too close. In less than 20 minutes, I had counted seven adults, one a mother with a tiny clinging baby.

AUTHOR NOTE: *Three-toed sloths look like little flat-faced "banditos" with dark brown masks. The two-toed species have longer faces without masks, so it's easy to tell them apart.*

◆ On Water

Beaches

There aren't any beaches in Bocas town proper, and the ones close by aren't good for swimming. **Sandfly Beach** – the name covers it all – is an easy walk from town but isn't very attractive, and you'll need plenty of insect repellent. Continuing along the coastal road, you'll come to surfing beaches **Playa Punch**, **Playa Dumpers** and **Playa Bluff**. Although they're lovely, all three are usually too rough for swimming, with undertows a clear and present danger. **Playa el Isthmo** and **Playa Ispeta** are smoother and safer.

Isla Colón's best swimming beach nudges up to **Boca del Drago**, a small community on the island's northwest side about five miles from Bocas town. Pleasant, open-sided, sand-floor **Restaurante Yarisnori** specializes in local seafood, and there are plenty of hammocks strung beneath the coconut palms. You can rent a small rowboat, pedal boat or snorkeling gear from the restaurant. There are a few small coral formations offshore, although snorkeling is good only when the sea is very calm. **The Institute for Tropical Ecology and Conservation**, a US-funded non-profit organization that provides scholarships for Panamanian students, has its base camp here. There are no phone lines to Boca del Drago, so if you are here and would like to overnight in one of the Institute's cabins, ask at the restaurant or the cabin with an "office" sign posted on its door. Classes are not usually in session between mid-January and mid-May, so beds might be available then. Expect to pay about $30 per night. To get here, you can take a taxi ($20 round-trip) that will leave you at the beach and come back to pick you up at an agreed-upon time. For a less expensive way, try the bus that transports Boca del Drago residents to and from work in Bocas town. It parks each morning around 8:30 am between the fire station and Hotel Las Brisas on Calle 1. If you want to spend a day at Boca del Drago beach, ask the driver if he'll take you there. He makes another run in the late afternoon to take the workers home to Boca del Drago, assuring you of a lift on his return to Bocas town. Expect to pay around $2.50 per person each way.

> **AUTHOR NOTE:** *The cooling sea breezes can keep you from realizing you're getting sunburned. Use plenty of sunscreen, wear sunglasses and a hat. If you're going to be on the water for an extended time or if you burn easily, wear a long-sleeve white shirt and consider hiring a boat with a canvas top.*

Fishing

Wahoo, dorado, tuna, several varieties of grouper and snapper, kingfish, barracuda, tarpon, snook and permit are caught in the archipelago's waters. **Bocas Fishing Company** operates the only fully appointed sportfishing vessel in Bocas. A full day of sportfishing with heavy tackle, cold drinks, and lunch costs $500 for a party of six (four anglers and two nonanglers). A half-day is $300.

J&J Boat Tours and **Transparente Boat Tours**, next to El Pirate Restaurant, ☎ 507-757-9915, offer sportfishing at $200 for a full day; $125 for a half-day. If this is too steep for your budget, or you want to go for only a couple of hours, ask around town for a local who'll take you.

Boat Tours

BASTIMENTOS NATIONAL MARINE PARK

Consisting mostly of sea, this 32,700-acre/13,226-hectare park includes the **Cayos Zapatillas** (Zapatilla Cayes) and a large part of **Bastimentos Island's** rainforest, mangrove forests and beaches. Sea turtles nest on beautiful **Playa Larga** (Long Beach) from April to October. Zapatilla's lovely white-sand, palm-fringed beaches are a 45-minute to one-hour boat ride from Bocas town. There's an ANAM ranger station on Zapatilla Major and a glorious rainforest trail crosses the island. Birds, sloths, monkeys, butterflies, lizards and frogs are easily spotted and a small interior lake hosts turtles and caimans. Snorkelers can explore the nearby offshore coral reefs inhabited by neon fish and small invertebrate critters. But don't venture out too far, as there are often strong currents. Only experienced divers should attempt to explore the 50-foot wall and its small caves. Bring a picnic lunch and spend the day or camp overnight on either Zapatilla Major or smaller Zapatilla Minor. The only facilities are at the station and you'll need to bring all of your own gear and food.

You'll pass other paradisiacal islands on the way to and from the cayes. Ask your guide or boatman to show you the shallow areas where hundreds of easily observed starfish lurk on the sea's sandy bottom. If coming with a local tour operator, be sure to ask beforehand if the $10 park entrance fee has been included in the price. If you hire a water taxi or local boatman, it generally isn't. If you plan to camp, get a permit from the **ANAM** office, ☎ 507-757-9244, in Bocas town on Calle 1, east of Parque Bolívar.

To get here, see page 251 for a list of boat tour operators, water taxis and local boatmen who provide transportation from Bocas town.

Surfing

The best surfing beaches are on Colón and Bastimentos islands. Surfing season here is December through March, when waves are consistent. Big waves are fewer and less predictable from April through July. **Loco Pollo** ("Crazy Chicken") **Surfboard**, on H Street in Bocas town, rents, buys and sells surfboards. You can get yours repaired or take lessons. Isla Colón's surfing beaches are all accessed from the one road that runs across the island from Bocas town.

Playas Punch, Dumpers and Bluff are along the beach road from Bocas town. Hire a 4X4 taxi in town to transport you and your boards. **Playa Punch** is the closest, with swells that average five feet/1.5 meters high, but can get up to 12 feet/3.6 meters. It has a reef bottom with left and right breaks and, sometimes, decent tubes. Next one up is **Dumpers** (named for the supposedly closed dump across the dirt road from the beach). Also a reef bottom, Dumpers is a short ride with six- to eight-foot waves (1.8-2.4 meters) that have been known to reach 12 feet/3.6 meters. A big tube and steep drop make it dangerous for beginners, so don't attempt this one unless you have some experience. Long and lovely **Playa Bluff** is the most distant, about 30 minutes from town. With powerful left and right breaks and some great tubes, it's only for pros and kamikazes.

Bocas' best surfing beach, **Silverbacks**, on Isla Bastimentos, offers a point and right break over a reef bottom. On a good day waves can get up to 16.4 feet/five meters, and its monster faces have been known to reach 25 feet/7.5 meters. Silverbacks is not for beginners. Also on Isla Bastimentos, **Red Frog Beach** has both left and right breaks over sand

and reef bottoms. The waves pound here, but when I last visited in March, swells were only about three feet/.9 meters, and no one was surfing. Hire a water taxi (about $8) in Bocas town to take you to Silverbacks or Red Frog Beach.

AUTHOR NOTE: *For more information on surfing in Bocas, surf the Web: www.panamasurftours. com, www.wannasurf.com, and www.panamatours.com.*

Sea Kayaking

I can't think of a better place for this sport. There's always something to see in **Almirante Bay's** warm (85F°/29°C) translucent waters, which has dozens of white-sand or mangrove-rimmed islands to explore – hundreds if you count the tiny islets. There's challenging surf along the bay's outer edge and, when you get tuckered out, plenty of places to pull onshore and rest up. If you didn't arrive with a kayak, you can rent one from **Bocas Water Sports**, on Calle 3, ☎ 507-757-9541.

Diving & Snorkeling

Beneath Almirante Bay's warm protected waters you'll find a wonderland lush with coral reefs and neon fish, starfish, sponges, peppermint shrimp, eels and dozens of little invertebrate creatures. Fully 74 of the Caribbean's 79 known coral species, including elkhorn, staghorn, fire, lettuce, sea fan, brain and black, have been identified in Bocas del Toro's waters. Although diving is best from the end of August to early November when waters are clearest, it's a year-round sport here.

The PADI professionals at **Starfleet Eco Adventures**, Calle 1 in Bocas town, ☎ 507-757-9630, www.explorepanama.com/starfleet.htm, know all the good dive and snorkeling spots. If new to the sport, you can take a three-day open water certification course in English, Spanish or German for $195. Not sure scuba is for you? Take their half-day session to find out. All-day snorkeling trips are bargain-priced at $15 per person, group rate. Two-tank, two-site dives with all the gear included average $50. Starfleet enjoys a spotless reputation and their personalized, professional service is top-notch.

Bocas Water Sports, ☎ 507-757-9541, Calle 3, across from Restaurante Da Claudio, offers competitive dive and snorkel trip rates, and they'll also take you water skiing or rent you a kayak. Both dive operators can arrange discounted package rates with local hotels.

AUTHOR NOTE: *Although the local hospital can supply oxygen, the closest decompression chamber is in Panamá City. Don't take unnecessary chances, and never dive alone.*

Hospital Point, on the western edge of **Isla Solarte** (also called Nancy Caye), was named for the hospital built here by the United Fruit Company in 1899. By 1914, the complex contained 16 buildings, including a separate hospital for black workers, a surgery, lab, pharmacy, administrative buildings and housing for the doctors and management personnel. After only 20 years of operation, the hospital was closed when Panamá Disease wiped out the bananas. The buildings were dismantled and jungles reclaimed the island. Today there are sprinklings of private homes, including one on a magnificent bluff – once the site of the old hospital – owned by Clyde Stevens, a former United Fruit researcher and botanist/historian. A beautiful protected reef at the edge of the jungle below the bluff is perfect for snorkeling. Developers have bought up a chunk of the island and there is a lovely hotel on another bluff above the sea. To get here, contact any of the tour operators or boatmen listed on page 251.

Birding

Although forests still cover 92% of the islands, birding here isn't quite as good as on the mainland. There are, however, plenty of species to be seen along forested trails. For now, there is good bird watching near and along the **Changuinola Canal** (see below), but this may not continue as traffic between the mainland and Isla Colón increases. The canal begins roughly nine miles/14.5 kilometers west from Bocas town at the mainland's edge, then runs parallel to the coast for 9.3 miles/15 kilometers through forested tropical wetlands to the Changuinola River. The boat ride to its mouth takes about a half-hour, with another 45 minutes or so to reach the river. Hire a boatman or boat tour operator (see page 251) to take you from town.

BOCAS DEL TORO

❖ TOURING THE CHANGUINOLA CANAL

Started in 1889 and completed 1903, the canal connecting Almirante Bay with the Changuinola River was used to transport bananas to the mainland. The nine-mile/15-kilometer canal was abandoned when the mainland railroad was completed. It cuts through one of Central America's largest expanses of tropical wetlands. A slow boat tour through the canal passes wading blue herons, jacanas foraging among lavender water hyacinths, iguanas perched on overhanging branches and little slapped-together wooden houses on stilts. Zebu cattle, pigs and goats have replaced much of the wildlife, but we still managed to see woodpeckers, laughing falcons, and dozens of smooth-billed parakeets. A flock of turkey vultures flew overhead, blocking the sun like a black cloud. Freshwater dolphins and manatees inhabit the canal, but we didn't see any. Although much of the habitat has been lost to cattle pastures and subsistence farms, birding is still good here. Ask your guide to go all the way to the vast, wild beach of black volcanic sand that washed down from the mountains. Environmentalists are lobbying to make the wetlands a protected area, but it may be too late. Much of the forest is already gone, and a new ferry service roars through twice a day transporting passengers to and from the mainland.

Swan Caye, a 131.2-foot/40-meter-high chunk of rock poking from the sea about 45 minutes by motorboat northwest of Isla Colón, is one of Panamá's few nesting places for the beautiful red-billed **tropicbird**. Numerous other species also nest on its craggy ledges among the few scrubby bushes and palm trees. The caye is a protected bird sanctuary and humans are forbidden to set foot on it. Content yourself with watching the birds from a boat. If you are with a guide or boatman who offers to take you ashore, please don't go. These rare birds are easily disturbed.

◆ On Wheels

Posada Los Delfines, Av H, ☎ 507-757-9963, rents bicycles for $8 a day, mopeds for $18 a day plus gas. **Roberto Small**, across from the park, rents mopeds for $8 an hour. He also rents bikes, but didn't give me rates. Make sure you have a sturdy mountain bike if venturing from town on the rough, hilly, potholed coast road.

Taxi driver **Roberto Smith**, taxi #153, ☎ 507-623-2933, provides a fascinating island sights and highlights tour that includes a visit to **La Gruta** (The Cave). The cave is also called Santuario Natural de Nuestra Senora de la Gruta (Natural Sanctuary of our Lady of the Cave), for the statue on a ledge above the small stream that flows from its vine-curtained entrance. A second, smaller statue of another saint on the stream's opposite side is said to have suddenly and mysteriously appeared one day. If you don't mind a little bat poop on your boots, walk into the cave a few feet and shine a light into the dark recess above. You can see thousands of roosting fruit bats. Roberto's tour includes local lore, the beaches and forests. He'll tailor one to suit your time, interests and pocketbook, and can also take you directly to Bocas del Drago. Like most Bocas natives, Roberto speaks English with a Caribbean accent, and Spanish as well.

Where to Stay

◆ Isla Colón

Bocas Town

La Veranda, Hospital Street at the town's north end, ☎ 507-757-9211, www.laverandahotel.com, $. Heather Guidi has turned this wonderful old Caribbean-Victorian house into a comfortable showplace with a collection of authentic local turn-of-the-century furnishings, antique doors and accessories. Polished hardwood floors,

❖ HOTEL PRICING	
Based on double occupancy	
No $	under $20
$	$20 to $39
$$	$40 to $79
$$$	$80 to $124
$$$$	$125 to $199
$$$$$	over $200

diaphanous mosquito netting just for show, and ceiling fans add to the ambiance of its six uniquely different rooms with super-comfortable beds and private baths. Guests can cook in the fully equipped veranda kitchen, there's a book exchange, and a convenient supermarket is one block away.

> **AUTHOR NOTE:** *Many Bocas hotels charge seasonal rates. High season is usually January through April and mid-July through November, but can vary by property.*

Hotel Angela, H Street on the seafront, ☎ 507-757-9813, www.hotelangela.com, $$, is one of the friendliest, most welcoming hotels in Bocas. The 12 rooms in this charming, Bocas-style former residence have private baths, air conditioning and orthopedic mattresses. Three have private balconies, and there's an expansive honeymoon suite with full kitchen, Jacuzzi and magnificent ocean views. Other perks include a book exchange, laundry, private bar and free Internet access for guests. Communal meals on the seafront terrace allow you to meet other guests and perhaps share activities. Best of all, you'll get to know Hotel Angela's owner, Claudio Talley, a poet at heart and a gentleman in every sense of the word.

La Estrella de Bocas, Calle 1, ☎ 507-757-9011, www.bocas.com/estrella.htm, $, more for apartments, is a new, two-story aparthotel with both hotel rooms and apartments of varying size. All are done up in spotless white with hardwood accents, have air conditioning, telephone and cable TV. The apartments have kitchenettes with refrigerator and dining areas separated from the bedrooms. Weekly rates are offered, and all rates include a full day's tour of the islands.

El Limbo on the Sea, Calle 1 South, at the Calle 3 fork, ☎ 507-757-9062, www.ellimbo.com, $$. This lovely new hotel is a favorite. Constructed of native hardwoods in typical Bocas style, it's a charming place, and was built to house European *Survivor* TV producers and crews. Its 18 tasteful rooms are simply furnished and exceptionally comfortable. Some have sea or street-view balconies, all have air conditioning, cable TV, and in-line hot water heaters to ensure a plentiful supply. Comfortable wicker love seats, bistro tables and chairs furnish the delightful indoor-outdoor bar/lounge and connecting over-the-sea terrace. Breakfasts, generous drinks and tasty snacks are served. There are docking facilities as well.

Hotel Bahia, Calle 1 South, ☎ 507-757-9626 or 757-9852, fax 507-757-0602, www.hotelbahia.biz, $$, is Bocas' grand old lady. Built by the United Fruit Company in 1905 to replace the company's original headquarters that was destroyed by fire in 1904, it once housed three consulates and the Tropical Radio and Telegraph Station. It's been Hotel Bahia since 1968. Salvaged from the fire and now on display in the hotel lobby is the original, massive safe used by United Fruit. A hint of yesteryear pervades this fine hotel, which has 18 large rooms, all with private bath, air conditioning and cable TV. Recent renovations have preserved its charm. The restaurant here is excellent (see *Where to Eat*, below).

BOCAS DEL TORO

Lula's Bed and Breakfast, Av Norte, ☎ 507-757-9057, www.lulabb. com, $$, opened in April 2002 with six charming, air-conditioned second-floor rooms in a wooden house with wide fretwork verandas. Gleaming native hardwood floors complement soft floral print bedspreads, and filmy window coverings with matching valances let in the sea breezes. Hostess Jean, an American who grew up in Bocas, is always on hand to provide friendly, personalized service, and the ice chest on the second-floor veranda is a nice touch for keeping your drinks cold. Breakfasts are served downstairs in Jean's breakfast nook or on the second-floor veranda overlooking the sea.

Cocomo on the Sea, Av Norte, ☎ 507-757-9259, www.panamainfo. com/cocomo, $$. Open the white picket fence and walk through a flower-filled garden to this charming B&B at the edge of the sea. This first of Bocas' B&Bs changed hands a couple of times and had gone downhill a bit until it fell into Douglas Ruscher's capable ones. Douglas, who hails from the US Midwest, woke up one day and realized he'd had enough of the rat race. Since he "found" Bocas a couple of years ago, Cocomo has enjoyed a revival. He's upgraded everything, including widening the lovely veranda over the sea where you can enjoy a delicious breakfast or simply relax in a hammock. The four soundproofed guestrooms, two with sea views, have orthopedic beds, and are a few steps from the main house and kitchen. Breakfast is included in the rates, there's a lending library and you can get your laundry done.

Posada Los Delfines, Av H, ☎ 507-757-9963, fax 507-757-9075, www.posadalosdelfines.com, $$, has 10 immaculate rooms and two junior suites, all with private bath, air conditioning, cable TV and comfortable king-size beds. Rooms paneled in wood are especially welcoming. Seaview balconies and custom wood furnishings add to the attraction of these quality accommodations. The new **Spa Flora Bella**, with a luscious assortment of relaxing treatments, just opened here. The hotel restaurant, **Arco Iris** (see *Where to Eat*, below), features outdoor terrace dining. Order a mouthwatering barbeque, grilled hamburger, or delicious rotisserie chicken, then cool your tastebuds with homemade Italian ice cream or a specialty drink concocted of fresh tropical fruit juices. This well-maintained property is on a quiet street, a few minutes' walk from the central park.

Bocas Inn, at the north end of Calle 1, ☎/fax 507-757-9226, or 507-264-1713 in Panamá City, www.anconexpeditions.com, $$, is operated by Ancon Expeditions, Panamá's top naturalist tour outfitter. There are seven rooms in a comfy older building on the sea and five brand new ones in a building in front. The newer rooms were not yet completed when I visited last but, by all indications, they are equally comfortable. The simple and pleasant rooms in the back building have good beds, private baths and, miracle of miracles, real bars of soap rather than those little chips you get in most places! The rooms are on the second floor, and the two best face the sea. There's a wide second-floor veranda strung with hammocks and comfortable seating, and the first-floor restaurant and bar are open to the sea. You'll feel comfortable and welcome here. Rent only the room or, for the best deal, get a package that includes meals and day tours, or a complete one that has meals, tours and transfers and airfare from Panamá City.

Hotel Swan's Caye, Calle 1, north of the park, ☎ 507-757-9090, fax 507-757-9027, www.swanscayhotel.com, $$, is more European in flavor than any other place in town. The main hotel is built around a central garden. Magnificent oriental rugs highlight the dramatic lobby and there's a lovely restaurant. An annex hotel building, private pool club with bar, grill and boat dock are one street away. A European flavor pervades in the air-conditioned rooms and suites highlighted by delicately inlaid imported Italian furnishings. The mattresses are firm and there are in-room telephones. Some have private balconies and some open to the interior garden. Like everywhere else in town, the rooms vary, and the smaller ones are quite small.

Hotel Hipocamo, Calle 1, ☎ 507-757-9073, fax 507-757-9261, www.bocas.com/hipocampo.htm, $, has seven spotless second-floor rooms of varying sizes with comfortable beds and lovely wooden walls. There's an attractive second-floor balcony and, although there is a casino downstairs, the rooms are quiet.

Casa Max, Av G, ☎ 507-757-9120, $, offers six charming rooms in an old house painted in eye-shattering colors. Inside however, the immaculate rooms are restful, cheerful and breezy. All have private baths, fans and ceiling fans and some have balconies. Cold drinks and tourist information is available and guests are treated to morning coffee and fresh tropical fruit.

Hotel Laguna, Calle 3 near the park, ☎ 507-757-9091, fax 507-757-9092, www.hotellaguna.net, $$, has beautiful cedar walls and ceilings that lend a cozy atmosphere to charming, recently renovated rooms. They're beautifully furnished and decorated and little extras like dressing tables add to the ambiance. The tasteful rooms vary but all have orthopedic mattresses, air conditioning, private bath, telephone and cable TV. There is a junior suite with coffee maker and a large suite with kitchenette, refrigerator and private balcony overlooking Calle 3. Ask about the special package for two that includes round-trip air from Panamá City, lodging and full daily breakfasts. The property has its own internal water purification system. Internet use is available for guests and Restaurant Da Claudio here has the best breakfasts in Bocas.

Hospedaje Heike, Calle 3, ☎ 507-757-9708, www.bocas.com/heike.htm, is an immaculate little place, perfect for budget travelers. Its seven second-floor rooms, all with shared bath, are comfortable and simply furnished with good beds, mosquito netting and fan. Some of the rooms are brighter than others, so look at a couple before deciding. The pleasant, breezy veranda is supplied with reading material and guests can use the large downstairs former restaurant's kitchen and dining room. Rates start at $8 single, $12 double. English, Spanish and German are spoken here.

BOCAS DEL TORO

Hotel Las Brisas, Calle 3 at Av Norte, ☎ 507-757-9248, bendi69@ya-hoo.com, $, was Bocas town's first hotel. Built at the turn of the century, it was originally called a "boatel," as part of it is constructed on stilts above the sea. There are 40 rooms in two buildings – the original, large boatel and a newer, two-story building across the street. The old building was recently upgraded without loss of character. Look at a few rooms – although all have private baths and air conditioning, they vary in size, price and décor. Some have skylights, cable TV, VCRs, refrigerators and microwaves. Check out the old maps and original Bocas artworks decorating the lobby and unwind on the wonderful covered veranda over the sea. The management here is very friendly and welcoming.

❖ **CHOCOLATE**

Chocolate is derived from beans inside the seed pods of a plant in the orchid family. The Maya called chocolate the "food of the gods." So valuable were the beans, they used them as currency. It was the Maya who first ground the beans into a powder and mixed it with water to make an unsweetened drink consumed only by royalty and during religious ceremonies. The Aztecs later followed suit, calling it chocolatl (warm liquid). If you've a craving for a delicious bar of the food of the gods, head over to La Veranda Caribbean Chocolate and purchase a few made from local beans. The rich, dark chocolate lacks preservatives and is less processed than that found on store shelves. These sensuously exquisite bars are indescribably delicious. Sorry, Godiva.

Punta Caracol

Punta Caracol Acqua Lodge, ☎ 888-535-8832 in the US and Canada, 507-612-1088 or 507-676-6186, www.puntacaracol.com, $$$$$, is on Isla Colón's protected south side, a 20-minute boat ride from Bocas town. Good old Webster didn't come up with enough superlatives to describe this enchanted place, which is built on boardwalks along a coral reef above the translucent sea, and is rife with romance. This family-owned and -managed operation is a natural paradise that sustains itself without harm to the local environment. Spaced apart for privacy, the five lovely two-story cabanas with typically "Bocas" exteriors are built of native hardwoods, wild cane and bamboo, and roofed with palm fronds. The exotic hardwood interiors tastefully blend natural elements with sophisticated elegance. Downstairs sitting rooms have two comfortable sofa beds and charming bathrooms. Each second-floor bedroom has handcrafted furnishings dominated by a king-size poster bed draped in diaphanous mosquito netting (the net is only for mood, as biting critters can't make it this far from shore). Each cabin, cooled by sea breezes, has a private veranda facing the sea and outer islands.

The palapa-roofed, open-walled restaurant and bar/lounge combination is on its own large veranda, and there is a small gift shop. Delicious meals rely largely on fresh fish and seafood and organic vegetables. Other foods are native to the area or freshly made locally. Spanish and Caribbean cuisine is prepared with the élan one expects from such a unique place. Full breakfasts and candlelight dinners are included in the room rates and vegetarian or special meals can be provided upon request. Non-guests can dine there with advance reservations. With its own water purification system, organic gardens, bio-digester to render waste harmless to the environment and solar panels to heat water and supply electricity, Punta Caracol gets a big thumbs-up!

◆ Surrounding Islands

Bastimentos Island

El Limbo on the Beach, ☎ 507-757-9062, www.ellimbo.com, $, is a rustic getaway set on a white-sand beach in the midst of a private nature reserve. Sure to please Robinson Crusoe types, it isn't fancy and isn't meant to be. Nestled in coconut palms, this big wooden house with a wrap-around balcony has six guestrooms, wide verandas and windows that open wide to let in sea breezes. Catch some rays on the long wooden dock, snorkel the pristine reef just offshore, swim, hike a jungle trail and kayak to your heart's content. Breakfast, dinner and non-motorized water sports equipment are included in the rate and sometimes discounts are available with Internet bookings.

Al Natural, 30 minutes by boat from Bocas town, ☎/fax 507-757-9004, 507-623-2217 for last-minute reservations, www.bocas.com/alnatura. htm, $$ to $$$. This is a perfect island getaway for honeymooners, romantics, and naturalists. It has five gorgeous bungalows isolated in a cathedral of green jungle at the edge of the sea. Built of natural materials in the rounded, stilt-house style of the region's Ngöbe-Buglé Indians, these unique bungalows are a conservationist's dream come true. Solar electricity powers the lighting, ceiling fans – and your electric shaver or hair dryer. Gleaming native hardwoods are used for the floors, and walls extend only halfway up to overhanging, conical palm-frond roofs – and then only on the jungle side. The fronts are open to the sea. Designed to ensure absolute privacy, each minimally and elegantly furnished natural house has a private bathroom and terrace. There are three types: natural house, natural house deluxe, and two-story. The larger houses will accommodate up to four adults. Some have queen beds, some have king and twin, and all are draped in custom-made mosquito nets for optimum comfort. Go for the two-story house if available – it's awesome and only $5 more than the deluxe. The lovely outdoor dining/bar area, also circular and palapa-roofed, is designed for savoring delicious, imaginative seafood dinners with wine. Wake to birdcalls and chattering monkeys, drift off to the sound of waves lapping the pristine white shore. All room rates include meeting and transfers to the resort from Bocas del Toro's airport, three delicious meals daily, and use of windsurfing equipment, kayaks, snorkeling and fishing gear, archery. A special all-inclusive package with a two-night minimum stay includes all of the above plus a three- to four-hour boat tour each day to area attractions, and all alcoholic and non-alcoholic beverages. French, English and Spanish are spoken.

Isla Solarte

Solarte del Caribe Inn, 10 minutes by boat from Bocas town, ☎ 507-757-9032, fax 507-757-9043, www.solarteinn.com, $$ double, $$$-$$$$ 3/4-room suites. This beautiful inn, handcrafted of native cedar, crowns a breezy island hilltop above the sea. Slowly turning ceiling fans, soft tropical breezes and public rooms opening to expansive views exude an atmosphere of peace and tranquility. Opened in February 2000, the inn was designed with ecological water and waste systems and uses only biodegradable products to protect the island's natural integrity. The same careful attention to detail enhances the comfortable, tastefully furnished rooms and suites. Bathrooms have oversize tiled showers, good lighting, decorator linens and composting toilets. There's satellite TV in the cozy great room and a reading area furnished in tropical rattans. The delightful dining room is open to sea views above expansive, landscaped grounds. Host Steve Hartwig has thoughtfully supplied a selection of board games, books for adults and children and informative literature about local wildlife and ecosystems. Patricia Witaker rules the kitchen, and can that lady cook! Her wonderful breakfasts – with fresh-baked muffins – are included with the room rates. You can enjoy lunch here or take it for a beach picnic. Patricia's superb dinners, available upon request, are $5 to $12. Be sure to let her know in advance if you'll be dining at the inn. Solarte del Caribe has its own covered *panga*, a large, flat-bottom boat, which can transport up to 12 passengers. The inn provides its guests with boat transportation to and from Bocas town.

Where to Eat

You'll find almost any cuisine your palate desires in Bocas town. Read on, because there are some really, really good restaurants here – lots of them Italian or international due to an influx of restaurateurs from Bella Italia. And do try the local Caribbean cuisine. It's wonderful and innovative. Note that most of the restaurants do not have telephones, but reservations are not necessary here.

❖ RESTAURANT PRICING	
Entrée & non-alcoholic drink	
$	under $5
$$	$5 to $10
$$$	$11 to $20
$$$$	over $21

AUTHOR NOTE: *Many hotels and restaurants in Bocas do not accept credit cards. If you need cash, there is an ATM at the National Bank of Panamá, next to the town's central park.*

Restaurant Da Claudio, $, features terrace dining at Hotel La Laguna on Calle 3 in the town center. Claudio makes his own fresh pastas – 10 to 15 different ones each day – and breads and pastries in amazing variety. I'm a pushover for his exquisite fettuccine Alfredo; with a crisp salad or antipasto, hot garlic bread and a glass of wine, it's heaven. Try papardelle with basil and salmon, anything with pesto sauce, lasagna or spaghetti. The restaurant is open all day and serves the best breakfasts in town. Healthy fruit and yogurt, almond or chocolate pancakes, omelets and a dozen more choices include Claudio's outrageously yummy pastries. Daily specials are listed on a blackboard outside.

Alexander Restaurant, $$$, in the Hotel Swan's Caye, is beautifully decorated with fresh flowers and elegant table linens. It has a romantic atmosphere. The Italian owners have put together a menu of mostly northern Italian and international specialties that include a seafood platter with lobster, shrimp, fish fillet, calamari and octopus that will set your tastebuds singing. You can order a platter of pastas nested in an array of different sauces; tortellini with spinach; spaghetti with fresh tomatoes and basil; and a perfectly prepared lobster or catch of the day. Be sure to save room for a scrumptious tiramisu for dessert. There's a fine selection of wines, too.

Restaurante El Refugio, $$, serves innovative food in a candlelight atmosphere at the edge of the sea. It's at the south end of Calle 3, around the corner from the business district. Husband-and-wife team Pilar and Flavio, from Spain and Italy respectively, offer up imaginative, delicious international specialties with an accent on gourmet Italian and fresh local fish. Start off with an antipasto of delicate Serrano ham, mozzarella, olives and tomatoes dressed in olive oil and basil with hot bruschetta or crostini, then move on to exquisite paella. Best bet is to ask what Flavio has prepared as the special for the day. Yummy fresh fruit drinks are featured. Sandwiches, salads, pizza and vegetarian dishes are always available.

El Pecado da Sabor, $$, on Calle 1 near the town center is an enchanting little place on the second floor of a tipsy old Bocas-style house. Ask for a balcony table and watch the nightly parade below. Billed as exotic international, this is delicious fusion food at its best. I seldom eat my favorite, lobster, because it's becoming rare in this area, but fresh ones had just arrived during my last visit, so I gave in to temptation. Before me appeared three generous-size succulent grilled lobster tails with crisp cooked veggies, a delicious salad, hot rolls and butter, baked potato and all the trimmings heaped on a huge platter. Everything is cooked to order and seasoned to perfection. Gregarious host Stephan heads up the bar's camaraderie, and his lovely wife, Olga, is in charge of the food. Thanks, Olga! There is always a daily special. If you don't eat here at least once, you're cheating yourself.

Le Pirate, $, on Calle 3, serves heaping portions of mostly seafood and pasta dishes on an outside terrace above the sea. Don't pass up one of the delicious specialty fruit drinks or an ice-cold beer from the pleasant

BOCAS DEL TORO

bar. I've had some good meals here, but last time the shrimp was over-cooked.

Kum Ja, on Calle 3 at the Calle 1 fork, is Boca's only Chinese restau-rant. The friendly owners arrived from China a dozen years ago and the food is authentic, inexpensive and good. This large, recently remodeled restaurant is plain, but immaculate and airy. Fresh herbs and spices, grown in planters on a private back terrace above the sea, impart wonder-ful flavors to heaping meals that cost $3 to $4 (more for shrimp and lobster).

Restaurant Hotel Bahia, $, south end of Calle 3. Dine outdoors on a graceful balcony or a paved garden terrace with umbrella-shaded tables prettily done in fresh green and white. Delicious Italian-Mediterranean and traditional Caribbean dishes rely on plentiful supplies of fresh sea-food and coconut. Cooling tropical fruit salads are luscious here and the pasta is always al dente. The service is first-rate, too.

Arco Iris at Posada Los Delfines, Av G, ☎ 507-757-9963, three blocks north from the park, specializes in delicious rotisserie or barbecue chicken, burgers and scrumptious homemade Italian ice cream. Cocktails made with fresh fruit juices are a specialty. To get here, walk north on Calle 3 and turn left when it ends three blocks from the park. Pick up a whole chicken for a picnic.

Om Café, $, north end of Calle 1, is the only place to get refreshing homemade yogurt fruit shakes or luscious carrot and orange juice with ginger. Sunanda cooks up delicious, healthy Indian dinner specialties that include succulent tandoori chicken, shish kebab with tamarind or cilantro chutney for omnivores. Vegetarians and vegans can choose from a list of taste-tempting daals, vegetable curries, lentil-based dishes and more. Yearning for a bagel and cream cheese? It's on the varied breakfast menu.

Café Paradiso, Calle 3, opposite the park, is the first place to open for early, prepared-to-order breakfasts. They stay open all day to serve fast, so-so cafeteria-style food at very reasonable prices. A few sundry items, candy bars and the like, are sold here. There's satellite TV in the small dining room and a bulletin board with all sorts of interesting, helpful infor-mation posted. The few outdoor café tables attract an interesting crowd of people-watchers.

Dessuz, $, Calle 3, south of the park. Talented local chef Dessuz pre-pares exquisite gourmet Creole cuisine in Bocas style. Using the freshest ingredients, he cooks as the spirit moves him. Hope it moves him to make rondon soup – seafood simmered in coconut milk and spices – when you're here. Potcover fish is another of his mouth-watering specialties, but don't expect a meat dish on Sunday. It's traditional to eat only fish on the Sabbath. Other cultural idiosyncrasies include never combining chicken with beef. Dinners come with coconut rice and peas and *platanos maduros*. The restaurant isn't much to look at but, ah – the food.

The San Blas Archipelago

The Kuna

"The earth is the mother of all things, the Great Mother. She is the Guardian who caringly watches over all that exists."
– Cacique General Enrique Guerrero (Ologuagdi), quoted from *Plants and Animals in the Life of the Kuna,* by Jorge Ventocilla, Heraclio Herrera and Valerio Nuñez

History

An estimated 50,000 of Panamá's most colorful indigenous group, the Kuna people, inhabit the San Blas Islands and a rugged swath of mainland coast stretching from Colón Province south 200 miles/322 kilo-

❖ CHAPTER HIGHLIGHTS	
➢ Kuna history, lifestyle, art	267
➢ Getting Here	273
➢ Tour Operators	274
➢ Where to Stay & Eat	275

meters to the Colombian border. Coral reefs protect the archipelago's 377 islands, only about 60 of which are inhabited. This is Dulenega, or **Comarca Kuna** Yala, the land of the Kuna, an autonomous region governed by the Kuna themselves. According to Kuna lore, their Chibcha forefathers were driven from their ancestral lands in what is now Colombia, sometime around the 16th century. Old Spanish records indicate that the Indians that Balboa befriended were Kuna. Pedrarias' systematic campaign to wipe out the Darién's indigenous people forced the surviving Kuna to retreat toward the Caribbean coast and, as the Spanish advance continued, they finally retreated to the archipelago's uninhabited islands.

Wherever they might have originated, the Kuna have been island dwellers for only the last two centuries or so. Sixteenth-century chroniclers mention San Blas as uninhabited and visited by only a few pirates and Spaniards. In 1925, after declaring their independence, these fiercely independent people staged a bloody civil uprising in which 22 Panamanian policemen were killed. Restrictions imposed on fishing and farming territories they had long considered their own, brutal treatment by Panamá's police and an edict forbidding the women to wear their traditional clothing and gold nose rings had driven them to revolt. The US military intervened and forced both sides to negotiate a settlement. The Kuna agreed to withdraw their declaration of independence and the Panamanians agreed to allow them to live autonomously. The women again proudly donned traditional molas and gold nose rings and have worn them ever since. Only those on Nargana, an island heavily influenced by missionaries, continued to wear Western clothing. In 1938, the Kuna comarca (autonomous region) was officially created. Kuna men dress in Western clothing. During World War II, many of them worked for the US military. As a result, some speak English.

> **AUTHOR NOTE:** *An American adventurer named **John Marsh** was instrumental in the 1925 Kuna Rebellion against the Panamanian government. Marsh got involved while searching for a mythical tribe of white Indians and helped lead the Kuna in the armed revolt that led to American intervention.*

Government & Education

The Kuna have one of the world's most highly organized and cooperative indigenous societies. Each community is headed by a *saila* (chief), who presides over weekly or twice-monthly meetings (congresses) to discuss important matters and resolve problems. The village saila reports to the overall Kuna Congress, led by three elected Supreme Sailas. Today, they're represented in Panamá's legislature and have the right to vote in Panamanian elections. Panamanian schools are permitted on their lands, and most Kuna recognize the value of education.

Although the Congress is presided over by men only, Kuna society is matriarchal. Daughters are prized because, when they marry, the new husband lives with his wife's family group and contributes to their labor pool and financial well-being.

No "outsiders" (called *uagmala* or *waga* by the Kuna) are allowed to own property or live on the *comarca*. A case in point is Kwadule, a gorgeous little acre of white sand with a few ubiquitous coconut palms. A few years ago, an outsider formed a partnership with Kwadule's Kuna owner to finance a small, attractive lodge. The lodge operated for a time before the Kuna authorities ordered it closed. It has since burned to the ground. No reparations were made to the foreign investor.

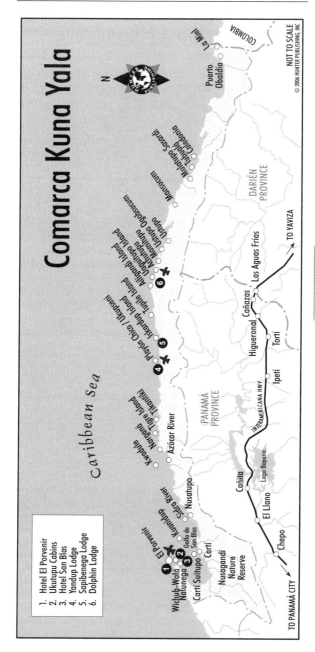

Comarca Kuna Yala

1. Hotel El Porvenir
2. Ukutupu Cabins
3. Hotel San Blas
4. Yandup Lodge
5. Sapibenega Lodge
6. Dolphin Lodge

NOT TO SCALE
© 2006 HUNTER PUBLISHING, INC

COLOMBIA

La Miel

Puerto Obaldía

DARIÉN PROVINCE

Mulatupo Sasardí
Tubualá
Caledonia

Mansucun

Ustupo
Ustupo Ogobsucum
Achutupu
Mamitupu
Uaguitupo Island
Algandí Island

TO YAVIZA

Las Aguas Frías

Cañazas

Higueronal

Tupile Island
Lkwdup Island
Playón Chico / Ukupani

INTERAMERICANA HWY

Torti

Ipetí

PANAMÁ PROVINCE

Tigre Island
Narganá
Kwadule
Tkantiki
Azúcar River

Cañita

El Llano

Lago Bayano

Nusatupo
Sidra River
Kuanidup

Golfo de San Blas

Carti

Nusagandi Nature Reserve

Chepo

Wichub-Walá
Nalunega
Carti Suitupo

El Porvenir

Caribbean Sea

BOCAS DEL TORO

TO PANAMÁ CITY

N

The Kuna Lifestyle

Only about 60 of the paradisiacal white-sand islands are inhabited, and most are less than three miles/1.86 kilometers from the coast. The rest, if large enough to support a few coconut trees, are "farmed" for the fruit that is sold or bartered, mostly to the Colombians, for cooking oil, hammocks, batteries, clothing and non-perishable goods. To keep the economy intact, the Congress establishes coconut prices each year, and anyone caught selling for more or less is punished. After you've seen a few claustrophobically overpopulated villages, you might wonder if they could do with a few less coconuts. As many as 5,000 people may live on a tiny island, packed so tightly with bamboo and thatch huts that there is barely space left to squeeze between them. Community cooperation is essential in this crowded culture where your neighbors live inches away and there is little privacy. You'll notice how quietly island people speak.

> "There have been several attempts to develop tourism within the Indian territory. Even when isolated and discrete, the progressiveness, possessiveness and perpetuity of modern hotel management clashes with Kuna traditional philosophy and intuition. The unique democratic process keeping this society intact also assures that any successful modern business will not long endure." – John Mann, Saibibi's San Blas, 1975

Motorized *cayucos* are generally used for fishing and transportation and a few ancient supply boats transport water – there is no potable water on the islands – and food from the mainland. Precious rainwater, captured in pots, pans, pails and huge plastic barrels, is used for most other purposes, including the washing of clothes and bodies. The Kuna men fish from small *cayucos* rigged with colorful sails, and subsistence farm rice, corn, plantains, manioc and a few vegetables on small plots slashed from the mainland jungle. It's not unusual to see a whole family set sail at the break of dawn. Only coconuts, a few watermelons and breadfruit trees will grow on the sand-covered islands. There's also a noticeable absence of livestock. The only animals I have ever seen are a couple of dogs and a pitiful captive keel-billed toucan tied to a stick. A few chickens don't take up much room, so I asked a lady why there were none. Her shocked reply was, "We eat only fish here." I thought this odd, as mainland Kuna hunt animals for food.

If you have the romantic notion that native peoples protect their environment and food sources, you're in for a rude awakening. In traditional Kuna culture, one takes only what is needed. However, the same culture is based on a "get what you can, when you can" teaching. When commercial enterprises began offering money for sea turtles, lobsters and small tropical fish, the Kuna began to hunt them indiscriminately. Five lobster species once flourished throughout the archipelago. Today, they are in danger of extinction. Sea turtles are seldom seen anymore, and overfishing has severely decreased large fish species. Mainland native peoples kill tapir, one of the tropical New World's most endangered animals, without compunction. If you stay for a few days at one of the Kuna lodges, you will probably be offered lobster for dinner one evening. If it's brought cooked to your table without advance notice, by all means, enjoy. If you know it will be specially purchased only if you order ahead – let your conscience be your guide.

> **AUTHOR NOTE:** *The Kuna say they have 365 islands – one for every day of the year. The official number is 377, and other counts vary by a few more or a few less.*

Unlike most New World indigenous populations that are steadily declining, the Kuna are increasing. It is not unusual for a family to have eight to 12 children. They are also one of the purest races left in the world, as Kuna law forbids intermarriage. It does happen, of course, but the perpetrators are usually banished from the *comarca*. I have heard of only one instance where a "foreign" marriage partner was allowed to remain, and then only after long debates in the Congress.

❖ A STORY FROM A KUNA SCHOOLBOOK

Child: Mother, where did I come from? Mama, is it true a dolphin brought me? My brothers and sisters, too?

Mother: Yes, the dolphin brought you.

Child: Mama, did the dolphin put me in the sand?

Mother: If I hadn't picked you up someone else would have.

Child: Who would have been my father and mother then, I wonder?

Once you get past admiring the women's beautiful traditional dress, you'll notice the physical characteristics of the people. The stocky men usually reach only about five feet/150 centimeters in height, and the delicate, fine-featured women are even shorter. Most outstanding, however, is the high incidence of albinism. The Kuna have the world's highest rate of this genetic anomaly. Albinos are called "moon children" and treated as special. I hadn't known any of this before my first visit to Kuna Yala. Needless to say, it was quite a surprise to see five pale, white-haired people with pinkish-blue eyes within the first few hours after arriving. Later, I noticed the pale children hustled out of sight at our approach. As I came to know more, I began to understand why. Much of it has to do with history and the fact that, with good reason, the Kuna are mistrustful of outsiders. Centuries of encroachment on their homelands and attempts to make them conform to Western standards are now complicated by disrespectful tourists who treat them like nothing more than "Kodak moments."

❖   **KUNA DRESS**

The complexity of the women's stunningly beautiful dress contrasts strikingly with the simplicity of their surroundings. A Kuna woman's costume consists of a mola blouse with short, puffed sleeves, a brightly printed, long wrap skirt (usually with a blue background) called *saborete*, a short underskirt (*pecha*), a contrasting print sash and a print kerchief head covering. *Winnis* – tightly strung rows of tiny, colorful beads – cover their legs and sometimes their arms as well. Huge gold medallion necklaces, gold earrings and a few gold bracelets complete the ensemble. Traditional women include gold nose rings and a straight black line drawn from the forehead to the tip of the nose. Gold is very important to the Kuna, who once called themselves "gold people."

AUTHOR NOTE: *Visitors clad in short shorts and bikini tops are shocking to these very modest people, who keep their bodies covered. You'll notice the men always wear shirts and women cover even their heads.*

Mola Art

Since the late 1990s, sales of handcrafted mola art have brought the Kuna more income than have sales of coconuts. And as mola sales represent cash money rather than bartered goods, Kuna women now earn more than most men. You'll seldom see a Kuna woman's hands idle.

Mola art began when Kuna women gained access to modern, store-bought fabrics. The first designs represented their culture, mythology, native animals and plants. Today's molas are still made in the traditional, geometric designs, but might also be inspired by comic book characters, advertising or political posters. Over the last few years, a mad rush of North Americans and Europeans have made mola folk art one of the hottest new collectibles.

The word ***mola*** refers to the traditional Kuna woman's blouse and to the beautiful, colored fabric panels sewn on its front and back. Mola panels are made by placing layers of fabric, one on top of another, then cutting a design through and stitching each one to reveal the color beneath. The method is called reverse applique. Kuna women begin to make molas when they are young girls. The smallest molas measure roughly 16 inches/41centimeters by 13 inches/33 centimeters, and the average size is 18 inches/46 centimeters by 15 inches/38 centimeters. You'll seldom see one larger than 20 inches/51 centimeters by 18 inches/46 centimeters. Expect to pay about $30 for a mola of average quality, but the price for one that is exceptionally well-made and intricately designed can go as high as $300.

❖ Molas are made from two to six layers of fabric; those with the most layers are the most colorful and sought-after.

❖ Stitching should be very fine, even and practically invisible.

❖ The designs should be well balanced. Look also at the width of the cutouts; narrower ones take more time and skill.

❖ Additional details such as embroidery, lattice work or zigzag borders also add to the beauty and value.

❖ Overall artistic merit of the color combinations and design is also important.

Visiting the Area

These poster-pretty white-sand islands, blanketed with swaying palms and surrounded by cerulean sea, are an escapist's dream come true. But there are a few things you should know before you go. Visiting San Blas isn't logistically easy if you want to see more than two or three inhabited islands. There are few hotels. Don't expect the Ritz; lodgings are simple, bathrooms are usually shared outdoor affairs, and communal meals are served at specific times. There are no menus – the choice is fish, rice, a simple salad or vegetable and fruit. Stays include your room, meals, and tours to nearby islands – usually to visit another community and a second, uninhabited island for swimming and snorkeling. Only one hotel uses solar power, the rest have gas generators to provide the electricity that is seldom turned on before dusk and usually turned off around 11 pm or midnight.

Keep in mind that San Blas hotels open and close with regularity. Those listed in this chapter have been around for some time and it looks as if they'll continue to be.

Getting Here & Getting Around

Flights to island airstrips depart Panamá City's Marcos A. Gelabart Municipal Airport (Albrook) in the early morning hours. The following airlines operate small planes that accommodate 18 to 24 passengers: **Ansa**, ☎ 507-315-7521; **Aerotaxi**, ☎ 507-315-7520 (e-mail address for both of these is iflyab@aeroperlas.com); and **Aviatur**, ☎ 507-315-0311, e-mail aviatur@sinfo.net. Be sure to make advance reservations. Seats are not assigned, so try to board early. The islands are strung along a 250-mile/

403-kilometer strip of Caribbean coast and, as some of the planes make several stops, flying time can vary from 45 minutes to 1½ hours. Getting here usually includes the flight and a short boat trip. For instance, if you're going to **Nalunega** (the nearest to Panamá City), you'll land on nearby **Porvenir**, and be transported by boat to Nalunega, a 10-minute ride.

Transport between islands is by motorized *cayuco*. Traditional *cayucos* are made from hollowed-out logs, and some of these babies are huge. The Kuna are not adverse to modern conveniences when it suits them, so there are a few actual boats now serving the purpose. I've never seen a *cayuco* with a canvas top, so be sure to take plenty of sunscreen, sunglasses and a wide-brimmed hat.

◆ Tour Operators

It's best to book your San Blas visit with a tour operator who will make all the necessary arrangements. See page 52 for a list of operators.

Following Local Customs

Kuna people do not drink alcoholic beverages except during celebrations, but will permit tourists to drink as long as they don't make fools of themselves. If you want wine with meals, you'll have to bring your own, although some hotels now sell beer. Women are asked to wear one-piece bathing suits and should not wear short-shorts or halter-tops. Men should wear boxer-type swimsuits. The snorkeling is excellent – there are some lovely reefs. Scuba, however, is not permitted. Expect to be out of touch with the rest of the world, although there are a few public telephones on some inhabited islands. Relax, respect that other people don't think as you do, and enjoy the experience.

Just as the Kuna are shocked by Western behavior, you'll probably be taken aback by their attitude toward money. These otherwise aloof, reserved people are blatant about getting as much of it as they can. Most hotel stays include tours to other islands, so be forewarned: you'll be expected to pay $5 per person for the privilege of visiting a community, and $1 to visit the islands that have only one or two families. The women can be insistent and persistent when trying to sell you molas and beads. Never take a photograph without asking first. Whip out your camera and you'll be expected to pay from 50¢ to $1 for each person photographed. Shoot a photo of mother and baby, and it will cost $2. I've been asked to pay up to $10 for a village shot without a single person in sight! However, if you buy a couple of molas, the ladies who sold them might grant you permission to take a photo. Whether you use it or not, expect to be charged $50 to carry a video camera onto some of the islands. Credit cards are not accepted, not even at the hotels. This is a cash only society, so if you are not using a tour operator, take a sufficient amount to pay for your hotel stay and incidentals. And take plenty of $1 and $5 bills – you'll need them.

AUTHOR NOTE: *Please **don't** swim near inhabited islands. During my first visit, I noticed little sheds at the end of the many docks that circle the island like outstretched tentacles. Naturally, I assumed the sheds were for storing fishing gear, gasoline cans and the like. Wrong! They're outhouses. In addition, anything considered trash is unceremoniously dumped into the sea.*

Where to Stay & Eat

Hotel El Porvenir, ☎ 507-229-9000, $. Little El Porvenir Island is the region's seat of government. There are a few official buildings, residences and a police station here. The hotel is right next to the landing strip and *bohio* that serves as an airport lounge. There's nothing to do except walk around the island – it'll take about eight minutes – or

❖   HOTEL PRICING
Based on double occupancy
No $ . . . . under $20
$ . . . . $20 to $39
$$ . . . . $40 to $79
$$$ . . . . $80 to $124
$$$$ . . . . . . $125 to $199
$$$$$ . . . . over $200

BOCAS DEL TORO

watch people waiting for the planes that land a couple of times a day. The hotel is very welcoming, and the rooms have private showers and toilets, but they're cell-like and drab. The rate is $35 per person, per day, including meals and a boat tour. A better place to stay is Hotel San Blas (see below), a 10-minute boat ride away on nearby Nalunega Island. Airfare from Panamá City to El Porvenir is about $60 round-trip.

Hotel San Blas, ☎ 507-262-5410, $$, is the largest in the archipelago, and the oldest. It's on crowded Nalunega Island, about 10 minutes from the El Porvenir airstrip. Its owner, genial Luis Burgos, speaks Kuna, Spanish and English – learned when he worked for the US military in Panamá during World War II. He's quite a character and full of great stories – if you can corral him long enough to get him to talk. Although he's less reticent than most Kuna, I couldn't pry any information about the "moon children" from him. The hotel has 28 rooms in two, two-story concrete thatch-roof structures and there are four typical huts with sand floors. A new building containing six more rooms was under construction and should be completed by now. The rooms are reasonably comfortable, but some have really awful mattresses, so ask to see a few before deciding. And request a corner room if one is available – it's the only way to get cross-ventilation. There's a pleasant sea-front *bohio* with hammocks strung beneath it and a little store where you can buy cold drinks, snacks and beer. The small beach is attractive and the sea tempting, but don't swim here. The shared bathrooms have cold-water showers and flush toilets. Luis's cook, Sipu Solis, is one of the best, so the food is better than usual. The $35 per-person, per-day rate for a double room includes meals and two daily excursions, one to even more crowded Carti, and one to a gorgeous small island that's safe for swimming, snorkeling and lazing on white-sand beaches.

> **AUTHOR NOTE:** *If you would like to rent a Kuna house, ask around on Nalunega. One or two families there will move in with relatives and charge you about $10 per person, per night. Nothing is supplied other than the hut and a hammock, so you will have to bring your own food or hire someone to prepare meals. If you're really down and out, Luis might let you sleep in a hammock under the hotel's bohio for a couple of bucks.*

Dolphin Lodge, ☎ 507-225-8435, cdolphin@sinfo.net, $$$, is the most attractive lodge, an hour by plane from Panamá City and about 60 miles/ 97 kilometers north of the Colombian border. It's on small, private Uaguitupu Island, four minutes by boat from neighboring Achutupu, a larger island with a good-sized village and the landing strip. Dolphin's nine large trim and tidy thatch-roof cabins, with queen beds and good mattresses, are built of wood rather than traditional bamboo. Private outside bathrooms have compacting flush toilets and fresh cold-water showers. The dining room is open *bohio*-style, set away from the cabins at the edge of the sea. Lunches and dinners are typically local fish, plain white or coconut rice, a salad and fruit. Expect them to have a boring sameness. Electricity is generated from 6 am until 8 pm every day and kerosene lanterns are supplied for lighting after it's shut down. One-night package rates are $95 per person based on double occupancy, and each additional night is $80 per person. The rate includes your room, breakfast, lunch and dinner daily, transfers to/from Achutupu, and two daily guided tours – one to Achutupu and a second to an uninhabited island for swimming and snorkeling. Other excursions are offered to visit some of the islands and to the mainland. Don't hire a boat to go by yourself, as permission to visit is required. This is the best lodge in the archipelago, owned by the friendly De la Ossa family, who speak some English. Round-trip airfare to Achutupu via Ansa, Aerotaxi or Aviatur is $81 (tax included). For children under 12 years, the lodge charges $65 (every night, no discounts for longer stays), and airfare is $41 round-trip.

> **AUTHOR NOTE:** *Although the Colombian trading boats that ply the archipelago's waters don't present any danger to visitors, the islands are a hotbed for drug traffickers. These guys don't fool around. If you want to go adventuring through the islands by boat, go only with an experienced guide or tour operator.*

Sapibenega, The Kuna Lodge, ☎ 507-225-8819 or 507-676-5548, fax 507-225-5505, $$$, is on Iskardup, a small, private island with white-sand beaches, close to the larger island of Ukupseni (Playón Chico) and to the mainland. It's located about halfway down the archipelago. The lodge's 14 raised wood-floor cabins with private bathrooms are constructed of pole and thatch. Electricity here is solar-powered and always available. There's an attractive restaurant and a bar. One-night packages include a visit to Ukupseni village and one to a nearby uninhabited island. Longer stays include excursions to the mainland, jungle and medicine trail walks. The meals here are similar to those of all island lodges. The $90 per-person, per-night rate, based on double occupancy, includes transfers from the landing strip at Ukupseni, lodging, three meals daily and local tours. Children under two years of age stay free. Those two to six years receive a 35% discount, and ages six to 10 years get a 25% discount. Round-trip airfare from Panamá City is $76 for adults, $36 for children under 12.

The lodge at **Yandup**, e-mail yandup@cableonda.net, $$, is only 1,090 yards/1,000 meters from the large island of Ukupseni (Playón Chico), in a cluster of little islands. The cabins here are pole and thatch with wood floors and are built near the beach. The beds are okay, but not as good as those at nearby Dolphin Lodge, and the rooms are plainer. Meals and excursions are the same as Sapibenega's. And since you'll arrive at the same landing strip on Playón Chico, the airfare is the same. Room rates are $75 per person, per night, based on double occupancy.

Staying on the Water

The very best way to enjoy San Blas is aboard a chartered cruise. You'll see much more, the food is better and, surprisingly, the cost is usually less. The custom-built 40-ft trimaran **Naylamp**, ☎ 507-683-8841 or 507-682-6825, e-mail trinaylamp@hotmail.com, offers short or long journeys that include shore excursions, Kuna village visits, kayaking, snorkeling, fishing, gourmet Mediterranean-style meals with wine, cold beer and more for $125 per person, per day.

San Blas Sailing, ☎ 507-226-2005, fax 507-226-8565, www.sanblassailing.com, offers a variety of itineraries aboard chartered monohulls, catamarans and engine-powered yachts.

If you prefer a larger ship, US based Windjammer Barefoot Cruises offers a six-day San Blas Islands cruise aboard the tall ship **S/V Mandalay**. This beautiful 236-foot/71-meter three-masted barquentine transports 72 passengers in casual comfort. Rates for a standard cabin with upper and lower berths, private head and shower start at $1,485. All prices include round-trip airfare from Miami to Panamá City, one night's hotel accommodations in Panamá City with breakfast, round-trip transfers airport-hotel-ship-airport, a Panamá City Tour and visit to the canal's Miraflores locks, six days of cruising, all shipboard meals and port charges. For more information, contact **Windjammer Barefoot Cruises** in the US, ☎ 305-672-6453 or 800-327-2601, www.windjammer.com.

BOCAS DEL TORO

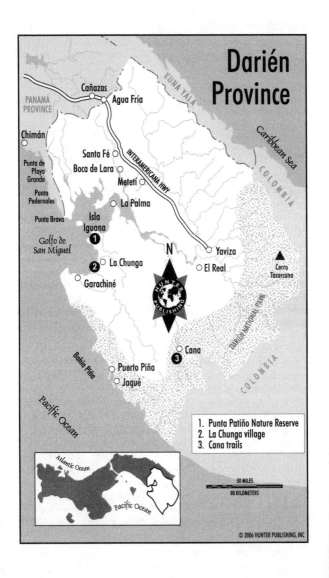

Darién Province

PANAMÁ PROVINCE

KUNA YALA

Caribbean Sea

COLOMBIA

Cañazas
Agua Fría

Chimán

Punta de
Playa
Grande

Punta
Pedernales

Punta Brava

Santa Fé
Boca de Lara
Metetí

La Palma

Isla
Iguana
1

Golfo de
San Miguel

2 La Chunga

Garachiné

INTERAMERICANA HWY

N

HUNTER PUBLISHING

Yaviza

El Real

Cerro
Tacarcuna

DARIÉN NATIONAL PARK

COLOMBIA

Bahía Piña

Cana
3

Puerto Piña
Jaqué

Pacific Ocean

1. Punta Patiño Nature Reserve
2. La Chunga village
3. Cana trails

Atlantic Ocean

Pacific Ocean

50 MILES
80 KILOMETERS

© 2006 HUNTER PUBLISHING, INC

Darién Province

The Land

Panamá's largest and least populated province (6,500 square miles/16,671 square kilometers) contains one of the world's most diverse ecosystems and the largest remaining

tract of primary forests in all Central America. Its landscapes rise from sea level flood plains to 6,150 feet/1,875 meters at the cloud forest summit of **Cerro Tacarcuna**, its highest peak. Several mountain ranges, including the **San Blas**, **Darién**, **Sapo** and **Pirre**, fringe Darién's deep valleys. Clear streams and sluggish, mud-brown rivers snake through marshes, swamps, mangroves and tropical rainforests that never quite dry out, thundering waterfalls burst from walls of green foliage and plunge down deep rock canyons. Rare plants and animals abound in this virtual laboratory of biodiversity, where clustering orchids grow nearly as big as Volkswagens. Towering **cuipo**, **rosa del monte** and **ceiba** trees soar into tangled canopies 150 feet/45 meters above the forest's shadowed floor. In anticipation of drier seasons, the cuipo's trunk bulges with conserved water. The **jacaranda's** trunk base is shaped like a wrinkled elephant's foot – an odd contrast to its beautiful lavender-blue flowers – and **chunga palms** are covered with three-inch spines that can cause nasty wounds.

There is no road all the way through Darién. The Pan-American Highway (InterAmericana) breaks at the town of Yaviza, leaving a 54-mile/87-kilometer stretch of wilderness before it picks up again across the Columbian border. Paving of the pot-holed, pitted road is well underway and, as it progresses, it's spreading ecological disaster. You can drive all the way to Yaviza, but when time is limited, a flight is a much better option. There isn't much to see during the drive east from the capital other than the purplish-blue shadows of the San Blas Mountains and disheartening stretches of cattle ranches, rice farms and barren hillsides.

History

Vasco Nuñez de Balboa left Santa Maria as its unofficial leader, hacked across the Darién, reaped gold and pearls, and on September 26,

1513, discovered the Southern Sea (Pacific Ocean). However, during his long trek Spain's King Ferdinand sent **Pedro Arias de Avila** (Pedrarias) to replace Balboa and govern the region then known as Castilla de Oro. Balboa couldn't have cared less. He congratulated Pedrarias and sent news of his discovery and Ferdinand's share of the treasure to Spain. Incensed with jealousy over Balboa's successes, the spiteful Pedrarias had him imprisoned. But when news of Balboa's discovery and the share of gold and pearls reached Spain, a delighted Ferdinand appointed him" Governor of the Southern Sea and the vindictive Pedrarias was forced to release him.

To separate himself from Pedrarias, Balboa, with a contingent of faithful conquistadors, left Santa Maria and sailed across the Bay of Urabá to a place where, in 1514, he founded **Acla**. As his popularity and power increased, so did Pedrarias' obsessive jealousy. Eventually, Pedrarias managed to have Balboa arrested on a trumped up charge of treason and forced a hurried trial. In January, 1519, the innocent Balboa was executed in Acla. The town was abandoned and reclaimed by the jungle. Soon, most of Santa Maria's residents moved across the isthmus to the new city of Panamá after its founding in 1519. In 1524, hostile Indians destroyed what remained of Santa Maria.

Gold found in Darien was so plentiful that the Spanish brought African slaves and indigenous slaves from as far as what is now Nicaragua to work the mines. The largest mine, **Cana**, in the remote Pirre Mountain range, operated for more than 150 years. By 1700, the Darien's remaining indigenous people – those who hadn't been killed or died in slavery or the diseases brought by the Spanish – had retreated deep into the jungles. The dreams and failed ventures that died here — Santa Maria, Acla, New Edinburgh, the mining towns, a Scottish trading colony, and French Huguenots families wanting freedom – have been relegated to history.

◆ New Edinburgh, The Scottish Colony

In the late 1600s a wealthy Scot named **William Paterson** attempted to establish a peaceful trading colony in Darién. To ensure that no British traders would arrive before him, he founded his own company, deceptively named **The Indian and African Company of Scotland**. Funds for the endeavor were raised by subscriptions sold in Scotland, directors were appointed and five ships had been built when the company advertised for settlers. A destination wasn't revealed, but times were hard and thousands of Scots, lured by the promise of 50 acres of "plantable" land and a house, lined up to volunteer. On July 17, 1698, the first 1,200 volunteer settlers set sail from Leith. None, other than Paterson, not even the ship captains, knew where they were going until they arrived in Madeira, Spain. The fleet sailed across the Atlantic to a beautiful Darién bay that Paterson named Caledonia Bay and the settlers came ashore to a place they named New Edinburgh. Paterson couldn't have known they were a stone's throw from Balboa's jungle-reclaimed Acla.

The industrious colonists built rudimentary homes and a fort named after Saint Andrew, but the venture was doomed from the start: Their five ships were no good to windward, Paterson was usurped and the councilors appointed to replace him argued among themselves and could not make decisions. Their constant infighting, the British government's obstruction, hostile Indians, torrential rains, crop failures, and storm-battered and sunken ships compounded the mistake of their unwanted trade goods that included heavy woolen fabrics, thick stockings, delicate slippers, women's kid gloves and 4,000 wigs. The rainy season brought the mosquitoes and soon the Scots began to sicken. After more than 300 had died, they deserted New Edinburgh. Deathly ill, Paterson made it to New York. But even as the colonists fled, more were on the way. The new volunteers fared no better. They too, soon left Darién and sailed to Jamaica, where most of them died. Not one ship made it back to Scotland.

During this time there had been no communication between Scotland and Darién; more shiploads of volunteers arrived. But by this time, news of their presence had reached the Spanish who attacked the Scots. After several bloody battles, the Scots were trapped inside Fort St. Andrew; their water supply and access to the bay cut off. After a final bloody bathe, the Spanish offered the sick and defeated Scots 14 days to leave Darién. With drums beating, the proud survivors marched aboard their remaining ships. Not a single one made it home to Scotland. Paterson, who had remained in New York, eventually recovered and returned to Scotland, but was too late to save his company. He believed it would have been successful if backed by England and proposed another attempt. When it came to nothing, he began to promote the union of England and Scotland.

◆ The French Huguenots

Persecution of the Protestant Huguenots (dissenters) by the Catholic Church began in Germany during the early 16th century. In 1535, as the Reformation spread through France and Italy, the Church issued an edict ordering extermination of the Huguenot "heretics." Some escaped to more tolerant countries, but thousands were systematically tortured and executed. The extermination edict was revoked 63 years later by the Edict of Nantes, but later withdrawn and the persecutions resumed. On August 14, 1742, an uprising of Catholic clergy and French soldiers led to the St. Bartholomew's Day Massacre, which brought violent and bloody death to more than 100,000 Huguenots.

Between 1690 and 1750, the Huguenot diaspora spread throughout the world. A few of the French came to the isthmus and established small colonies in Bocas del Toro and Darién, but the Spanish refused them autonomy. Most who settled in Bocas del Toro were killed by the Spanish. The Darién settlement ended when the Kuna, armed by the British, massacred 60 families. Still, every now and then, the tale of a "lost" tribe of white Indians filters from the depths of the jungles.

The People

The province's population is estimated at about 45,000, mostly **Emberá** and **Wounaan** people, **Kuna**, and **Black Panamanias**, called Dariénites – many of them descendants of the **Cimarrones**, black slaves who, almost five centuries ago, escaped the Spaniards' harsh treatment.

Most Emberá and Wounaan live deep in Darién National Park's wilderness, and the Kuna generally live near the Caribbean coast. Only a slight language variation separates the Emberá and Wounaan people, often called **Chocoes**, as both emigrated here from Colombia's Chocoe River region. These traditional forest dwellers live in small villages, usually in extended family groups, along the rivers that provide fish, their main protein source. Farming is done on a subsistence level, although some Emberá and Wounaan now grow small amounts of additional food for sale or trade. These gentle, artistic people that rely mostly on fish for protein sometimes hunt with poison-dipped lances and blow guns. Quite likely, it was the fierce Kuna who annihilated entire regiments of conquistadors.

Wounaan and KEmTheir homes, which are set slightly apart for privacy, are open-sided platforms raised 10 to 12 feet/three to 3.6 meters above the ground as a protection from marauding wild creatures and insects. Accessed by lashed-together log ladders, the homes are roofed with palm-frond thatch, and the floors are made from fragile-looking but deceptively strong strips of **gira**, a native palm. Men are excellent wood-carvers and the women make exquisite baskets, some so tightly woven they will hold water. Once only utilitarian, these beautiful baskets now provide a source of income. The Emberá and Wounaan also make dugout canoes (called *paraguas*) from giant, hollowed out logs. Some of these sturdy canoes last for generations, and are large enough to transport a dozen people at one time.

Visiting the Area

Parque Nacional Darién

Most of southern Darién is within Panamá's largest and most remote national park, 1.4-million-acre/576,000-hectare Darién National Park. The park was established in 1980, declared a UNESCO World Heritage Site in 1981, and a Biosphere Reserve in 1982. More than 450 bird species have been recorded here, including the world's largest populations of endangered **harpy eagles**. Mammals include all five big cat species, tapirs, peccaries, giant anteaters, five monkey species, sloths, and giant pocket gophers. Reptiles and amphibians include endangered American alligators, crocodiles, several species of poison dart frogs and a goodly helping of snakes, many of them venomous.

There are no roadways into the park; it must be accessed by air or by river. Visiting any part of Darién isn't a Sunday stroll. The park is no exception, and under no circumstances should you try to go it alone. You can count on your fingers the number of people who speak anything other than Spanish or native dialects. Towns and settlements are few and far between and even the toughest adventurer can get hopelessly lost, or worse –much worse. Even if you're not fazed by poisonous snakes, herds of raging peccaries or getting lost (the Indians will probably find you eventually – scratched, blistered, tick-covered and half-starved – and get you to safety), you should be aware that drug traffickers, guerillas and paramilitaries infiltrate the area over the border from Colombia. Unlike La Amistad, where the lost always turn up eventually, in Darién they don't. This isn't to say you shouldn't go. You should. There aren't many places like this in the world. But go only with a responsible tour operator familiar with the territory.

◆ Getting Here

Based on the Darién's remoteness and assuming you want to get the most out of your visit, I recommend you go only with a qualified nature tour operator who knows the territory. Only a few schedule trips to Darién, and none is better than **Ancon Expeditions**, ☎ 507-269-9415, fax 507-264-3713, www.anconexpeditions.com. Their bilingual conservationist guides are natural history experts and are, quite simply, the best of the best. Ancon – they're affiliated with Panamá's National Association for the Conservation of Nature maintains three lodges within Darién National Park.

❖ KIDNAPPED, OR AMONG THE MISSING...

Don't even think about trekking beyond Yaviza without a knowledgeable, reputable guide. The Darién is no simple walk in the woods. Consider this: In1990, two British orchid hunters captured by Columbian guerillas were held six months before their release. They never knew if their captors were members of the Revolutionary Armed Forces of Columbia (FARC), the National Liberation Army (ELN), or the paramilitary United Self-Defense Forces (AUC). These groups, dubbed narco-guerillas by the Miami Herald, are terrorist organizations that traffic in narcotics and heavy-duty weapons. They aren't freedom fighters folks.In January, 1993, three New Tribes missionaries were kidnapped. They haven't been heard from since and in 2002, were declared dead. Ten years later, on January 18, 2003, an AUC group invaded the Kuna villages of Paya and Pucuro. After murdering Paya's cacique, his second cacique and a village administrator, the group continued on to Pucuru where they murdered that village's cacique and burned some of the homes. Both villages were looted of valuables and food. Called on for assistance, the US military flew supplies to village residents and helped relocate them to a safe area. Almost simultaneously, journalist Robert Young Pelton, author of *The World's Most Dangerous Places*, and two companions were captured by an AUC splinter group and held for 10 days. Pelton's account of the kidnapping appeared in the April, 2003 issue of *National Geographic Adventure* magazine. In August 2003, a group of young backpackers were kidnapped. Two managed to escape within a few days, but the others were held captive in deplorable conditions for several months before their release.

Cana

Cana, the site of a former gold mining camp, lies in the wilderness of a Pirre Mountain plateau. There are no roads to Cana, only a rough trail through mountainous jungle leads to the nearest little village, a two-to-three day walk distant. Transport here is by air from Panamá City, a flight of less than an hour. When your plane lands on Cana's grassy runway, clamber out and look around. You've come to worship in nature's cathedral.

The Spanish found gold here in the early 16th century and mined it until they left the isthmus in the mid-18th century. Cana was deserted and reclaimed by the jungle until the early 20th century, when a British company discovered there was still some gold in "them thar hills." The British mining concession petered out in the 1960s and the jungle again reclaimed Cana. This remote wilderness today is so complete that it's almost impossible to imagine that 20,000 people once lived and worked here. Now an Ancon Field Station, Cana is in a small clearing on the eastern slope of the Pirre Mountain range, an area known for its vast amount of endemic wildlife and one of the world's best for bird watching. Minutes after arriving, I had seen four blue-and-yellow macaws, a small flock of great-green macaws, quibbling toucans and circling hawks. Much to my amazement, they are all quite common, unlike the beautiful tree runner, golden-headed quetzal, Pirre warbler, Pirre bush tanager, rufous-cheeked hummingbird, and green-naped tanager that are among some of the rarest and endemic to the region.

Unless there are visitors, Cana's only human inhabitants are a few staffers and border policemen. The old mining camp headquarters Ancon once used as guest quarters has been demolished and new lodge accommodations built with eight comfortable bedrooms, shared hot water bathrooms, screened windows and solar-powered electricity. Excellent meals are served in the separate dining hall. In addition to the station's base camp, there is a tent camp on a cloud forested mountain ridge at 4,300 ft/1,300 meters.

Although the steep 3.75-mile/six-kilometer **Pirre Mountain Trail** from the base lodge to the tent camp can be walked in about three hours, there is so much to see along the way that it usually takes about seven. Expect to see myriad bird species and plenty of wildlife. Jaguars, pumas, jaguarundis, margays, ocelots, and tapirs all live here, but you'd have to be awfully lucky to see one. However, howler, black-handed spider and capuchin monkeys are often encountered. All you need to take is your pack with overnight supplies. The staff lugs all the food and water necessary to prepare meals in the camp's full field kitchen. While they're working to get you properly fed, mosey to the lookout point, which offers awesome views of Darién National Park.

The **Cloud Forest Trail** continues to the top of the Cerro Pirre ridge (5,200-feet/1,600 meters) where the habitat changes to transitional cloud forest. The **Machinery Trail** loop is an easy 1.2-mile/two-kilometer hike into gorgeous secondary forest and, as the name implies, past bits of rusting machinery left over from gold-mining days. Remains of a huge smelter and the yawning mouths of liana draped tunnels are visible, but please don't attempt to enter them. They're old and crumbling, and who knows what might lurk inside. The **Seteganti Trail** is an easy hike down to the Seteganti River, where you can take a cooling dip or soak your tootsies. Also easy is a short hike along a rusty track to a little locomotive frozen in time.

◆ Getting Here

Visits to this magical place can be arranged with **Ancon Expeditions**, ☎ 507-269-9415, fax 507-264-3714, www.anconexpeditions.com, via chartered flights (non-stop from Panamá City's municipal airport to Cana). The flight, over magnificent mountains and jungles splashed with flowering trees, small clearings, snaking rivers and thundering waterfalls, takes about one hour. Ancon's all-inclusive itineraries include expert guides, air travel to/from Panamá City, lodging, all meals and a variety of naturalist and/or birding adventures. Private five-day/four-night itineraries are priced at $1,327 each for a party of two; eight-day/seven-night adventures are $1,650. The group rate is $995 per person for the five-day/four night package and $1,350 for eight days/seven nights.

BOCAS DEL TORO

Reserva Natural Punta Patiño

(Punta Patiño Nature Reserve)

Located on the Pacific Gulf of San Miguel, this is the country's largest private nature reserve (65,000 acres/26,000 hectares), and is owned by Ancon. The lodge here is about an hour by river from La Palma, Darién's provincial capital, and it's the most comfortable of any you'll find in the province. The reserve's habitats, different from Cana's, include beaches, mangrove, primary and secondary lowland and tropical dry forests. Along with many lowland and coastal bird species, capybaras, foxes, collared peccaries, tayras, sloths, Geoffrey's tamarins and iguanas inhabit the region. A guided hike through **Sendero Piedra de Candela**, the main trail, offers an opportunity to watch for birds and learn about the dry forest. There is a fine swimming beach close to the lodge. Visits to an Emberá community up the nearby Mogue River and the village of Punta Alegre, whose residents are the descendants of African slaves, are included with Ancon Expeditions' itineraries.

❖   EXTREME ADVENTURE

If you're up to it, Ancon Expeditions offers the trip of a lifetime – a trans-Darién trek. This one requires stamina, guts, and a desire to experience a journey that few people are fortunate to even imagine. Contact **Ancon Expeditions**, ☎ 507-269-9415, fax 507-264-3713, www.anconexpeditions.com, for information on Cana, Punta Patiño, the Trans-Darién Expedition and other itineraries throughout the country.

Río Sambú & La Chunga

Aviatur Airlines worked with Cacique Ricardo Cabrera of La Chunga village to help purchase the supplies necessary to welcome visitors to his community. As a result, a few visitors have found their way here, so you may not find it quite as authentic as some that are more remote. On the other hand, the accommodations are more comfortable than in other Darién Emberá communities.

Surprisingly, and although no one else in the village speaks English, Cabrera does. He learned during a six-month visit to the US. La Chunga's four spacious guest cabins are 16.5 yards/15 meters from the village, and each has two rooms, some with double beds, others with twin. All have mosquito netting. And there's yet another surprise – real flush toilets and running water. A large circular building houses the separate dining room and lounge. There's good bird-watching and beautiful hikes through the forest to a swimming area beneath a small waterfall. Local wildlife includes sloths, peccaries, monkeys, iguanas, squirrels and crocodiles. You can arrange river fishing, and the village chimán (medicine man) will explain medicinal plants and their uses.

◆ Getting Here

Flights from Panamá City's Marcos A Gelabart (Albrook) Municipal Airport to Sambú village in Darién take less than one hour. Motorized cayucos depart from Sambú for a 45-minute journey up the Sambú River to a riverbank that is a 10-minute walk through the jungle from the village. **Aviatur Airlines**, ☎ 507-315-0311, e-mail aviatur@sinfo.net, offers a complete package that includes an overnight stay in the village, all meals, and transportation for $175 per person; additional nights are $55 each. **Aeroperlas**, ☎ 507-315-7500, e-mail iflyap@aeroperlas.com, www.aeroperlas.com, provides a similar package on alternating days for about the same price.

Boca de Lara & La Palma

Exotics Adventures, ☎ 507-673-5381, 507-223-9283 or 507-673-5381 (cell), e-mail exoavent@cwpanama.net, offers a three-day, two-night trip to Boca de Lara, a Wounaan community downriver from Santa Fé. Transportation is by 4X4 from Panamá City to Santa Fé, then by motorized canoe to Boca de Lara. The trip includes all meals, rustic accommodations in a typical Wounaan home furnished with air mattresses, outdoor showers and bathrooms. Included are demonstrations of traditional dances and crafts, fishing with flying nets, a jungle trek to see monkeys and other wildlife, a boat tour, and a visit to La Palma to explore its interesting culture. Mangroves along the river harbor an astonishing variety of tropical marine birds. Cost for the package is $350 per person, based on two passengers, $300 per person for three or more. Exotics Adventures also offers three- to four-day kayak adventures on the Chucunaque River to the Emberá community of El Salto, and a shorter kayak adventure that covers 37.2 miles/60 kilometers on the Chucunaque in two days, with an overnight stay in the community.

> **AUTHOR NOTE:** *The National Geographic Society filmed a documentary series about an American family living with the Wounaan. Michel Puech of Exotics Adventures, one of the Wounaan's staunchest supporters and friends, was chosen to select the village and the family who would host the Americans and to provide logistics for the film crew. The series, titled* Worlds Apart, *aired on the National Geographic channel in March, 2004.*

Appendix

Recommended Reading

◆ Nature and Ecology

Leigh, Egbert G., Jr. *Tropical Forest Ecology: A View from Barro Colorado Island.* Oxford University Press, *1999.*

Royte, Elizabeth. *The Tapir's Morning Bath: Solving the Mysteries of the Tropical Rain Forest.* Mariner Books, 2002.

O'Keefe, M. Timothy. *Sea Turtles, A Watcher's Guide.* Larsens Outdoor Publishing, 1995.

Carr, Archie F. *The Windward Road: Adventures of a Naturalist on Remote Caribbean Shores.* University Press of Florida, 1979.

Ridgley, Robert S. and John A. Gwynne. *A Guide to the Birds of Panamá.* Princeton University Press, 1992.

Dressler, Robert L. *Field Guide to the Orchids of Panamá and Costa Rica.* Cornell University Press, 1993.

◆ Indigenous Peoples

Howe, James. *The Kuna Gathering: Contemporary Village Politics in Panamá.* University of Texas Press, 1983.

Salvador, Mari Lynn. *The Art of Being Kuna: Layers of Meaning Among the Kuna of Panamá.* University of California, 1997.

Kane, Stephanie C. *The Phantom Gringo Boat: Shamanic Discourse and Development in Panamá.* Smithsonian Institution Press, 1994.

Hemmers, Paul and Anne. *The Kunas of San Blas.* Stuart, Florida, 2000. A photographic presentation of the Kuna people.

◆ General Non-fiction

Greene, Graham. *Getting to Know the General: The Story of an Involvement.* Simon & Schuster, 1984. An oldie but goodie about Greene's friendship with Torrijos.

Donnelly, Thomas, Margaret Roth, and Caleb Baker. *Operation Just Cause, The Storming of Panamá.* Rowman & Littlefield, 1991.

Dinges, John. *Our Man in Panamá: How Noriega Used the United States – and made Millions in Drugs and Arms.* Random House, 1990.

Espino, Ovidio Diaz. *How Wall Street Created a Nation: J.P. Morgan, Teddy Roosevelt, and the Panama Canal.* Four Walls Eight Windows, September 2003.

McCullough, David. *The Path between the Seas: The Creation of the Panama Canal, 1870-1914*. Touchstone Books, 1978.

◆ Fiction

le Carré, John. *The Tailor of Panamá*, Ballantine Books, 1997.
Zencey, Eric. *Panamá: A Novel*. Berkley Publishing Group, 2001.

Information Sources

◆ Useful Web Sites

www.panamainfo.com – A very helpful site with loads of good information.

www.ipat.gob.pa – The Tourism bureau's official website. Plenty of information, but all in Spanish.

www.visitpanama.com – Built and maintained by the tourism bureau's public relations agency. Pretty site, but not a great deal of information.

www.cometoboquete.com – Helpful, but limited information.

www.escapetoboquete.com and **www.theboquetetimes.com** – These sites are the brainchildren of publisher Juan Antonio (John) Villegas. *Escape to Boquete* features plenty of local interest items, geared to visitors and newly arrived expats. The new *Boquete Times* is chock-full of news, interesting articles, restaurant reviews, forums, and an extensive local events calendar.

www.thepanamanews.com – On-line biweekly English-language newspaper. Check the restaurant reviews, list of upcoming events and entertainment venues.

www.chitrenet.com – Information about the Central Provinces. In Spanish.

www.gaypanama.com – A good resource for GLB travelers.

www.panamaaudubon.org – A "must" for birders. The Society also offers birding adventures.

www.planeta.com – Ron Mader's environmentalist site often posts information about Panamá.

Foreign Embassies

Embassies in Panamá City include:

United States, Avenue Balboa . . . . ☎ 507-207-7000
United Kingdom, Call, 53, Marbella. . . . ☎ 507-269-0866
Canada, World Trade Center, Calle 53. . ☎ 507-264-9731
Spain, Calle 33 and Avenue Peru . . . . . . ☎ 507-227-5122

France, Plaza de Francia, Casco Antiggo . ☎ 507-228-7824
Italy, Avenue Balboa . . . . ☎ 507-225-8948
Germany, World Trade Center, Calle 53 . ☎ 507-263-7733
Sweden, Av Balboa and Calle Uruguay . ☎ 507-264-3748
Switzerland, Calle Victoria & Miraflores . ☎ 507-261-1530
Greece, Avenida Manuel E. Batista . . . . ☎ 507-260-7814

APPENDIX

Index

INDEX